FAMILY RESOURCE MANAGEMENT

This book is dedicated to our families, students, and friends.

*To the men in our lives—Pat, Ted, Patrick, Aaron, Christopher, Alex, Taylor,
and Austin—who spent many hours taking care of themselves
while we were immersed in the completion of this text.
We love you and learn something new every day we spend with you.*

*Our students have been instrumental in the development of this book,
pointing out the things we missed and adding their own
unique perspective to this body of knowledge.*

*Friends and colleagues have been most supportive and forgiving during
this process. We look forward to reconnecting after this process is completed.*

FAMILY RESOURCE MANAGEMENT

Tami James Moore and Sylvia M. Asay
University of Nebraska at Kearney

SAGE Publications
Los Angeles • London • New Delhi • Singapore

For information:

Sage Publications, Inc.
2455 Teller Road
Thousand Oaks, California 91320
E-mail: order@sagepub.com

Sage Publications India Pvt. Ltd.
B 1/I 1 Mohan Cooperative
 Industrial Area
Mathura Road, New Delhi 110 044
India

Sage Publications Ltd.
1 Oliver's Yard
55 City Road
London EC1Y 1SP
United Kingdom

Sage Publications Asia-Pacific Pte. Ltd.
33 Pekin Street #02-01
Far East Square
Singapore 048763

Printed in the United States of America

Library of Congress Cataloging-in-Publication Data

Moore, Tami James.
Family resource management/Tami James Moore, Sylvia M. Asay.
    p. cm.
Includes bibliographical references and index.
ISBN 978-1-4129-3750-4 (cloth : alk. paper)
   1. Family life education—United States. 2. Family—Study and teaching. I. Asay, Sylvia M. II. Title.

HQ10.5.U6M66 2008
306.850973—dc22   2007025408

Printed on acid-free paper

07   08   09   10   11   10   9   8   7   6   5   4   3   2   1

Acquisitions Editor:	Cheri Dellelo
Associate Editor:	Deya Saoud
Editorial Assistant:	Lara Grambling
Production Editor:	Sarah K. Quesenberry
Copy Editor:	Heather Jefferson
Typesetter:	C&M Digitals (P) Ltd.
Proofreader:	Theresa Kay
Cover Designer:	Bryan Fishman
Marketing Manager:	Stephanie Adams

Brief Contents

Detailed Contents

Unit II: Discovering Family Needs

Preface

Structure, Understanding, and Application

The goals of *Family Resource Management* are focused on structuring the concept of the topic in an understandable format that allows students and instructors to apply both knowledge and theory to the study of how families manage their resources for both survival and fulfillment. Multiple perspectives are utilized to broaden the base of understanding in a contemporary environment.

Family Resource Management unlocks the complexity of family decision making for students, enabling them to grasp both the concepts and underlying explanations of family behavior. A strong theory base and the organization of material within the decision-making process facilitate both understanding and retention.

Unit I: The Study of Family Resource Management presents a framework for understanding the discipline of Family Science/Family Studies in the context of the decision-making process. An in-depth analysis of the concept of family and family structure presents the complexity of how families identify and fulfill their needs. Students are provided with a structured approach for comprehension of how cultural diversity and differing worldviews impact that decision-making process. Another important concept explored in this unit is that of the contextual influences that impact family resource management. Management—principles and application—is presented in both historical and contemporary contexts. The interdependence of family management and business management is explored and synthesized through theory and practice.

Unit II: Discovering Family Needs requires recognition of how needs and wants differ and how families determine priorities when necessary. This includes a discussion of Maslow's hierarchy and an analysis of how values, attitudes, and behaviors impact need recognition and the actual perception of need. It also includes an understanding of how external forces, such as marketing and social changes, impact family value sets over time.

Unit III: Understanding Resources presents economic and social resources in a family-based framework. Although students may be exposed to the field of economics and financial planning in previous courses, it is essential that practicing family service providers and educators understand the reciprocal relationships between families and these social systems. Financial problems are often cited as catalysts in family dissolution, and the complexity of social services, especially Social Security and Medicare, has created a new family service niche—family life education programs and consulting services.

Unit IV: Making Choices moves the decision-making process into the action mode. The planning process and implementation of choices are presented within real-life applications, such as financial planning and emergency action preparation. The importance of communication in the family decision-making process is validated with strong theoretical support and clear illustrations. Understanding the choices made by families requires an understanding of leadership concepts and group dynamics.

Unit V: Implementing and Evaluating Decisions wraps up the five-step decision-making process. Reflection on actions and behaviors, and evaluation of the actual impact these decision have on the family, are perhaps the most important steps, although often neglected. Breaking the cycle of bad choices requires postdecision analysis. Life satisfaction and the impact of decisions on individuals, the family unit, the community, and society are essential to student learning and professional development.

Family Resource Management Is Flexible and User-Friendly

After years of experience in the undergraduate classroom and discussions with students as to their preferences, the authors selected a conversational style of material presentation, rich in application and discussion. Understanding that the core concepts within this topic are complex and dynamic, the decision to include descriptive scenarios at frequent intervals strives to connect new material to existing student understandings. This method encourages readers to control their own learning process. Drawing from multiple disciplines and preparing university students for personal, career, and possible graduate study success, it is imperative that material be drawn from scholarly resources and properly referenced in an academic fashion.

The abundance of material and the multiple opportunities for application in this text allow the instructor the opportunity to provide a structure for presentation and the possibility of gearing the material to any college/university course level needed. The material can be integrated into a multiple-level approach of studying family resource management, or it can stand alone as a one-term principles course. The flexibility of material and the presentation style utilized allow usage in both the degree-specific study of this topic and the more generalized elective courses across multiple major programs of study. The authors recognize that all students in post-secondary education are members of existing families and that they will find the material applicable to both personal and professional experiences.

Understanding Family Diversity

Presenting a framework for students to use as they explore the challenges presented by an increasingly diverse clientele is essential for positive development of diversity skills and understanding. The authors have chosen the worldview framework introduced by Kluckhohn and Strodtbeck (1961). Others have built on this over the last four decades, but the original remains most adaptable to multidisciplinary approaches.

Although difficult when presenting diversity within scenarios, use of ethnic names has been deliberate as a purposeful effort to be inclusive. The examples created for explanation of complex concepts are not always negative, nor are they positive. No stereotypes are implied through the use of these names. Families of all races, ethnicities, income levels, and other defined characteristics experience similar decision-making situations. The worldview framework helps students realize that decision making will differ between and within family units based on how situations are defined and viewed by the individuals involved. This framework is helpful both with intranational diversity of groups and international group differences.

Real-World Examples

Each chapter strives to present current, reality-based supporting information for the chapter's objectives and content. *Reality Checks* include information from contributing families and/or media accounts of real individuals and families in specific circumstances. *Worldview* pieces are drawn from both the media and academic sources to provide concrete examples of how families from different cultures might perceive similar concepts differently. *In the News* features have been extracted from contemporary news sources to further inform students of issues facing society on a daily basis that are directly connected to the material they have just been presented.

Case Application Opportunity

The casebook for use with this text provides students with the opportunity to explore what it is like to be part of family structures that might be different from their family of origin. In this casebook, there are five different families, each with unique strengths and problems inherent to family resource management. Thirteen case application assignments, designed specifically for each family, are provided to use with individual chapters. Students may be assigned one specific family for the course term. Then students can participate in community groups, where classmates representing the other four families can share their success and concerns in working with the other four challenging case families. This approach to application of concepts has proved effective with past courses. Each section of the text presents complementary information that can be used to problem solve in hypothetical situations presented. The cases utilize writing and practical skill-building assignments.

When appropriate, instructors have the flexibility to adapt the casebook material included in this edition to meet the needs of upper level students by adding assignments and activities that enhance higher order thinking skills and application.

Acknowledgments

We are grateful to those at Sage Publications who have encouraged us in this journey: Jim Brace-Thompson for bringing us on board, and Deya Saoud and Cheri Dellelo for the guidance and patience necessary to complete this project.

We are also thankful for the substantial contributions of the reviewers to this book, who provided objectivity and perspective to the material: M. J. Alhabeeb, University of Massachusetts; Maria Canabal, Illinois State University; Michael Cheang, University of Hawaii; Faye Griffiths-Smith, University of Connecticut; Celia Ray Hayhoe, Virginia Polytechnic Institute and State University; Jeanne Hilton, University of Nevada, Reno; Diane Klemme, University of Wisconsin-Stout; Wendy Reiboldt, California State University, Long Beach; Kathryn D. Rettig, University of Minnesota; Deborah A. Sullivan, Ashland University; and Betty Young, Minnesota State University, Mankato.

Our students, who have suffered for years without a textbook, were also an important source of direction, providing suggestions and critique when necessary. Finally, our colleagues at the University of Nebraska at Kearney have been both supportive and understanding.

Unit I

The Study of Family Resource Management

The Complexity of Managing Family Resources

1

Objectives

- Be aware that the family is the basic unit of society that has continued and is maintained over time.

- Recognize that the family is in transition both as a result of changes outside the family and in family structure.

- Understand that family resource management is a process that requires decision making and evaluation skills.

- Acknowledge that families need education about the opportunities and limitations of resources.

- Be familiar with how the words *family, resource,* and *management* identify the study of family resource management.

- Comprehend the five-step decision-making process.

- Acknowledge the impact that contextual influences have on family resource management.

Family Resource Management is an understanding of the decisions individuals and families make about developing and allocating resources including time, money, material assets, energy, friends, neighbors, and space, to meet their goals.

—National Council on Family
Relations (2003)

D espite the challenges facing families across time, the family remains the world's oldest form of relationship, a universal phenomenon (Sokalski, 1994). For centuries, families have been organized as a basic unit of society. This social unit has continued to be maintained over time, and, until recently, the family unit was generally considered to be a private institution. The contemporary family is now, more than ever before, a political entity. Family values are emerging in campaign slogans, drawing increased attention to the importance of family units within the social framework of communities, locally, nationally, and globally. This surge of interest in the family unit has resulted in increased research, expanding our knowledge base of family functions and evolution over time.

Although family life does give individuals a strong sense of continuity, Skolnick and Skolnick (2005) call attention to the fact that the family is in transition. Emerging communications and technology capabilities have accelerated this transition. Families of the future will not only need to be aware of changes that are taking place, but they will also need the skills to adapt resource management to fit new realities.

Paralleling the changing social, political, and economic climates surrounding families are changes in the structure of families. Coontz (2000) points out that favored traditional family structures carry privilege, whereas Doherty (1997) speculates that, as a result of environmental changes, our current society may be the first in history that cannot clearly define the family. These complexities necessitate the need for ongoing education and evaluation about the ways families function.

The key concepts of family resource management include an interdependency of individuals, a dynamic environment, and a conscious effort to meet basic needs for all individuals within the family unit. Managing family resources has always been a process, requiring individuals to recognize that effective decisions cannot be made quickly and that the evaluation of those decisions is essential for future decisions.

Families cannot effectively manage resources without an awareness of their opportunities as well as a consideration of their limitations. They need to be aware that living in the 21st century presents numerous challenges to the family. Families will continue to consume large amounts of resources, be engaged in the world economy, and provide safety and security for its members. Each of these functions requires management. Thus, the concept of family resource management is imbedded in those three individual words: **family**, **resource**, and **management.**

What Is a Family?

Contemporary families are diverse in nature, reflecting the socioeconomic environments surrounding them. The idea that a traditional family exists, from which students can compare and contrast other **nontraditional** family units, is nonproductive to the goals and objectives of family service providers. It is necessary, however, to categorize and define families when public and private programs assess needs and determine qualified services for citizens based on that designation. Chapter 2 presents a framework for understanding contemporary family definitions and structures.

Joe and Rocia have three children. Joe recently lost his job. To qualify for financial assistance through various local and state programs, they must meet the criteria of those programs in terms of how a family is defined. Some programs may only be available to them if they are legally married. Some assistance may be available based on their household status regardless of whether they share a home. If Joe is not the biological father of the children, his assistance may only be based on what is deemed necessary for a single male.

In terms of family resource management, it is assumed that families are units where members strive to meet the needs of all members while maintaining that family unit over a period of time. Thus, families have both individual and group needs. Identification and communication of these needs are continual. To satisfy these needs, resources must be identified and secured. Money and material possessions are easiest to identify as important family resources; however, the human resources available among all family members are just as important, if not even more essential, to the family's survival and maintenance.

The processes of identifying needs and securing **resources** are dynamic within a family unit. Situations arise in frequent, repetitive ways that allow many decisions to become subconscious and almost habitual. Family members shopping for a weekly supply of groceries may cruise down the store aisles identifying and purchasing an assortment of products with little deliberation. These products have been identified through previous decision-making processes; until family members decide that these basic products are no longer meeting their needs, they are habitual purchases. Other situations require more deliberation and information seeking. The working parent who is confronted on Monday morning with an ill child-care provider must find a specific resource to meet an acute need. The stress level in this type of decision is much higher because this decision impacts the family unit on multiple levels.

How Do Families Use Resources?

Humans consume and require massive amounts of resources for survival, physical growth, and personal growth. Basic needs such as food, water, shelter, and clothing are obvious. Other resources are necessary to facilitate education, community, and recreation. The study of family resource management considers both the consumption of resources and the availability/ expenditure of human resources by family members.

The identification of resources to meet specific needs is guided by **culture, availability**, and **accessibility**. Tap water quenches thirst, yet an individual may choose to buy bottled water for family drinking purposes. A single-family detached house may be preferred, but if apartments are the only choice available, a family may make do until other options surface. An Ivy League college may be a student's choice, but if he or she does not meet the requirements for admission, another selection must be made.

As families identify needs, their focus turns to finding ways to fulfill those needs. The number of possible solutions will vary depending on the particular need. These solutions, however, always require resources. The larger the pool of resources, the higher the probability that needs will be met **efficiently** and **effectively**. In managing family resources, sufficiency is also an important consideration. Will family members accept a solution that just meets their minimum expectations? Old newspapers suffice for bathroom use, but not everyone would accept this choice. Because family needs are dynamic and ongoing, any one particular resource may prove useful on some occasions, but not even be considered at other times.

Families may substitute some resources for others depending on the situational variables. Lunch may consist of a peanut butter sandwich when time is limited, but may be a multicourse feast when time is not an issue. Money is often substituted for time in resource selection. Fast food, airline travel, and lawn-care services are examples of this resource transfer or exchange. The complexity of individuals and families elevates the complexity of resource identification and selection when compared to resource management in the business setting.

In the News

Two Cities, Two Careers, Too Much?

By Cybele Weisser

January 1, 2006

(MONEY Magazine)—On a typical Monday morning, David Meyer wakes up at 4:45 A.M. in St. Louis and embarks on a seven-hour-plus commute to Providence. During a two-hour layover in Chicago, he grabs breakfast at McDonald's and catches up on academic papers. He won't see his wife, Judith Wangerin Meyer, until Friday, when he completes the trip back to Missouri. The two have been happily married for 40 years, but for much of the time they live 1,200 miles apart: David is a tenured sociology professor at Brown University; Judith is the president of the Lutheran high school association in St. Louis. And neither plans to retire or change jobs anytime soon.

The Meyers, both 62, became long-distance spouses five years ago, when Judith was offered a job in St. Louis. Because it would have been nearly impossible for David to find as good a position as he had, they opted for the commute, despite the emotional and financial costs. The Meyers estimate that they spend $15,000 to $20,000 a year for travel and extra housing, which puts a strain even on their comfortable six-figure income. "We've made sacrifices," says Judith. "But we decided it was important for both our careers to make this work."

One family, two homes: Think you couldn't find yourself living apart from your family, at least for a while? Think again. According to the U.S. Census Bureau, 3.2 million married Americans (including military families) live in different homes, a 26% increase since 1999. And it's often for good reason. Employers increasingly expect high-level workers to relocate, says Linda Stroh, a business school professor at Loyola University Chicago, who has studied commuter relationships and their effect on the family. Plus, a greater number of women with high-paying jobs, as well as a growth in late-in-life marriages, when both spouses are well entrenched in their careers, are increasing the likelihood of a temporary separation. "Families today are often dependent on two healthy incomes, so losing one job can have a huge financial impact," says Stroh. "That means more couples are thinking, let's just try the commuter hat on for a while."

But being far away from your loved one can create a host of challenges, from fatigue to financial hardship. "This is an expensive way to live," says Jay Lebow, a clinical professor of psychology at the Family Institute at Northwestern University, who has seen an increase in the number of patients in commuter marriages over the past decade. "You have two homes, travel expenses—even if you are making a fair amount of money, the drain on cash is still considerable." Fortunately, there are ways to minimize the financial damage, as well as the emotional strain.

(Continued)

(Continued)

Face Up to Higher Costs

The total expense of a commuter marriage can easily cause sticker shock, says Burlingame, Calif. financial planner Barbara Steinmetz, so create a budget before you take the job—and then look for ways to save. Housing is often the greatest sinkhole for long-distance couples, but depending on how many nights a week you spend apart, a hotel or short-term rental may be a cheaper alternative to two homes. The Meyers, for example, found that having David stay in a bed and breakfast near the Brown campus was not only less expensive than paying monthly rent, but also eliminated the need for them to keep a car in Providence or furnish two homes.

Living apart can easily lead couples to blow their budget on smaller items as well, says Olivia Mellan, a Washington, D.C. therapist who specializes in family and money issues. "It's a stressful situation, and when people are under stress they have a tendency to overspend," she notes. Don't use retail therapy to fight loneliness or anxiety, filling your closet with extra clothes and eating nothing but takeout. Do allow yourself extra cash for a second set of toiletries, a set number of on-the-go restaurant meals—or a periodic splurge to keep your marriage healthy. "The ultimate goal is to have a meaningful relationship," says Alison Piepmeier, 32, a college professor in Charleston, S.C. whose husband, Walter Biffle, 37, is studying for a fine arts graduate degree in New Bedford, Mass. "If that means we aren't always frugal, so be it."

- Ask Your Boss to Share the Tab

Workers often assume that their company won't be sympathetic to a commuter arrangement, but employers are frequently willing to pitch in, says Dan McLaughlin, an executive recruiter in Seattle. You're more likely to get a deal if the company has requested that you transfer, but even if you're accepting a new job, it's worth asking before you sign on. "Tell them allowing you to visit your family frequently is the best way for them to make you happy," says McLaughlin.

Companies are most likely to cover travel expenses, but they may also be willing to pay for some housing costs. That was the deal that attorney Amy Krallman, 39, struck when she was recruited three years ago for her current job as a vice president and corporate counsel for a financial services company. Her boss pays for weekly flights home to Long Beach, Calif. to see her husband Stephen, 40, an accountant, and for corporate apartments in both Philadelphia and Portland, Ore., between which she splits her time during the week. "I have to maintain three sets of wardrobes, toiletries and cosmetics, but otherwise there isn't a big financial impact on the relationship," says Krallman.

- Master the Mileage Game

Most airlines offer discounts if you buy a block of tickets well in advance, so book as far ahead as you can, and stick to one airline to maximize frequent-flier miles. You should keep enough miles "in the bank" to avoid paying exorbitant prices for a last-minute ticket. David Meyer, a Southwest loyalist, pays extra for two separate tickets (one from St. Louis to Chicago, the other from Chicago to Providence), because adding a leg to each trip lets him accrue free tickets faster.

- Make Time for Your Money

Money management can become a big headache in a commuter marriage because each partner doesn't always know what the other is doing. Some couples find it easier to keep money in separate bank accounts and pay bills on their own; others prefer to make one person largely responsible for everyday finances. Either way, "agree ahead of time who is going to pay for what, or get at least 90% of the bills to go out automatically," suggests St. Louis financial planner M. Eileen Dorsey. Online banking gives both spouses easy access to the family money. (Technology, of course, can be your secret weapon in a commuter marriage. Piepmeier, for instance, keeps an online blog with her husband. "I log on every day to see if Walter's posted something, and he does the same," she says. "It's a fun way to have a conversation that includes our friends and family.")

Faced with higher expenses and a constant lack of time, it's easy for long-distance couples to forget about long-term planning. Therapist Mellan recommends having a formal sit-down no less than once a month to discuss short- and long-term goals, as well as to make sure you are staying within your budget. "In this situation it won't happen spontaneously," she notes. Sign up for automatic investing in your 401(k) or IRA and contribute as much as you can. After all, if you've spent many of your working years apart from your spouse, you'll eventually want to retire in the same place. Even dedicated commuters like the Meyers are looking forward to the day when they can both settle in the same city. In the meantime, they have no immediate plans to return to a more traditional arrangement. "I love my job," says Judith. David agrees. "It's a balance of career and marriage. I love my wife, and we do what we have to do."

Source: "Two Cities, Two Careers, Too Much?" Cybele Weisser. Originally published January 1, 2006, in *MONEY Magazine.* © 2006 Time Inc. All rights reserved.

Managing Families

The history of family sciences is closely linked to that of business management. Both fields emerged in academia at about the same time, and both began with efforts to facilitate efficient and effective use of resources. Many of the management theories applied to individual and family resource management stem from business management. Many of the human resource theories are supported by research in family science and other social sciences. Business management focuses on planning, organizing, leading, and controlling the use of resources to accomplish performance goals. The goal of any business is the maximization of this process. It is a conscious effort and a constant process. Choices must be made and evaluated continually.

Although the family is not a **business**, it does have many of the same goals that a business addresses. Management theories are explored from both the business and family conceptual frameworks in Chapter 3. Business decisions generally have a stronger hierarchical base and more tangible factors available in the decision-making process. Most family management activity begins with that same decision-making process, but family management exists on a higher personal level with more emotional, intangible types of factors to consider. The decision-making process is a major concept addressed and explored throughout this text.

The Decision-Making Process

There are many ways that individuals and families go about making decisions. Janis (1989) proposes the rational model, presuming that, in the process of making decisions, there are purposeful goals and objectives. Rational decision making involves searching for alternatives, assessing consequences, estimating risk or uncertainty, determining the value of consequences, and selecting the action that maximizes attainment of those desired objectives. Decisions that have long-lasting impact on a family unit would benefit from this type of structure. Selection of educational programs and disease treatment options are often approached within this type of framework.

Pfeffer (1987) proposes another model that draws from rules, procedures, and processes, rather than the effort to maximize values. The bureaucratic model relies on habitual ways of doing things and is appropriate only

Photo 1.1   Technology enhances a family's search for alternatives.

Source: © Paul Kline/istockphoto.

for low-risk and uncontested decision situations. Although this model is more appropriate for business decisions, there are some frequent, low-risk decisions that must be made by families. Grocery shopping, especially for staple items, often operates this way.

The political model of decision making (Pfeffer, 1987) produces outcomes that are related to the power of individuals within the group. This model recognizes that individuals within the unit may have differing interests and acknowledges that conflict is normal or at least customary. Although decisions made within this model are seldom perfect for all members, the acts of bargaining and compromising result in member support for the final decision. Decisions specific to family relocation are often reached using this approach. Although children are greatly affected by such moves, it is generally more of a negotiation among the adults where power becomes a crucial influence.

Realizing that family decision making may be served by any, all, or a combination of these basic models, it is necessary to create a flexible framework for analysis of a variety of individual situations. The **five-step decision-making process** is the framework chosen for this text. Although family decisions are not always methodical, they follow a general framework of need identification and clarification, identification of alternative resources available, analysis and comparison of those resources, selection and implementation of resources chosen, and postimplementation evaluation. This model also gives the family the tools for rational, bureaucratic, or political thought found in the other decision-making models. By analyzing these steps separately and then synthesizing them as a process, the learner can more fully understand the complexity and occasional unpredictability of family choices and behaviors.

The Decision-Making Process

- Recognize existing need(s)

- Identify alternatives to fulfill identified needs

- Evaluate identified alternatives

- Select and implement alternatives

- Reflect and evaluate alternative selected

Contextual Influences in Family Resource Management

Families do not exist in a vacuum. Outside influences come into the family environment to change the way the family thinks and behaves. These influences come from history, culture, and the environment.

HISTORICAL INFLUENCES

Throughout history, there have been ideas and circumstances that have influenced the way families manage their resources. New ideologies and ways of thinking have impacted existing family behaviors. New child-care practices, new medical discoveries, and even changing marriage expectations may alter the way a family carries out its functions. Historical events also influence the family. Wars, recessions or depressions, terrorist attacks, and other events all have an impact on families.

The history of family resource management has influenced the way a family manages today. The early Greek and Roman cultures left a wealth of information about family management that can be found in the writings of the ancient philosophers. The word *economy* comes from the ancient Greek *oikos nomos*, which means *house* and *management*. Hesiod (ca. 715 BCE) wrote, "You should embrace work-tasks in their due order, so that your granaries [grain storage] may be full of substance in its season" (Hesiod, 1999). The 13th-century Church of England also left a legacy of instruction for management. As the church experienced a reform movement, more clergy were encouraged to speak out on marriage and family issues (Murray, 1987). One of the earliest recorded writings was by Robert Grossesteste, Bishop of Lincoln. This was written for his friend, Countess Margaret of Lincoln, after the death of her husband to help her manage his vast estate. He wrote, "And with the money from your corn, from your rents, and from the issues of pleas in your courts, and from your stock, arrange the expenses of your kitchen and your wines and your wardrobe and the wages of servants, and subtract your stock" (Henley, Lamond, Cunningham, & Grosseteste, 1890). In contemporary terms, he was suggesting how this new widow might balance her budget—income and expenses.

By the turn of the century, the world was changing at a rapid pace. Social mobility and invention would change the way many families managed. Although the Western family was still patriarchal, the Industrial Revolution forced men and women to move into different spheres of influence. Men gave their energies to their work, now outside the home, whereas women gained more power over the household. Isabella Beeton's *Book of Household Management* (cited in Hughes, 2006) sold thousands of copies in England. Her ideas have been compared to modern small business management techniques. According to Mrs. Beeton, good management included setting an example for and giving clear guidance to the staff, controlling the finances, and applying the benefits of order and method in all management activities (Wensley, 1996).

In the United States, another reference during this time was Beecher's (1869) *The American Woman's Home.* This volume was written as a training manual for women in the duties of the home in the same fashion as training for other trades at that time. According to Beecher, a woman's profession included "care and nursing of the body in the critical periods of infancy and sickness, the training of the human mind in the most impressionable period of childhood, the instruction and control of servants, and most of the government and economies of the family state" (p. 14).

The influences of science (ecology and biology) and technology (invention) in the home precipitated the Lake Placid Conferences in 1899 and 1909. The **discipline** of Home Economics or Domestic Science was developed as a result of these conferences.

Since the early 1900s, many changes have taken place in living conditions, equipment, and values and standards. During this time, the development of management also changed. The way in which today's egalitarian family acquires and uses resources is radically different than in previous decades.

ENVIRONMENTAL INFLUENCES

The resources that are available for use also influence family management. Some families may have a limited amount of resources available because of their geographic location or economic status. The needs of a family may not be met because necessary resources are not available. In other cases, if a resource is limited, the family may have to pay more to get that resource than if it were plentiful. The availability and accessibility of resources greatly influence how they are used. These factors also influence how resources are managed. More discussion about how resources influence family management can be found in Unit III.

Reality Check

When Uncle Sam Calls

What impact does military deployment of a parent have on a family? The United States has fought many wars in the past, but the most recent efforts in Iraq and Afghanistan have disrupted families in ways that were not typical in past deployments. The majority of soldiers did not come through a draft of young men. In the Vietnam and Korean wars, the average soldier spent less than a year overseas and was a young recruit or draftee. In Iraq, much of the burden has fallen on older reservists, National Guardsmen—family men and women (Skipp, Ephron, & Hastings, 2006).

One such family, the Arrendos (name changed for privacy),

Photo 1.2   Family members serving in the military leave more than emotional voids behind them.

Source: © Joanna Pecha/iStockphoto.

(Continued)

(Continued)

agreed to share its experience with our readers. Kathy and Mike were young professionals with two small children, ages 2 and 3, when Mike was called to duty. Kathy shares how her needs and resources changed during the course of her husband's absence. Payne's (1998) five resource categorizations are used as a framework for understanding.

Financial Resources

My husband's income increased through deployment. He made more money as a Major than he was making as a civilian. Our expenses changed, also, with his absence. He was not spending money and was no longer part of the budget for food, clothing, gasoline, and entertainment. I continued to work, and with both of our incomes and this decreased spending, we were able to accumulate a large savings account.

This situation is much different than in previous wars, when young men entered the service at much lower pay rates and, if married, their wives were usually not professional, career women, so money was often tight for those military families. Kathy shared her discomfort initially in this situation.

I met many military wives in a support group. They were in similar economic situations and their spending was unbelievable. I think I tried hard not to increase spending with our savings goal in mind. Some spending, I believe, is tied to emotions. When I was feeling angry about our situation, I spent money. As the savings account grew, I relaxed a little and spent a little more on myself—haircuts, dining out, clothing, and makeup. Other wives were remodeling their entire homes, buying new homes, and getting new vehicles. When my husband returned, we went on a bit of a spending spree, and we don't feel the same financial pressures we did before we accumulated the savings account.

Not all military families experience such increased financial resources. However, without the draft, enlistment demands have changed the level of incentives currently offered.

Emotional Resources

Initially, I couldn't focus or concentrate. How am I going to be a single parent? We always did everything together! When he left, it was almost easier because the anticipation of his departure was so emotionally draining. I went into automatic, doing what had to be done. I realize now that I did take some of my frustration out on my daughter. My mother recognized this early on and set me straight. I had relaxed control over both children, and I needed to reclaim it. Eventually the kids and I were functioning normally, again.

At the 6-month point, I quit feeling sorry for us and changed my thinking. The hardest thing emotionally is the loss of companionship. I was very lonely and found myself grasping every opportunity to converse with another adult. I found myself drinking alcohol more frequently, not more, just one or two drinks each night.

His return was much more emotionally taxing than I anticipated. It took at least 3 months for the kids and me to get used to another adult making and enforcing some of the rules. I didn't deal well with his disciplining of the children, and he seemed to be talking down to the children. It had been 18 months, and the three of us seemed to have grown and matured, but he returned at the same level he was at when he left. He resumed managing all bills and the checking account. It drove me nuts for a while! It seemed like when he had called me from over there almost every day, we really talked! He listened. At home he was returning to his old routine of avoiding conflict and controlling things. I was unwilling to go back to that relationship. We have had to work through a lot and that probably should include counseling.

When asked to discuss how her relationships with family and friends changed during Mike's deployment, Kathy noted several things that surprised her.

My father, who hates emotions, came with me to the "send off" and came to visit us every 3 months from his home in another state. Usually on past visits he wanted to be taken care of and entertained, but not during this time. He mowed, fixed things, winterized our home, and did everything that needed to be done. My mom watched the kids when I needed to be away for days at a time for work. I didn't hear from my mother-in-law at all, but I didn't before the deployment, either. No one from his family really stepped up to help. His little brother called more than usual, but never spent time with us. My siblings were supportive, my sister most. My brother did take my children to his home for 2 weeks over Christmas and made it an incredible holiday for all of us.

Friends . . . well, I really learned who my friends were. Most of those we believed to be friends before Mike left disappeared. Some we had never really done a lot with suddenly appeared and gave me tremendous support. When Mike returned, his old buddies started calling. I insisted that we had new friends and he was understanding enough to change friendships, himself.

Mental Resources

At first it was difficult to go from two adults making decisions to one adult in a high-stress, emotional state solving problems. However, as time went on, I was more and more confident in solving problems

(Continued)

(Continued)

myself, and I think that I actually grew and became more independent and better at decision making.

I became a very good time manager. I was forced to be more efficient. I think the hardest thing was being a working parent and wanting to spend as much time with the children as possible, but cleaning, mowing, laundry, cooking still had to be done. I simply decided to choose my battles. We ate out a lot, and we found more time to play together on the weekends.

Spiritual Resources

I am not a real spiritual person. I think through deployment you have to maintain a high level of trust and believe that our troops are well trained and that your spouse will make good decisions. I wasn't able to even think about what if . . . I maintained a level of confidence that things would be OK and I had a greater appreciation for God. During this time, my 18-month-old neighbor was diagnosed with cancer. I couldn't play the "poor me" card after that. I developed an ability to focus on the positives in life.

Although my husband is the religious member of my family, I continued to take my children to church each week. At first it was nothing more than a hassle with a 2-year-old and a 3-year-old to watch and control. I got nothing out of the sermon. Over time they became more manageable, and, although I did not receive support from the church, it was a nice quiet time to reflect.

Physical Resources

At first I was exhausted, but after about 6 months my stamina improved. I did hit a wall at 12 months. I had had enough. I was frustrated and angry, and I wanted it to be over! We all stayed in very good health through this time. When the kids did get sick, I brought them to work or they went to a neighbor's house. I felt neglectful, but I didn't have a choice. Once I got sick, myself, and had to ask for help, but I actually was the most physically fit I have ever been during this time. Cooking for me and two little ones was easy. The kids and I walked every day.

Kathy and Mike did what had to be done and coped in the best ways available to them. Their resources expanded with increasing needs. Sources of support shifted and changed completely in some ways. They will never be able to return to the same relationships and decision-making style present before deployment. Time, circumstances, and priorities have changed their family unit markedly. The year following a service member's return to civilian life will often determine the family's ultimate adjustment.

The toll on families caught up in the wars in Iraq and Afghanistan will be analyzed for years to come. Divorces in the military increased by 100% in 2004 (Skipp, Ephron, & Hastings, 2006). The army has spent millions of dollars on programming designed to positively enhance marital relationships of deployed men and women. All branches of the military have engaged in conscious efforts to strengthen support systems on both sides of the globe. Kathy appreciated this.

The army family support group meetings were helpful, and I really respected the army chaplains and their wisdom. It was a good place to air frustrations and anger, but it was only once a month.

CULTURAL INFLUENCES

Any study of individuals and families in the context of a global community could not ignore the enormous impact that **culture** and **diversity** have on the identification, use, and production of both material and human resources.

One cultural influence is family experience. When individuals marry, they bring with them a wide array of experiences from their own family of origin, including their unique cultural heritage, which ultimately influences their expectations for the new family. How their family managed resources will follow them into their newly formed relationship, and the two individuals will explore these experiences as they formulate their own unique way of managing resources.

Yuki and Eric have been married for 4 years. They are planning to begin a family soon. Eric announces that they must find a larger, two-bedroom apartment before a baby arrives. Yuki doesn't understand this need. In her home country, Japan, it is not uncommon for infants to share their parents' bed for the first few years.

Another important cultural influence on family resource management is **worldview**. Kluckhohn and Strodtbeck (1961) developed a framework for comparing and contrasting the different value systems between and among different cultural groups. The assumptions underlying their work include the following:

- There is a limited number of common human problems for which all people at all times must find some solution. Most families, at one time or another, must match needs and resources to feed, clothe, educate, and protect members.

- Although there is variability in solutions of all the problems, it is neither limitless nor random, but is definitely variable within a range of possible solutions. Each family and each situation is unique; however, experiences have common factors between and among families.

- All alternatives of all solutions are present in all societies at all times, but are differentially preferred. Choices made by any family at any given time may differ from those of others because of cultural expectations and beliefs. (p. 10)

As a result of these different value frameworks, they identified five distinctive **orientations** that exist within any particular cultural group, yet differ between groups. These orientations are human nature, man nature, time, activity, and relational.

The orientation of human nature may be viewed by a cultural group as evil, a mixture of good and evil, or basically good. Often cultural practices are based on these beliefs. Consider the judicial system. The practice of imprisoning criminals for certain periods of time with rehabilitative treatment suggests a culture that believes that humans are basically good, but can be misled. Religions that believe in original sin purport human nature as basically evil, with possible salvation through ritual.

The relationship between humans and nature is an orientation that can be categorized in three perspectives. Humans can be subjugated to, in harmony with, or have mastery over nature. Refusal of medical treatment is illustrative of a subjugation orientation. Air-conditioning and heating systems are used by many to gain mastery or control over the weather elements. Today, emerging concerns over environmental quality and sustainability of natural resources have forced a reconsideration of harmony between man and nature.

Every cultural group must deal with all three time orientations—past, present, and future—to maintain existence over time. The preference or dependence on a particular time orientation separates cultural groups. To participate in a financial savings plan implies that an individual is preparing for the future. Investing 4 or more years to obtain a college degree is another example of future-time orientation. Cultural groups that devote a great deal of time to the study of and the continued practicing of past rituals, art forms, and doctrine are reflective of past-time orientation.

The value placed on human activity is an orientation that also differs between cultural groups. Some focus on being or living only for the day. Others focus on becoming, searching and working for self-growth and improvement. A third orientation places more emphasis on accomplishments that are measurable by external standards. All three orientations may exist within any large group of people; however, the group as a whole shows a preference for one. Members who show evidence of that preferred activity are then deemed to be successful.

The last orientation identified to differentiate between cultures is that of human relations. Three different patterns emerge: lineal, collaborative, and individualistic. The lineal pattern is characterized by dominant group goals, a chain of command, and a commitment to maintaining the group over time. A collaborative pattern is reflected in the concept of a team. Someone operating from the individualistic pattern will place primary emphasis on personal goals and objectives and on personal autonomy.

How does this worldview framework impact family decision making? Each and every decision made by a family reflects cultural preferences at multiple levels. For instance, when a parent decides to participate in a college savings plan for his or her child, this decision reflects core beliefs that education is important, that sacrificing today for something that might come to be in the future is a worthy action, and that a college degree is an accomplishment viewed positively by the larger social group.

A human service professional operating from his or her own worldview will find that his or her ability to serve individuals and families functioning within another orientation is problematic. When an individual is devoted to collaborative relationships (i.e., family, gang, religion), he or she will not consider solutions that involve competitive actions or individualistic accomplishments. If a parent believes that children are inherently good or bad, behavior modification plans will be viewed as illogical. A family struggling for many generations with intense poverty may see no value in saving or planning for the future when surviving each day requires so much of its resource base.

Table 1.1   Impact of Differing Worldviews

Common Decision: Selection of Family Housing Family Members: Same ages, income, location, and educational levels		
Orientation	*Family A*	*Family B*
Human nature	*Harmony* Considerations: Energy conservation Natural building materials Simplicity of furnishings	*Mastery Over* Considerations: Comfort regardless of weather Popular building materials High-tech, personalized interiors
Time	*Present* Considerations: Provide for the present Meet current needs	*Future* Considerations: Invest for the future Plan for future needs
Activity	*Being* Considerations: Housing is merely shelter Changing situations will require moving	*Accomplishing* Considerations: Housing reflects social position Neighborhood implies status

Possible decisions	Modest rental unit that is
	  conveniently located
		Purchase of acceptable home
		  with mortgage commitment

Worldview

Using the structured form below, analyze the following family decisions in terms of differing worldview perspectives:

- a dual-career couple decides that the wife will leave the workforce until the youngest child enters middle school

- your neighbor refuses to use weed killer on his or her lawn because it is harmful to the environment

- a 16-year-old high school student drops out of school to take a full-time job to help support his or her family during an economic crisis

- a high school graduate decides to attend a 4-year college instead of entering the workforce immediately

Table 1.2   Worldview Applications

Orientation	Perspective	Possible Decisions
Human nature	Humans are evil? Humans are good? Humans are a mixture?	
Humans and nature—The relationship	Humans are subjugated to nature? Humans are in harmony with nature? Humans have mastery over nature?	
Time orientation	Look to the past? Look to the future? Live in the present?	
Human activity— What is valued	Focus on being? Focus on becoming? Focus on accomplishments?	
Human relations— What is expected	Lineal decision making? Collaborative decision making? Individualistic decision making?	

As Payne (1998) states, "the role of the educator or social worker or employer is not to save the individual, but rather to offer a support system, role models, and opportunities to learn, which will increase the likelihood of the person's success. Ultimately, the choice always belongs to the individual" (p. 149). Awareness and understanding of cultural differences or different worldviews provide the human service professional with increased options and heightened objectivity.

Multidisciplinary Perspectives

The study of families and behaviors of individuals and family units depends on research methods and disciplines that provide a variety of perspectives. The field of family studies integrates existing theory, new research findings, and cross-disciplinary works into a framework for understanding the complexities of family study. Utilizing that framework, professionals are able to engage in further research and/or practical application of knowledge in the field. Although the following discussion illustrates a few specific disciplines that contribute to this knowledge base, several others are possible contributors over time.

Psychology

In ancient Greek, the word *psyche* meant *soul* or *mind* and *logos* was the study of something. Psychology, as a field, has evolved into an academic and applied field focusing on the study of the mind and behavior. In the applied sense, psychology also refers to the use of the knowledge accumulated through that study to mental illness and behavioral analysis. Psychologists study mental processes and behavior of individuals, alone or in a group, not on the group itself. Wilhelm Wundt opened the first psychological laboratory in 1879.

Sociology

Sociology is the study of society, with a focus on the study of the social interactions of people, groups, and entire societies. This academic discipline emerged in the early 1800s and evolved through that century as struggles for global leadership emerged. Scientific methods were used to understand how and why groups come together and continue across time. From this inquiry, theories about social rules and governing structures give insight on why individuals are motivated to be a part of groups. In an applied form, sociological research benefits educators, lawmakers, administrators, families, and others who seek resolution of social problems and creation of public policy.

Social Psychology

The ancient philosopher Plato believed that humans organize themselves into groups and form governments to solidify their groups because they cannot achieve all of their individual goals alone (Goethals, 2003). Through the ages, students have pondered the question: How much of our behavior is determined by external constraints vs. internal drives? Triplett (1898) put social psychology into the realm of academic discipline by conducting studies that focused on the impact of other people on the individual. Allport's (1935) textbook, *Social Psychology,* grounded the study of social psychology in scientific methods. Many studies have focused on the development of norms within groups and the transmission of those norms across groups—interpersonal influence.

Social psychology is a field devoted to understanding how individuals impact the groups they associate with and how groups impact their individual members. Research within this discipline includes studies of marriage, religion, and parenting, as well as adolescent behavior.

Cultural Anthropology

Anthropology is the study of humanity. The cultural branch of anthropology seeks to make sense of difference or variation among humans. Because culture is acquired through learning, people living in different, separate places or under differing circumstances will develop different ways of thinking about similar things. This belief is exemplified by the earlier discussion of worldview.

Although understanding the differences among cultures is important to understanding how families manage their resources, it is also important to this discipline to seek universalities among humans across cultural and geographic boundaries. Are beliefs and behaviors completely learned, or is there a biological, hereditary basis to them? Anthropologists have surmised that people adapt to their environments in nongenetic ways—through culture. Current concern for the global environment and international relationships has redirected study in this field to the tensions among cultures.

Economics

The study of economics is not only about business, but also about human behavior within existing structures of production, distribution, trade, and consumption of goods and services. As a science, it functions to predict and explain the consequences of choices made by consumers and producers. Economics is a quantified field of research depending on numerical methods of analysis.

Microeconomics studies individual agents, like households and businesses. Macroeconomics focuses on the economy as an entirety. Key concepts include supply, demand, competition, and pricing. The research and models derived from the study of economics help explain how families identify and evaluate resources in their decision-making processes.

Behavioral economics is an emerging field of study that focuses on application of scientific principles to human and social dimensions of decision making. Research questions seek to answer how consumer decisions impact pricing and the allocation of resources in a society.

Biology

The field of biology is the study or science of living things. Family resource management derives important information on reproduction, physical health, and safety from biological findings and implements biological research methods and theories to answer questions about how the environment and humans interact. Genetics is an associated field that provides families with guidance when making important reproductive and health decisions. Medicine is also a related field that plays an important part in family decisions and resource allocation.

Professionals in family studies utilize multidisciplinary research methods and integrate research generated by all of these fields, which allows a multifaceted exploration of topics. For instance, if we want to understand maternal employment and its impact on the family, we can approach the question from multiple frameworks. Psychologists might focus on the emotional and cognitive impacts on family members—parents and children. Sociologists may consider the motivations that lead to the mother's participation in the workforce and how social expectations influence that behavior.

Social psychologists may view the topic in terms of how employment impacts the female's self-esteem or power base or how females impact the working environment they occupy. Cultural anthropology might be more interested in how maternal employment participation varies between and among different cultures and across time. Economics would be interested in how maternal employment impacts resources available to families and how that, in turn, impacts their consumption. Another topic of interest to economists is the potential for increased production through more fully participating adult female labor pools. Biology might study the issue from a physical perspective. The spread of contagious diseases through on-the-job contact or within child-care centers might be of interest.

In combination, these disciplines provide us with a holistic view of family resource management. All are important to the study and understanding of family behavior.

Summary

The family unit has been and continues to be the basic unit of society. As such an integral part of the larger social system, the family is impacted by all social, economic, political, and environmental changes. Thus, the family is dynamic in nature, responding and adapting to change. To allow such flexibility, families must engage in the management process, using basic decision-making tools and accessing necessary resources to maintain over time.

Questions for Review and Discussion

1. Why and when is it necessary to create limiting definitions of the family?

2. Other than money, how many resources can you list that would be important in the management of families?

3. How has culture and worldview influenced your decision to study family resource management?

4. Individuals and families use the basic decision-making steps for even small situations. Trace your most recent eating experience through the process.

5. Using the worldview framework in this chapter, determine your personal combination of the five dimensions.

6. Marriage and divorce are two important topics in this field. How might researchers in economics and social psychology differ in the way they approach these topics? Psychology and sociology?

Understanding Families 2

Objectives

- Be aware of the history and origins of the family.

- Recognize that the family today is in transition.

- Acknowledge the variety of definitions of family and the sources of those definitions.

- Be familiar with the functions of the family both in the past and today.

- Be aware of the purpose and usefulness of theory in understanding families.

- Be familiar with the basic family theories or conceptual frameworks.

- Acknowledge the strengths and weaknesses of family theories/perspectives.

- Be aware of the two basic types of research methodology, both quantitative and qualitative.

The family. We were a strange little band of characters trudging through life sharing diseases and toothpaste, coveting one another's desserts, hiding shampoo, borrowing money, locking each other out of our rooms, inflicting pain and kissing to heal it in the same instant, loving, laughing, defending, and trying to figure out the common thread that bound us all together.

—Erma Bombeck

The most basic unit of society is the family. It is hard to imagine someone who has never experienced being part of a family. In fact, almost everyone can tell a story about his or her family. For most, this unit is where we learn strength and courage to face the outside world. Effective management of the family is critical not only to the family, but to the individual members within the family. The family is where we learn to make good decisions and experience the consequences of bad decisions. A study of the family begins with the history of the family.

History of the Family

The origins of the family are unclear. Some have suggested that there is evidence that families have existed for thousands, perhaps millions, of years (Gough, 1971). Anderson (1997) speculates that although prehistoric clans were organized around a patriarch with the development of agriculture, it became necessary to organize around geographic areas ruled by political figures, rather than by the head of the family. In medieval Europe, the family was influenced by the church and feudalism, generally extended in form (Seufert-Barr, 1994). Tadmor (1996) studied the definition of a family as it appeared in 18th-century English writings. She found that the term included not only immediate blood relatives in the household, but also servants and other relatives in residence. The criterion for inclusion as a family unit at that time was an individual's dependence on the head of household for basic needs.

The institution of marriage within the family is also varied. As early as 1922, Westermarck described the origin of marriage as

It was, I believe, even in primitive times, the habit for a man and a woman to live together to have sexual relations with one another, and to rear their offspring in common, the man, being the protector and supporter of his family and the woman being his helpmate and the nurse of his children. This habit was sanctioned by custom, and afterwards by law and was thus transformed into a social institution. (pp. 27–28)

Gibbs and Campbell (1999) reported that religious and social groups experimented with different forms of familial social bonds in America during the 19th century. The practice of **polygyny**, having multiple wives, existed in certain religious factions and in some Native American cultures. Larger households meant an increase in children and wealth. Multiple adult members provided resources necessary to fulfill the many daily needs of large family units.

In America, the preindustrial family was largely an economic unit. Those who lived together were needed to help provide for existence. Families sometimes included nonfamily members whose purpose was to care for the children or carry out household work. Children, once old enough, were often sent to help other families if they were not needed at home.

After the Industrial Revolution, work was no longer centered in the home. Men went away from the home to work, and family roles were more defined. As the middle class emerged, the family became a symbol of stability and the domestic ideal (Skolnick, 1993). The **modern family** consisted of a bread-winning husband, a housewife, and their children. According to Aulette (2002), the modern family included two distinct phases. First, the **democratic family** emerged at the end of the 18th century as a separate and private group in society where mates were selected through preferences and children were nurtured. Creating and maintaining a family was an expected, almost obligatory, role for adults. Husbands went to work outside the home, and wives were expected to stay home. By the 20th century, the second phase, the **companionate family**, had become the most common family form. In the companionate family, husbands and wives were partners who married because they loved each other, rather than out of a sense of moral duty (Mintz & Kellogg, 1988).

The **postmodern family** implies that families at this time in history are so diverse that comparison with those in the past is impossible. Another implied concept within the term *postmodern* is that, in trying to rely on past research and theory, one would be unable to study current family structures and relationships.

The Family Today

Throughout history, researchers have been unable to find a picture of family that would represent what it has come to mean today or what it will be in the future. How we define the family today must be broad and flexible. One definition would not be able to accurately characterize every family in the United States. The **traditional family** or **nuclear family** implies a husband, wife, and children in one household. Although this idea has come to symbolize the American family, it is far from representing the vast majority of families.

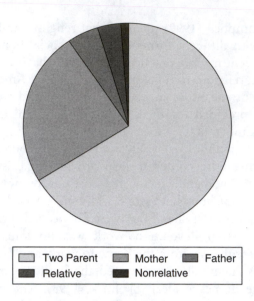

Figure 2.1   Contemporary Family Composition

Source: www.census.gov/population/socdemo/hh-fam/.

The functions of the family will lead us into our discussion throughout the text. Before we look at these functions, it is helpful to look at the diverse ways that family units are defined.

Defining the Family

The word *family* still brings to mind the image of an intact, two-parent home with two children, a dog, and gray-haired grandparents. In reality, we have just learned that in the United States we can no longer define the family in this way. In the past, the definition of family has been selective and often rigid in description, leaving many to wonder about the validity of their own family. Given the various configurations of families today, creating a contemporary definition of *family* can be a difficult task. The definition of family takes on diverse meanings depending on the context from which it comes.

THEORETICAL DEFINITIONS

Within the study of family resource management, interdependence of members and the continual need for decision making to meet needs of members are key concepts. Although no single definition meets all situational needs, those within the field of family sciences incorporate core concepts founded not only as a result of research and the development of family theory, but in response to the changes that have taken place within society. Existing definitions that address the study of families include the following:

> A group of persons united by the ties of marriage, blood, or adoption; constituting a single household; interacting and communication with each other in their respective social roles; and creating and maintaining a common culture. (Burgess & Locke, 1945)

> A range of household structures that meet people's needs at various points in their lives or that are forced on them by circumstances. (Hess, 1995)

> A consuming unit that is highly dependent on the economic system beyond the home, over which the family members have little control. (Hess, 1995)

> Two or more persons who share resources, share responsibility for decisions, share values and goals, and have a commitment to one another over time. (American Association of Family and Consumer Sciences, 2003)

As families search for public and private resources, they must navigate the multitude of definitions held by different institutions. It is hard to put the family into one philosophical box. Throughout history, the family has changed to meet the needs of its members. Family will be defined in this text based on three core concepts drawn from Lamanna and Reidmann (2006):

(1) an economic unit that strives to provide for the needs of its members,

(2) two or more people who self-identify as part of the family unit and are significantly attached to that unit, and

(3) members who are committed to maintaining that group over time.

All three criteria have major implications for resource identification, access, and management.

VARIATIONS ON A DEFINITION OF FAMILY—WHEN NUMBERS ARE NECESSARY

U.S. Census—Two or more persons sharing a household and who are related by blood, marriage, or adoption (U.S. Bureau of the Census, 1998).

Worldview

Polyandry is a form of polygamy in which one woman is married to several men. Its occurrence is rare and assumes a specific concentration in the Himalayan areas of South Asia. However, it is sporadically distributed in Africa, Oceania, and Native America. Two forms have been recorded: fraternal polyandry, in which a group of brothers share a wife; and nonfraternal polyandry, in which a woman's husbands are not related. The Nayar case discussed in another section represents a nonfraternal form, in the sense that a woman engages in sexual relations and has children with several different men, any of whom may be called on to acknowledge paternity. Fraternal forms are common in the mountainous areas of Nepal and Tibet. Among the Tibetian Nyinba, brothers live together throughout their lifetimes in large patrilineally constructed households. They share a common estate and domestic responsibilities. They also share a common wife with whom each maintains a sexual relationship. Generally, each child of the marriage is acknowledged by and develops a special relationship with one of the possible fathers, even where biological paternity cannot be determined. This arrangement can partially be understood as a response to a shortage of women due to a lower survival rate in comparison to men. It also has important economic implications. Because brothers share a wife, their joint estate remains intact from generation to generation and is not subject to the fragmentary and inefficient divisions that might occur if each belonged to a separate conjugal unit (Stone, 1997).

Polyandry is generally found in areas where difficult physical environments or high populations impose extreme pressures on agricultural systems. It works to limit population growth and ensure the coherence of agricultural estates. Some theorists suggest that this institution more often occurs in societies in which women hold relatively high social status (Stone, 1997, p.194). However, it does not reflect the same stratification pattern as polygyny because a woman's social position and prestige are not determined by the number of husbands she can amass. Female status is more apparently marked in woman–woman marriage options in polygymous societies.

Source: © Brian Schwimmer. All rights reserved. Department of Anthropology, University of Manitoba. Created October 2003. www.umanitoba.ca/anthropology/tutor/marriage/polyandry.html.

Data gathered by the U.S. Census are used in a multitude of ways. Business institutions focus on these households as consuming units, further categorizing them into socioeconomic, cultural, age-specific, and other target market groups. Financial analysts use these data to forecast the economic health of the country. Social scientists apply these data to the analysis of behavioral shifts and actual or possible impacts of such changes.

Public Opinion—Surveys administered to the general public collect information about behaviors and configurations of family units that are then presented as being acceptable or deemed to be normal in that particular society. Depending on the scientific rigor used in the creation of the instruments used in these polls, results may be generalized to the larger population or may be biased and unreliable.

Policy-Specific Definitions

The Legal System—The legal definition of a *family* has become much more flexible and nonspecific and not limited to people linked by legal marriage, blood, or adoption. Judges use these criteria: common residence, economic interdependency, stability, and commitment (Scanzoni & Marsiglio, 1993).

> Based on the functional and psychological qualities of the relationship: The "exclusivity and longevity" of relationship; the "level of emotional and financial commitment"; the "reliance placed upon one another for daily family services"; and how the members "conducted their everyday lives and held themselves out to society." (New York Supreme Court; see Gutis, 1989)

Life Insurance

Employers offering life insurance in the benefits package will usually limit coverage of an employee's family members by defining such terms as *spouse* and *child*:

> A spouse is a husband or wife, as recognized under the laws of the state of Nebraska. He/she is a common-law spouse if the common-law marriage was contracted in a jurisdiction recognizing a common-law marriage. A child is defined as a natural-born or legally adopted child who has not reached the limiting age of 19. A stepchild is one who is living in the employee's home and is chiefly dependent on the employee for support, and who has not reached the limiting age of 19. A child is one for whom the employee has "legal guardianship" and who has not reached the limiting age of 19. Appropriate documentation must be provided to verify the court appointed "legal guardian" status. (University of Nebraska Benefits, 2006)

The Family Medical Leave Act (FMLA)

Employees working for qualifying employers have the legal right to take unpaid leave to care for infants, ill children, spouses, and parents, and new parental time with adopted or foster children under this law. The following definitions illuminate qualifying situations.

- birth and care of a newborn child

- placement with the employee of a child for adoption or foster care and to care for the newly placed child

- care for an immediate family member (spouse, child, or parent—but not a parent in-law) with a serious health condition. (*The Family and Medical Leave Act: AFSCME's Comprehensive Guide*, 2007).

Social Security Survivor Benefits

To determine eligibility for someone to begin receiving these benefits, the following documentation is necessary on application:

- your marriage certificate if you are a widow or widower

- your divorce papers if you are applying as a surviving divorced spouse

- dependent children's Social Security numbers, if available

U.S. Income Tax/Internal Revenue Service

To determine tax liability, U.S. citizens file annual tax returns. The terms used in this process are defined by accompanying literature. A **Head of Household** is an unmarried person who pays over one half the cost of keeping up a home for a qualifying person, such as a child that lived with you or your parent whom you can claim as a dependent. A **dependent**—There are five tests that must be met for a person to qualify as another's dependent:

1. The Relationship Test. The person must either be a relative or have lived in your home as a family member all year.

2. Joint Return Test. If the person is married, he or she cannot file a joint return with another person.

3. Citizen or Resident Test. The person must be a U.S. citizen or resident alien, or a resident of Canada or Mexico. There is an exception for certain adopted children.

4. Income Test. The person's gross income must be less than $3,000. However, your child's gross income can be $3,000 or more if he or she was either under age 19 at the end of the year or under age 24 and a student.

5. Support Test. You must have provided over half of the person's total support in 2002. Two exceptions to this test are children of divorced or separated parents and persons supported by two or more taxpayers. As taxpayers complete the reporting forms, it is important that they understand the implications of how they define their family and how their family functions as an economic unit during the year. (www.irs.gov)

> *Should an expectant mother hope for a New Year's Eve delivery?*
>
> For a married couple, a child born on December 31 could result in a tax savings. That child would qualify as an exemption from the adjusted gross income, which would reduce the taxable income amount. Ultimately, this could save the family hundreds of dollars that year.

THE GRAY AREAS

Other definitions of *family* tend to be influenced by social factors. Family definitions that include cohabitation and domestic partnerships may be seen as gray areas by some, but are becoming more socially accepted, and these families are often granted "family" legal rights.

> **Cohabitation** is defined as two unrelated adults of the opposite sex sharing the same living quarters. (U.S. Bureau of the Census, 1998)

Despite the concerns, it has gained widespread social acceptance over the past 30 years. Current legal debate has centered on **domestic partners** entitled to legal rights and/or employee benefits. Loosely, two people who have chosen to share one another's lives in an intimate and committed relationship, live together, and be jointly responsible for basic living expenses qualify for such programs in states that recognize this designation. Federal regulations have permitted unmarried low-income heterosexual and homosexual couples to qualify as "families" to utilize public housing (Bishop, 1989).

Yorburg (2002) defines *families* as groups related by marriage, birth, adoption, or **mutual definition**. According to this definition, when people define themselves as a family, they essentially are a family. Within that mutual definition are elements of emotional involvement and identity attachment that connect individuals at the present time and create a need for continuation or maintenance of that family unit over time. This maintenance function requires acquisition and utilization of resources.

Changes in the Family

Yorburg (2002) proposes that families in industrial societies are experiencing dramatic changes in many dimensions, most obviously in terms of forms, functions, expectations, and values. Changes in demography mark the contemporary family. These represent the changes to the various forms or configurations of families today. The U.S. Census Bureau (2002) reported that married-couple households represented 56% of families in 1990, but dropped to 53% in 2000. Other demographics point to changes as well. The 2001 Census data reveal an increase in median age at first marriage, a decrease in the average size of the nation's households, and an increase in the number of persons living alone (U.S. Census Bureau, 2001). Although some may see these changes as a lack of commitment to the family, others suggest that these changes reveal caution. Individuals may be waiting for marriage or finding alternatives to marriage in an effort to avoid failure.

Changes in family expectations serve to alter the emphasis of the family within society. DeGenova and Rice (2002) point to changes in the way individuals view the family. They suggest that today the family is fulfilling more of an expressive role by meeting personal needs, such as emotional security and companionship, rather than solely fulfilling the traditional role of the family as an institution that meets the needs of society. Coontz (1992) found that only 22% of those polled in 1989 defined a family solely in terms of blood, marriage, or adoption. In contrast, 74% agreed to a definition that identified the family as any group of people who love and care for one another.

The National Marriage Project (2001) found that the institution of marriage has also changed. This project recognizes that marriage contributes to the social health of our nation and that most Americans still desire that type of relationship. Using data from 1960 to 2000, this project sought to find the indicators of the social health of marriage in America and identified the following key findings:

> Young adults today are searching for a deep emotional and spiritual connection with one person for life. At the same time, the bases for marriage as a religious, economic, or parental partnership are receding in importance for many men and women in their 20s. Taken together, the survey findings present a portrait of marriage as emotionally deep and socially shallow. (p. 6)

- Marriage trends in the United States in recent decades indicate that Americans have become less likely to marry, and that fewer of those who do marry have marriages they consider to be "very happy." (p. 18)

- The American divorce rate today is more than twice that of 1960, but has declined slightly since hitting the highest point in our history in the early 1980s. (p. 21)

- The number of unmarried couples has increased dramatically over the past four decades. Most young Americans now spend some time living together outside of marriage. (p. 22)

- The presence of children in America has declined significantly since 1960, as measured by fertility rates and the percentage of households with children. Other indicators suggest that this decline has reduced the child-centeredness of our nation and contributed to the weakening of the institution of marriage. (p. 24)

- The percentage of children who grow up in fragile—typically fatherless—families has grown enormously over the past four decades. This phenomenon is mainly due to increases in divorce, out-of-wedlock births, and unmarried cohabitation. (p. 26)

- Surveys of teen attitudes over the past few decades point up a growing disparity. Teenagers' desire for a long-term marriage has increased, especially for boys, but girls have become more pessimistic about ever being able to have such a marriage. Both boys and girls have become much more accepting of the alternatives to marriage. (p. 30)

Although many changes have taken place and the family may be difficult to define, the concept of family is an integral part of the fabric of American culture. Policymakers, educators, and service providers acknowledge the importance of the family as the core to individual well-being and growth.

In the News

The American family has been at the core of many media productions—radio, TV, movies, and even music videos. The family has been portrayed as comical, cynical, dysfunctional, and even macabre. The public is easily drawn to these odd, yet interesting, imaginary families. So much so that when these shows are discontinued, viewers mourn their loss as if the characters are real, not imaginary, friends.

Growing Pains, a family sitcom, ran from 1985 to 1992. Viewers became so attached to the Seavers that two full-length movies have been made since the show's departure from prime time more than 15 years ago. The movies' writers attempt to continue the original storyline while explaining and allowing the cast members and their characters interesting adult experiences. (www.abc.com)

The Simpsons, one of the most successful and critically acclaimed TV shows of all time, has built its reputation around the bizarre interpretation of real-life family and social issues. As an animated series on FOX, none of the characters is required to age, allowing the pseudo-middle-American family great freedom of interpretation of current social issues through the last two decades. www.thesimpsons.com/index.html

Family Guy, another hit from FOX network, lacks blue hair and the radioactivity of Springfield, USA, but packs a punch with quirky characters of its own. Stewie, the unnaturally mature baby, has his own unique, perverted perspective of family life. His older siblings provide insight into the world of adolescence, and his mother and father struggle with all of the day-to-day problems that parents face. (www.familyguy.com)

The Addams Family debuted in 1964 as a weekly prime-time, comical, yet dark, production. Scripts were focused on the traditional family of Gomez, his wife Morticia,

(Continued)

(Continued)

and their two young children, Pugsley and Wednesday. Living with this family in the frightening mansion were Uncle Fester, Grandmama, Cousin Itt, and Thing, under the faithful care of the butler, Lurch. This family unit became so beloved and well known that even though the original series only lasted for 2 years, subsequent animated series based on these characters and full-length movies brought them back to life again and again. They have most recently been on TV advertising the dark chocolate version of the popular candy M&M's.

The list of old and new media hits based on "the family" is long. What makes viewers so anxious to follow the escapades of imaginary families? Some might say that it is an attempt to make sense of their own. Others might suggest that it is an attempt to escape their own, if only for a few minutes each week.

Family Functions

Perhaps it would also be beneficial to look at the various structures of the family and concentrate on the critical functions of the family. As noted earlier, families provide the individual with a sense of belonging and emotional security, as well as to provide for their physical needs. The family is the most basic economic unit in society and is responsible for reproduction. The family is also the principal component in the socialization process. It is in the family setting that a child learns his or her place in society, as well as the roles and behaviors that give him or her status in that society.

In the past, one of the most popular theories about family was the structural-functional theory. This theory views individuals as members of many interrelated systems, one of which is the family. Parsons (1968), one of the creators of this theory, believed that four basic functions were necessary for any system to survive. These functions help to explain functions that families perform and that have caused the family to continue throughout history. These functions are latent pattern maintenance or loyalty, adaptation or ability to adjust to change, integration of members, and goal attainment or the ability to mobilize resources. This theory has been criticized for its patriarchal views, as well as for not being able to explain the differences between culture and ethnicity (Aulette, 2002).

Mitchell (1984) suggested that families provide four activities or functions: production (producing or purchasing food and shelter, preparing workers to earn wages, and consumption of goods and services), reproduction (bearing and raising children), socialization (teaching the rules of society), and sexuality ("legitimate" sexual activity).

Although some social scientists have acknowledged that many families have lost some of the functions of previous generations, such as growing their own food and educating their own children, they generally agree on three basic functions (Lamanna & Riedmann, 2003): responsible reproduction, economic support, and emotional security. Reproduction, meaning bearing and raising children, has been largely the responsibility of the family. Although the family is no longer self-sufficient in the production of goods, the family is responsible to meet the basic economic needs (food, clothing, and shelter) of its members. In addition, families can provide individuals with an important source of emotional support that includes affection and companionship. Identification of the functions of families describes the family by defining the work of families.

Families Within Cultural Contexts

Photo 2.1   Family diversity brings multiple cultures together.

Source: © lijlexmom/istockphoto.

Reality Check

Arranged marriage is a common practice in many Indian cultures, yet among non-Indians in the United States, it is widely misunderstood. Vani is a university undergraduate student who moved to the United States with her parents 10 years ago. Her family operates a retail business, and she is an education major. Vani was anxious to share marriage customs from her homeland.

Interviewer: Are you considering an arranged marriage when it is time?

Vani: It is very likely. My parents want me to return to India when it is time to begin looking for marriage. We visit about once a year, and family members who remain there would help me through the process.

Interviewer: Can you describe that process?

Vani: Most marriages where I come from are "arranged"; that is to say, the parents choose their children's mate. A key point is making sure that the mate is from the appropriate caste and is able to pay the dowry price.

Interviewer: What is a dowry?

Vani: Dowry is the payment in cash or kind by the bride's family to the groom's family when they give the bride away. The bride's family can give land, jewelry, and/or money as the gift.

Interviewer: Dowry is a very unfamiliar concept for many. Having lived in the United States, do you still think the dowry system is a good idea?

Vani: The Hindu religion is more likely to practice the dowry system, so it has religious history in my family. This practice has been responsible for many crimes against women in India, including domestic violence, bride burning, and wife murder. But my family and the families from our area are not as violent.

Interviewer: What purpose does a dowry serve?

Vani: There are three purposes. First, it is like a gift from the bride's family to the groom's, a friendship bond. Second, it is a means of compensating the groom and his family for taking on the economic burden of the bride. Third, it is a premortem inheritance for the bride.

Interviewer: You mean, it is like a life insurance policy. If the groom dies, the bride will get that back?

Vani: Maybe not exactly the same things back, but she will be assured some assets if her husband dies.

Interviewer: Let's get back to the "arranged" part of arranged marriage.

Vani: My friends in the United States have a real problem with that concept. I think people have the idea that parents find a girl for their son, and that the two never meet until their wedding day—that they have to take whatever they are given. That rarely happens. Those types of arranged marriages may still happen in smaller, conservative communities, but it's not likely.

Interviewer: How do you think your marriage will be arranged? What is the process?

Vani: Don't get me wrong. Some couples in India marry for love, but most are arranged. Since I am here, going to school, my family back in India will look for a possible husband for me. They talk to people—uncles, cousins, neighbors—and find out if anyone knows of a suitable man. Eventually someone will say, "My friend's brother has a son...." The girl's side always takes the first steps, making everyone aware that they have a marriageable female family member. When a family has a possible husband, they will ask questions and get information to help them decide if I might be good for him.

Interviewer: So if they think you are a possible match, what happens?

Vani: We will meet. If we like each other, arrangements will start.

Interviewer: You have seen your U.S. friends date. What do you think of dating?

Vani: I think it is a lot of bother. My friends seem to be attracted to guys for the wrong reasons—cars, clothes, looks.

Interviewer: How quickly do marriage arrangements happen?

Vani: Maybe half a year. During that time, sometimes, the couple finds out they are not compatible. They can stop the process when that happens. They get together a few times, not overly much. Maybe two times a month, minimum.

Interviewer: What about divorce?

(Continued)

(Continued)

> **Vani:** I have had a few classes that explore "love." That seems like a very shaky thing to me. In my country and in my group, marriage and family is built on more strong points—compatibility and possibilities. Marriage isn't expected to be perfect or always joyful. I think our way is more realistic.
>
> **Interviewer:** Then there are no divorces?
>
> **Vani:** No, there are. I know some people who have divorced. The reasons aren't about love or stopping love, it is usually about drunkenness or violence. I approve if it's needed—if he's a drunk or if he's beating her. Many of my American friends have divorced parents. Children back home don't have that kind of insecurity.
>
> The United States has citizens from many religious and cultural backgrounds. Dating and mating behaviors will differ between and among groups—even within the same group. These behaviors have evolved over long periods of time, reflecting values and experiences of group members. They are all valid on some level. It is difficult, if not impossible, to evaluate behaviors from outside your group without the necessary context for understanding why those practices continue.

Families exist within the cultural contexts of race, ethnicity, religion, politics, and economics. These frameworks impact the way individuals and families define and evaluate their relationships. As the global community continues to evolve, it is important to recognize, understand, and be responsive to cultural differences between and among cultural groups.

Families pass learned behaviors and experiences, or a cultural heritage, from generation to generation (Johnson, 1998). Drawing from the worldview framework introduced in Chapter 1, the values held by cultural groups are expressed in unique patterns through formation and perpetuation of family units. Kluckhohn and Strodtbeck (1961) propose that the three primary cultural expressions of group membership are lineal, collaborative, and individualistic. Family units within these cultural groups reflect the orientation of the larger social group. For instance, Native-American families reflect stronger lineal relationships, often defining family membership from a clan or group of related families (Johnson, 1998). However, few cultural groups will fit neatly into any one of the three orientations. Although many Native Americans may have a more developed awareness of their tribal membership (lineal), the basic functions of these tribes have historically been collaborative in nature.

The African American family has been the focus of numerous studies. Murry (2000) states, "just as black families are different from white families, black families are also different from each other" (p. 336). Peters and Massey (1983) suggest that when studying situations and coping models about African American families, we must understand that the experiences of these families continue to be influenced by racism and that the existence of that social condition requires extraordinary efforts of African American families to lead ordinary lives.

Demographic information illuminates a few unique family structural differences within the contemporary African American family. A larger proportion of African American families are headed by single parents (Murry, 2000). Norton and Moorman (1987) report that, although 9 out of 10 White women can expect to marry within their lifetimes, fewer than 3 out of 4 African American women can expect the same. These emerging patterns could further impact the family experiences or the cultural heritage of future generations.

As cultural groups coexist within a larger society, individuals from different racial, ethnic, and religious groups begin drawing life partners from distinctly different cultural groups. Interracial marriages include the joining together of individuals from the White, African American, Asian, or Native-American races with someone from outside their race. In comparison to all marriages, interracial marriages have increased from .7% in 1970 to just over 5% (U.S. Bureau of the Census, 2006). Interethnic marriages consist of partners who marry within their ethnic groups, such as unions between Hispanic groups or between Asian groups.

Although religious homogamy is still prevalent, **interfaith** marriages are increasing in the United States and have an influence on the economic and demographic characteristics of families (Lehrer, 1998). Adler (1997) reported that 15% to 20% of marriages represent differing religious preferences between spouses. Still others switch to their partner's religion, or the couple chooses a new religion to practice. Religious homogamy is not as frequent as racial and ethnic homogamy in marital statistics; however, it is an important factor within some marriages. Religious orientations often affect decisions about money, children, social networks, and relationship issues.

Researching the Family

Those who study the family recognize that the field is diverse. Not only are there many structural variations that describe families and numerous ways of defining the family, but there are many ways to explain how families function and operate in society. Formal **theory** involves a set of propositions that can be tested or proved to explain a phenomenon in society such as the family. Borrowing from various fields of study, family theory depends on multiple **theoretical perspectives** or **conceptual frameworks.** Some of these involve scientific explanations, whereas others are based on personal experience and observation. All seek to understand the family.

There are several reasons that it is necessary to examine the theoretical perspectives of families. These perspectives help explain "why" or "how" families work. They help us to make sense of how families behave. This information is helpful to those who assist families as well as those who guide policy that affects families. Theory also provides structure for future studies—a place to start when looking for answers. They give the researcher a guide for his or her inquiry.

At this point, it becomes important to explore eight theoretical perspectives that help in understanding families. Particular attention is given to how these perspectives relate to family resource management.

FAMILY SYSTEMS THEORY

The family systems theory (also referred to as the family systems framework) is a popular perspective among professionals who work with families. This theory grew out of the general systems theory developed by Bertalanffy (1969) in the 1960s from the science field. Several components of this theory are distinctly applicable to the family as a system. According to the family systems theory, when something occurs to one family member, all members of that family are affected. It is assumed that the members are part of the group or system and function as a system. Family therapists find this theory especially helpful in working with individual family members, and their treatment may need to include the whole family.

Charles and Bonnie have always enjoyed the finer things of life, and throughout their married life rationalized their need for expensive clothing, fine dining, and a lavish lifestyle. They frequently spent more than their income to support their habits, not being able to build savings or retirement as a safety net for the future. For Charles, this way of living was a model that he saw from his own parents. When Bonnie, who grew up in a very poor family, met Charles, she was enamored by the lifestyle and quickly adopted his principles of the "good life." Although they recognized that their way of living was probably not responsible, they were not willing to change. They often remarked "Most people have no idea how to live!" They knew that others did not approve of their lifestyle but Charles would announce, "We are not hurting anyone . . . I wish they would mind their own business!" After a few years, Charles and Bonnie's son graduated from college and announced his engagement. The newlyweds were married in a lavish ceremony and began their new lives in a beautiful new home in one of the finest areas of town. After a few months, their son called to tell them that he and his wife were getting a divorce and that he would have to declare bankruptcy. Charles was shocked and replied, "How could this happen, you have everything you want?"

This story illustrates the idea that the actions of individuals within a family affect all the family members. Parents model behavior that is passed down from generation to generation unless there is a conscious effort to change. Furnham (1999) suggested that habitual economic behaviors established early may be encouraged by parents or other adults. If Charles and Bonnie's son is ever going to make responsible decisions about his financial future, he will have to make a conscious decision to make changes that will help him to learn new strategies about spending and saving money.

Another aspect within the family systems framework is the assumption that what families do within their units not only impacts other family members, but also impacts their communities.

SOCIAL EXCHANGE THEORY

Family members have individual motivations influencing the behaviors they select. These differences between and among members create situations where personal resources can be bartered or exchanged to further one's self-interests. Exchange theorists explain that families continue to exist because the family group is viewed as a source of rewards for individual members (White & Klein, 2002). Family members bring to the family unit personal resources that can be used to maintain that unit. Infants and children are heavily dependent on the resources of older family members, but will be expected, at some future time, to contribute their own time, energy, and skills to the family's functioning. Adolescent and adult family members may participate in a type of cost-benefit analysis when they feel uncomfortable or unappreciated by other members. The degree of self-sufficiency perceived by individuals will impact their decisions to either leave or stay within the family group.

The exchange framework is often used to study power bases within the family. Obviously, the ability to provide necessary resources to the family unit will increase one's value in that group. Depending on the circumstances or the types of resources necessary at any one time, an individual family member's personal power may increase or decrease. That power base may impact an individual's role in the decision-making process. When a parent has the money and ability to make a purchase contract, he or she will have more actual power in the decision process for buying a teenager an automobile. Regardless of whether he or she exercises that power will depend on the family's communication process and the history of that particular child–parent relationship.

Application of the exchange theory also emerges in the study of courtship, mate selection, and implementation of the decision-making process across family life situations. By the end of the 1970s, exchange theory had become one of the most widely used theoretical frameworks in family research (Edleson & Tan, 1993).

Monty and Frank are brothers in their mid-40s. After the death of their father, Bill, they jointly inherited the family farming operation. Monty is married with three children. Frank is single and has no children. Their mother is to receive an annual living allowance from their operational profits. This change of ownership has created a great deal of stress between the brothers and between Monty's wife and her mother-in-law. They decided to bring the conflicting issues before their lawyer for advice.

"I know Bill meant well," Monty's wife offered, "but we have children to support and Frank is single. Surely he didn't mean for his grandchildren to go without at the expense of their uncle."

"Having children was a choice you and Monty made," her mother-in-law responded. "We wanted our hard-earned estate to be equally divided between the two boys."

"How does this inheritance continue, then?" asked Monty's wife. "When Monty and Frank die, is the entire farm operation split equally among our kids?"

Inheritance can be viewed as a set of long-term exchange relationships, linking different generations of the farming family (Kennedy, 1991). Land and earning power are both examples of resources that are used as bargaining capital in the exchange process within families. Historically, this division of farming lands among surviving heirs seriously compromised the ability of farm families to make a living on shrinking pieces of land. Much of what used to be family farm ground is now part of large corporate-owned businesses. The increasingly complex legal ramifications of such actions has made the creation of legal wills and trusts a common action of families with inheritance that is to be passed from generation to generation.

SYMBOLIC INTERACTIONISM

Symbolic interactionism has a long-standing tradition in family theory, tracing back to the early 1900s and continuing to add to the theoretical framework through the last century (LaRossa & Reitzes, 1993). Social and psychological concepts are woven into this conceptual framework. This theoretical perspective looks within families at the process that creates a family unit in the minds of those family members.

Drawing from both qualitative and **quantitative research** studies, theorists avoid identifying any natural or typical family structure. Instead, families are viewed as unique creations of participants as they spontaneously relate to one another. Interactions of family members, such as talk, gestures, actions, and shared beliefs, create that family's particular reality. Individuals develop a sense of self through these interactions.

Family identities emerge over time as the family creates rituals and shared meanings or **symbols** (Bossard & Boll, 1943).

The shared meanings that emerge through interactions and defining of member roles allow the family unit to define situations in unique ways. Behaviors, such as decision making and resource identification, are based on meanings that group members have created regarding both the situation and possible actions that individuals and family units have available to handle that particular situation (Mead, 1964).

This theory does not ignore the impact of larger social groups on the family unit. Researchers have sought ways to explain how family units and members within families seek to present themselves to others. Turner (1970) refers to this as **impression management.** As consumers of goods and services, individual within the family unit are aware that choices made will be interpreted by other social groups outside the family and social value judgments will result.

Samuel, a PeeWee baseball player, and his parents are shopping for shoes to wear during practices and games. Prices range from $20 to $120 in his size range. "I've got to have those white ones on the top shelf. My favorite professional baseball player talks about them on television and Bobby said he was going to get them, too." "But those are twice as much as these," his father counters, pointing to a similar looking pair on a lower shelf. What are the odds that Samuel will walk out of the store with the more expensive shoes?

Shoes are shoes. Why is it that some consumers will pay higher prices for athletic shoes that are similar in construction to less expensive choices merely for an athlete's endorsement or a company's insignia? Building on the symbolic interactionist theory, Laverie, Kleine, and Schultz (2002) explored how and when consumption and products purchased impact a person's self-identity or "how products make the person." The results of this study found that not only do the actual possessions (apparel and equipment used during athletic activities) lead to more positive self-evaluations, but social ties and the media promotion of those products also enhance the owner's feeling of self-definition. A contemporary term, **conspicuous consumption,** is used to describe situations that result from purposeful selection of products to create an image of the self when judged by others. Designer labels, expensive automobiles with identifying symbols, and even specially bred pets are examples of this concept.

The media's advertising implications and peer pressure may have a significant impact on Samuel's ultimate possession of new baseball shoes. The process utilized by his parents to decide which shoes to buy will include the possible impact of this purchase on young Samuel's self-identity, as well as the reflection such a purchase will have on the entire family as decision-making criteria. Prioritizing such criteria will determine the ultimate impact such factors will have on the shoes selected.

CONFLICT THEORY

Although the conflict theory surfaced as a popular framework in the 1960s, its roots are in the 19th-century works of Karl Marx (Marx & Engels, 1967). Marx revolutionized the way human society was viewed, focusing on the negative impact of the European Industrial Revolution. He felt that the capitalistic environment encouraged the exploitation of the workers. To combat this, he purported that when those being oppressed join forces and challenge their oppressors, conditions can be changed.

Conflict theorists agree that conflict is natural and expected in human interaction. Family units are no different than other organized groups in this respect. There are unequal power bases within each family, resulting in situations of competition, coercion, and conflict.

Conflict theory can be analyzed through three central themes: (a) humans are driven to want and to seek certain things, (b) power is at the core of all social relationships, and (c) groups have self-interests that they use to advance their own goals, rather than those important to the entire society. Thus, families are social institutions where some members benefit more than others from the existence and maintenance of the family unit. Marriage is often viewed as a relationship ripe with inequality, subordination, and male dominance. Other family situations that are often studied from this framework are domestic violence, divorce, and single parenting.

Application of conflict theory challenges the presentation of families as stable, harmonious, and peaceful social units. For that reason, many researchers avoided using this framework in family research until society experienced stressful change periods, such as the civil rights movement of the 1960s and the dramatic increase of women in the workplace over the last four decades. It emerged as a major player among theories in the late 1960s, and the body of research since that time has established this framework as a strong base for the study of contemporary family issues. Feminist theory is often considered rooted in basic conflict theory thought.

Marta and Pete are disagreeing about more and more day-to-day parenting decisions concerning their twin daughters. Frequent struggles over power within their personal relationship have ensued since Marta returned to her job after the girls started grade school. Marta had left her flight attendant career when she became pregnant. Pete is beginning to feel that his job as a travel agent is becoming a dead-end endeavor. The advancement of travel arrangement via the Internet has brought about lower commission earnings at his current office. Marta has been very pleased to be able to supplement his declining earnings with her own paycheck. Recently she has been promoted to a higher level of crew management and received a large raise in pay.

When the girls were exposed to chicken pox at school and had to spend a few days recuperating at home, tension boiled over.

"Pete, can't you stay home with them and do your work on your computer, here?" Marta pleads when she gets a call for a well-paying flight.

"The girls want you, and you know that they are impossible. You've spoiled them rotten," he retorts as he grabs his bag and heads out the door.

"They're just not used to you being so involved with them," Marta continues, "if you'd just spend more time with them." Pete is already out the door.

When parents are struggling within their own relationship over power issues, how are relationships with their children affected? Lindahl and Malik (1999) found that clashes over power and control in the marriage were associated with diminished support of the children. Mental and physical resources are limited, and when they are channeled into negative discourse, they are unavailable for other tasks. Pete may be trying to regain his earlier power base of breadwinner by forcing Maria to choose between her daughters' well-being and her job at the economic detriment to the entire family unit.

FEMINIST PERSPECTIVE

Although the field of family sociology has been in existence for decades and women's rights emerged as early as the late 1800s, the study of the family was largely dominated by men. Since the early 1970s, feminists have stressed that the widely used frameworks that describe families are often void of the women's point of view or experiences.

Gordon (1979) identified three essential themes within the feminist perspective: the "emphasis on women and their experiences; recognition that under existing social arrangements women are subordinated or oppressed; and commitment to ending that unjust subordination" (p. 107). Osmond and Thorne (1993) suggest that, as a result of these themes, a fourth theme has emerged: "attention to gender and gender relations as fundamental to all of social life, including the lives of men as well as those of women" (p. 592).

Although the feminist perspective has gained some popularity in the past few years, there are others who argue that the theory isolates the role of women in relationships and forgets that both genders should have equality within family relationships. There is no doubt that gender plays a large role in family studies or that researchers should take both genders into account.

> *Charlotte was recently widowed after a long and happy marriage of 48 years. Following the shock of losing the only man she ever loved, she was faced with the overwhelming task of taking care of the financial affairs of the estate. Realizing how helpless his mother felt, John decided to help her sort through the papers. "Where did dad keep all the insurance policies and the statements from your retirement account? Did he have a safety deposit box or did you have a savings account?" Charlotte responded, "I don't know where anything is! Your dad took care of all our finances . . . I guess he never thought I would need to know. I was only a housewife."*

Charlotte is not alone. Many older women have had similar experiences. Macdonald (1995) suggests that the very nature of economics is male-dominated, and thus the two spheres of paid labor market economics and unpaid/informal household economics are separate. In this case, the feminist perspective could help to understand how these two spheres interact and impact each other.

FAMILY ECOLOGICAL THEORY

The family ecology theory joins the concepts of human development and family relationships with the structure of family resource management to identify a wide range of problems that families face given the environment in which they live. Bubolz and Sontag (1993) suggest that this theory is particularly useful today because it is not limited to certain groups, and it applies to a wide range of family configurations and cultural backgrounds.

The origin of the ecological theory as it relates to the family began as the ideas of human ecology were being promoted by Haeckel in 1873 (Bubolz & Sontag, 1993). According to Haeckel, who was intrigued by Darwin's theories of evolution, there is a link between science or biology and the environment. During this same time, Ellen Swallow Richards announced the beginning of the science of oekology (derived from the Greek word meaning *household management*) that she described as the "science of living" (Clarke, 1973). Oekology was a way of using scientific principles to improve the lives of families. The name that eventually became associated with this science was *home economics.*

Although the ecological theory does not have a formal set of theoretical propositions, Hawley (1986) put up some general propositions that describe the family within the surrounding ecosystem. Some of the propositions Hawley suggests are that change and growth occur through experiences with the outside systems, new information from the outside causes change to the relationships within the family, and the family is closed to the ecosystem around it to ensure stability.

Sheila and Michelle are cousins and are both single mothers. Their children are the same age, but have responded to the demands of life in very different ways. Michelle reports, "Ben is getting into trouble at school almost every day but I just don't know what to do. It has upset me so much that I started seeing a therapist. He suggested that I take an antidepressant to help me." Although Sheila is sympathetic, she doesn't agree with the way that Michelle is handling her situation. Sheila replies, "Michelle, have you talked to Ben about what is bothering him? Have you met with his teachers? Are you sure that medication will solve this problem? I know that when Ethan gets in trouble, it helps to get all the information I can in order to help him." Sheila silently wonders if Michelle is making decisions about medications that are based on societal expectations without knowing the consequences to herself and her family. Is Michelle neglecting to address her own physical, emotional, and even spiritual needs?

The ecological theory requires that the whole person within a series of systems—the external environments—is taken into account when a problem is presented. Meyers, Varkey, and Aguirre (2002) found a significant association between these systems and family functioning. In this case, Michelle opts to solve the problem at hand by taking an antidepressant drug instead of examining the various systems involved in her son's behavior as well as her own.

FAMILY STRENGTHS FRAMEWORK

The focus of the family strengths framework is on what is right rather than what is wrong with families. According to Olson and DeFrain (2003), one advantage of this framework is that the focus of study is changed from just solving problems to emphasizing what is working well in that family. Once strengths are identified, a foundation is established for continued growth and change in that family. As a result, strong families can become a model for families that want to succeed.

The strengths perspective can be traced back as early as the 1930s, but Herbert Otto's work in the 1960s is often credited with building a foundation for the current work in family strengths (Otto, 1962). Within the structure of the family strengths framework, there are six major qualities of a strong or healthy family (Stinnett, 1981; Stinnett, DeFrain, & DeFrain, 1999): commitment to the family, spending enjoyable time together, spiritual well-being, successful management of stress and crisis, positive communication, and showing appreciation and affection to each other. The researchers continue to study family strengths and have found these qualities have been reported by more than 21,000 family members in the United States and more than 25 other countries around the world. Families everywhere are unique in their own cultures, yet strong families commonly seem to be guided by these basic qualities.

Greg and Cindy are newlyweds. They thought that they had prepared for marriage in every way. They attended premarital sessions, talked to other newlyweds about their experiences, and read several books about marriage. Six months into their marriage, they began to see differences in the way they each wanted to spend money. After realizing this, Cindy said, "This doesn't change the way I feel about you but I am concerned that when we have children, we will have trouble deciding on how to save for their education, and other expenses." They began to talk about the origin of these differences and traced many of their ways of thinking back to the models that they saw while growing up. Will Cindy and Greg ever be able to work through this issue in their marriage?

Through the discussions, they started to realize neither one had an inherently flawed idea of money, but that they needed to understand each other's views and develop financial goals that met the needs of their own newly formed family. DeFrain and Stinnett (2002) identified several propositions of the strengths perspective that are illustrated here. Greg and Cindy were able to look at their own families and identify differences focused on the issue of money. Instead of continuing to disagree and argue about who was right, they focused on the positive by appreciating the values that the other person brought to the discussion. They also used positive communication to discuss ways to change and manage positive growth in this area.

FAMILY DEVELOPMENT THEORY

Of all the theories introduced in this chapter, family development theory is the only one that is solely based on the discipline of family studies. It does not claim to have broader applications to other social groups (White & Klein, 2002). The two major components within this theory are time and history, focusing on the changing social expectations unique to each stage of a family's existence. Thus, it views the family as a dynamic system. The roots of this theory have moved through three distinctive periods.

Tracing back as far as the American Revolution (1770s), the definition of a family and the life course of individual families were recorded and reflected on. White and Klein (2002) refer to this phase as the descriptive phase of the theory. Shortly after World War II, research on family stress ensued. Within this research, the family unit is described as having social roles and relationships within that change as the family moves through stages over time. The theory was embraced, and research efforts further solidified it as a major theoretical idea.

Most recently, the family development theory has struggled to maintain a distinctive position in family theory. Proponents have tried to answer criticisms and incorporate new methodologies. Core to this current theoretical framework are the ideas that families are identifiable groups that mature and change as they move through a time continuum. Time is measured in stages. A **family stage** is an interval of time in which the roles and relationships within the family change in observable ways. The theory works most easily with traditional families—wife, husband, and two children. Considering the current diversity in family constructs, this theory becomes problematic. Even traditional family structures with several children become confusing as the number of stages and the overlapping of stages increase.

Alvin has recently retired from his lifelong career and is making adjustments to his daily schedule. He has spent the last 40 years in a fast-paced, 60-hours-a-week position and has been looking forward to relaxing and pursuing his special interests that have long been postponed. He is also anxious to spend more time with his family and to travel extensively.

Martha, Alvin's wife of 42 years, has devoted most of her time to managing the home and family and actively volunteers for several charity organizations. She has been anxiously awaiting Alvin's retirement and looks forward to spending more time with him. As a couple, these two are transitioning from one family stage into the next—retirement. They adjusted to the empty-nest stage years ago.

After 2 weeks, Martha explains to Alvin, as he places his breakfast dishes into the sink, "Let me show you how to load the dishwasher and run it. I've been wanting to talk about how you could help me more around the house, anyway."

Housework was not one of the things Alvin had been planning to add to his new role. "But I already take care of the yard and the car."

As families move from one stage to the next, roles must be renegotiated. Gupta (1999) studied the effects of transitions in marital status on men's performance of housework. One conclusion from that study was "with respect to housework time at least, the formation of households with adult partners of the opposite gender remains more to men's than to women's advantage" (p. 710). This notion would lead us to believe that Alvin will probably not rise to meet his wife's new expectations. However, family member roles may be age- and stage-graded (White & Klein, 2002). If the surrounding culture views cleaning as a more acceptable expectation for a retired male than for a working male, Alvin may likely accept these new duties willingly.

The theoretical or conceptual framework utilized in a research project will both enhance and constrain the information collected. All of the theories and perspectives presented in this chapter have a history within the study of families. Each has its strengths and weaknesses. Together they have created a broad, useful knowledge base for family problem solving and understanding.

Table 2.1   Theory Strengths and Weaknesses

Theory/Perspective	Strength	Weakness
Family systems	Focuses on the interconnectedness of family members and their experiences.	Assumes that all family members are functioning as active participants of the family system.
Social exchange	Focuses on individual resources and the bartering of these resources, seeking to explain the power bases within families.	Becomes problematic when analyzing the roles of children in family units.
Symbolic interactionism	Combines social and psychological concepts, and views families as uniquely self-created units.	Focuses on the uniqueness of family realities and lessens the generalizability of research findings.
Conflict	Recognizes that conflict is natural and expected in human interaction.	Challenges the view of families as stable social units.
Feminist	Incorporates women's views and experiences into the research framework.	Isolates the role of females and ignores male experiences.
Family ecological	Links the family experiences to its environment.	Broadens research efforts and raises level of complexity for findings.
Family strengths	Focuses on emphasizing what is working well for the family rather than problem solving.	Focuses on problem solving.
Family development	Views the family as a dynamic system.	Becomes difficult with nontraditional family structures.

Family Research Design

Questions about how families work lead to research. Research methods are selected to answer these questions and are chosen based on the researcher's theory preference. Research traditions fall along the lines of either quantitative or qualitative methodology (see Table 2.2). Quantitative methodology is used when quantifiable data are needed to show a measurable correlation between phenomena. One example of a research project that would require a quantitative design involves a researcher who wants to find out whether an increase in single-parent homes has a possible connection to an increase in juvenile delinquency. The researcher would need to have a large sample and collect enough data to show a statistical correlation. In contrast, qualitative methodology is used to develop a deeper understanding about something in which little is known. **Qualitative research** involves details that are difficult to present in quantitative terms. An example of a qualitative study with families would include describing the complexities of homelessness (Marshall & Rossman, 1995). This study would involve the researcher conducting interviews and possibly observing the homeless in an effort to understand their lived experiences. Whatever methodology is chosen, the results of research are meant to inform. This new information can then be used to improve education or change policies in that particular area.

Table 2.2   Family Research Design

Quantitative	Qualitative
• Data are collected with an instrument. • The search is for a correlation. • Results are reported using numbers or percentages. • Findings are generalized.	• The researcher is the instrument. • The search is for a pattern. • Results are reported using words or description. • Findings are centralized, but specialized.

Summary

The family is one of society's most basic institutions. Historically, the family has existed for centuries and was organized for economic purposes. Today, the family has changed. Although it is still an organization that depends on economics, family members

(Continued)

(Continued)

may also rely on each other for emotional support and security. Throughout history, researchers have been unable to find a common definition that would describe the family. Today, it is still hard to find a definition that would represent what the family has come to mean today or what it will be in the future. Such a definition must be broad and flexible. The family has also experienced a change in function. Although functions such as the production of goods and services have changed to the procurement of goods and services, basic functions of emotional security and economic support still apply. Family theory is another way to define and understand how families work and family researchers draw from one or more of these theories or conceptual frameworks. Today family researchers use quantitative and qualitative methodology that leads to a better understanding of the family.

Questions for Review and Discussion

1. What is the history of the family?

2. What are some examples that illustrate how the family today is in transition?

3. Why are there so many different definitions of family?

4. How have the functions of the family changed over time?

5. What is the purpose of theory in understanding families?

6. What are the strengths and weaknesses of each family theory?

7. What are the two types of research methodology used in family research? What are the differences between the two?

The Management Process 3

Objectives

- Be familiar with the common history of business management and family management.
- Acknowledge the importance of management to family success.
- Recognize the need for active management processes in the decision-making process.
- Understand the connections between management and family choices.

*American families have always shown remarkable resiliency, or flexi-
ble adjustment to natural, economic, and social challenges. Their
strengths resemble the elasticity of a spider web, a gull's skillful flow
with the wind, the regenerating power of perennial grasses, the cooperation of an ant colony, and the persistence of a stream carving
canyon rocks. These are not the strengths of fixed monuments but
living organisms. This resilience is not measured by wealth, muscle
or efficiency but by creativity, unity, and hope. Cultivating these
family strengths is critical to a thriving human community.*

—Ben Silliman, Family Life Specialist
with the University of Wyoming's
Cooperative Extension Service

Management is an ongoing process. It involves matching resources and
needs on a continual basis. It could be argued that management continues until failure is accepted. The largest, most successful companies in the
United States have survived because their management approaches have
evolved with the social, political, and economic changes characteristic of the
business environment.

Families also exist within a dynamic environment. Because family members experience personal, individual growth and development, managing a
family unit requires high levels of flexibility and resourcefulness. Although
business and family management differ in many ways, they share many
threads, in both historical development and contemporary application.

Management as a Field of Study

Management is essential to human existence. One could argue, then, that
management has been practiced since the beginning of humankind. The
word *manage* has its roots in two distinctive sources. The Italian word *man-
ageggiare* is defined as handling things, especially horses. However, it is
believed that at the turn of the 16th century that word became confused with
the French word *menager*. This new meaning was to be used carefully, especially in a household. Also of interest is the fact that the word *economy* can be
traced to ancient Greek where it meant *house management* (Wensley, 1996).

Stone (1998) suggests that even as late as the 1940s management as a
discipline of study was yet undeveloped: "Most managers did not realize that
they were practicing management" (p. xi).

Crainer (2000) believes that management, as a profession, came of age
during the 20th century, but it would be foolish to assume that it did not
exist before that time. Obviously, management was involved in the creation

of all historic civilizations, evident in their cultural expressions of arts and political structures.

In Weir's (2001) biography of King Henry XIII of England (1491–1547), she presents several managerial scenarios within this single royal court. Managing a kingdom and a court of great size required both structure and recordkeeping. To maintain a royal blood line, it was necessary to exert high levels of control over even the most personal aspects of the royal family's life.

> Back in his nursery, the Prince was subject to an orderly regimen. . . . Henry's Lady Mistress supervised his wet-nurse and dry nurse, who were assisted by four chamberers known as rockers, whose chief duty was to lull their charge to sleep by rocking his cradle. . . . A physician stood by to supervise every feeding. (p. 137)

Surely, the construction of ancient artifacts, such as the pyramids and the Great Wall, required massive management campaigns. Management, as a process used by humans, is evident in historic written records as well as artifacts left behind from each great civilization. To accomplish goals and objectives, resources must be managed, either consciously or subconsciously. The same is true of both businesses and families. If a business or family unit is to maintain, grow, and be productive, it must be managed well.

PARALLEL HISTORIES

The post–Civil War United States was heavily involved in reconstructing the country and its government. These activities required a great deal of organization and resource management. During this time, the culture of the United States remained dependent on the family unit. Commerce and industrialization were rising, yet the transfer of wealth from one generation to the next was still connected to inheritance through family lines. Families lived in household units that required management of facilities, food, clothing, and education. As early as 1861, a publication on how to manage such a unit was released and received by the general public quite favorably. As mentioned in Chapter 1, Beeton's *Book of Household Management* (cited in Hughes, 2006) presented three principles of good management:

- set an example and provide clear guidance to your staff,
- control the finances of the family carefully, and
- strive for order and method in all management activities.

Some argue that Mrs. Beeton was the first author of the operations management perspective (Wensley, 1996).

Not long after this publication, Fayol (1949) proposed four key managerial concepts: plan, organize, lead, and control. Although these concepts were intended for business management, they were equally applicable in household management. When viewed as a social organization and a productive unit, the family resembles the business unit in many ways. As the discipline of business management emerged during the 20th century, there are several parallel developments in the field of home economics, from which family resource management has its roots.

Two influential people lived and worked for similar things at the turn of the 20th century. Frederick Taylor was busy applying scientific analysis to the workplace and the nature of work itself, and Ellen Swallow Richards was working diligently toward a similar end—the application of science to the family and the household.

Ellen Richards

Richards was the first woman admitted to the Massachusetts Institute of Technology as a special student in chemistry. In 1876, she became head of the science section of the Society to Encourage Studies at Home. Her scholarly contributions included the study of sanitation of the home, nutrition, and health, and the management of the home in terms of time, energy, and money. As a contributor in the noted Lake Placid Conferences at the turn of that century, Ellen ensured that the field of home economics was recognized by the academic community. She was also instrumental in the formation of the American Home Economics Association (now the American Association of Family and Consumer Sciences), formally organized in 1908 and devoted to improving living conditions in the home, the institutional household, and the community (Pundt, 1980).

Frederick Taylor

Frederick Taylor had a passion for efficiency. Perhaps his greatest contribution was to invent management as science. He focused on the nature of work, proposing that any change in the process of work that brought about increased efficiency and resulted in increased productivity was worthy of both study and implementation. In 1911, he published his beliefs in *The Principles of Scientific Management.* Taylor also believed that the fundamental principles of scientific management were applicable to all human activities (Crainer, 2000).

Both Richards and Taylor were working toward similar ends at about the same time in history. They wanted their personal passion for scientific study of management to be legitimatized as a field of study, recognized, and appreciated by the scientific minds in higher education. The realms of application differed, however. Home economics would strive to improve the lives of individuals and families where they lived, the home, whereas business management would strive to improve efficiency and productivity in the workplace, the assembly line, and other production venues.

The Evolution of Home and Business Management: The 20th Century

Aspects of both home and family management and business management continued to coexist and to even thread together on occasion through the last 100 years. Vickers (1984) delineates this period of time into four separate eras of household production and consumption patterns. Because the changes in the social, political, and economic environments of the United States had a profound impact on both household management and business management, the changes emerging within the science of business management are presented within the discussion of each era that follows.

ERA ONE (CA. 1900–1930s)

Building on the foundation set forth by Richards, the study of household management continued focusing on health, sanitation, and hygiene. The study of how households function as units of consumption and production in the overall economy was also considered. Programs and curriculum in both high schools and universities were built around cleaning, cooking, meal planning, and organizing housework.

In 1918, the first Home Management House opened (at the University of Nebraska), where students actually lived and received practical instruction in keeping up a home as part of their coursework . . . in 1922, the Home Management House grew to include a baby, giving the women opportunity to have practical training in child care. The babies were "borrowed" from the State Home for Children . . . Each baby stayed about four months before it was adopted. (Kroesche, 2002)

Another illustration of how the fields of both family and business management become intertwined is the story of Lilian Gilbreth. Lilian and her husband Frank were pioneers in "motion study." When Frank died in 1924, companies that had employed the couple as consultants refused to continue employing a widowed woman in that capacity. Lilian turned her study of efficiency onto what was possible, her family's home life. She charted her 12 children's daily activities—chores, hygiene, and education.

The field of business management underwent several important changes of direction during this era of time. Weber moved beyond Taylor's work in efficiency to the development of a highly structured **bureaucratic** system. Barnard introduced rational decision making into the management process, proposing that the chief officer of any company is more of a parent than a dictator, nurturing the values and goals of the organization. He also incorporated the systems theory into his framework. A female, Mary Parker Follet, worked within the business management field to humanize industry at a time when her male colleagues were moving in the other direction. She saw the manager's tasks as coordination, defining the purpose, and anticipation (Crainer, 2000).

To summarize Era 1, both fields of study embraced the idea that units, whether family or company, operate within a greater system, impacting and being impacted by that system. Both fields focused on the value of application of their emerging sciences through simulated learning opportunities, and both factions were continuing to establish their relevance to the society in general.

ERA TWO (CA. 1940s–1950s)

World War II and the emergence of the United States from the Great Depression years combined to bring intense change to the environment surrounding homes and businesses. Invention and production of goods and services was at an all-time high. The attitudes and imaginations of the American public were equally charged. Demand for and consumption of goods and services quickened to a frantic pace. The entire nation was in a consumption mode.

The study of home economics came into direct alignment with the field of business management during this time. New household equipment was tested, improved, and incorporated into the vision of the modern home. Efficiency of completing household tasks, saving wasted steps and movements in the process, and simplifying and standardizing work units became key research and application projects.

The U.S. business sector was frantically involved in keeping up with product development, production, and marketing. Although the rebuilding of Japan at this time was changing management thought at a basic level, it was not really apparent to the American business realm until much later.

ERA THREE (CA. 1950s–1960s)

This era is best characterized as the time that home economics, as a discipline and field of study, began the metamorphosis to better serve the changing needs of both its mostly female constituency and the changing social scripts of both men and women. As the nation struggled with civil rights issues and the escalating women's movement, traditional female roles were being questioned, and the definition of family was being modified to align with emerging social programs and practices.

In response to these environmental changes, the focus of this discipline moved heavily into what is now characterized as family resource management—family values, goals, standards, resources, decision making, organization and process, and **optimization** of families. Less emphasis was placed on work performance within the home and more energy was devoted to understanding the family unit and its interaction with the greater social structure. This family structure, or family culture, became a model for new developments in the field of business management.

Schein (2004) coined the phrase *corporate culture* to explain how companies were becoming both self-contained and self-perpetuating. He proposed that employees within a company slowly create norms, acceptable behaviors, role expectations, and unique communication processes that differentiate that company from others. In essence, they create a faux family unit at the workplace. Executives and workers were primarily men, and this emerging devotion and expected loyalty to the company has often been portrayed as "men in flannel suits."

It was also during this time that Abraham Maslow presented his theory of motivation, with its famous visual pyramid of needs. This pyramid has since been applied to the study of psychology, sociology, economics, families, and business. It is explored in more depth in later chapters. Maslow was also interested in how values and goals impacted the behavior of workers and how teamwork may be utilized in the realm of business.

ERA FOUR (CA. 1970s–1980s)

It was during these two decades that many long-standing home economics programs in universities across the nation were threatened with elimination during budget crises. It became increasingly important to shore up the mission, objectives, and curriculum of these programs. A key approach was to illustrate how essential these programs were to society in terms of employment and social impact. One outcome was the development of a systems framework that emphasized the interconnections among family, home, and society.

Another outcome of this time was the movement toward a closer alignment of home economics programs with vocational education. The Carl D. Perkins Vocational Education Act was passed in 1984 with financial support in the form of state-based grants for secondary and postsecondary educational vocational programs. The **vocational** framework within this alignment is obvious in the program restructuring at this time. The five majors (or fields of study) within home economics programs were Food and Nutrition, Human Development and the Family, Clothing/Textiles, Family Economics, and Home Economics Education. Each had elements from the field's original foci—food selection and preparation, raising children, sewing, and managing the home. The topics, however, were encased in possible job or career clusters.

The realm of business management during this time was delving into two distinctive camps—protecting and empowering employees. The success of Japanese business was intriguing American business leaders. Quality control, and especially **quality circles**, became popular management techniques. The principle underlying the quality circles was that when employees participate in decision making and problem solving, the quality of work is enhanced.

Kanter (1985) reintroduced the humanistic approach to management. She proposed that the corporation is merely a minisociety that shapes individuals to collective ends. Another concept illuminated in her works was empowerment of employees. While the home economics discipline was moving to connect the field with business in terms of specific jobs and career training, the business world was looking at research in the area of personal growth and development from a holistic perspective.

CONTEMPORARY MOVEMENTS

The field of home economics has undergone many transformations since the 1980s. One obvious change is in the way the field identifies itself. Few programs still exist under the title of Home Economics. As it became necessary to reposition and reframe its mission, the discipline found the old title too restrictive and too laden with incorrect assumptions about contemporary research, application, and curriculum. One problem is a lack of consistency in program names. Students, professionals, and the general public can be confused by the variety of titles used (see Table 3.1).

Table 3.1   Diversity of Program Titles

Family and Consumer Sciences	Family Science
Human Sciences	Family Studies
Human Ecology	Family and Community Studies

The field of business management continues to struggle with its quest for efficiency and its need to avoid depersonalization of employees. The technology explosion of the past two decades has presented new problems for managers. They and their subordinates must be able to think differently, frequently seek additional training, and respond to change in positive ways.

The Interface of Business Management and Family Resource Management in the Context of the Family

Why is it important to understand the history of business management and its connection to family resource management? Both have a parallel

Reality Check

It is not unusual for business and family to become intertwined. The United States, like many other countries, has a strong economic base of family-owned and -operated businesses. Some have evolved over several generations. New family businesses often arise from perceived needs within a family. The Burns family launched a large-scale specialty service business to fulfill a personal need.

Jan Burns, owner and manager of her own small business, catered to the pet grooming needs of her community. For 15 years, she had been moderately successful, establishing both her skills and relationships with loyal customers. The flexibility of her schedule and the home-based location allowed her to raise her two children with little outside child care. Joanna, Jan's daughter, was now in high school, and what had been a syndrome of learning and developmental difficulties was becoming an obvious problem for both her teachers and her parents. Jan shares the decision-making process that followed this recognition.

Joanna's teachers are wonderful. They are very supportive and have challenged her in the special education classrooms as best they could. When she was a junior in high school, her classmates began talking about college and future careers. Her father and I hadn't really accepted the fact that she wouldn't be capable of at least some training program in the local community college. Joanna was even more belligerent. She insisted on sending in college postcards that were coming in the mail on a daily basis. She even signed up to take the ACT test. Her father and I had never applied to a junior or a regular college, so we had no idea what that really was.

Of course, we weren't prepared for Joanna's reaction—frustration and despair—when she went to take that test. Her coursework in middle and high school had been modified, and although she performed adequately in those specially designed situations, she had elementary math skills and science comprehension. Reality hit us all hard. Joanna would never be fully independent and socially functional. Her counselor began talking to her and us about group home living and vocational work programs in the area. We were devastated.

While her parents dealt with their new realization, Joanna turned to self-therapy and began spending more and more time at her mother's grooming shop. Jan took notice and expanded her customer services to include short-term boarding. Joanna was given the responsibility of taking care of boarded dogs and cats at night and on weekends. She was both capable and responsible in these duties. Jan started thinking about a possible future for her daughter in her own business field.

(Continued)

(Continued)

> *I don't remember just when it hit me, but one day a customer told me about a pet resort she had toured in a neighboring city. I did some surfing on the Internet and realized that there was a growing market for high-service pet care. Within the year, we had expanded my small business with the construction of a large grooming, retail, training, and boarding facility—Jan's Pet Resort!*
>
> Like many new businesses, this endeavor started slowly. However, within the first year, it proved to be a huge success.
>
> *Our grooming business more than tripled, and the boarding is at capacity every holiday season. Joanna feeds these pampered pets, plays with them, and even does some front desk customer relations. I can see her working full time here when she graduates. We, as a family, have accepted the fact that she will always need our attention and support. The increased income from this new business takes some of the stress off, however.*
>
> Creating a business to meet the needs of one family member proved to be both a positive family experience and a profitable business endeavor. Basic management skills provided Jan with answers to both personal and professional challenges.

developmental dateline. Because both are concerned with sustainability and improvement of a group of people, it is natural that they will reflect one another at any period in time. Both borrow new and old ideas from the other. One only has to compare the popularized family living programs of the last few years with the management gurus and their programs to see the connections. Authors apply the same basic core concepts of management to family and business structures.

- *The 7 Habits of Highly Effective Families* and *The 7 Habits of Highly Effective People* by Stephen Covey
- *Principle Centered Leadership* by Stephen Covey, and *The Purpose Driven Life* by Rick Warren
- *Family Meetings: How to Build a Stronger Family and a Stronger Business, Second Edition* by Craig E. Aronoff and John L. Ward
- *Settling Disputes: Conflict Resolution in Business, Families, and the Legal System* by Linda R. Singer
- *Keep Your Business Close and Your Family Closer* by Larry Hollar

Photo 3.1   Technology impacts the management process.

Source: © Jeffrey Smith/istockphoto.

Technology has also had a profound effect on both business management and family management. Historically, the United States has moved through periods of overdependence on labor, materials, and fuels. Its greatest challenge in the future may be that of information acquisition. Knowledge may be the most important resource available to both families and companies as computerization continues to expand on both fronts.

Another factor that connects these two fields closely is the interdependence of the family unit and business. Families realize that the wages and status earned through employment have an enormous impact on their success. Businesses realize that employees are members of families and their obligations to the family unit will impact their motivation, loyalty, and willingness to commit to company objectives. A great deal of mutual research has been done in the areas of child care, job design flexibility, and family-friendly benefit packages.

The Foundation of Family Resource Management

As mentioned previously, the study of family resource management has a long history woven throughout home economics. Originally based in microeconomic theory, theorists moved toward sociology in the 1960s and 1970s, connecting to systems theory (Buckley, 1967; Key & Firebaugh, 1989). Cushman (1945) structured her textbook, *Management in Homes,* around case studies. Her cases presented traditional family units across the lifespan, focusing on resource identification and problem solving. Everything from kitchen space planning to values and body mechanics were part of the proposed curriculum. Knoll (1963) encouraged the development of a conceptual framework for the field of home management. Her framework centered on the "decision-making organization process" (p. 335).

Hill (1971) presented the family household as a semiclosed system composed of a group of individuals with responsibility to maintain the group and a level of interdependency that made the group cohesive. The family, as a social system, was viewed as transforming energy, information, and matter that enters that system into outcomes that the family needs and wants. To accomplish this goal, families participate in decision making and communication, which leads to goal setting, planning, implementation, and evaluation.

Deacon and Firebaugh (1975) included events in their model of family resource management. The family is viewed as a decision making unit that requires human and material resources to fulfill demands. Demands are specific objectives based on the family's values structure. Events are unexpected, low-probability situations that must be met with action. Meeting objectives and responding to these events require the use of human and material resources with a constant tension between the two.

Paolucci, Hall, and Axinn (1977) designed their textbook around the decision-making process within the family ecosystem. Their premise was that families have decisions to make and a certain level of freedom in that process. However, decisions are influenced by many things, most significantly, in their estimation, the environments within which individuals and families operate. A central concept to their discussion was the "Family as an Energy Driven Organization" (p. 25), which coincides with the emergence of computer terminology—inputs and outputs—in academia during that decade.

Although a great deal of time and energy had been exerted in the attempt to create a theoretical foundation for family resource management prior to 1990, Key and Firebaugh (1989) reflected on the shift from economics to systems theory and the ultimate impact on the theoretical foundation of the field. They proposed that the 21st century would present unique and challenging problems for families. Specific issues in their discussion were changing family structures, uncertain economic times, and demographic changes of the U.S. population. W. Bryant (1990) published an entire book on the "economic organization of the household," thus igniting more research on families in the economic systems of their environments. He based his work on the emerging interest of economics courses and women's issue courses on the family unit.

Avery and Stafford (1991) presented a new theory—the scheduling congruity theory of family resource management—incorporating works from behavioral psychology, cognitive psychology, economics, business management, and Deacon and Firebaugh's seminal work in family resource

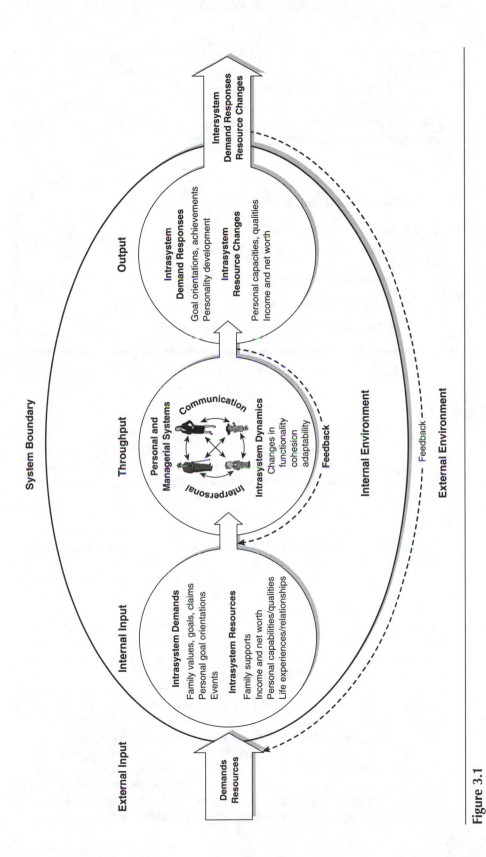

Figure 3.1

Source: From Deacon, Ruth E., & Francille M. Firebaugh. *Family Resource Management: Principles and Applications, 2/e.* Published by Allyn & Bacon, Boston. Copyright © 1988 by Pearson Education. Used by permission of the publisher.

67

management. Their intent was to design a theoretical structure that would both explain and predict family resource-allocation behavior. The strengthening of existing theoretical structures in family resource management continues. A common theme drawn from all of these past approaches is the inherent need for families to make decisions. Thus, this textbook focuses on and organizes information within that process.

The Decision-Making Process

- Recognize existing need(s)

- Identify alternatives to fulfill identified needs

- Evaluate identified alternatives

- Select and implement alternative

- Reflect and evaluate alternative selected

Worldview

In the United States, many choose to buy their groceries on a weekly or monthly basis. The ability to stock up on some items both from a standpoint of disposable income and the ability to store large quantities seems to be an American practice. However, many families in European countries shop for their food on a daily basis. Being able to use the freshest produce is one reason that many choose to buy food so often. Another reason is the limited storage space. Many kitchens have small refrigerators and limited counter and cabinet space.

In the days following the fall of communism in the late 1980s, there were other reasons that people in Eastern European countries bought their food on a daily basis. One reason was that the devaluation of currency left many families uncertain about their purchasing power for necessities such as food. In addition, shortages in goods, including food, was common during this time in many areas. Many previously government-run food sources were no longer in business, and make-shift markets were set up in vacant lots, empty buildings, and street corners. One never knew whether the man that was selling eggs (by the piece, rather than by the dozen) would be on that same corner the next day. The availability of fresh fruits and vegetables during the winter and other foods not readily available in the local area were especially dismal. The author experienced this in the spring of 1994 in Romania. Fresh vegetables were so scarce that the markets were selling tiny carrots that were pulled out of the ground prematurely just to make this product available as soon as possible. Grocery shopping around the world can be very different!

Specific Applications of Management to the Family Unit

Family members possess many types of resources that are discussed in detail in later chapters. To understand the importance of managing those resources, time management, family planning, dependent care, and financial planning are discussed briefly.

TIME MANAGEMENT

Although not all cultures believe that time is manageable, the general belief in American culture is that time is a **commodity**. One can measure time, keep time, save time, and waste time. Major activities that require the expenditure of time in the family setting include sleeping, eating, grooming, learning, working, maintaining the environment, and relaxing. A common problem expressed by working parents is the lack of sufficient time to accomplish all of these tasks. It is often a fine line on which working parents balance.

Imagine that Maggie and John are both employed outside of the home and they have two children, a toddler and a grade-school child. Not only is this family juggling schedules for four different individuals, it is also trying to mesh schedules of the two workplaces, the elementary school, and the day-care provider. Even with the highest commitment to organization and planning, there will be times when one change in one of these schedules causes intense discomfort for one or more family members.

If both parents work 40-hour weeks and work 8-hour shifts each work day, they must make arrangements to ensure that each child will be delivered to the child-care and/or school setting as needed daily. These children may need to be picked up and delivered to multiple locations at times. The flexibility of parents' work hours enhances a family's ability to juggle such arrangements. Stringent, depersonalized work schedules and demands can elevate the pressure this family must endure

In the News

By Marilyn Gardner

Modern childhood, for all its abundant privileges and advantages, keeps falling on hard times.

Nearly a quarter of a century ago, David Elkind sounded one of the first alarms in his eloquent book, "The Hurried Child: Growing Up Too Fast, Too Soon." He warned

(Continued)

(Continued)

that pressure in the media, schools, and homes was forcing children to hurry through life, creating an assault on childhood.

That was also the era when Neil Postman published "The Disappearance of Childhood," making a case that the growth of electronic media exposes children to sophisticated information formerly out of bounds to them. That, he said, blurs the line between children and adults, eroding innocence.

In the decades since those books appeared, the pressures on children have only intensified. Dr. Elkind's classic book remains so relevant, in fact, that his publisher will soon issue a 25th-anniversary edition for a new generation of parents.

Another urgent warning comes from 110 teachers, children's authors, and psychologists who signed an open letter to the Daily Telegraph in London this month. They wrote darkly that "junk culture" is "killing" childhood, and that children are "being poisoned by modern life." They spoke of "toxic childhood" and "the death of childhood" as they listed negative influences, among them computer games, poor diets, and the stress brought on by highly competitive education.

No less eminent a figure than the Archbishop of Canterbury joined the chorus by describing a "crisis" of modern childhood. The Very Rev. Dr. Rowan Williams warns that parents are failing to demonstrate the right mix of love and support. As a result, they are rearing children who are growing up too fast, becoming "infant adults."

Sobering talk indeed.

Such cautionary tales can be useful reminders of the need to protect children. But if there truly is a "crisis" here and that attention-grabbing word does tend to be overused perhaps it's not just a crisis of childhood but of parenthood as well.

As carefully synchronized fathers and mothers shuttle between home and work, chauffeuring children to school, soccer practice, and music lessons, they may feel part of what some call a "family unfriendly" culture.

They also face criticism. Madeline Levine, author of "The Price of Privilege," charges that many parents are pushing their children to be high achievers. That raises a question: Where does encouragement end and pushing begin?

To add confusion, a report being released in early October challenges the notion that children have too many activities. Yale psychologist Joseph Mahoney, who conducted the study, found no negative effects on students who take part in high amounts of organized activities.

Only 6 percent of the children in his study spend nearly 20 hours a week in organized activities. A surprising 40 percent of children have no extracurricular activities, the report finds.

Too many commitments? Too few? Each family must find its own balance.

Even if children aren't overscheduled, some of their parents are. Dr. Levine cautions that "marriages suffer under the barrage of child-centered activities."

Parenthood may be the world's longest, hardest, and ultimately most satisfying job for which there is no real training. We are all, in our own ways, winging it, doing our best, and hoping we do it right.

The reassuring news is that as children and parents in every generation navigate the shoals of their particular era, most families prevail. They find their own solutions to meet the needs of their children. They write their own definitions of success and happiness.

Which doesn't mean they don't need help. Perhaps it's time for a book titled "The Hurried Parent," outlining ways to reduce the pressure on families.

Offering one bit of comfort, Sue Palmer, a former teacher and a signer of the letter to the Daily Telegraph, says simply, "Childhood is not a race."

Neither, she might add, is parenthood.

Source: By Marilyn Gardner. Reproduced with permission from the September 27, 2006, issue of *The Christian Science Monitor* (www.csmonitor.com). © 2006 The Christian Science Monitor. All rights reserved.

FAMILY PLANNING

Never before in the history of science has a woman had as much control over childbearing decisions as she does today. However, not every woman finds herself in a position to exercise all options available to her. Nevertheless, it is assumed by many that having one child or multiple children is something that can be managed or planned. The average age of women giving birth in the United States has gradually increased over the last few decades. Lamanna and Riedmann (2006) suggest that there are three emerging options for those of childbearing age: remaining child-free, postponing parenthood, and having only one child. These options are discussed in more detail later in this book, but serve as important references in this discussion of management.

The choice to have one child or multiple children has a substantial impact on the resources needed and how those resources will be managed in any family. Each additional member creates multiple ripples in the family system. The roles and expectations of children have also been changed in light of new childbearing attitudes and behaviors. A child within a large agricultural family during the 1920s may have been viewed as another source of labor for family farming operations, whereas a child today may be viewed more as a visible extension of his or her family's social position.

DEPENDENT CARE

Adults who do choose to have children are faced with competing needs for time and energy resources. Working parents must secure adequate child care, and those who leave the workforce to care for children in the home must adjust income and expense expectations. Seventy-four percent of women with children between the ages of 6 and 17 and 90% of fathers are employed outside of the home (Mannes, 2006). A two-career household juggles multiple work, child care, school, and activity schedules. Time management is essential.

Working parents appreciate family-friendly employer efforts. Onsite or contracted child care, flextime, and job sharing are becoming more common. When the pool of qualified employees is tight, employers realize the long-term cost savings that such options provide. Workers who worry about their children and struggle with competing needs at home and at work are less productive and less satisfied with their jobs. Inflexible work hours may add to the stress faced by employees with family obligations, resulting in more sick time and more frequent job turnover.

Mothers who leave their careers to care for young children must realize that their loss of income will have an impact on family dynamics and financial resources. Those who choose to reenter the workforce at a later date may face up to 37% less in income than those who do not leave in the first place (Hewlett, 1991). Opportunity costs are associated with all decisions. Although difficult to assess, there are lost possibilities with every choice made.

Janell has a college degree in marketing. She has been working for 5 years for her current employer and has risen to middle management. When she discovers that she is expecting her first child, Janell decides to leave her job and stay home with her young family until the children are school-age. Her cousin, Sara, has two small children, but chooses to continue working full time after her maternity leaves end. Both must adjust to changes in financial resources. Janell no longer has a steady income and must rely on her husband's income and savings accumulated. Sara, while still bringing a paycheck home, must pay for day care. At the end of 5 or 6 years, both cousins have sacrificed financially for their decisions to have children. However, Sara has continued her career path and statistically will earn about one third more over the course of her working years than will Janell. Each will have to individually determine how her decision impacted the level of life satisfaction achieved.

Caring for dependents—children, parents, and other family members—is a responsibility facing many adults within family units. Cost, quality, and availability are weighed against the family's resources. Matching the needs to the resources is an important and often frustrating management task.

FINANCIAL MANAGEMENT

Families must manage the flow of resources into and out of the family unit to maintain the needs of the group. Long-term financial management is explored in Chapter 9, but it is important to understand the impact of purposeful, continual management on a family's monetary resources. Money, once earned and received, must be exchanged as cash, check, or electronic transfer funds. This transformation of income into expendable forms is a management procedure.

Payne (1998) explores the difference in management styles inherent to differing socioeconomic levels. Those with a tremendous amount of financial security actively manage their money through investments or allocate financial resources to pay others to manage their money. Middle-class families focus on shorter term savings plans and are more active in the management of their monthly cash flow with checking and savings accounts. Middle-class families also save for retirement, but in passive ways, most often through employer plans. Individuals and families operating at or below the poverty line depend much more heavily on cash and much less on bank-centered transactions. Savings are lower in priority, and money is more easily shared among family and friends.

Summary

Management is a key process for any group's survival, whether businesses or family units. There are limited resources and limitless needs of group members, and the matching, evaluation, and distribution of resources within the unit are a continual challenge. Whereas businesses measure success in terms of financial gains and losses, families must focus on less tangible things, like relationships, health, and wellness. Financial security is important to both businesses and families, but interpersonal linkages are more essential to families. The decision-making process is the key to the management success of both.

Questions for Review and Discussion

1. Do you believe that business management and family management continue to impact each other in this new century? If so, how?

2. The number of women with children participating in the workforce has increased greatly during the last 50 years. Do you think that the workplace has incorporated major changes that reflect their needs? If so, what? If not, what might be changed?

3. Explain how management is a culturally defined behavior.

Unit II

Discovering Family Needs

The Decision-Making Process

- Recognize existing need(s)

  Chapter 4. Categorization of Needs

  Chapter 5. Values, Attitudes, and Behaviors: Understanding Family Choices

- Identify alternatives to fulfill identified needs

- Evaluate identified alternatives

- Select and implement alternatives

- Reflect and evaluate alternative selected

Categorization of Needs 4

Objectives

- Recognize the difference between needs and wants.

- Understand the hierarchy of needs and its application to family life.

- Be familiar with the Consumer Resource Exchange Model.

- Be aware of the categorization and changing perceptions of needs.

- Recognize the purpose of needs assessment.

- Explore the role of technological progress on human needs.

All humans have the same basic needs . . . members of every society have the same basic physiological resources for satisfying their needs . . . humans everywhere develop a variety of derivative needs and desires that reflect their experiences as members of society.

—Lenski, Nolan, and Lenski (1995, pp. 27–29)

All families spend a great deal of time making decisions. On a daily basis, families must decide where to live, what to buy, and how to spend their leisure time. Others decisions may be life-changing, such as the decision to become parents or how to treat a life-threatening illness. The decision-making process is an essential tool for families. The first step in making any decision is to recognize existing needs.

Needs and Wants

It is not uncommon to hear a phrase such as, "I need a cup of coffee" or "I need a new car." Although someone may need a drink or his or her car may be the only mode of transportation, the coffee or car may not actually be a need, but a want. What is the difference between a need and a want? A **need** can be described as a necessity such as food, clothing, or shelter. Needs are requirements for living. A **want** is something that you would like to have, but it is not essential.

The difference between needs and wants can be blurred by the contexts of our society. Time changes needs. At one time, owning a computer was considered a luxury. Today, the benefits of owning a computer have caused some to see it as a necessity. In fact, now you may not even consider the possibility of being without one. The context of place also affects wants and needs. It is dependent on where you live and the lifestyle you choose. For example, in a country like the United States, the standard of living is so high that even those who are considered poor may have more than the basic necessities of food, clothing, and shelter. In 2001, more than 18 million Americans whose income was less than $15,000 per year owned a color TV (U.S. Energy Information Administration, 2001). Many people around the world would consider a TV a luxury, but in the United States, it is often viewed as a necessity. The United Nations' Millennium Development Goals focus on global human needs that include reducing hunger, increasing access to primary education, and addressing childhood mortality. Many of these human needs are taken for granted in industrialized countries such as the United States.

Even within the United States, the needs of one person may not match the needs of another. Those who live in a large city have different needs than those who live in a rural area. Needs and wants are determined by personal choice. What is extremely important to one person may not be important to another. We choose between needs and wants every day. We are given hundreds of options, and we are influenced by the power of the media. Making the distinction between needs and wants can be relative to the individual making the choice.

Aaron, a college student, is planning a trip to New York City. Although he has visited New York before, he is excited to see it again and to take in some of the sights that he missed the first time. He is especially looking forward to watching the Yankees play. Aaron needs a hotel room.

While looking online, he discovers a room for less than 20% of what even inexpensive hotels charge per night. Although the hotel is farther away from his destinations, there is a subway stop a few steps away. He also realizes that the location of this hotel may not be as safe as another area and it does not have many amenities. He decides to book the room. Aaron's need is to have an inexpensive place to lay his head after a long day of sightseeing, whereas another person may have a need to feel safe, require room service, or need alternative modes of transportation.

HIERARCHY OF NEEDS

According to Maslow (1954; Maslow & Frager, 1987), there is a common **hierarchy of needs** that individuals climb on the path to life satisfaction (see the following figure). On the lowest level of this hierarchy are *physiological needs* such as food and shelter. Individuals who are without these basic needs are motivated to meet these needs before looking ahead to fulfill other needs. The next level represents *safety needs*. These needs are also basic to living and include the need to be free from fear, danger, or deprivation. *Social needs* illustrate the need to relate to others in a meaningful way. According to Maslow, everyone seeks love and acceptance. *Esteem needs* include self-respect, status, and recognition. These needs are based on others' reactions to us and our own self-assessment. To fulfill this need, competence may be required. Although all of these needs may be met, Maslow and Frager (1987) reveal that individuals may still feel unfulfilled unless they feel that they are doing all they can to reach their potential—*self-actualization*. Although Maslow believes that few ever achieve self-actualization, the need for self-actualization is what motivates someone to be the greatest athlete, the finest novelist, or even the best parent.

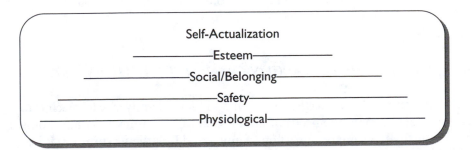

Although Maslow is best known for his hierarchy of needs theory, his work on management should not be overlooked. Maslow, Stephens, Heil, and Maslow (1998) suggest that applying the concepts of basic psychological needs to an organization provides an advantage.

The principles of Maslow's theory of needs apply not only to the individual, but to the group, "developing him via the community, the team, the group, the organization—which is just as legitimate a path of personal growth as the autonomous paths" (Maslow et al., 1998, p. 4). Stephens and Heil (Maslow et al., 1998) suggest that too much time is spent in organizations that do not support an individual's movement toward his or her true potential. In addition, Maslow suggests that any organization includes long-term relationships, loyalty, and communication. The family is such an organization. Family management depends on the identification of needs and progress in meeting those needs. Only then can family members begin to move toward realizing their potential as individuals. At the same time, family members love and care for each other in meaningful relationships over time. Let us examine more closely the hierarchy of needs as it applies to the family.

Worldview

In the book *Hungry Planet: What the World Eats,* Peter Menzel and Faith D'Aluisio present photos of 30 families in 24 countries and show what each family eats in one week. Each family has a different selection and amount of food based on their location, size of family, and income.

Go to the following Web sites for a look at a few of the photos:

- The photo at www.menzelphoto.peripix.com/viewdetails/item/3672/size/800/shows an Australian family.
- The photo at www.menzelphoto.peripix.com/viewdetails/item/3542/size/800/shows a Japanese family's kitchen.
- See www.menzelphoto.peripix.com/viewdetails/item/3461/size/800/for a photo of an Indian family's food.
- The photo at www.menzelphoto.peripix.com/viewdetails/item/3384/size/800/shows a family in Ecuador.

APPLYING THE HIERARCHY OF NEEDS TO THE FAMILY

All families have needs. Just as individuals identify needs specific to their own desires, the needs of families vary from family to family. Some things that are important to one family could be the least important to another. However, the lowest level of Maslow's hierarchy of needs, **physiological needs,** cannot be overlooked.

Emily is a single parent. She has struggled to make the best of her situation with her three children. Although Emily has a good job, recently her landlord threatened to kick them out if she didn't pay the rent. There is never enough food either. Emily is addicted to cocaine. Because Emily has determined that the need for cocaine will take precedence over the basic needs of the family, the physiological needs of her family go unmet. According to Maslow, not meeting these basic needs keeps the family from meeting higher level needs, such as safety or social needs. Unless things change, Emily's children may risk shoplifting at the grocery store to meet their food needs.

Safety needs are met as the family seeks to protect each other from danger or the fear of danger. Parents will take the steps necessary to ensure the safety of their children by building a fence, installing a security system, or fastening them into a car seat.

Mark and Debbie, a young couple in their early 20s, live in an urban setting. Although they were not impressed with the condition of their apartment, it was one of the only places they could afford, and it was near where they worked, eliminating the need for transportation. Shortly after moving in, they experienced several burglaries. Debbie was uneasy when she was home alone and often stayed late at work if she knew Mark would be late. Once home, they avoided going out with their friends, not wanting to risk another break-in. Eventually, Mark and Debbie decided to move to a safer area. Even though it cost them more, they decided that the need to feel safe was more important than other things they could do without.

Ideally, the family is able to address the **social needs** of its members. Maslow suggests that this need is met when one has meaningful relationships. Family members who feel a sense of belonging create an atmosphere of love and acceptance that meets the social needs of the members.

Photo 4.1   Homelessness illustrates survival at the physiological needs level.

Source: © David Freund/istockphoto.

Matt and Jenny have been married for 18 years. Each has a high-profile career, and they find it hard to spend time with their daughter, Angela. Jenny has always made sure that Angela had the best of everything and was given the opportunities that some of her friends didn't have. Each summer she attended the best summer camp, and she took violin lessons from the finest teacher in the area. Angela knew that she was privileged, but she longed to have the kind of relationship that her best friend had with her parents—especially her dad. When Angela was 16, her parents learned that she was pregnant. As Angela's need for love and acceptance went unmet, she looked for that elsewhere.

Esteem needs are those that allow families to be the best they can be within their environment. Individually, family members look for self-respect, but as a family, they look for status and recognition within the community.

Cain and Beth wanted a big family. Early in their marriage, they talked about and planned for children. By their 10th anniversary, they were expecting their fifth child. Beth knew that not everyone approved, including her own mother. "How are you going to feed all these kids?" her mother would say. She was aware of the whispers as her family attended community functions or when she was shopping for school supplies. Cain noticed that there were less and less invitations to get together with other families. As a result, Cain and Beth decided to curtail their desire for more children. Their need for approval from the outside was greater than their need for a large family.

Although Maslow believes that individuals become **self-actualized** by reaching their potential, the family also benefits. Family members who are able to move ahead and realize their own potential are able to help other family members in their quest to be the best they can be.

Consider the lives of two brothers—Ned and Nick. Ned attended college right after high school, but he just couldn't seem to find a direction and soon dropped out. He went to work as a plumber's assistant. When he became disgruntled by the hours and hard work, he quit. Still living with his parents, he was able to be unemployed for months at a time, jumping from job to job. Nick's plan after high school was very different from Ned's plan. Nick sought the advice of his counselor to determine a career goal in Physical Therapy. Even while still in high school, he took classes that prepared him. Tragically, Ned and Nick's parents were killed in a car accident in Nick's senior year of college. Relatives were not surprised that Nick was able to make all the arrangements and handle the estate of his parents. Ned, on the other hand, could not seem to move ahead. Ned's physiological needs, safety needs, social needs, and esteem needs went unmet as a result of his parents' death. Until these needs are met, the potential for Ned's success will be limited.

THE CONSUMER RESOURCE EXCHANGE MODEL (CREM)

Bristow and Mowen (1998) used the earlier human need research to develop a model that is based on the concept that consumers manage resources to meet their needs. In the development of CREM, four basic assumptions are made and theoretically justified. The assumptions are as follows:

Assumption 1. Consumers seek to manage resources that enable them to function more effectively in their world. Those resources include physical, social informational, and financial resources.

Assumption 2. Individual differences will exist in the level of importance consumers attach to each of the four resource types.

Assumption 3. Resources exist as part of an interrelated/interdependent system; each resource need type supports and is dependent on the other.

Assumption 4. Time is a finite temporal space in which activities are performed. Time is not a consumer resource. (pp. 91–94)

Physical resource needs are those that maintain life, such as exercise and good nutrition. Social resource needs involve a person's relationships and interactions. It also involves the need to belong to a group. Financial resource needs focus on money. This need is satisfied by money or goods. Information resource needs are those that drive a person to satisfy intellectual curiosity. It is the need to know. Bristow and Mowen (1998) point out that these resources may not be all-inclusive. For example, the need for spiritual connection may be an additional need for someone. They also recognize that people will attempt to manipulate their resources to meet their needs. Finally, they propose that individual importance is placed on each resource.

The following is an example of how the CREM is reflected in how a family met their needs.

The Peterson family is getting ready for another vacation abroad. Although the family is not wealthy, Jack and Sharon feel that these experiences are valuable for their family, especially the children. They have been planning this trip for several weeks. Sharon has made sure that they will have access to the money they will need by checking the PIN numbers of their ATM and credit cards and has ordered the Euros they will take from their bank. Jack has carefully planned their itinerary to include plenty of exercise and has gone online to choose hotels that are close to a good variety of restaurants. He has also looked in several travel guides for local festivals that will be going on while they are there (assumption #1). The Petersons realize that many families do not place the same priority on travel. Giving up cable TV and limiting the number of times they eat out has given them the resources to travel more. Jack and Sharon have been careful to solicit input from each of the family members about their preferences for how they will spend their time while there (assumption #2). They cannot imagine not being able to see new sights, eat new foods, experience different cultures, and broaden their knowledge of the world (assumption #3). They only wish that they had more time to spend each day as they set off on their new adventure (assumption #4).

CATEGORIZATION OF NEEDS

Needs are met at different levels and for different reasons. Not all families have the same needs nor are they met in the same way. For example, a family that lives on a ranch in western Texas would have different needs than a family that lives in inner-city Los Angeles. At the lowest stages, needs are critical. Tomer (2001) describes the lower needs as a craving or striving, whereas the needs in the higher stages can be described as an aspiration. The needs of families can be divided into several categories.

Economic Needs

Of course, all families have economic needs that are met by adequate resources. Having enough money to buy the basic necessities is important for the well-being of the family. Family income may come from a variety of sources, such as employment, but may also come from gifts or inheritance. Successful management of income is a factor in meeting this need.

Physiological Needs

Physiological needs represent basic physical needs, such as nutrition and health care. Families need to be able to provide members with adequate food and the availability of a doctor when an illness arises. Zuluaga (2000) suggests that this need "may mean either the absence of disease or disability or the satisfactory adaptation to existing conditions" (p. 320).

An individual's perception of good health may vary according to his or her desired quality of life.

Psychological Needs

Psychological needs involve intrinsic needs such as self-esteem. In their study of family caregivers, Irvin and Acton (1996) found that basic need satisfaction was directly related to high self-esteem. Timmerman and Acton (2001) later added to that by finding that individuals with higher levels of basic need satisfaction are also better able to deal with stress, resulting in healthier behaviors.

Social Needs

A family's social needs reflect their relatedness or affiliation within society. Some families have a difficult time recognizing their needs and may spend a great deal of time helping each other cope with situations caused by their inability to meet their needs. Other families are able to identify the needs and meet those needs in a short period of time.

An alcoholic family member is using his paycheck to support his habit. Although he may need to get professional help for his addiction, the family may focus only on the need for the family to make more money.

The ability to measure whether needs are being met is not universal. Doyal and Gough (1991) argue that it is difficult to measure need satisfaction. They point out that, although the government has some indicators that show the health of our economy, such as the Gross National Product (GNP), human behavior is not considered and thus may not be a good way to measure if the people feel their needs are being met. In addition, it may be easier to see whether people's basic needs are being met; however, the problem lies with the "intermediate" needs. Everyone needs food and clothing, but as Doyal and Gough (1991) point out, there are second-order goals or needs that build another layer within advanced societies. Some of these intermediate needs are

- Nutritional food and clean water
- Protective housing
- A nonhazardous work environment
- Appropriate health care
- Economic security
- Safe childbearing
- Security in childhood

Chris was transferred by his company to Pakistan. The company promised an increase in salary and extra benefits that included housing. When he arrived with his family, he was disappointed in the apartment that had been arranged. Although it provided the basic needs of shelter, security, and belonging, he and his family had other expectations. His children, Alison and Jacob, were used to their own rooms, and this apartment only had two bedrooms. The building was near a factory, so fine white ash formed on their furniture each day. In addition, the apartment faced a major street with lots of noisy traffic 24 hours a day. The family had "intermediate" needs that were not being met in this situation. Once the company realized the needs of Chris and his family, they were able to find other accommodations. Their intentions were then turned toward meeting their needs for safe food and clean water.

CHANGING PERCEPTIONS OF NEEDS

Photo 4.2   Safety restraints meet parental needs for child safety and social mandates.

Source: © Randy Faris/Corbis.

The way that individuals within families view their needs often changes over time. The needs of a family may change due to circumstances, **personality,** economic status, technology, culture, **lifespan,** and gender differences.

Circumstances

Circumstances often change the perception of what a family needs. There are many situations that families face that will alter the needs that they have. Some situations may cause needs to be altered for a short time, and others realize that their needs have changed permanently. For example, a child who has chicken pox may cause a family to have to change its schedule and sleeping arrangements for a short time, whereas a debilitating illness such as a stroke that results in permanent disability will cause the family to change indefinitely. Situations such as illness, disability, death, and natural disaster all have an effect on the needs of individual families. Although it seems that monetary resources would be important in a crisis situation, recent research indicates that the most immediate need for those who are dealing with a critically ill family member is information and assurance (Bond, Mandleco, & Donnelly, 2003; Ward, 2001).

Social changes also require family needs to change. During the Great Depression of the 1930s, family needs were greater for basic survival. At this time in history, high unemployment, drought, and an unstable monetary system led many families to think differently about their needs (see Box 4.1).

Box 4.1

During the Great Depression of the 1930s, First Lady Eleanor Roosevelt received more than 300,000 pieces of mail in her first year of office. Many of the letters pleaded for relief from the conditions of unemployment, poverty, and homelessness. Many of the letters were from children. Although most children are unaware of the financial situations of their parents, these children were fully aware of the struggles they and their parents were living. The following letters illustrate the differences in the needs of these children, as opposed to the "needs" that children might identify today.

Royse City, Texas
Sept. 6, 1934

Dear Friend:

Well I don't suppose you know who I am. But I'm a 16 year old motherless girl that has to work hard for all she gets. I have a brother and a sister and daddy. We

---

(Continued)

(Continued)

are working as day labor for a living and don't get much of that to do. In the winter I could piece quilts if I had any scraps. We are trying to keep off the relief this winter so we are keeping every penny we can to buy groceries this winter. Whether we have sufficient clothes or not. We haven't even enough furniture. We haven't any bedsteads, a stove, or cabinet. Some of our neighbors are letting us use their stove, cabinet, & one bedstead. I thought you might have some old clothes, coats, and shoes, or any kind of clothing you could sent to us. I have read so much about your kindness I know if you have any you will send them. I would send some money for postage but haven't any. Address to your loving friend Miss D. H. (p. 48)

Gettysburg, S. Dak.

Jan 8, 193[4]

Dear Mrs. Roosevelt:

A young girl from a God forlorn country is writing to you. I will be 16 years old Jan 16. We are so poor we haven't hardly enough to eat. I have 2 sisters and I brother and father. Mother is dead over 5 years. She was killed in a railroad collision. I have to keep house. We haven't had a crop for 8 years. We get about ¼ can of cream in two weeks and that is only 10 cents so we can't buy anything. Eggs we haven't any. Would you be so very kind and send us a little money to buy a few necessary things. I suppose you get many letters like this but if you can please send a little I would thank you from the bottom of my heart.

As ever your Friend.

A. N. (p. 60)

L. B., an eighth-grade student from Illinois, to Eleanor Roosevelt, February 1934

I have a brother younger than I, and he's in the same grade with me. My mother would want both of us to go to school, and be something when we grow up. Yet, she can't afford to send both of us. My brother being the youngest, he's also the lucky one. He would go to school while I will have to stay home. Oh, I just hate to think of it. I just would love to go to school. I do not like to go to school just to spare time, like some do, but I would like to go to learn . . . Maybe you will help a girl that doesn't want to quit school . . . If you could help me, nothing would be so dear to me than you. Education is more than anything in the world to me. (p. 89)

Source: From *Dear Mrs. Roosevelt: Letters From Children of the Great Depression* by Robert Cohen. Copyright © 2002 by the University of North Carolina Press. Used by permission of the publisher.

During times of war, the United States experienced **rationing**, which also led to a reevaluation of needs for many families.

During World War II, people were encouraged to plant "victory gardens," to conserve rubber, paper, aluminum, tin cans, toothpaste tubes, sugar, coffee, and even kitchen fats. Drivers were limited to three gallons of gas per week, leading to the formation of carpools or "car clubs" (Rauber, 2003, p. 32).

Personality

Personality differences play a role in perception of needs. Personality measures point to differences in the need for closure or structure (Leone, Wallace, & Modglin, 1999), the need that introverts have to avoid communication (Opt & Loffrendo, 2000), and the need that risk-takers have for novelty, change, and excitement (Zuckerman, 2000). Individual desires, motivation, and behavior are assembled as a person grows and develops and has an influence on what is important to them. For example, peer group pressures that someone experiences as an adolescent will influence his or her behaviors and motivations as an adult.

Sandy grew up in a family that stressed conservative values. She was not allowed to have many of the popular styles in clothing that her friends wore. As an adult, it is important to her that her daughter has the newest and most trend-setting clothes to help her fit in with her peer group.

Economic Status

The **socioeconomic status** (SES) of a family will have an influence on its needs and how it meets those needs. For those families with resources, the choices they make regarding their perceived needs will be different than the family that is barely surviving. According to Tan (2000), low-income families that are receiving public assistance have different spending habits than other families. "Overall, for families with three or more types of assistance programs, the average annual expenditure on food, housing, and clothing make up 70 percent of average total expenditures, compared with 53 percent for families with one type of assistance, and 48 percent for non-assisted families" (p. 31). For families that are struggling financially, basic needs such as health care, adequate housing, and healthy foods may not be met. Even the lack of educational experiences that children need becomes a disadvantage for some low-income families. Feldman (2001) points out that a significant number of children from low-income families lack the preliteracy, premath, and social skills that other children have when they start school. Educational needs are critical to families' ability to rise out of poverty. Sclafani (2002) reports that 85% of the job market in 2000 represented professional or skilled labor, compared with only 40% in 1950. The need for adequate education is important not only to the individual and their family, but to the nation as a whole.

Technology

Perhaps more than at any time in history, technology plays a major role in the needs of families. Technology is woven into the fabric of our lives in every way. Everything we see and do involves technology from the media, the production and consumption of goods, and the workplace to reproduction and our physical quality of life.

Reality Check

In the age of information and communication, the needs of families have expanded as we learn more about the world and what it has to offer—news, advertising, movies, and music. How has the media changed family lives?

- ○ Shopping. Can retail stores continue to exist when consumers have the ability to shop via TV, telephones, and computers? Will families become more home-bound?

- ○ TV. Does more equal better? Are hundreds of TV channels enhancing or confusing the public? Will attention spans continue to shrink with habitual channel surfing? Will the line between reality and fiction be blurred?

- ○ Education. Will all schools be equally capable of providing technology for student use? Will that technology increase knowledge or confuse it?

- ○ Politics. Is computerized voting an enhancement to democracy or a threat? Will politicians become more obsessed with creating positive images and less involved in bringing about necessary changes that would enhance family situations?

- ○ Work. How will workers with obsolete skills be retrained for newly emerging jobs? Will technology replace human labor?

- ○ Society. Will the increase in information access draw countries together or split them apart?

Source: The Media: The Impact on Our Lives (Petley, 2001).

To be on the right side of the **digital divide**, families need to be current with technology. Crandall (2001) suggests that "families would improve their educational, cultural, and professional status, if they owned a PC or connected to the Internet" (p. 40).

Culture

Cultural differences point out the differences in needs within families that have different priorities and structures. Meeting the needs of all racial and ethnic groups in the United States is a challenge. For example, the need for belonging takes on a different meaning between cultures. Some cultures place a great deal of emphasis on civic responsibility, whereas other cultures place more emphasis on family responsibility.

Doyal and Gough (1991) identified four preconditions that are necessary for needs to be met within any society: production, reproduction, cultural transmission, and authority. **Production** is necessary for goods to be made available for meeting basic needs such as food and clothing. To continue, all societies must reproduce. In addition, **reproduction** involves caring for the young and their socialization. Another precondition involves the culture's ability to pass on cultural norms, rules, and values through communication with each other. Whereas production and reproduction involve the physical environment, **cultural transmission** involves human behavior necessary to cause the cultural group to move in a certain direction. **Authority** ensures that the cultural rules will be carried out.

It is difficult to identify needs that are common to all groups or cultures. Not all cultures agree on identifying basic needs. An American may see a car as a basic need, but in a Third World country, a car is a luxury or want. In addition, the range of need satisfiers varies greatly. Differences in foods, clothing, and traditions magnify the differences in the way various cultures met their needs.

Donna is a registered dietician in a large hospital; she is responsible to meet the nutritional needs of the patients in that hospital. One of her patients was diagnosed with anemia. In visiting with the patient, Donna discovers that his religion does not allow him to eat any meat. The patient needs complete protein to regain his strength and red blood cells, but Donna helped him to design a diet that also met his need to practice his religion by introducing incomplete protein sources such as beans, nuts, and other legumes. Although the foods available in his native country meet his dietary needs, once he moved to the U.S., he was no longer getting the nutrition needed.

These cultural differences can also involve the standards that are set within those cultures. The standards in the United States may differ from other countries. For example, the Occupational Safety and Health Administration (OSHA) set minimum standards to ensure safe and healthy workplaces. Standards are also set for education, child care, buildings, and other areas that affect families. Some standards are set by world organizations such as the Convention on the Rights of the Child, adopted by the General Assembly of the United Nations in 1989.

Cultural rituals are another way that perception of needs differs among people. The importance that is placed on the rituals that families perform can vary greatly. One family may see burial as a ritual that has a high priority, and a good amount of resources may be allocated toward this ritual. Another family would view burial of their loved one as a low priority in light of their other obligations. Some cultures place a high priority on specific rituals. In the Hispanic culture, a *quinceanera* is a celebration of a girl's 15th birthday. It is a special occasion because it is when a girl becomes a woman. Hispanic girls all over the world celebrate this occasion. Although the family may be struggling financially, this rite of passage cannot be overlooked, and a great deal of resources may be allocated to this event.

Lifespan

Changes throughout the lifespan can also bring changes for families as they go from being just a couple to a family and back again to being a couple. Each of these stages signals changes in their needs.

Infants have a way of letting us know they have a need. Parents are often able to distinguish the different cries of their infant because it is their only form of communication. Infants also have a need to bond or attach to their caregiver, which usually results in building trust that will follow them throughout life. Brazelton and Greenspan (2000) suggest that infants need loving relationships that offer encouragement and communication, and that can provide a stimulating environment for emotional and intellectual development. As children grow, they still need opportunities for physical development and exposure to language, as well as to have a sense of belonging in their family. Older children need encouragement for their accomplishments, consistency in the way that boundaries and limits are set, and to learn how to get along with others.

When a child becomes an adolescent, a new set of needs is identified. Hersch (1998) described the adolescent culture as a separate community: "More than a group of peers, it becomes in isolation a society with its own values, ethics, rules, worldview, rites of passage, worries, joy, and momentum" (p. 21). This social dependency creates needs that may not be identified within any other age group. In addition, many adolescents' risk-taking behaviors, such as drug and alcohol experimentation, risky sexual activity, and poor eating habits, require different health care needs.

Adults have different needs as well. According to Levinson (1978, 1990), both men and women follow a series of transitions as they progress into and through adulthood. Each transition represents changes that include separating from parents, forming meaningful relationships, and developing the ability to have control over their own lives.

Cyndi is spending her first holiday season away from her family. After finishing graduate school, she took a job several hundred miles away from her family. Her limited budget and the amount of time she could be away from work prevented her from going "home" for the holidays. Cyndi's mother knew that the holidays would be hard for Cyndi, and she decided to send several care packages. Although the packages were nice, Cyndi realized that her needs were changing. What she missed wasn't her mother's gifts or cookies but the longing to be with the people she loved. Over the next few weeks, she invited her new friends and coworkers to cele-brate the holidays with her.

As adults age, their needs often return to physical needs. Older adults need more help in carrying out their daily tasks. These needs may requires them to seek shelter in assisted living facilities, choose foods that are more easily digested, and buy clothing that is easy to get on and off. Pandya and Coleman (2000) found that one in four American households is provid-ing caregiving services for an older family member.

In addition to physical needs, Brubaker and Roberto (1993) identified educational needs for older adults and their families. They suggest that older adults need more information related to marriage, sexuality, inter-generational relations, and caregiving. As adults live longer and more active lives than in the past, their needs include maintaining their inde-pendence and increasing their satisfaction with life. Coleman (2000) points to motivation research that reveals competence, relatedness, and autonomy are essential needs for humans and especially as they age.

Gender Differences

Despite that the basic needs of families affect both males and females, men and women have different needs. Physically, there are differences that affect health care needs. DeLorey (2003) reports that, "while women live longer than men, they are more likely to suffer from long-term activity lim-itations and chronic conditions such as osteoporosis, arthritis or migraine headaches" (p. 1). Although men have been plagued by stress-related dis-eases such as heart attacks, strokes, and hypertension, more health profes-sionals are beginning to recognize the danger for women as well.

Personality differences also affect the needs of men and women. Bakan (1966) identified two groups of traits that describe these differences. **Communal traits,** more common for women than men, are related to forming and maintaining social relationships with others. Thus, women would be more likely to need companionship and social connection. **Agentic traits,** which are more associated with men, focus on indepen-dence, control, and completion of tasks, signaling more of a need for self-reliance and self-motivation.

Newlyweds Jim and Janet just bought their first house. Although they are satisfied with the structure and floor plan of the house, they plan to make some major improvements. They began to make plans for a weekend where their friends and family could come and help them tear out the old paneling. Jim is looking forward to making progress on the house. Janet, on the other hand, is looking forward to the time they will spend with their friends and family members. Their needs for the workday are different.

Needs Assessment

In the News

Could Rising Gas Prices Kill the Suburbs?

By Marilyn Lewis

When a high-cost commute reaches the point of no-return, home buyers will start finding houses closer to work. In fact, some already are.

Rising fuel costs are being blamed for everything from soaring utility costs to lower retail sales and higher airline tickets. And now, experts say high gas prices could reshape U.S. cities.

"Most analysts believe that crude oil prices in the $50s and $60s will be with us for some time," says Stuart Gabriel, director of the Lusk Center, a think tank at the University of Southern California devoted to studying real estate forces and trends. There's even talk of crude hitting $100 per barrel—or 10 times what it sold for in the summer of 2005.

Once the realization soaks into the American consciousness that high-cost gas is here to stay, Gabriel predicts, those high commute prices will pull more homeowners—even young families—to live in central cities and create a push for more public transportation.

Trading Miles for Mortgage Dollars

But with the cost of gas hovering around $3 per gallon on average in the U.S., it's worth considering whether a shorter commute would pay for the incremental cost of a more expensive in-city home.

Assuming a full-time job, $3 gas, 26 mpg and 50 cents a mile for maintenance and no parking fees, a 50-mile roundtrip commute costs $646.15 a month, or $7,753.80 a year, according to the City of Bellevue, Wash.'s, Commute Cost Calculator.

Moving closer to work boosts your house-buying power. Everything else being equal, a 10-mile, roundtrip commute costs just $1,550.76 yearly—saving about $6,200 per year, or $517 monthly. That can add about $80,000 to the total amount of a mortgage loan, says one Chicago lender. The rule of thumb: Each $250 a month you can free up for mortgage payments equals roughly $40,000 more you can borrow at current rates (using the recent national average of 6.5%), says David Kasprisin, district sales manager for National City Mortgage Co. in Chicago.

Of course, if you're driving to work in a city, you're likely to pay up for parking. But even factoring in $200 per month for those fees, you'd still save $3,800 a year with the shorter commute—good for at least another $40,000 on your mortgage. And chances are city living would make public transportation a viable option. Taking the bus—in Bellevue, at least—cuts the cost of the commute to between $600 and $1,000 per year, depending on whether you need a one- or two-zone bus ticket. This puts your savings back up around $558-$590 per month.

Kasprisin says it's not hard to make the argument to his underwriters that a low-commute applicant should get a bigger loan: He says, "Look, these people live near public transportation, you can take that into account. We're pretty flexible and look at the entire person's picture for getting their loan approved. We're not just looking at debt-to-income ratios; we're looking at a whole mixture."

Additionally, Gabriel predicts that "in-fill" developments eventually will make city living even more affordable. The key is building homes closer together—say, 20 units on a site, rather than five, he says. Such homes are smaller than suburban homes, but closer to work and priced right.

Source: "Could Rising Gas Prices Kill the Suburbs?" By Marilyn Lewis. Retrieved from http://realestate.msn.com/buying/Articlenewhome.aspx?cp-documentid=742526.

Although accurate and timely reports provide demographic information about individuals and families, the real needs of those populations are not always known. Policymakers and human service providers often conduct **needs assessments** to determine the needs of those they serve. A needs assessment is an important tool used to communicate. Okerlund and Parsons (1995) describe the needs assessment as "the most valuable decision-making tool for human service providers and planners" (p. 49). A needs assessment should be representative of the population, current, and used to meet the needs for the population in which it is intended.

A needs assessment that is representative of the population will provide accurate information about the population to be served. Thus, information about culture/ethnicity, family structure, age, education, employment, health, and so on will be included.

A needs assessment must also be current. Conducting a needs assessment that will be utilized years later is not acceptable when the needs of people are changing rapidly. A need that is important can become critical in a short period of time. It is also possible that what is considered a need today could no longer be needed tomorrow.

Several years ago, Community X conducted a needs assessment of low-income families and determined that they needed better jobs with higher wages and more family benefits. Community leaders began searching for a manufacturer that would consider relocating to their community. A beef-packing plant was soon built outside the city limits. After the first year, the plant was unable to staff all the shifts and within three years, the plant closed. Later, it was discovered that a major problem for many potential workers was the lack of transportation to and from the plant. The community failed to assess the new needs following the initial assessment and solution. As a result, the needs of the community were not meet.

Finally, a needs assessment must be used to meet the needs for the population for which it is intended. To carry out this task, assessment must include a clear understanding of the perception of the problem(s), the barriers to accessibility, and who is responsible for the outcome(s). In addition, if new policy is set as a result of the assessment, there should be a good understanding about the implications that will result from the changes. Identifying and meeting the needs of individuals and families can be difficult depending on the definition of need. Grant (2002) reveals that needs can be felt (what people say they need), expressed (expressed in action), normative (defined by experts), or comparative (defined and compared by groups).

Human Needs Versus Societal Needs

Meeting individual or family human needs does not automatically mean that the needs of society are fulfilled. Meeting human needs, as we have discussed in this chapter, must combine socioeconomic and technical progress. Corporate America has manipulated consumers into believing that they need the products being sold through advertising. **Planned**, or **artificial obsolescence**, a phenomenon that appeared early in the 20th century, came about to ease the fear that the economy would be slowed by a saturation of products. In the 1920s, the auto industry was facing a crisis; by 1926, by the most accurate estimates, everyone who could afford a car would own one, and sales would decline. The president of General Motors, Alfred P. Sloan, suggested that the industry create a demand by creating dissatisfaction with past models as compared to new ones (Marling, 1994). In 1934, presenters at the Society of Automotive Engineers suggested that the lifespan of an automobile should be limited (Beder, 1998). Ethical concerns were raised about the responsibility of the manufacturers to provide quality products. Artificial obsolescence also creates a new need for consumers. A good example comes from the fashion industry. Each season "new" styles and colors replace those of the previous season. The need for change creates the need to buy the newest and latest fashion. Even when the style is repeated from a previous generation, superficial changes cause the consumer to buy the new product.

Not only are there ethical concerns involved in planned obsolescence, but meeting human needs must also include the desire to conserve the earth's natural resources. The consequences of our "disposable" society will impact our world. Sage (1999) suggests that the needs of any society should be closely tied to the idea of sustainable development. He defines **sustainable development** as "activities that improve the human condition and which can be maintained over time" (p. 195). Just talking about a family's need for food will not ensure the family that the future will be bright. The societal needs of producing food at a fair price, the guarantee of food safety, and the assurance that the soil used to grow that food will not be depleted are just as critical to that family's future.

In thinking about the needs of individuals and families, it is important to look at the larger picture. Societal needs influence and expand the family's decision-making process. As in any problem-solving process, asking questions that lead to an understanding of how decisions influence and impact those outside of ourselves is critical. It may be important to consider whether improving our lives *is* better. Siegal (1998) suggests that we are at the point in our society where we may have reached the limits of human needs. He suggests that we have moved from consuming necessities to consuming luxuries. Consumerism creates problems when "growth brings diminishing benefits as social and environmental costs climb" (p. 41). Although his writings may be viewed as somewhat controversial, Illich (1978) stated over 20 years ago that in our society the proliferation of commodities has become requirements. Eventually, these become needs on demand. What *are* the costs for getting what we need?

Summary

It is critical that every family begin to recognize the difference between its needs and wants. Maslow's hierarchy of needs and the CREM are two ways to explain the needs of families. Each family has a different way of determining needs, and the way that a family perceives its needs changes over time. A needs assessment is used to determine needs and takes into account the culture/ethnicity, family structure, age, education, employment, and health of the family. Needs assessments are important tools in determining policies. Technological progress and consumerism have changed human needs. In many cases, the media has influenced our perception of needs.

Questions for Review and Discussion

1. What is the difference between needs and wants? Are they different for everyone? Why or why not?

2. Discuss the different levels of Maslow's hierarchy of needs. What kind of person is able to achieve the highest level of self-actualization? Apply these questions to a family.

3. Compare Maslow's hierarchy of needs with the CREM.

4. How do changing perceptions of needs affect a family?

5. When conducting a needs assessment, what should be included?

6. How do human needs affect societal needs? How do societal needs affect human needs?

Values, Attitudes, and Behaviors 5

Understanding Family Choices

Objectives

- Understand the concepts of values, attitudes, and behaviors and how they impact family decision-making.

- Become familiar with the factors that impact development, maintenance, and changing of personal and family value sets over time.

- Become aware of how external forces impact value expression in the identification of needs and alternatives and in the decision-making process.

- Be able to apply understanding of values, attitudes, and behaviors to the critical analysis of family decisions and behaviors in society.

Not everything that can be counted counts, and not everything that counts can be counted.

—Albert Einstein

Individuals and families discover, rank, and create evaluative meanings for their needs. Every step of the decision-making process is impacted by one's values, attitudes, and behaviors. When family members are contemplating or discovering needs, they rely on these subjective measures to rank order or prioritize the multiple needs. For instance, family members need clothing. *When* that new clothing is required is a function of existing resources and environmental conditions. Beyond that, in American society, new clothing purchases are motivated primarily by social expectations and how deeply the family unit is persuaded to follow fashion and social pressure. A bride needs a wedding dress, right? Well, actually, legal marriage ceremonies do not mandate participants' dress. If a traditional wedding dress is perceived as a real need, it is processed as such. From that point, values and resources are weighed to determine what type of dress is obtained and how it is secured. Will it be borrowed? Purchased? Created? To understand the impact of values, attitudes, and behaviors on family resource management, we must understand the definitions of many terms that are often used loosely.

Values

Value is a term used often in the discussion of human behavior from two unique perspectives. When discussing economics and consumer behavior, the term *value* is used as a measurement of exchange. If you spend money on goods or services, you expect satisfaction from that exchange of resources. It is determined to be a good value if the person exchanging resources feels that he or she received a fair return. This determination of fairness is subjective. A baseball card collector may feel that one single card is worth several hundred dollars. Someone who is not involved in this hobby may feel that such a purchase would be a waste of monetary resources. A grandmother's collection of photographs may be priceless to one grandchild, but of little perceived value to another.

Another common use of the term *value* is perhaps even more subjective and personal in nature. Guiding principles of thought and behavior are often referred to as one's values. It is believed that these principles develop slowly over time as part of the individual's social and psychological development. Researchers have focused on these dispositions in numerous scientific studies in an attempt to measure, predict, and understand how values guide thought and action.

A search for universal values has been troublesome to theorists. **Human rights** are discussed and presented as universal values, yet some of these rights are not embraced by all groups. The practice of female genital mutilation, or female circumcision, is one such debated violation of human rights. Boulding (1985), an economist and philosopher, purports that human betterment is an appropriate goal for everyone across all cultures and nations. Human betterment, or an increase in the quality of life for all, is reflected in four dimensions: economic adequacy, justice, freedom, and peacefulness.

Universal values may be difficult to define, but cultural or social values are not. When a group of people embrace a set of understood values, members operate within those beliefs and are judged accordingly. The discussion of worldview in Chapter 1 illustrates this concept.

In the United States, especially in business and educational institutions, punctuality is highly valued. Teachers expect students to be in class when that class is scheduled to begin. Not every American accepts that one particular value, but being late is generally unacceptable and carries consequences. Being late for a commercial airplane flight may result in the loss of the price of that ticket and the loss of travel via that medium. Being late for a meeting may result in missed leadership opportunities or, in some cases, unwanted responsibilities.

PERSONAL VALUES

Values, when framed within a religious or spiritual framework, are often referred to as **morals**. Using morals in decision making is placing value judgments on a continuum of right and wrong. Kohlberg (1984) proposes that humans develop a set of morals as they mature, both socially and intellectually (see Table 5.1). One's sense of justice and how he or she makes judgments about what are good and bad decisions evolve over time primarily due to changes in cognitive abilities. Young, school-age children think concretely. Something is always right or always wrong,

Table 5.1   Kohlberg's Sequence of Moral Reasoning

Level	Stage
Pre-conventional	1. Obedience and punishment 2. Individualism, instrumentalism, and exchange
Conventional	3. "Good boy/girl" 4. Law and order
Post-conventional	5. Social contract 6. Principled conscience

there are no shades of gray. Adolescents, who are capable of abstract thinking, will begin to contemplate each **situation** in terms of context, alternatives, and impact of actions on self and others. Some adults, according to Kohlberg's sequence, will consider universal moral principles even at the risk of breaking their own civil laws. One example frequently used to explain this concept is the husband who would break into a pharmacy to steal a medication that would keep his wife alive, rather than let her die because he couldn't pay for it.

Although this model of moral development assumes a progression through stages, it does not assume that every individual moves through each and every stage. Thus, any group of adults may have individuals functioning at different phases of Kohlberg's model. Obviously, a multigenerational family will also have members operating at different levels. Adults in family units are most often the final decision makers, but that does not mean that family decisions will then reflect the higher moral levels. If those adults are functioning at lower levels, decisions will reflect that.

Mr. and Mrs. Jones set aside an entire day each February to prepare their income tax returns. They read the directions carefully and report both their earnings and deductions honestly. Mr. and Mrs. Smith wait until the last day to file taxes. They claim only the income they have received that can be traced through federal reporting forms and exaggerate many deduction amounts to reduce their final tax payment. The Jones' are functioning at a moral level that reflects their beliefs in what is right and what is wrong and their sense of obligation to the government. The Smiths may feel that the government is misusing funds collected through taxation or may rationalize their behavior in other ways.

Moral beliefs that are held strongly enough within a group may ultimately become laws with punitive legal consequences. Accurate reporting of information on tax reports has legal consequences, but only when discovered.

When faced with decisions that impact society, but aren't mandated by law, family members responsible for making decisions regarding resource management must rely on their values, morals, and past experiences to reach decisions that they are comfortable making. One purchase decision faced by many families is the procurement of a vehicle for transportation. This decision has personal, family, and social ramifications.

When contemplating the purchase of automobiles in the United States, consumers have many options. The selection includes many sizes, configurations, materials, and fuel sources. Some vehicles are fuel-efficient, whereas others are gas-guzzlers. Current laws do not impose restrictions on gas mileage of automobiles. A conscientious consumer may forgo some size capacity and styling options because he or she wants to reduce the pollution and consumption of gasoline. Another may be determined to buy larger, less efficient vehicles because he or she needs the size to transport others and/or materials. Neither is breaking a law. Both are expressing their consumer rights. Both may value the need to reduce air pollution and fossil fuel consumption. The second owner, however, is rationalizing his or her purchase by prioritizing existing needs (hauling capacity) above environmental concerns.

FAMILY VALUES

Reality Check

Jeremiah was born and raised in a conservative, Catholic community in the Midwest. He was the oldest of five children in a family that struggled to stay at the poverty line. He is approaching retirement age and reflects on the choices he has made over his adult life that were directly related to his inability to operate within the values and attitudes of his hometown.

At 22, I hitchhiked across four states to the East Coast. I had completed a college degree in journalism, but knew that I wouldn't be happy in the geographical area I had grown up in for many reasons. One major reason—I was gay. In the sexual revolution of the 1960s, that wasn't such a radical thing, but in my home community, it was unacceptable. I went to Woodstock and hung out in New York City for a while and really enjoyed the lifestyle there. I met my life partner shortly after arriving. Eventually we moved to a small coastal community between New York and Washington, DC.

Jeremiah physically separated himself from a value set that had discounted him and his sexual orientation, which resulted in a physical and emotional separation from his family of origin.

My younger sister knew why I had moved away. My parents and extended family probably knew, but never acknowledged that, even now, 40 years later. I sent cards and letters home occasionally. My siblings, and even my mother, made short visits to Virginia and spent time with me, in my home, where my partner was also living. He was always referred to as my friend and roommate by family members. I was always up-front about our joint ownership of property and our growing investment portfolio. Eventually, I think they saw him as a "business partner" of sorts.

(Continued)

(Continued)

> *I missed some important family gatherings, but always traveled back for anniversaries and weddings. Holidays were usually spent with my partner and our large extended family of friends and neighbors in our neighborhood. As I get older, I visit home more often. My partner has never gone back to the Midwest with me. It wouldn't be comfortable for him. Recently, his father died, and I was included in the obituary as his "life partner." That was a very emotional event for me. He was not acknowledged in that way in my parents' obituaries. But I do think my siblings and their families would be okay with it now. They address cards to both of us now and include my partner in invitations.*
>
> Values, attitudes, and behaviors are slow to change. Jeremiah's family journey spanned almost half of a century.

Because families consist of more than one individual, the probability that family members' values will clash with one another on occasion is quite high. To understand how values impact the decision-making process of families, group dynamics must be explored. Do families develop unique value systems over time that might differentiate one family from another?

Homogamy is a term used to describe the purposeful selection of mates from a pool that has similar characteristics to our own. Homogamy is most visible in terms of race, religion, and social class. Although many contemporary thinkers may claim that this practice is fading, what do statistics indicate? Kalmijn (1998) reports that marriages are largely homogamous, in both the United States and around the world.

Although laws forbidding interracial marriages are no longer legal or enforceable, according to 1994 data, less than 1% of Whites married non-Whites (Starbuck, 2006). This rate is much lower than would be expected if mates were selected without regard to race. The number of interracial couples has increased in the United States since 1960. However, they remain a small percentage of all marriages. By the 1990s, attitudes toward interracial marriage remained unfavorable. Survey results indicated that 66% of Whites still opposed the marriage of a close relative to an African American, and 45% opposed a relative's marriage to an Asian or Latino (Wilkerson, 1991). A more recent survey of college students by Bonilla-Silva and Forman (2000) found that only 30% approved of marriages between Whites and African Americans. Johnson and Jacobsen (2005) suggest that for Whites, educational and religious institutions provide social arenas for positive attitudes about interracial marriage, whereas work sites and neighborhood contacts do not.

In North America, between 80 and 90% of Protestants are married to Protestants. The marital homogamous rate among Jews is 90% and Catholics between 64 and 85% (Eshleman, 1994). These figures imply a purposeful search for a partner with similar religious morals and values. Educational levels may be even more important in mate selection than religious affiliation. Blackwell and Lichter (2000) reported that married and cohabiting couples are highly homogamous with respect to education. Another possibly confounding variable is the strong interrelationship between religion and race. American Mormons are overwhelmingly White, and African Americans are predominantly Protestant. Determining which factor—race or religion—guides mate selection becomes problematic.

Homogamy, in terms of social class affiliation, has been a factor in mate selection in all known societies. Although there is probably more mixed-class marriage in the United States than in many other countries, intraclass pairings are the norm. A pattern of finding mates whose parents have similar occupations to one's own parents is also firmly entrenched in U.S. courtship and marriage. Even geographical location impacts this type of homogamy. Neighborhoods are often delineated by income level and social class. Although transportation and career mobility have changed the opportunities for mate selection across geographical distances, most couples still find each other in relatively narrow geographical areas—community or state of origin.

Peggy was born and raised in an affluent suburb of Washington, DC. Her family was White, upper-middle-class, and Catholic. She attended private religious schools from K-12 and then attended an Ivy League college. Rarely was Peggy in a social situation where there were children or adults from minority groups. Her pool of dating partners reflected little diversity.

Jolie grew up in Harlem, New York City. Her mother was African American, and her father was of Cuban descent. Her neighborhood, schools, and church were culturally and racially mixed, with the exception of Whites. Few White children attended her schools, and even fewer participated in her religious and social activities. Although her pool of dating partners was more diverse than Peggy's, it still reflects a segregated sample.

Odds are that both of these females will select mates that are similar to them in terms of socioeconomic class and race. This is not necessarily purposeful homogamy, but more likely experiential in nature. When diverse families live and interact together, the rate of interracial relationships should be higher. Statistics in such cases, however, still indicate that purposeful selection of mates is impacted by race and ethnic preferences.

According to the data and theory on homogamy, it appears that couples forming new households and family units bring similar backgrounds with them in terms of race, religion, and social class factors, which would suggest that they have similar value and moral bases. Although probably true in the majority of cases, it is still essential that compromise and negotiation take place initially in newly formed families, thus resulting in a unique blending of values and approaches to decision making. These sets of **family values** will guide family resource management over time. As with all social memberships, family members may deviate from established family values, but there will be consequences for them in doing so.

Patrick and Katria are both college students in the central region of the United States. Although they have both grown to adulthood in different states, their educational, religious, and social experiences have been quite similar. When they decide to marry, there are minor differences between the families in terms of wedding details and living arrangements, but nothing extremely out of the ordinary.

Derrick and Charlene are both Hispanic. Derrick has been raised in the Midwest in a foster home with a Euro-American family and middle-class social and educational experiences. He moved to the Southwest for employment and met Charlene. Charlene has grown up in a border town with language and economic challenges. Although, by all outward appearances, the marriage of these two young people would appear homogamous, they have many more obstacles and much more intense negotiation to work through as a new family unit.

Changing immigration patterns in recent decades have had a major influence on family and household behaviors in the United States (Taylor, 2002). As previously presented in Chapter 1, worldviews shape the values and behaviors of newly immigrated families and individuals. Over time, these families may **assimilate** to the value system of the majority, or they may create a unique blending of the two. Since early in the 1900s, the largest wave of immigrants has been from Latin America, Asia, and other Third World countries. Although studies have varied greatly in reporting structural differences in the family unit that are culturally derived, it is important to remember that the family unit is essential within all minority communities. Differences among these groups in family practices and living arrangements are the result of "unique demographic and ancestral backgrounds, cultural histories, ecological processes, and economic origins and statuses" (Wilkinson, 1987, p. 204).

Food consumption choices are deeply embedded in values—personal and cultural. Choosing to be a **vegetarian** is a conscious decision of many Americans. This choice is often in opposition to that of other family members. The main reasons for choosing a vegetarian diet today are health, animal ethics, and environmental issues (Bryant, De Walt, Courtney, & Schwartz, 2003). All of these reasons reflect certain values held by individuals and their social groups.

Photo 5.1   Thanksgiving meals reflect family values on many levels.

Source: © Larry Williams/Corbis.

When one or more family members practice vegetarianism and other family members do not, meal planning, food procurement, and food preparation increase in complexity. Restrictive diets of any kind require advance planning and continual monitoring. Thus, family resources— time, effort, and economic—must be expended to enable family members to follow specific dietary regimes.

Religious commitments often impact food selection and consumption in the United States and across the globe. Hinduism promotes a strong tradition of vegetarianism rooted in more than 2,000 years of history (Bryant et al., 2003). Vegetarianism is widespread in Buddhism and Jainism, which promote nonviolent treatment of all beings and so prohibit the killing of animals for consumption (Whorton, 2000). Hunger fasts and product boycotting are also expressions of values held by individuals and social groups.

Economic values are also expressed in food consumption. When families purchase food in bulk, stockpile, or devote time and energy to the growing of raw foodstuffs, they are expressing their values or beliefs about materialism and the efficient use of family resources. When families depend on fast food and restaurant catering to meet their food needs, they are expressing their values of time and financial expenditures. Purposefully selecting foods and planning meals to meet nutritional requirements is also an expression of values—health, longevity, and self-discipline.

The phrase **family values** also has been used to discuss socioeconomic concepts pertaining to the family as a social institution. Folbre (2001) offers a simple definition of this concept—love, obligation, and reciprocity. Members of a family care about other members' welfare and happiness. They devote a certain amount of mental, physical, and spiritual resources to those other individuals to maintain both the group and the members. In turn, it is expected that other family members will do the same.

Within the family, values are expressed through behaviors toward one another. Folbre (2001) warns that the "work" within the family is unpaid and, thus, devalued by society. She notes a trend toward transferring economic activities from family and kin-based systems to the larger, less personal institutional levels, such as government and service industries. The movement away from family-based care for aging adults and toward the institutionalization of frail elderly family members would be a reflection of this concept. The same could be said for the reliance of working parents on day care and educational facilities for child care.

Politicians often expound on the negative changes they perceive within families as declining family values. Although touted as important parts of a candidate's platform, family values are not always clearly defined. Often the phrase is used in the discussion of the "breakdown" of the family unit, which is then illustrated through a series of examples highlighting the diversity of family structures operating in contemporary society. Correlations are then made between these diverse structures and the success or failure of family members. The general consensus from all major political parties is that the United States needs to "get back" to family structures and behaviors that had more positive effects on society in *better times*.

The phrase **family values** also is used to express an external concept. The value and expectations that the larger social system places on the family seem to have shifted through recent history. In recent years, tax deduction discrepancies for single and married citizens suggest that the federal government has a bias for one or the other. Availability and quality of child care have been identified as important national issues. The importance of, or the value placed on, families in the United States continues to reflect the level of attention devoted by the media.

VALUES ACROSS THE LIFESPAN

Do our values change over time and across the lifespan? When psychological constructs are developed slowly and over long periods of time, as are values, they become deeply ingrained in individuals and family units. Experiences, cognitive development, and moral maturity can force one to reconsider current values and, with enough justification, can move one to actually change previously held convictions and beliefs. When microwaves were first introduced for household use, many families were reluctant to use a new technology that they did not understand. Over time, the perceived value of time spent preparing food became more important than perceived risks or fears, and now the majority of households in the United

States own at least one microwave. New inventions and discoveries force us to revisit our values and behaviors and bring both into alignment or balance.

Through shared experiences, cohorts or **generations** develop. People born within a few years of one another are likely to experience similar economic, political, historical, and technological changes through the life course. Baby boomers, born between 1947 and 1964, have experienced the rise of computerization, the fall of major world powers, and the increasing influence of media on consumption. They can remember how things were before September 11th, 2001, and before the assassinations of John F. Kennedy, Robert Kennedy, and Martin Luther King, Jr. They experienced hours standing in line to register for college courses or to change college schedules. They can remember when gasoline was less than 25 cents per gallon. These shared memories have an impact on how those between the ages of 40 and 60 process and evaluate new products, situations, and proposed changes. They may value security differently because they can reflect on how it *was*. Those born after 2001 will not have a memory of when airline travel did not require extensive security checks, so they will not be as disturbed or as grateful (depending on the individual's disposition) for this process as their grandparents might be.

Travel, domestic and international, is another example of how values may change over the life course. Less than a century ago, traveling 100 miles was a day-long event for most families. With the increasing availability and affordability of airline travel, people are developing an expectation of distant travel in their lifetimes. College students are encouraged to take advantage of international study opportunities. Newly married couples are expected to travel to exotic places for a honeymoon if they can afford it. Retired adults have come to expect and plan for travel opportunities once they have time to devote to such activities. The value of travel, as an entire concept, has changed during the last decades. Personally, individuals value travel experiences differently as they age and participate in the workforce.

VALUE CONGRUENCE ACROSS GENERATIONS

Is there a generation gap in terms of values? A great deal of research has been devoted to the study of adolescent values and the impact of peers on values and behaviors. From that research emerged insights on how parental value systems impact adolescent decision making. Chilman (1983) reported that a number of previous studies showed that parents were less approving of cohabitation than were their children, creating intergenerational conflict. She proposed that later studies showed a positive shift of parental attitudes toward that behavior, aligning it more closely with the attitudes of their young adult children. Thus, values change more slowly among older individuals, but eventually an alignment between generations may be achieved.

Other studies support the idea that children look toward adult values expressed within their families for guidance in decision making. In a nationwide survey funded by the Henry Kaiser Family Foundation (Blum, 2002), researchers found that 64% of teens between the ages of 15 and 17 who had decided not to engage in sexual activity attributed their decisions to fear of what their parents might think of them. Miller (2002) found that parent–child closeness or connectedness and parental supervision or regulation of children, in combination with parents' values against teen intercourse (or unprotected intercourse), decrease the risk of adolescent pregnancy.

Decision making regarding adolescent educational participation has also been linked to central family value systems. Featherman (1980) reports that the vocational aspirations of adolescents are strongly correlated with their parents' jobs. Parent–child similarity emerges as a function of educational attainment. Read (1991) found that one reason female high school students cite when asked why they purposefully drop out of gifted programs and select a less academically challenged track in school is that they were discouraged by their parents from continuing rigorous subjects. Hence, not all adults have embraced the idea of female financial independence through vocational accomplishments in their parenting practices. Seabald (1986) found that peers are more influential in short-term, day-to-day matters, such as appearance management, but parents have more impact on the basic life values and educational plans of their adolescent children.

Parents and other adults within the family are the first teachers of values and morals in a child's experience. Their value systems will guide and support the developing value foundation of younger family members. Although later experiences and education may bring about changes to that initial set of values, past research suggests that a core set of values created early in life and supported over time will likely endure.

Attitudes

Values are abstract constructs. Feather (1990) suggests that values affect behavior by influencing one's evaluation of possible consequences of his or her actions. Attitudes are expressions of how we feel about any given thing, reflections of the values we hold. An **attitude** is a learned predisposition to respond in a consistently favorable or unfavorable manner to any given object (Fishbein & Ajzen, 1975). Attitudes are values couched within social situations. Sherif and Sherif (1967) believed that attitudes are expressions of how individuals conceive "their ways of life, their ways of doing things, their stands on the family and on social, religious, economic, and political issues, and how they conceive the ways and stands of others" (p. 1). Thus, the focus is on how they expect their expressed beliefs will be judged by others. Allport (1935) defined attitudes in cognitive terms. He

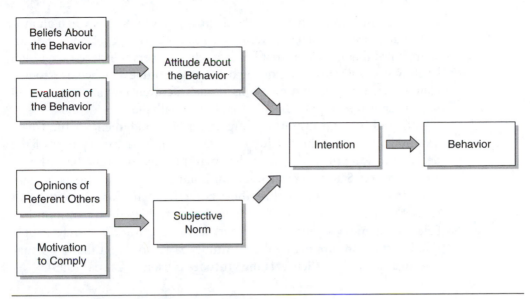

Figure 5.1   Fishbein-Ajzen Theory of Reasoned Action

Source: From Moore, T. J. (1995). Unpublished doctoral dissertation, University of Nebraska at Lincoln.

proposed that an attitude is a state of readiness that will impact an individual's response to any situation.

Fishbein and Ajzen (1975) studied the formation and expression of attitudes and proposed that attitudes are learned, and therefore are dynamic (see Figure 5.1). They can and do change with experience and education. These **predispositions** are assumed to also predispose one to certain actions and behaviors. If one believes that human life begins at conception and is to be protected, he or she may purchase prolife t-shirts and bumper stickers. The attitude is expressed or communicated to others in this way. Statements could also be made to express this attitude. Attitudes are values couched within context. If this person were consistent in his or her attitudes, abortion would be wrong in any case. Humans aren't always consistent, however. Under certain circumstances, such as rape or severe malformations, people may believe that abortion is an option.

Theorists have long held the belief that attitudes are created and maintained through interactions over time with parents, family members, and other socially significant individuals in a child's realm. The field of behavioral genetics has begun to address a possible genetic component within attitude formation. Arvey, Segal, Bouchard, and Abraham (1989) reported that approximately 30% of the observed variance in job satisfaction in a twin study conducted by that research group was attributable to genetic factors. Other studies (Eaves, Eysenck, & Martin, 1989; Tesser, 1992) support the idea that some attitudes are more resistant to change perhaps because they have psychological protection mechanisms around them exhibited by biological discomfort when faced with change. For example, when an attitude is an expression of a core value, such as a religious belief, and evidence is presented that questions that belief, a religious person is faced with high levels of stress. Because the existing belief, and attitude attached, is strongly connected to many other dimensions of one's life, even a small change would have an enormous ripple effect in that individual's life.

Attitudes have an important impact on one's judgment of the world around him or her. These value judgments can impact every part of the decision-making process, especially when information must be gathered and processed. **Selective interpretation** is illustrated in the efforts of cigarette smokers who rationalize their addictive behavior, claiming that research reporting negative health findings are biased and unfounded. **Selective memory** is one of the oldest ideas in attitude research. People find information supporting their attitudes easier to accept than information that contradicts their existing attitudes (Olson & Zanna, 1993).

Martha has been following a popular, restrictive diet and has successfully lost 20 pounds in a short time. When information is presented from a recent large-scale study that this particular diet presents the possibility of future serious physical complications, she quickly dismisses that information as sensational and unfounded. When asked by a concerned family member if these new findings frighten her, Martha insists that the data are flawed or the researchers are misleading the general public. If she were to seriously consider this new information, she may experience psychological discomfort. Dismissing it eliminates that unpleasant state, at least for a time.

Behaviors

Choices made and actions taken by individuals and families are the **behaviors** that become important in the family decision-making process. After a century of research on attitude and behavior, predicting behavior based on attitudes assessed is still problematic. There are several reasons that the two are not perfectly matched.

Fishbein and Ajzen (1975) propose that the connection between attitude and behavior is multitiered:

- One's behavior can be predicted from intention.
- Intentions can be predicted from one's attitude toward the behavior and one's perception of what others think one should do.
- Attitude is a function of how one perceives the action's outcome will be received by others.

Research conducted using this set of beliefs has included cigarette smoking, seat belt use, self-monitoring of health, and selection of career behaviors. Those applications have been successful in predicting intentions and behaviors.

As discussed in Chapter 4, individual and family needs are important triggers to the family decision-making process. Dupont (1994) included the dimension of needs to the explanation for behavior. He believed that all of our actions are motivated by our needs and values. Kurtines and Gewirtz (1991) added situation into the mix of factors that impact the connection between attitude and behavior.

Studies in the field of social psychology have provided insight into the impact of behavior on attitudes, the reverse of previous studies. Bem (1972) proposed the self-perception theory, where individuals attempt to bring their attitudes into alignment with their behaviors without losing face among others who observe those behaviors.

Jed is daydreaming in class. When his teacher calls attention to his distraction and assigns a detention penalty for it, he focuses on how the situation might negatively impact his social situation within his peer group. After class, while walking with friends to another classroom, Jed comments on how dull and boring that last class had been. He insists that his inability to attend to the situation was not his fault, but the teacher's.

The dissonance theory internalizes the same types of situations. If Jed has consistently been an attentive student during his school years and he prides himself on that personal attribute, daydreaming and the act of being caught in that activity causes him personal discomfort or internal dissonance. Jed is uncomfortable and needs to bring this current behavior into alignment with his long-held attitude.

Just as individuals develop tendencies to behave or react across situations in fairly consistent ways, families exhibit similar characteristics. Some family behaviors may be purely reactionary, especially when the unit or individuals within the family are threatened in any way. When a family member is diagnosed with a terminal disease, the family may pull inward initially. As the unit works through the process of handling immediate needs, there is little energy focused on doing what others outside of the family would expect them to do. However, most behaviors occur on a more conscious level and are actually the result of a complex thought process. The way family members choose to present the family group to others in the larger social environment guides much of the decision-making process. For instance, when a family member dies, members will initially react in instinctual ways, focusing on self and the immediate needs of other family members. Eventually they will turn time and attention to planning the funeral for the deceased. Acceptable practices are firmly embedded in religious, cultural, and social layers. Choices will be made by family members based on their perception of "how it should be done." The focus often shifts from the deceased to the social expectations of those outside the family circle—friends, neighbors, and community members.

At a higher level, membership within a social group and an identified cultural group depends on a person's acceptance and demonstration of certain values, often referred to as ethics. **Ethics** consist of a set of moral principles that exist in formal or unwritten modes. Professional organizations often create, publish, and encourage members to follow a set of behaviors based on unwritten values embraced by that profession. Family units rarely have such formal value and behavioral structures in place, but their values and behaviors may be consistent with such structures.

Values, Attitudes, and Behaviors in the Decision-Making Framework

In the News

Media Overplayed "Moral Values" as "Decisive" Election Issue

Exit polls conducted during the November 2 (2004) presidential election showed that more people (22 percent of voters) selected "moral values" as their primary issue of concern than any other issue, including terrorism, Iraq, or the economy, and that 80 percent of those who picked the "moral values" issue voted for President George W. Bush. Since then, many members of the media have accepted as fact the notion that "moral values" was the decisive issue of the campaign. But those who propound this conventional wisdom offer little to explain or define what voters meant by "moral values."

On the November 9 edition of CNN's *Inside Politics*, host Judy Woodruff suggested that Democrats fared poorly in the election because of a disadvantage in the "moral values" arena: "How do the Democrats close the gap on this 'moral values' question?" Despite the absence of any concrete definition, other media figures have echoed the idea that "moral values" was the pivotal issue of the election. Here are a few examples:

○ *Dan Rather* (CBS anchor): "Moral values—we'll give you a look at the surprise issue that trumped the war, terror, and the economy as the decisive issue in the election." [*CBS Evening News*, 11/3/04]

○ *Anderson Cooper* (CNN anchor): "Well, for months, the presidential campaigns and pundits have debated whether the driving issues of this election would be Iraq or the economy. Turns out it was neither. Moral values ruled this election, with 22 percent of voters citing moral issues as their No. 1 concern." [CNN, *Anderson Cooper 360*, 11/3/04]

○ *Paula Zahn* (CNN anchor): "Tonight, it is the decisive issue, the one pollsters didn't see coming—millions of people voting their moral values. . . . The exit polls are quite stunning, at least to some folks looking at these numbers for the first time, when it appears that moral issues trumped just about every other issue on the map here." [CNN, *Paula Zahn Now*, 11/3/04]

○ *Pat Buchanan* (MSNBC analyst and former presidential candidate): "It wasn't the economy or the war in Iraq or even the war on terror. Exit polls tell us moral values were most important in choosing a president." [MSNBC, *Scarborough Country*, 11/3/04]

○ *Bill Plante* (CBS White House correspondent): "In the end, it was not the Iraq war or the economy, the two issues most often mentioned as voters' biggest concerns, but moral values, which were the biggest factor in motivating people to go to the polls." [CBS, *The Early Show*, 11/4/04]

In fact, the meaning of the "moral values" polling and its merit as an indicator of voter sentiment remains widely contested. Andrew Kohut, president of the Pew Research Center, contended in a November 6 article in *The New York Times* that the exit polls were, in fact, "misleading" because "moral values . . . was an ambiguous, appealing and catchall phrase." "If you put moral values on a list," Kohut noted on the November 3 edition of PBS's *The NewsHour with Jim Lehrer*, "it's hard for many people to say they weren't thinking of moral values when they were making their decision." On MSNBC's *Deborah Norville Tonight*, Kohut called the "moral values" option a "horribly flawed question on the exit poll"; host Deborah Norville added: "I mean, who isn't going to say they're for moral values?"

Although 80 percent of those who selected "moral values" as their primary issue of concern in exit polls voted for Bush, it doesn't necessarily follow that the issue favors Republicans. Norville debunked this assumption on the November 8 edition of *Deborah Norville Tonight*, noting that on three of the issues generally grouped under the "moral values" category—abortion, gay marriage, and stem cell research—Democrats are actually more aligned with the American public than Republicans are:

I want to just throw up some statistics where you look at what the numbers say, first starting off with abortion. And *55 percent of voters, and this is from the National Election Poll, say that abortion should be legal in all or most cases.* That's not that different from what a *Washington Post* survey found eight years ago, in '96. Going on now to gay marriages—when you add it all together, *60 percent of voters say they support either gay marriage or civil unions.* And then stem cell research: two-thirds, *68 percent of voters support federal funding of stem cell research. It doesn't seem like there's a great divide . . . on these "life issues."*

On the November 7 edition of NBC's *Sunday Today*, co-host Campbell Brown asked: "What do you think they were talking about in terms of moral values? Was this driven by opposition to gay marriage?" But the notion that support for same-sex marriage

(Continued)

(Continued)

bans in eleven states was the driving force behind many "moral values" voters also appears to be mistaken. As author and University of Virginia associate professor of politics Paul Freedman observed in a November 5 article for Slate.com, Bush's share of the votes in states considering same-sex marriage bans actually *decreased* in 2004 as compared to 2000. Freedman noted that this fact raises questions about the conventional understanding of the "moral values" issue, and asked: "Did people in these states mention moral issues because gay marriage was on the ballot? Or was it on the ballot in places where people were already more likely to be concerned about morality?" Further, Freedman explained that Republican turnout did not increase disproportionately as a result of the "moral values" issue:

> [T]he morality gap didn't decide the election. Voters who cited moral issues as most important did give their votes overwhelmingly to Bush (80 percent to 18 percent), and states where voters saw moral issues as important were more likely to be red ones. *But these differences were no greater in 2004 than in 2000.* If you're trying to explain why the president's vote share in 2004 is bigger than his vote share in 2000, values don't help.

Even conservative *New York Times* columnist David Brooks agreed that little can be concluded from the "moral values" responses, asking in his November 6 column: "Who doesn't vote on moral values? If you ask an inept question, you get a misleading result."

Source: Material reprinted with permission of Media Matters for America. Retrieved from http://mediamatters.org/items/200411100010.

When used as a verb, *to value* implies that individuals develop a ranking order of what is important to them. Based on that unspoken ranking, resources are expended to a higher degree to protect or build certain other resources. As discussed in relation to the culture of poverty (Payne, 1998), when monetary resources are limited, families tend to judge their success or status based on relationships within the family and throughout the community. Time and energy are devoted to further developing personal relationships and maintaining interpersonal connections between and among group members. When money is readily available or when one desires to be accepted by others who have monetary resources, material goods take on increased importance.

Values are beliefs that guide behavior of family members and the decision-making process. They must be expressed through words or actions to bring about decisions within a group. Some beliefs are so central to the family unit's functioning that they are assumed in almost all decision-making activities. After several decisions are reached, basic values and beliefs may move to the subconscious level of family members. Only when their decisions are challenged by outsiders will they recognize the importance of those values.

Mr. and Mrs. McCallister were both college athletes. During training they were encouraged to eat high-protein, low-fat foods. Breakfast, for them, consisted of skim milk, juice, and cereal or a bagel. Years later, their daughter has a friend spend the night. At breakfast, this friend is distraught because the McCallisters do not have bacon, sausage, or eggs, which she is used to having at her house. For the first time, these parents have to explain their dietary choices to their daughter.

Values and Behaviors in Family Purchasing Decisions

Marketing and advertising specialists have devoted a great deal of time and energy studying family buying patterns and motivations. Manning and Reece (2001) describe product buying **motives** as reasons consumers purchase one product in preference to another. They propose that consumers operate on one of four possible sets of motives: brand preference, quality preference, price preference, or design preference.

BRAND PREFERENCE

Long-standing, well-established manufacturing companies have the opportunity to develop positive product images of quality and performance in the minds of prospective buyers. *Brandweek*, a weekly publication serving media and marketing professionals, is actively involved in surveying consumer brand loyalty utilizing the Brand Keys Customer Loyalty Index. This research is conducted through phone interviews with 16,000 active brand users twice a year. Participants rate brands that they use regularly based on categories of products. The results of these surveys are published in both this publication and a multitude of other media sources interested in consumer behavior. Recent survey results indicate that consumers are less loyal to brand names than they have been in the past.

Companies providing products and services for families continue to spend a great deal of money to convince these buyers that name-branded products have benefits beyond the obvious. Consumers are encouraged to consider the benefits of established company guarantees and histories of customer satisfaction when weighing the choices available in the marketplace. When comparing similar products, these intangible attributes may convince buyers to pay more for the peace of mind that well-known brands give them.

Another aspect of brand loyalty stems from the desire for families to present themselves in specific ways to the larger social groups in which they function. Identifying logos, obvious or subtle, visually presented, imply a level of discrimination in one's purchasing decisions. This behavior may also be a reflection of perceived quality preference.

QUALITY PREFERENCE

Manning and Reece (2001) suggest that the contemporary consumer exhibits higher levels of quality standards than past generations of buyers. When product and service competition is high, quality is one of the factors that differentiate one from the other. Quality can be the result of better materials, workmanship, or quality control, or quality can be a perception of higher standards. Consumers may believe that products with higher price tags indicate higher quality, they may equate name brands with higher quality because they have had positive experiences in the past with those brands, or they may have been exposed to promotional information aimed at setting that brand apart from competitors.

Large-ticket purchases, such as automobiles and appliances, include an expectation of performance for multiple years. Quality may be perceived as an indicator of such performance. Although the competition among and the number of models within automobile manufacturing firms have increased over time, the selection available to consumers could be considered somewhat limited when other types of products are considered. Factors cited as obstacles to new producers include development and production expenses, but another important hurdle to entering the automobile industry is the perception of quality and the sense of security buyers perceive when dealing with the same number of well-established companies.

PRICE PREFERENCE

Family resources are used in exchange for goods and services. Even when a family is resource-rich, product selection usually factors in price differences into the decision-making process. For many products, especially electronics, technological advancements and creative product development have created a "wait for the price to come down" expectation among consumers. Table-top calculators sold for as much as $1,000 in 1975. Smaller calculators with several more features are now available in hand-held versions for under $50.

When two products that both meet the criteria set by a family have noticeable price differences, price increases in importance in the selection process. Price can also be used in the initial phases of decision making if an acceptable price range is established before exploring all available options. That range may screen out several options, thus making the decision less time-consuming. Generic prescription drugs are a good example of how price can become the primary discriminating factor among competitive products. Generic equivalencies of certain drugs have been identified by insurance companies and physicians. FDA requirements imply that all approved drugs are safe and effective. Because generics use the same active ingredients and are shown to work the same way in the body, they should have the same risks and benefits as their brand-name counterparts. Once generic drugs are approved, there is greater competition, which drives the price down. Many insurance companies provide limited coverage of name-brand equivalencies, forcing patients to pay more out-of-pocket expenses if they select these drugs. When faced with that trade-off, most patients select the generic equivalents.

DESIGN PREFERENCE

A lawnmower cuts grass. A riding mower provides wheels, a seat, and blades. How many variations of this product can there be? Thousands. Once a family's needs move beyond the level of security, preferences for style, size, color, and comfort begin to emerge. These preferences reflect personal and group values that have evolved over time. Producers invest a great deal of money in product design and development and in redesign and redevelopment to position their products among competitor's offerings.

The Marketing Profession's Interest in Family Values

Worldwide, businesses search for crystal balls that will help them know what consumers want in terms of products and services. One tool, the VALS™ system, is based on a personality trait survey that is used to predict consumer behavior. This system was originally developed by Mitchell, a consumer futurist in the 1970s, to explain the changing values and lifestyles reported during that decade. The original VALS system was redefined in 1989 by experts from SRI International, Stanford University, and the University of California, Berkeley. The results of that effort focused on segmenting consumers on the basis of personality traits, which were believed to be more salient than social values over time. The premise is basically that personality traits drive consumer behavior.

The VALS framework suggests that consumers are driven to buy products and services that fulfill their preferences and enhance their lives. Each consumer has a primary motivation that determines his or her action in the marketplace. Some are motivated by ideals, basing decisions on criteria such as quality, integrity, and tradition (see Figure 5.2).

Others are motivated by achievement, basing their decisions on anticipated acceptance or rejection of behaviors by members of the groups to which they aspire to belong. The third motivational orientation is that of self-expression. These individuals make choices on an emotional level, stressing individuality and personal challenge. Further identification of motivators and environmental influences of consumers utilizing this model creates profiles and data that can be used by both consumers and producers in product development, distribution, and marketing.

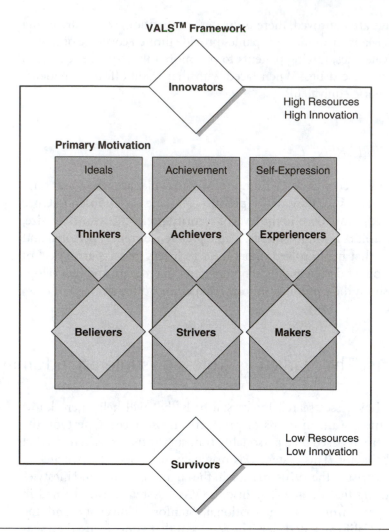

Figure 5.2   Standardized Method of Classifying Consumers by Value Sets

Source: SRI Consulting Business Intelligence (SRIC-BI); www.sric-bi.com/VALS.

Impact of Culture on Values, Attitudes, and Behaviors

Individuals operating within social or cultural systems learn the important values of that group. If they accept and live by those values the majority of the time, they will be able to exist in that group and depend on group membership when seeking necessary resources. If they do not accept or display the majority of these values, they risk being cast out and cannot depend on group support when needed. To maintain a cultural group, this important set of values must be transmitted to future generations and new members. The cultural environment and social interaction have tremendous influence on an individual's set of values. Theorists

Worldview

In many cultures, there are practices and beliefs about the interdependence of individuals. "Do unto others," "You scratch my back, I'll scratch your back," "Quid pro quo." China has a similar concept—*guanxi* (pronounced "gwon-see"), a personal relationship between any two individuals with long-term benefits for both (L. Yu, Chan, & Ireland, 2006). Imagine a spider web of personal connections, cultivated over one's lifespan, functioning as a network of favors and obligations. In a society with rigid social hierarchies, those who have power are easily distinguished from those who do not. To survive, the powerless recognize the importance of *guanxi*, and those with power realize the benefits of maintaining connections with those in the lower levels.

As China emerges as an attractive global market for exportation of goods and services, *guanxi* is an important tradition for business analysis. Although China's younger generations are shedding many ancient traditional behaviors, *guanxi* holds steadfast, although slightly altered by modern technology. The Internet expands networking opportunities exponentially. Moving from personal, face-to-face contact, Chinese young people can build networks without such personal investment.

Cynthia needs concert tickets. She instant messages 20 of her network friends using a sophisticated social network site. The probability of someone in her network with connections to either ticket holders or ticketing offices is 20 times more powerful than her personal resources. Cynthia has a lot of "face," Chinese for status.

Lam and Graham (2007) stress the highly contextual aspects of doing business in China. Contracts and business deals are sealed in social settings, such as restaurants and karaoke establishments. Business relationships, within and between companies, include a complex system of gift exchange. L. Yu et al. (2006) present this system as an art form—it's not the thought, it's the brand and cost of the gift that secures *guanxi*.

propose that children are encouraged to accept existing value sets within their culture.

Individuals may affiliate simultaneously with more than one social group. They must then balance their value systems and behaviors carefully to retain membership in both groups. Within the United States, there are several different religious and professional groups. The U.S. legal system and governmental body operate within a code of ethics or system of values that reflects the beliefs of some of these subgroups more readily than others. For instance, federal offices and services build working holiday calendars around the Christian holiday, Christmas. Workweeks are generally scheduled with Sunday, or the Sabbath, as a nonworking day. Those seeking to observe other religious holidays must negotiate within the existing framework of employer expectations. Even higher education is wrapped around a system of beliefs that may inconvenience citizens exercising their right to participate in religious practices.

Sandra is an adolescent who has been raised within the Mormon religious community. Upon graduation from high school, it may be expected of her to spend 2 years as a missionary of her faith. Because the insurance industry in the United States adopts the idea that students graduating from high school should move directly on to postsecondary educational programs, health insurance coverage of family members pursuing college degrees generally ends on their 24th birthday. If Sandra follows her desire to be a missionary for 2 years, she may only be covered by her parents' insurance through 4 years of college study. Her peers who enter college immediately after graduation may be covered through their graduate or professional programs. Scholarship opportunities may also differ for her because she will be viewed as a nontraditional student when she enrolls.

IMPACT OF SOCIOECONOMIC FACTORS ON VALUES, ATTITUDES, AND BEHAVIORS

Do families with immense pools of resources approach the decision-making process differently than those with limited resources? Contemporary literature implies that they do. Aldrich (1996) devoted an entire book to the subject of *old money*. His premise is that America's upper class has significantly different values toward and meanings of wealth. These values differ from those of the marketplace and newly emerging rich. Other authors explore the unwritten code of family preservation among the families that have held wealth over several generations. From selection of potential marital mates to the simplicity and elegance of clothing, home, and automobile selections, this concept of **old money** continues to intrigue those aspiring to acquisition of wealth or those frustrated with what they view to be unfair advantage.

Stein and Brier (2002) provide guidelines for raising responsible children of wealth. They suggest that parents introduce their children to the attorneys, accountants, and financial planners that manage the family's wealth. Another piece of advice given to parents with large inheritances to pass on to their children includes how to teach those young people important tenets inherent to their social and economic positions:

- Children must be taught to share their good fortune with others.

- **Philanthropy** is a key factor in teaching children to be responsible managers of their money.

- Wealth is not an entitlement. (pp. 2–3)

New money, or large accumulations of wealth within the current generation, is also explored by many theorists and social science authors. Brown (2000) presents the idea of "the sudden wealth syndrome" as experienced by new millionaires in Silicon Valley. Rapid technological changes and the making of large fortunes at an early age may have serious consequences for those families. The term **affluenza** has made its way into books and the media as a way to describe the increasing value placed on money and the materialistic side of American society. Underlying the glib of new syndromes and maladies associated with money is the suggestion of an out-of-control society with success defined as acquisition of money and the power that is inherent to that commodity. This desire to get ahead, fast and furiously, seems to overshadow the values most often associated with the family unit—love, obligation, and reciprocity.

> **Af-flu-en-za. n.** 1. The bloated sluggish and unfulfilled feeling that results from efforts to keep up with the Joneses. 2. An epidemic of stress, overwork, waste, and indebtedness caused by dogged pursuit of the American Dream. 3. An unsustainable addiction to economic growth. (www.pbs.org/kcts/affluenza/)

Consistency Over Time and Situation

Capitalism, by its nature, results in a dynamic environment where one can rise and fall financially in short periods of time. Are values, attitudes, and behaviors impacted by changes in economic conditions? When needs are analyzed simultaneously with values and attitudes, one must remember that survival needs will always be more important than higher order needs. A middle-class family that finds itself suddenly in the throes of extreme poverty due to unemployment, disease, or accident will focus first on food and shelter. Only when a relative level of comfort and safety has been reached can the individuals within that family focus attention on evaluative dimensions of the choices they have available to them. Existing value systems will remain intact until they are challenged sufficiently to consider change and reforming of those core beliefs.

Summary

Values impact family decision making at every phase. They determine what and how needs will be determined and, once determined, how important each need is relative to all other needs. Once the need has been determined, the alternatives available to fulfill that need are processed in terms of values and attitudes of family members, especially those most responsible for the consequences of the decision to be made. The postdecision evaluation is based almost entirely on the value and attitude structures that lead the decision and implementation processes. Families consist of multiple human beings, inherently social beings. Outsiders will never fully understand the unique unfolding of this value-laden process, but the understanding and acceptance of the fact that families create, display, and maintain value systems allow all family service providers the opportunity to be as objective as possible.

Questions for Review and Discussion

1. How do values and attitudes differ?

2. Why might the same family come to entirely different conclusions on two separate occasions when the decision to be made is essentially the same in each situation?

3. How does brand loyalty reflect consumer values and attitudes?

4. How are family values used politically?

Unit III

Understanding Resources

The Decision-Making Process

- Recognize existing need(s)
- Identify alternatives to fulfill identified needs

  Chapter 6. Identification of Family Resources

- Evaluate identified alternatives

  Chapter 7. Families Within the Economic Environment

  Chapter 8. The Impact of Society on Family Decisions

- Select and implement alternative
- Reflect and evaluate alternative selected

Identification of Family Resources 6

Objectives

- Be aware of the nature and characteristics of a resource.
- Be familiar with resource theory.
- Recognize the different types of resources.
- Be familiar with how resources are measured and managed.
- Be acquainted with the way that resources are used and allocated.

My mother's menu consisted of two choices: Take it or leave it.

—Buddy Hackett

From the moment that humans inhabited the earth, they set about to learn and expand ways to use its resources. Hamilton (1992) defines a **resource** as "anything people use or might want to use to achieve an end" (p. 10). Foa (1993) defined a resource as "any item, concrete or symbolic, which can become the object of exchange among people" (p. 2). Zimmerman (1964) defined resources not in terms of substances, but as

127

"living phenomenon, expanding and contracting in response to human effort and behavior" (p. 7). Howitt (2001) expands on Zimmerman's definition to explain that resources are a "matter of relationships not things" (p. 4). In this definition, resources have more to do with the relationship or transactions between people and their cultures.

Resource Availability

Worldview

How many of you stopped to pick up your favorite cappuccino or latte today? A documentary film, *Black Gold* (www.blackgoldmovie.com), released in 2006, captures the surprise that workers in the hills of Ethiopia had when they are told how much their coffee earns around the world. At Starbucks, a shot of espresso costs more than $2.50. A coffee worker in Ethiopia earns less than half of that in a day. Here are some figures given in this film to illustrate the *real* cost of coffee:

2 billion cups of coffee are consumed every day worldwide
100 million people worldwide depend on its production
Coffee is the second largest commodity in the world after gasoline
75% of the world's coffee comes from small producers
15 million Ethiopians depend on the coffee trade
90% of Ethiopia's exports are coffee (54% of Ethiopia's GDP is coffee)
$1 a day is the average Ethiopian coffee worker's wage
$27 retail cost per pound for luxury coffee; Ethiopian producer would get about $1
Less than 10 cents is given to the grower when you pay more than $3.00 for cappuccino

"Coffee came first from Ethiopia," says Hailu Gebre Hiwot, president of the country's coffee exporters' association, as he sips on a cup of a deep, rich variety, "and so did mankind."

In a warehouse in Addis Ababa, where workers check the quality of tons of smooth, dark coffee beans, Mr. Hiwot is musing on the unfairness of trade in a globalised world. While espresso, cappuccino and latte drinkers are bringing huge profits to some of the world's biggest multinationals, the place where coffee originated remains one of the poorest on Earth.

Around the world more than 2 billion cups of the stuff are consumed each day. In Starbucks in south London the cheapest shot of espresso costs £1.35. A coffee worker in Ethiopia earns less than half of that in a day.

Now the country where coffee was first consumed around 1,000 years ago is trying to get a fairer share of the proceeds. Growers are clubbing together to try to squeeze more money out of the export trade.

International donors such as the EU are providing cash to try to develop the industry and keep more of the processing inside Ethiopia. More attention is being focused on creating top quality, more expensive beans. And an international effort is under way to raise consciousness over the plight of Ethiopia's impoverished workforce.

A documentary film, Black Gold, released this month, captures the astonishment of workers in the hills of Ethiopia when they are told how much their produce earns for foreigners. Coffee is sold for the equivalent of 2,000 Ethiopian birr a kilo (£121); they are paid one thousandth of that.

In Ethiopia at least 15 million people depend on the trade yet on Western supermarket shelves the fruits of their labour are hard to see. "Illy, Lavazza, they all buy our coffee and they use it in their blends which are both African and Central American," says Mr. Hiwot.

One of the most popular with Western firms is the high quality Yirgachefe which, as it happens, is what Mr. Hiwot is drinking. "This coffee grows in a particular area," Mr. Hiwot explains, "at a particular altitude. It has its own special climatic conditions. That's why we have the quality and flavour, why the aroma is so special." True though that may be, the fact that some of the world's best coffee comes from Ethiopia remains unknown to the millions around the world who drink it. "The brands are established by these big multinationals which spend money on brainwashing the consumer. Once they make you their customer you stick with them," Mr. Hiwot says. It is a vicious circle that condemns millions of people to poverty.

Ethiopia's efforts to get a greater share of the wealth its coffee beans create faced a major setback this week when the country was stopped from trademarking its coffee by the US National Coffee Association (NCA). Yesterday the British charity Oxfam accused Starbucks of being behind the bid to deny Ethiopian farmers a potential income of up to £47m, according to reports in the Guardian. Oxfam is reported as saying that the US coffee giant, which had turnover of $7.8bn (£4.1bn) in the year to 1 October, prevented Ethiopia from securing trademark protection for two of its best known beans, Sidamo and Harar.

Had Ethiopia been successful, it would have allowed the country to control the use of the beans in the market, giving its farmers more of the retail price and securing an estimated extra £48m, the charity said. Nevertheless, Starbucks had in the past provided support for coffee farmers in Ethiopia.

The importance of coffee to Ethiopia is difficult to overstate. The country is the largest coffee producer in Africa and the sixth-biggest in the world. Coffee accounts for no less than 90 per cent of Ethiopia's exports, half of which go to EU countries. The trade generates some 54 per cent of Ethiopia's gross domestic product.

As Yackob Yalla, the State Minister for Agriculture, puts it: "Coffee is crucial, because of the trade aspect, the share of the gross domestic

(Continued)

(Continued)

product and the proportion of jobs it creates." In recent years the price plummeted by almost 50 per cent and, though it has recovered somewhat, the consequences remain devastating.

Without its own port, landlocked Ethiopia must export its produce via Djibouti, adding to its costs. Moreover its economy and traditions hardly equip it for the modern, marketed world of designer drinks.

In Ethiopia every ounce of coffee exported must be bought at auction in the country's main exchange in Addis Ababa. Hi-tech it is not. Blocking the entrance to the building is a taxi resting on wooden blocks. Inside, the large, bare halls appear to have changed little over recent decades, with exporters seated along one side and local traders on the other. Above them sit the auctioneers on a wooden stage at the front and to the side is a blackboard and piles of paper. There is not a single computer in sight.

This being the off-season the coffee exchange is buying and selling the contents of 90 lorries a day. During the busiest part of the year that will rise to 200 lorries' worth. Looking around this hall it is hard to see how Ethiopia's coffee-growers can take on the multinationals.

One thing that can be done on the ground is to work through co-operatives which, as Black Gold illustrates, remove up to 60 per cent of the cost of transactions in the buying and selling chain. That helps put more cash in the pocket of the growers. Similarly, fair trade coffee can be an additional resource.

Ethiopian coffee exporters also want to raise the profile of their country internationally.

However Mr. Hiwot says: "European and American brands are better marketed and financed. It requires a lot of financial input to develop a brand in the European market." Realistically the best prospect may be to maximise the amount of money that can be won from exports and that means going upmarket.

The EU, which has been supporting the Ethiopian coffee sector for about 20 years, has invested around 100m (£67m) in developing it. Export of higher value coffee has increased seven fold, from 5 per cent to 35 per cent of total exports, though officials say there is still considerable room for improvement in quality and agricultural practice.

Visiting Addis Ababa, Peter Mandelson, the European trade commissioner, said: "Improving production methods, meeting common standards, marketing and distribution are vital. This is precisely where European Union technical assistance has been making the difference for the past two decades."

Mr. Hiwot says production of the highest quality coffee for export can be boosted by 10 to 20 per cent. "At the top level, where the competition is not so severe, the market is better for us."

One success story comes from Teklu Gabriel, chief of coffee quality at IPS, a company which works with 15 producers and which began to supply Starbucks this year. His firm is, says Mr. Gabriel, "exceptional" but its secret is simple. Firstly, it has worked hard to become a reliable supplier to big multinationals. Just as important, he says, "the coffee is very high quality."

Nevertheless, only a fraction of the wealth of the global coffee trade is likely to cascade down anytime soon.

Black Gold: The Figures

2bn cups are consumed every day worldwide

50p a day is average Ethiopian coffee worker's wage

15m Ethiopians depend on the coffee trade

£14retail cost per pound for luxury coffee; 59 pence the maximum an Ethiopian producer would get

90% of Ethiopia's exports are coffee

54% of Ethiopia's GDP is coffee

2nd to petrol in terms of being a global commodity

15th century: this is when coffee first arrives in Europe but it only becomes popular in the 17th century

$11.2bn Ethiopia's GDP in 2005

5% of the total UK coffee market is fair trade

75% of the world's coffee comes from small producers

31bn cups of coffee are drunk in the United Kingdom every year

$7.8bn turnover was recorded last year

5p on average is given to the grower when a £1.75 cappuccino is sold

100m people worldwide depend on its production

$8.7bn exports worldwide in 2000

—Debbie Gore

Source: www.netscape.com/viewstory/2006/10/27/the-real-price-of-coffee/?url=http%3A% 2F%2Fnews.independent.co.uk%2Fworld%2Fafrica%2Farticle1932728.ece&frame=true.

The lowest level of Maslow's hierarchy of needs, as discussed in Chapter 5, relies on the idea that people use resources to meet their physical needs of food, clothing, and shelter. There are certain conditions that cause resources to change. The industrialized world that we know today was created by uncovering and using new resources. However, nothing becomes a resource unless there is a use for it or unless someone determines that it has value, no matter how much of that substance exists. A good example of this is the diamond. Diamonds are mined in great quantity for industrial uses because of their hardness. Until people began to equate the diamond as a symbol of marriage, the value of the diamond was much different. Although the raw value of a diamond was not that lavish, the value of the diamond ring to romantic Americans is high.

Resources have certain characteristics that make them useable. A resource must have a purpose or **utility**. In the past few years, the penny has come to have less utility. Buying "penny candy" or feeding a parking meter with pennies is no longer possible. People may walk over pennies laying on the street all day without stopping to pick them up because they have less purpose or utility in our society.

Most believe that having money is all that is important for accessing what is needed. However, a resource must also be available before it can be used no matter how much money you have. As a result, accessibility is an important characteristic. For example, a person who needs a specialized type of surgery cannot access that service if he or she is not able to get to the hospital where it can be performed no matter how much money he or she may have.

Resources must also be transferable. Transferability allows consumers to move assets to where they are needed the most. Some resources are more transferable than others. For example, real estate may be a good investment and over time may increase in value, but it may not be able to be liquidated and transferred as quickly as cash or stocks.

Resources are interchangeable. Money can be exchanged for goods or services. We can go to the grocery store and exchange cash for food that we can take home to prepare or we can go to a restaurant and exchange our cash for the service of having a meal cooked and served. Any resource can be substituted as a means to gain assets. For example, someone might work to help tend a neighbor's garden in exchange for tomatoes and green beans, or those green beans might be exchanged for tulip bulbs from another neighbor.

Manageability of resources is a characteristic that allows consumers to make decisions about how resources are used, transferred, or exchanged. The ability to manage resources leads to more efficiency and maximum use of resources.

Resource Theory

Resource theory was first created by Foa (1971). The idea behind this theory has its roots in social psychology and maintains that people attempt to meet their needs in the context of social interaction. According to the theory, it is through relationships that people gather resources. The theory identifies six types of resources:

Love—an expression of affectionate regard, warmth, or comfort

Status—an expression of evaluative judgment that conveys high or low prestige, regard, or esteem

Information—advice, opinions, instruction, or enlightenment

Money—any coin, currency, or token that has some standard unit of value

Goods—tangible products, objects, or materials

Services—activities on the body or belongings of a person that constitute labor for another

These resources are those that are exchanged in relationships. For example, groceries are usually exchanged for money, and services are performed in exchange for money. In school, information is exchanged for status (a high school diploma or college degree).

The theory also identifies resources as particularistic, or their degree of concreteness. A resource that is particularistic is one in which the person is selective in choosing. A good example of this is love. Usually we are careful about those with whom we give and receive love. In contrast, money is the least particularistic because we don't usually care about with whom we exchange money. The degree of concreteness also helps to understand resources. When we sell a car, the car is gone. Exchanging goods has a high degree of concreteness in that the possession can be gained or lost. However, some resources are symbolic, as in the case of information. We may "give away" information, but after the transaction we still possess the information. We may use our skills to perform a service, but in the end we still possess that skill. Around the circle on the diagram of resource theory, the different types of resources are arranged by similarity. For example, money is next to goods, but opposite of love. Foa believed that this order predicts that people prefer to exchange resources that are similar. For example, most people would exchange money for goods or information more readily than exchanging money for love or status.

Although resource theory does explain a lot about human behavior and economics, it is not without weaknesses. Because the meaning of the exchange is more important than the exchange itself, it represents something different than pure economic behavior. For example, the relationship between the two who are exchanging can range from strangers to intimate partners. Therefore, the meaning of the exchange is different. Other factors may involve the intensity of communication between the exchangers, the self-esteem of the exchangers, or the nature of previous exchanges.

Human Resources

Human resources are those that are unique to people. People bring a variety of assets that enrich their lives and those around them. Cognitive or mental resources are the most common of the human resources and the most flexible. These resources include experience that has been gained from the past, the know-how that results from learning, the skills that are acquired, and inherent creativity.

Davenport and Prusak (1998) suggest the components of human capital are ability, behavior, effort, and time. Ability involves a person's knowledge and skills, but also his or her inborn talent. Most employers desire education. Although education may add to a person's ability to produce goods and services, it is also a signal of intellect, determination, and discipline. It may also signal motivation or the individual's ability to set goals and make plans to meet those goals. Behavior consists of observable ways that someone does things that contributes to accomplishing a task, including ethics, values, and beliefs. Effort is the component that activates or applies ability. It is the motivation to get things done.

Although time is not a resource within the person, it is the most fundamental resource that is under their control. Humans gauge their time or pace themselves by using the time they are given. Beblo (2001) observes that time can be allocated into three basic economic categories: paid labor (workplace or market), unpaid labor (household), and leisure. Each person is given a limited amount of time each day. Choices are made that determine the use of time. People may choose to go to work, collect a paycheck, and use that money to buy goods and services. They may also choose to use the time for their own leisure or to spend time with their family. The value of that time can be viewed differently among individuals.

Photo 6.1   Working mothers juggle available resources.

Source: © Images by Trista/istockphoto.

Shannon recently gave birth to her first baby. Before the birth, Shannon and her husband decided that she would stay home with the baby for the first few years rather than work outside the home. Shannon's friend, Julie, is in a similar situation. Julie has called several times to ask Shannon to have lunch, to go shopping together, or just visit over the phone. Shannon almost always declines. Shannon tells her husband, "I feel that it is a waste of time to spend the day with Julie. When will I do the laundry, prepare meals, and keep up with the housework?" Julie, in contrast, values the time that she can get out of the house and interact with other adults. Both Shannon and Julie value the resource of time, but in different ways.

As a resource, time may be more valuable than money. The busy working parent may choose to buy partially or fully prepared foods. This food may be less expensive for the family than the loss of more expensive work time. Although most workers cannot exchange work time for home time, buying convenience foods does afford parents more time to spend with the family at the end of a long day.

Eriksen (2001) suggests that because we live in the information age, the resource of time is the scarcest. The amount of information that is available causes a struggle to control our time. The Internet and other similar technologies, designed to improve and ease our lives, have in some ways served to complicate them. Those operating from a different worldview may not see time as a manageable commodity. Their perception of time, as a resource, may not be one of "limited," but rather as "renewable." Each new day has boundless potential.

Another human resource is energy. People possess the ability to use their bodies—legs, hands, and muscles—to accomplish tasks. These psychomotor skills allow people to create as well as maintain resources. For example, someone can take raw materials such as wood and create a beautiful cabinet. After the cabinet is finished, they can use their energy to keep that cabinet polished and clean, which helps maintain their investment. Personal energy is used in working and in leisure. These activities are central to living.

Economic Resources

Family economic resources are gained by either acquisition or inheritance. Family members earn economic resources by working. Workers are compensated by a wage or salary. Employees who earn wages are paid by the hour. The government sets minimum wage levels according to the Fair Labor Standards Act (FLSA). Debates over the minimum wage continue as full-time minimum wage employees hover close to the poverty level. Although proponents argue the need to raise employees' earnings for low-income families, those against argue that raising minimum wages only benefit teenagers in middle-class families. The term living wage has been used to describe a wage rate that would allow wage earners to provide for their families above the poverty level. According to Pollin (2002), since 1995, more than 60 cities have passed ordinances that set a standard for wages. Controversy around the living wage centers on the definition of poverty and the wide range of wage rates and benefits standards that have been set across the country. For example, the living costs for low-wage earners on the East or West Coast may be different from those in the South or Midwest. Pollin states that "living wage proponents have a large task ahead of them in establishing wage norms that provide all workers with the capabilities to support families, maintain self-respect, and participate meaningfully in the civic life of the community" (p. 273).

In contrast to wage earners, employees who are paid a salary are usually those who have spent time preparing for life-long work in a particular field or profession. These workers have engaged in training or education that allows them to move into careers that require specific skills. Although it is not uncommon to find an hourly wage earner who brings home more money than the person who is at an entry-level position on a salary, statistics show that the salaried person will probably move up the pay scale more quickly over time. Although the cost of a college education continues to rise, it is still a good investment over a lifetime for most. Bradbury (2002) reports that, in 1980, college graduates made 43% more than someone with a high school degree. At the end of the 1990s, that percentage rose to 71%.

Reality Check

What is the value of an education? Today, more than at any time in history, an education is directly related to economic success. Although there are many ways to define education, most agree that more education means higher wages. According to data from the U.S. Bureau of Labor Statistics (BLS), the financial difference between a bachelor's and master's degree is nearly $200 per week, while the difference between a bachelor's degree and a doctorate is nearly $500 per week.

Median Usual Weekly Earnings of Full-Time Wage and Salary Workers Age 25 or Older:

Doctoral degree: $1,421
Professional degree: $1,370
Master's degree: $1,129
Bachelor's degree: $937
Associate degree: $699
National median weekly earnings: $696
Some college, no degree: $653
High school diploma, no degree: $583
Less than a high school diploma: $409

Resources also come in the form of benefit packages that workers receive as part of their earnings. Benefits all have a significant impact on the total resources of the worker and their family. Some benefits are required by the government (see Chapter 8 for more information on Social Security), whereas others are voluntarily provided by employers. Employers must contribute to their workers' Social Security, Medicare, and unemployment insurance funds. Beyond those basic requirements, employers may decide to offer paid vacations, sick leave, health insurance, life insurance, disability insurance, and retirement savings plans. Benefits account for almost 28% of labor costs of U.S. employers (Collinge & Ayers, 2000). When the demand for employees exceeds the supply of laborers seeking employment, companies use voluntary benefits to attract and keep their labor forces. When unemployment figures exceed the number of job openings, employers may not need the incentives provided by benefit packages to fill empty positions.

It is crucial that working adults understand the benefits packages available to them before they accept a job and when they are considering changing jobs. A job with a lower salary may actually provide more resources when benefits are considered. One should be especially careful in reviewing optional benefits available with certain positions. These options are often referred to as cafeteria plans because employees can pick and choose from among several different kinds of benefits, meeting their unique current and forecasted needs. Employers may provide workers with a set number of benefit dollars and a menu of possible benefits priced individually. Employees can select what they want from this menu. Thus, if Employee A is single, he or she may select the $150 single health plan and a $50 disability insurance plan, whereas his or her married colleague may select the family health plan for $200 and forego the disability plan. If the company offered a straight health insurance option to all employees, Employee A would actually be receiving $50 less per month because of his or her single status.

Job A has an annual salary of $25,000, with a 3% contribution to the employee's retirement savings plan, and a contribution of $350 per month toward the employee's $450 health insurance premium. Job B has an annual salary of $28,000, no retirement contribution, and $150 toward the health insurance premium. Which job actually pays out more to the employee?

Gender also has an impact on earning potential. Wage differences between men and women historically have favored men. Reasons given for this difference have included the types of jobs, longevity and commitment to the job, and other factors. Bradbury (2002) reports that between 1979 and 1992, women's wages rose, whereas men's wages declined, reducing the gap between pay differentials. After 1992, men's wages increased even though women's educational attainment exceeded that of men. By 2006, the U.S. Department of Labor reported that women's earnings equaled 80.7% of men's earnings, which is up slightly from 78% in 2002. Avellar and Smock (2003) found that women pay a penalty for being mothers. Even over time, having children has a negative effect on women's wages. Heckert et al. (2002)

found women expect to earn less and that they place more emphasis on how their job will affect their family life.

The other way that family economic resources are gained is by inheritance. The history of inheritance can be found in antiquity, with various cultures establishing their own way of distributing assets after the death of a family member. In the United States, the inheritance practices followed the early settlers from their native country. In colonial times, if someone didn't make a will, the state would decide how the assets would be divided. Because many settlers owned their own businesses or farms, dividing the resources was difficult if it meant jeopardizing the operation. Deciding who would get the family business was complex. In addition, they were reluctant to adopt the English laws that so many were fleeing. *Primogeniture*, the English law whereby the eldest son inherited everything, was rejected by most of the colonies. However, male children continued to receive more of the inheritance.

Following the Revolutionary War, most states passed laws to give children equal shares. Also, unlike English inheritance laws, which bypassed widows, a woman could inherit provisions for her lifetime. Not until the late 19th century did states pass the Women's Property Acts, which allowed wives to inherit estates from their husbands. This act allowed women to keep ownership and control and to decide inheritance among their children after their husband's death. Today parents are living longer, and many are more concerned about retirement resources than inheritance for their children. When someone dies, the assets are usually given to the surviving spouse. When both spouses are gone, the assets are often liquidated and divided among the descendants. Although it sounds simple, there are two factors that often complicate inheritance. First, the emotions and expectations of the family members may make dividing resources more difficult. Families may find themselves faced with disagreements about fairness.

Dan has never considered any other profession than farming. Since he was a child, he enjoyed being outside with his father on the family farm. Although he attended and graduated from college, he always knew he would come back to the farm. When he married his wife, Sandy, they both assumed that they would continue to work the land together and grow old on the farm that they both loved. Dan and his father continued to work together until 2 years ago, when his father suffered a stroke that left him unable to do much of the work. This year, Dan's father passed away from another stroke. While working with the lawyer, Dan found out that the farm assets would be divided equally among himself and his three sisters. In order to continue to farm, he would either have to rent the land or buy the land from his sisters. Although the farm had provided enough income for Dan and his parents, the new expenses would make it impossible to continue to farm. When he came home he said, "I can't believe that I have given my life for this farm and my sisters don't care about it at all, and yet they still get their share!"

Disagreements over family heirlooms sometime erupt when one person feels they are entitled because of special circumstances or relationships. In addition, the value of some assets may be in dispute. For example, one brother may value a particular set of dishes because of the memories they create of family time, whereas the other brother may value the dishes because of their retail value. Which brother should have the dishes? Or should only a daughter have dishes and the brother get tools? These questions are at the heart of the emotional side of inheritance.

The other factor that complicates inheritance is the tax laws. In 1916, Congress enacted for the first time a tax on the transfer of estates. This estate tax was joined in 1935 by the Revenue Act, which allowed for inheritance tax to be collected. An inheritance tax is imposed on those who receive property, and estate taxes are imposed on the deceased's estate. Today the federal government collects estate taxes, and some states impose inheritance taxes. Sometimes these taxes force people to sell property to meet obligations to the government. Considering the prior example of the farmer; if the father and mother had not done any estate planning, the farm assets may have to be sold to pay the taxes, regardless of who inherits the land. Many people attempt to save these taxes by setting up trusts or other legal methods to bypass the tax system. Those who have the financial means and can afford legal advice are most often the ones who benefit from these legal loopholes. Even in death, those with the most resources have the advantage.

Environmental Resources

In the News

Federal Government Final Piece to Complete Water Settlement

May 2006
U.S. Water News Online
SANTA FE—A 40-year-old lawsuit over water rights on the Pojoaque, Nambe and Tesuque rivers is close to a settlement, but questions remain over how much the federal government will pay for a regional water system that is the agreement's cornerstone.

Representatives of the state, Santa Fe County, non-Indian well owners and the pueblos of Nambe, Pojoaque, San Ildefonso and Tesuque are to sign a settlement in the lawsuit, known as the Aamodt case after the first name in a lengthy list of water claimants.

(Continued)

(Continued)

The lawsuit was filed in 1966 by the state engineer's office to adjudicate water rights in the Nambe and Pojoaque areas north of Santa Fe. The case includes the four pueblos and thousands of non-Indian water users, including the city and county of Santa Fe.

Settlement talks began in 2000.

Under the agreement revealed earlier this year, the federal government will be asked to appropriate about $150 million for a regional water system, which will cost an estimated $172 million to $177 million.

The state has agreed to pitch in about $17 million. The county will pay up to $10 million.

A settlement proposal in 2004 fell apart when the Bush administration balked at paying most of a $280 million price tag to build a regional system to pipe water to the Pojoaque Valley from the Rio Grande. At one point, the administration refused to commit to more than $11 million.

The latest proposal scaled down the regional water system.

Leaders from the pueblos, county and state are to travel to Washington, D.C., in two weeks to discuss the settlement with New Mexico's congressional delegation.

"The wild card is Congress," said Bill Hume, the governor's director of policy and issues.

"I don't expect they'll go there and come back with a ringing endorsement" because New Mexico's finances look good, he said. "They'll say, 'Since you're so well off, why don't you pick up the cost?' "

Sen. Pete Domenici, R-N.M., agreed.

"In light of a tight federal budget, securing the funds necessary to implement this settlement will be very challenging," he said.

He said the settlement "will require an appropriate local and state contribution."

But Maria Najera, a spokeswoman for Sen. Jeff Bingaman, D-N.M., said the impediment is not Congress, but the president.

"The Bush administration hasn't been willing to invest in Indian water projects in the states, so we're concerned there won't be support for this," she said.

The settlement calls for non-Indians to reduce groundwater pumping from their wells by 15 percent, unless that's less than half an acre foot—as is the case for most of the wells.

In exchange, the pueblos would use the water imported from the Rio Grande to support development and would not assert their senior water rights during times of drought—meaning they would not try to cut off water supplies to non-pueblo users.

Earlier court rulings established that the pueblos had the longest-standing right to the water.

Negotiations are slated in the fall on rules to govern the water master, the division of the state engineer's office that will enforce the settlement and an "impairment fund," which will pay restitution to non-Indian wells harmed by pueblo pumping.

Finalizing the case "will still take years," said San Ildefonso Pueblo's attorney, Peter Chestnut.

Source: www.uswaternews.com/archives/arcrights/6fedegove5.html.

Environmental resources include those resources in the physical environment around us that are provided by nature. Families all over the world depend on the earth's resources to live and work. As environmental resources are used, they may be depleted and eventually exhausted.

Environmental resources are either renewable or nonrenewable. **Renewable resources** are those that can be used that will not deplete or those that can be used over and over again. Flow resources are those that are available on a continual basis. Good examples of these are the sun and wind. Other renewable resources are renewed by the biological process, such as plants, animals, and fish. Although we consider renewable resources to have unlimited potential for use, misuse or overuse will eventually deplete the supply. For example, although trees continue to reseed and grow voluntarily in the biological process, aggressive logging can remove enough trees in one area so that trees are not given a chance to replenish. **Nonrenewable resources** are those that are available in limited quantity. Once the resource is used, it is not replaced. Examples of these types of resources would include minerals and fossil fuels. Much of the physical environment is nonrenewable and needs to be protected for the generations that will live on the earth in the future. There are several ways to think about how natural resources should be used. Some view the use of resources in terms of restricting consumption. Conservationists want to educate and affect policies that will recognize and protect resources. Some generations have been more aware of and willing to protect the environment. Whenever a natural resource is threatened, there are those who rise up and call for more protection. Others advocate for new technologies that will allow more efficient use of resources or create alternative resources. A good example is the research being done on alternative power for automobiles, such as electricity or hydrogen.

Sterner (2003) suggests that the environmental resources are in danger for various reasons. First, the increase in population has caused depletion and shortages in natural resources. These can include the increased demands for natural goods, such as lumber and water, and the added chemicals associated from production of goods. Another danger comes from inadequate environmental policies. Politics is often in the middle of the debate over how to protect the environment. Environmentalists argue that nothing should allow the environment to be compromised, whereas industry pushes for less restriction to increase production and profits.

Social Resources

The previous types of resources discussed have been **tangible** (those that can be seen), whereas **social resources** are those that are felt. McDermott (2004) suggests that, in the past, the economic community has largely treated social resources as something that only individuals acquire. He suggests that social resources be brought to the social level. Putnam (2000) describes social capital or resources as "connections among individuals— social networks and the norms of reciprocity and trustworthiness that arise from them" (p. 19). In addition, human and economic resources can be owned individually, whereas social resources are collectively owned.

Social resources are resources that are found both inside the family and those that come from outside the family but affect the family. Social resources found inside the family include caring for and meeting the needs of the family members. Family social resources also include relationships skills. One of the most important family social resources is the ability to effectively communicate with each other. This social resource prepares children for future relationships.

Bernard and Jenny are newlyweds. They met and married after a short courtship. Even though Bernard was a quiet man, Jenny was convinced that he was the perfect mate. Jenny's family had always been very open and honest with each other and they were able to resolve any conflict fairly. It was a surprise to her that when she and Bernard disagreed, he would clam up and often disappear for a few hours. When he returned, he acted as if nothing had happened. At first Jenny let it go, but over the next year she became frustrated that the same disagreements kept coming up and Bernard would never stay and talk it out with her. When Jenny threatened to leave him if they didn't go to counseling, Bernard agreed. Jenny soon discovered that Bernard's family had never been able to resolve conflict. Bernard did not have the resource skills to effectively communicate or effectively resolve a conflict.

Another social resource within the family is archival family function. Families that pass on their history pass on an important social resource, whether it is through photographs, stories, or heirlooms. Although it is pleasant to reminisce about the past and to hear interesting stories of ancestors, the past is an important part of the future. Family members must come to realize that it is important to understand the past as a historical process that shapes the future. Passing on family history gives us a sense of belonging and attachment to the family that cannot be accomplished with any other social group.

Travis was in his third year of college. One night he and his friends were talking about their family histories. Although most of them didn't really know much about their families' histories, Travis was able to talk about how his great grandparents had emigrated from Scotland and settled in Ohio. He had read in a family diary about the hardships and challenges that they faced over those early years—financial hardship and harsh climate. The other young men were intrigued by how much Travis' own perseverance at school reflected that of his ancestors' determination generations earlier.

Social resources are also found within the community or environment outside the family, including the family's ability to connect to and utilize the social resources available in the community. In addition, collective socialization refers to how the community as a whole engages in family life (e.g., how adults look out for the children of the community and whether parents appreciate this or isolate themselves from their community).

The Lewis family is active in their children's school. Mrs. Lewis attends all the parent advisory meetings and often helps out at the school fundraising events. In the summer, the Lewis children participate in the recreation activities sponsored by the city. Mr. Lewis has volunteered as a soccer coach and helps with the Little League tryouts. The Miller family views their community quite differently. The Millers work long hours to provide for their family and have little time or money to participate in social activities. Mr. and Mrs. Miller are not active in their children's education and rarely interact with other families outside of their own family and extended family. They do not take advantage of the educational or sports opportunities that are offered through their community and rarely leave their children with anyone other than grandparents. In contrast to the Miller family, the behavior of the Lewis family is an example of collective socialization.

Photo 6.2   Passing on family history through photographs is an example of the archival family function.

Source: © Burke/Triolo Productions/Jupiter Images.

There are advantages to social resources. Communities in which people band together to improve and maintain a good quality of life have many advantages. Wickrama and Bryant (2003) found that, in addition to the previous literature that has shown that a lack of community resources leads to community adversity such as dropouts and substance abuse, the presence of community resources leads to effective parent–child relationships and less adolescent depression. Torquati (2002) stated that social support, whether formal or informal, is associated with positive parenting. In addition, social resources such as a basic trust of others foster acceptance of others within diverse societies (Hooghe & Stolle, 2003).

Local, state, and federal benefit programs are social resources that are available to families. Local governments provide services for families in the form of public libraries and public parks. State governments provide other opportunities such as state parks and state museums. Some examples of federal programs are Cooperative Extension Services, Federal

Emergency Management Agency (FEMA), Veterans Health Administration, and National Endowment for the Arts.

Economic social support is available through Social Security. The Social Security Administration began in 1934 to assist families that could not provide basic needs during the depression. One of the major purposes of Social Security is to provide a safety net for families that need social assistance. It was originally designed to be a short-term resource, however, and the idea of generational welfare is a challenge for the program today. Although most people support the idea of Social Security, many have doubts about its effectiveness. Reforms such as the recent replacement of Aid for Families with Dependent Children (AFDC) program with the Temporary Assistance to Needy Families (TANF) are working for change. Social Security is discussed more in Chapter 8.

Recently, concern has been expressed about the decline of social resources. Putnam (2000) observes in his book, *Bowling Alone,* that for the past four decades, declining volunteerism and participation in civic organizations, political apathy, and a rising distrust among cultural groups signal serious problems ahead. Others argue that belonging to a particular group or political party does not automatically ensure social resource benefits and may actually be detrimental to society if groups become closed and self-serving (Stolle, 2003). Rothstein (2001) contends that social capital is a result of how government institutions function, rather than the contributions of voluntary organizations.

Regardless of the purpose and future of volunteerism, the family may be most instrumental in raising awareness of societal needs by teaching children the value of social capital. It is parents who model the value of performing civic duty, who show the value of cooperation with others, and who teach their children about trusting or mistrusting others (Stolle, 2003).

Measurement of Resources

When an exchange of resources is made, most people prefer that they have an equitable exchange. In other words, we want to receive something equal to what we give, as in the case of paying a fair price for a gallon of milk at the supermarket. However, resources and the value of those resources can be measured in various ways. When we give something to a friend or family member, many would not expect something in return. There may be other times when you expect a better rate of exchange, such as getting a good deal on a swimming suit because it is the end of the season. To a child, $100 is perhaps more valuable than it is to the wealthy person. The value of an exchange may depend on the nature of the interaction and the relationship of those involved.

In relationships, the theory of relative resources (Blood & Wolfe, 1960) assumes that the balance of power in that relationship will be on the side of the partner who has the most resources. In the past, the balance has traditionally favored the male partner, whose contributions of earning power and status outweighed the value of homemaking and childrearing. As women entered the workforce and relationships became more egalitarian, the balance changed. This theory tends to view resources from the cultural context of the United States. However, Rodman (1967) argues that in traditional cultural settings, where the husband has all the authority, marital power is not associated with resources of each partner.

Mahavir and Sashi have been married for 5 years. They were both raised in New York City, but they continue to follow the customs of their native India. Sashi and Mahavir both have professional careers as attorneys, with Sashi's salary actually exceeding her husband's salary. Still, because of their cultural traditions, Mahavir has all the authority in their relationship.

The most effective way to manage resources involves improving people's lives while weighing the effects of culture, environment, and equity. Every culture has different meanings and places different values on resources. At the same time, the physical environment must be considered and guarded. Economic equity must also be considered. A society where gross economic inequities exist—extreme poverty existing side by side with extreme wealth—will face many future problems.

Family resources are used to meet basic needs. For some families, resources that are plentiful are used to satisfy wants as well. Unfortunately, most families have only a limited amount of resources and must find ways to effectively manage what they have to meet their needs. Effectively managing resources can help families. The family's ability to manage resources may come as a result of the combination of resources available to them. For example, Jenkins (2001) found that access to care for the elderly depends on their family's willingness to help, as well as their financial resources. For that same family, social resources such as public programs like hospice are also necessary when looking for help.

Resources can affect the family directly by providing economic stability or indirectly by helping the family to cope. When families are worried about how they will use their resources or whether they will not have enough resources, stress can result (Fox & Bartholomae, 2000). These stresses can come from expected events, such as marriage, or unexpected events, such as divorce. They may also be temporary, such as an illness, or long term, such as a chronic condition like diabetes. Individuals and families who implement adequate financial planning can diminish the vulnerability that leads to economic stress. Monetary resources help the family in tangible ways when there are doctor's bills to pay, but often other resources are needed when money cannot be used to "fix" the problem. Resources such as support from the community, counseling, or effective coping skills may be needed. Commitment to marriage, strong family relationships, good problem-solving skills, and higher levels of education contribute to successfully coping with financial stresses (Fox & Bartholomae, 2000).

Regulating the flow of resources is important in managing resources and helps the family to plan for the future. Of course when someone continues to work, resources continue to come into the household. However, job loss, crises, or unexpected events can interrupt the flow of resources. Careful management of resources can prepare the family in the event that resources stop.

In a family, the way that resources are managed may be influenced by a variety of factors. Traditions or celebrations that are yearly or milestone events will affect resources. Some families choose to manage their resources for future events such as college or weddings. Family roles may also affect resources. If both the husband and wife work outside the home, they may manage their resources differently than the family that chooses different work patterns.

Resource Allocation and Use

Resources are used in a variety of ways. In the discussion of resource theory, the idea of exchanging resources is presented. Giving up one resource in exchange for another is the most common use of resources. Other uses include producing and consuming. Many resources are produced today in mass quantity. Factories turn out millions of goods each day that are distributed to stores for consumers to buy. Consumers buy the goods to consume. Most families consume goods, and some families also produce goods.

In addition to exchanging resources, they can also be saved or invested. Saving resources will allow someone to have a reserve to be used in case of emergency or to be used later.

The Smiths live in the panhandle of Florida. During the hurricane season each fall, they need to be prepared by making sure that they have plenty of bottled water, ready-to-eat foods, and plywood for their windows. In September, the panhandle experienced a major hurricane. Because of the erratic behavior of the hurricane, the stores were not prepared to sell enough supplies and prices were much higher. Planning ahead for the eventuality of a hurricane by storing up and saving resources was an effective strategy.

Saving resources can also be a way to increase resources. Over time, antiques and real estate may become more valuable. Saving money yields interest at a bank or savings institution. Investing can also be a good use of resources. Families may choose to not use all their income as it comes in, but may choose to invest the money in hopes of increasing their resources over time. Investing may include stocks, bonds, mutual funds, and annuities. Investments are discussed in detail in a later chapter.

Most people want to protect their resources. Some resources are protected by insurance. Lenders who hold mortgages and car loans require insurance to protect against something happening to the property before the buyer pays it in full. Banks assure customers that their money is federally insured by the FDIC in case something happens to the bank. Others protect their resources by taking precautions. Locks, security systems, and even zippers on purses are all ways that people protect their resources.

Resourcefulness is the ability to identify and use resources to meet needs effectively. The resourcefulness of families or how they use their resources is not the same in all families. For example, it is assumed that spouses "pool" their money and use their resources, including income, equally, but that is not always the case. Woolley (2003) observes that economists, who look at resources in terms of individual men's and women's work income and consumption, often miss the influence of human behavior within a marriage relationship. She points out that, although most American marriages "cherish the ideal of egalitarian marriage, studies in developing countries show that family members frequently share unequally in the household's resources" (p. 108). Although most pool at least some of their money, women are more likely to have their own bank accounts, and those that have been married before are more likely to keep their finances separate.

As discussed in Chapter 2, the exchange theory explains how resources are balanced within relationships depending on income, status, skills, and other assets. That balance does not always come easily, and there is often conflict over how those resources will be distributed and used. Although some family members may cooperate to get the most out of the available resources, others may compete for the resources. One aspect of relationships that makes decision making about resources difficult is that there is a certain amount of power associated with deciding how resources will be used. Safilios-Rothschild (1976) uses the terms orchestration power and implementation power to describe the types of decision-making power within many relationships. Those that have orchestration power are given power to make major decisions that often determine the lifestyle of the family. Yet they often use that power to pass minor decision making to someone else (usually the other spouse) for day-to-day management. That person then realizes a certain amount of implementation power when they are given the responsibility of the day-to-day decisions. Woolley (2003) found that women are more involved than men in managing the money within a relationship; however, those with higher incomes have more control over the money.

The way that families allocate their resources is also related to the conditions in which they are making those decisions. Langholtz et al. (2003) suggest that the conditions of certainty, risk, and uncertainty have an effect on how resources are used. It is less complicated when the decisions about use of resources are made under the conditions of certainty. For example, a family with a stable income, substantial savings and investments, and adequate life and health insurance will find the decision to buy a new car fairly simple. Even the daily decisions are made easy under the certainty of a set amount of resources from a monthly paycheck. However, under the conditions of uncertainty, such as unstable work conditions or poor health, the decisions would be more difficult. Although a family has the stability of a regular paycheck each month, it may have the uncertainty of a family member who has a chronic illness. If that family member has to be hospitalized, they may not be able to bring resources in, and more resources will have to be used for the hospital bills, medicine, and other expenses. Under the conditions of **risk,** the family doesn't know what resources will be available and has to make decisions under assumptions that the resources will be there. These conditions make it difficult to make decisions about allocation of resources.

Robert and Lisa have been married 14 years and have two children ages 8 and 10. Due to a series of mergers in his company, Robert's job description has changed over the past 6 months, and he has become increasingly unhappy with his work situation. In his mind, either the job will have to change or he will have to leave. Last week, the 15-year-old family car began having problems. Both Robert and Lisa knew that it meant that they would have to buy a new car. The decision would be made under the condition of risk, knowing only that Robert's job was questionable. He could stay and negotiate his present job, he could quit and be unemployed, or he could find a new job that would pay more than he is making now. Because they need a car, it is a risk they will have to take.

Recent research on resource-allocation behavior (Langholtz et al., 2003) has examined possible strategies that people use when they make decisions about how to use their resources. Resource-allocation problems are different than common problem solving because the decisions are often multilayered. At first glance, there is usually not one obvious solution when deciding on how to use resources. Sources of resources, the way resources are valued, and multiple ways to allocate resources contribute to the complexity of decisions.

Carol loves to cook. After a long day at work, she finds it relaxing to spend several hours each evening creating a wonderful gourmet dinner for her family. Her coworker, Rose, would rather spend her evening hours reading or watching television with her family. Rose wants to spend as little time cooking as possible, so she often buys time-saving precooked meals or orders takeout. The relative amount of resources may be the same for both Carol and Rose, but the allocation is different.

Langholtz et al. (2003) found that many people tend to use resources without thinking about the future outcome. They tend not to think about whether using their resources would have either a gain or a loss and adopt an "assume-no-loss strategy," where they don't worry about the outcome until a loss actually occurs. However, those with less resources and more uncertainty tend to plan more for losses. In addition, people tend to use more of their resources early in the time period, using less toward the end. Most people save between 10% and 25% of their resources at the end. For example, at the beginning of the month, someone might spend more money on groceries than at the end of the month, making sure that there is money left before the next pay period for emergencies. Another strategy that people use is to make adjustments in how they use resources along the way. If necessary, people will change the way they allocate their resources midstream if it means the outcome will be more efficient and improve their results.

Deutch (2005) identified three principles of distributive justice to determine how resources are distributed and would guide the use of resources. The principle of equity can be based on fairness where distribution is contingent on contributions to the system. For example, those who pay taxes are the most deserving of public services. In contrast, equity can also be determined by how much someone deserves the resource, such as someone who has contributed in the past, but now finds that he or she needs help, such as the homeless. The principle of equality is purely based on equal distribution. Dividing resources equally among the group or family members certainly helps to create cooperation and harmony, but does not always address everyone's needs. The principle of need is also a way to distribute resources. This principle is what drives some programs, such as Social Security, or some organizations to give grants or scholarships. This principle is used especially when resources are limited.

The Sandoz family has four children ranging in age from 2 to 15. Maria Sandoz has always been sensitive about treating her children equally. She makes sure that she shows an equal amount of love and attention to all her children. When it comes to dividing their resources, however, distributing them equally is not the best solution. Fifteen-year-old Jose needs more than twice as much food as 2-year-old Rosa. As school starts, Jose will also need new athletic shoes for football and a special type of calculator for his math class. At this time in their family life, the amount of resources needed by Jose outweighs what is needed by the other children.

The concept of voluntary simplicity may affect the way that resources are used in some families. Although this concept may or may not be attached to political or religious organizations, it is rooted in a rejection of the ideas behind consumerism and is practiced by those who choose not to live a life where the main objective is to "buy" the good life in favor of simple living. Although some fear that consumerism has led to an insatiable desire for more "stuff," living a simple life is less about the amount of purchases than the underlying values that cause people to make those purchases. Examples of voluntary simplicity for families may include living with less technology, buying only biofriendly products, cutting down on work hours to spend more time at home, and downsizing living space and possessions.

How and why people use resources is often complex. Looking at the context of the situation in which decisions are made may be as important as the decision. How the need is presented, the values of the person making the allocation, past history, and even the practicality of using resources in a particular way are all factors that need to be taken into consideration.

Summary

Individuals and families utilizing the decision-making process first determine needs. Once needs have been identified, possible alternatives must be explored that could fulfill or meet those needs. Identification and evaluation of resources available to families provide choices and determine the success or failure of the process. Resources are tangible and intangible, bountiful and limited. Decisions based on solid understanding of alternatives available have a greater chance of satisfying and enriching family existence, presently and in the future.

Questions for Review and Discussion

1. How does someone's culture or family background affect the use of resources?

2. Considering resource theory, how is the exchange of love different from the exchange of money? How can status be exchanged?

3. Looking at the reasons that we invest our resources, how would the reasons be different for work and the family?

4. Why do gender differences continue to exist for paid work?

5. With parents participating more in paid work, does this limit the time they have to model the value of social capital in our society? If so, what will be the consequences?

6. Explain why families have differences in their definition of resourcefulness.

Families Within the Economic Environment 7

Objectives

- Understand the basic concepts of economic theory.
- Explore the interdependency of the economic system and families.
- Comprehend the impact of the economic system on the family decision-making process.
- Understand how a family's economic status impacts quality of life.

People who never do any more than they get paid for never get paid for any more than they do.

—Albert Hubbard

As discussed in Chapter 2, family systems theory explains how families impact their environments and are simultaneously impacted by changes in those same environments. Each family, individually, and all families, collectively, impact the economic systems locally, regionally, nationally, and globally, while they are impacted by those same systems.

151

Individuals within families exchange human resources in the production and distribution of goods and services. They pool the money they earn within the family and consume goods and services, thus stimulating the entire economic exchange process. The resources available to families determine how deeply they are involved in the marketplace.

Beginnings of Consumerism

How did families become so enmeshed in such a system? The exchange of goods and services is evident throughout recorded history. Artifacts found in ancient Egyptian tombs were created by skilled craftspeople who were commissioned by the ruling class to exchange their time and talents for protection or for the prestige that accompanied such assignments. Pioneer families in the United States were self-sustaining in terms of food, safety, and shelter. Eventually, however, these families produced more foodstuffs than they personally required and began participating in trade among other families in the area, eventually becoming an integral part of the economic system in nearby communities.

Early settlers in the Great Plains states left Midwestern travel centers like Chicago and St. Louis to carve out a place of their own in the land opened to settlement by the movement of the transcontinental railway. Their provisions on departure included basic farming tools, a few livestock, and food staples for the trip. These pioneers knew that their survival would depend on raising their own food, building their own shelter, and a great deal of luck. Although there were a few small towns already in existence at strategic points along the major trails westward, the availability of goods and services was limited. Farmsteads were regularly miles from these rudimentary marketplaces, anyway, so self-sufficiency was crucial.

Crops were planted, tended, and harvested. Food gathered during harvest was dried, pickled, salted, canned, and stored for use until the next harvest could be expected. Livestock were bred, raised, and slaughtered as needed. Meat was used fresh, dried, salted, and stored as best it could be. Game, such as birds, squirrels, deer, and other local fauna, was utilized when possible. All family members were actively engaged in sustaining their existence. Living and working was a family affair, with people of all ages toiling side by side from daylight to dusk. Recreation was unplanned, but a natural part of daily life. Their existence was quite different from that of relatives who stayed behind in the established cities with expanding retailing opportunities.

When these pioneer families depleted the monetary stores they had brought with them, they needed to participate fully in the trading network available to them. Extra foodstuffs, animals, and seed were carted to the nearest town and traded for supplies or cash depending on the needs and resources present at the time and location of the exchange. Once the transportation system of the railroad became the steady supplier of goods across the country, these farm families found better markets and prices for the goods they produced. Wholesale and retail businesses in these small towns grew to accommodate the exchange.

Over time, farm families became less self-sufficient. Crops and livestock were raised primarily for exchange in the marketplace. Gardens still provided some foodstuffs and the occasional animal was butchered for meat, but canned goods, frozen foods, and prepackaged foods were available through exchange of money received from crops and livestock. Farms evolved into full-fledged businesses. Farm families became dependent on the economy, and their success or failure is now rooted in global economics.

The American economic system is rooted in the European economic developments prior to the Revolutionary War. Much of the motivation for a separation of the colonies from England came from dissatisfaction with economic exchange between these two societies. McCracken (1988) explores how consumerism shaped the European economy of past centuries and suggests that the relationship between individuals and their economic system depends on the willingness of individuals and families to engage in the process of conspicuous consumption. He traces this phenomenon back to the royal court of Queen Elizabeth I of England in the late 16th century.

Queen Elizabeth I insisted that the nobility visit her personally at court. Until that time, these landholders and titled families could receive royal goods and favors through intermediaries who traveled to and from London. Elizabeth insisted that nobility plead their cases directly to her. Traveling to London and taking part in the lavish proceedings of the court were quite expensive. Payments for the required finery and privileges fed the royal coffers, thus allowing Elizabeth to maintain the opulent court system at their expense. These noble men and women, while at the top of the system back at their estates, found that they had to compete for the Queen's attention among other nobles at court. This need for competitiveness forced them to acquire magnificent wardrobes, larger and more elaborate townhouses in the city, and rarer and more noteworthy royal gifts, as well as to give bigger and better parties than their noble peers. McCracken (1988) called this "a riot of consumption" (p. 12).

This engagement in conspicuous consumption had an impact on both the function of the family unit and the purpose of family in society. The concept of acquiring material goods and financial wealth that would be passed to and enhanced by future generations was challenged by the need to spend large sums from the current family holdings to maintain family status at court. Spending shifted from a need to build future holdings for the entire family to a need to be fashionable. The increased demand for fashionable goods and services fueled the local community's production of both. What had once been an economy based mainly on sustainability evolved into an economy focused on an early version of mass production, marketing, and distribution (McCracken, 1988).

Another historical era that further increased the participation of U.S. families in the economic system was the capitalistic industrialization in both Europe and America during the 1800s. Before the Civil War, the U.S. economy was primarily centered on agricultural production and distribution. Production was usually done at or near the home, and trade was primarily within local market areas (Welch & Welch, 2004). Railroad transportation, telegraph and telephone lines, mechanical and electrical inventions, and mass production in large factory settings opened new markets and provided new goods and services. These developments greatly influenced American families. As presented in the last chapter, many adults, primarily male, began working in the production and distribution sectors of the economy. Instead of trading products from their home base, these adults now used their monetary wages to trade for goods and services. Mass production made goods readily accessible and affordable, so families increased their consumption.

The stock market crash of 1929 devastated the U.S. economy and sent companies, workers, and families into the Great Depression that lasted for over a decade. The economy eventually pulled out of the downward spiral, mainly due to the end of World War II. At that time, the U.S. government spent massive amounts of money, fueling a rebounding economy (Collinge & Ayers, 2000). Passage of the Employment Act of 1946 cemented the participation of families in the economic system by providing expectations of full employment, full production, and stable prices. Congress was given authority to manipulate taxes and government spending to bring the economy to a desired level of activity (Welch & Welch, 2004).

American families are an integral part of the U.S. economy for several reasons. First, families spend their resources on products that they believe will meet their needs. Together families represent one of the largest markets for goods and services, accounting for almost 68% of total spending in 1998 (Collinge & Ayers, 2000). Other large consumer groups include the government, institutions, and industry. Second, families provide the labor force necessary to maintain business operations. To better understand the symbiotic relationship between families and the economy, one must understand the economic process.

Economic Principles

Economics, like the decision-making process, is all about making choices. Families must meet their needs by selecting from limited resources. Regardless of income, a family establishes limitations on how much of their available resources will be traded for any particular need. Producers must decide what they will produce, and service providers must focus their supply of human resources to meet demand. Economics exists because the resources we need to fulfill our wants and needs are limited.

Economics is the study of how resources are expended to fulfill the needs and wants of individuals, families, and social groups. Resources are inherently limited and needs and wants are rarely limited, so decisions must be made continually to balance the two. Most often the focus centers on material needs such as food, clothing, housing, transportation, entertainment, and other things that consumers believe they need to live satisfying lives. However, essential to the cycle of production and consumption are intangible resources such as time, energy, and human knowledge and skill. Contemporary American economics is fueled by money. Money is obtained through the exchange of these intangible human resources, the promise of future exchange (credit), or through inheritance or chance.

Dreaming of winning the lottery and living the good life? Many social scientists warn us that sudden windfalls are not always the path to happiness. Knight (2004) reported that one lottery winner in the UK found her dream was really more of a nightmare. Callie Rogers won nearly 2 million pounds, roughly a little over $3 million U.S. dollars, in a British lottery. Within a year her home was robbed, she began receiving threatening phone calls, she was betrayed by two boyfriends, and she became estranged from her father. Her mother had also been brutally attacked with a knife in the home Callie had purchased for her with lottery winnings.

Callie admits that the winnings bought her a comfortable home and padded a huge savings account, but finds that she is now lonely and isolated. Callie confided, "Being able to buy anything I wanted did not make everything OK. I could not buy a happy family." She has decided to invest about one third of her winnings into a trust that she will not be able to access for 8 years and has put the remaining funds into bonds. She has enrolled in a counseling course and hopes to become a social worker, helping children in bad family situations. "I want to live a normal life," she confesses.

In the News

PlayStation Sales Take Demand to the Next Level

PlayStation 3 sales bring out EBay speculators and price gouging. Scuffles occur at some stores, and Fresno police threaten to use Tasers.

By Valerie Reitman, Times Staff Writer

November 18, 2006

Dollar signs danced in the head of business student Julian Perry, 25, when he learned that the much-anticipated PlayStation 3 would go on sale Friday—in limited quantities.

As demand outstripped supply, Perry knew the video game console's price would rocket past Sony's $599 list price—on EBay.

So Perry hired seven people to get in line with him. It would be a long wait.

They arrived Monday afternoon at the Circuit City in Torrance, where 100 machines were to go on sale at 12:01 A.M. Friday.

Perry bought a tent from a store across the street, only to return it the next day when a friend showed up with one large enough to house all of them.

He fed his crew breakfast, lunch and dinner. He gave them gas money so they could go home to shower or report to their jobs, while the others held their spots.

And he paid them $50 to $200 apiece.

Shortly after midnight, Perry and his crew drove off in a convoy with eight PlayStations, avoiding what he said were shady-looking characters lurking around the parking lot.

A few hours later, he had the first one listed on EBay, where bids for other consoles had already surged to $2,500 and up.

Things went smoothly in Torrance, but elsewhere in California and around the country, scuffles broke out as crowds grew anxious.

In West Covina, police struggled to restore order when patrons began pushing and shoving at a shopping mall where only 20 consoles were available.

In Palmdale, a Super Wal-Mart was forced to close for several hours as tempers flared among weary customers.

And in Fresno, police threatened to use Tasers on hundreds as they stormed a store, trampling some people.

There was also gouging. Stuart Dean, 50, of Studio City said he had placed an advance order for two machines at Aahs! in Sherman Oaks.

But when he went to pick them up early Friday, he was told the machines would cost $2,500 apiece.

He called the district attorney's office to complain but was told such price hikes were not illegal. Store manager Sunny Kohli said that Aahs! could adjust the prices because it wasn't an authorized Sony dealer.

"If I was going to resell them, I wouldn't care," Dean said, but they were for his son and daughter, ages 6 and 9. He said they need two because they "never share."

As for Perry, he hopes to make $3,000 to $4,000 for each of the seven PlayStations he's selling on EBay. He may have to settle for less. By Friday evening, dozens of the video consoles were listed on EBay, with most prices ranging from $1,600 to $2,600. Will he share the profits with his crew?

"No, uh, uh," said Perry, who hopes to soon complete his MBA at the University of Phoenix in Pasadena. "Everybody's all paid off. We negotiated in advance."

Times staff writer Dawn Chmielewski contributed to this report.

Source: "PlayStation Sales Take Demand to the Next Level" by Valerie Reitman, published November 18, 2006. Copyright © Los Angeles Times. Reprinted with permission.

SUPPLY AND DEMAND

At the center of the study of economics are the concepts of supply and demand. Buyers and sellers are key players in an economic system. When buyers are willing to exchange resources for a particular good or service, this is referred to as *demand* for that good or service. When sellers make the decision to produce and/or provide goods and services, this is referred to as *supply* of that good or service. A common example of this relationship is the demand and supply of greeting cards. Individuals purchase paper or e-mail cards to send, thus remembering or celebrating important days, events, and milestones of family members, friends, neighbors, or colleagues. The demand for Christmas cards exists only because of the holiday celebrated at that time of the year. Many families and individuals send greeting cards in December—demand. Manufacturers of greeting cards produce the anticipated number of cards many months before the actual season to make sure these cards are available in stores and online—supply. Which comes first, supply or demand? This is much like the chicken and egg controversy. Years ago, there was no Administrative Professionals' Day. Did the desire to honor these assistants create a demand that was then met by the manufacturing companies? Or did the official designation of Administrative Professionals' Day and the production of cards for this occasion (the supply) spawn the consumer demand?

Demand is a complex concept. Consumer demand fluctuates over time; if producers fail to predict these changes adequately, they may be stuck with goods and services that are no longer in demand. When product inventory increases against a decreasing demand, a surplus of unwanted products will result. When fewer products are produced than are demanded, a shortage exists. How can buyers and sellers work within this uncertainty?

PRICING

In an economy such as the United States, goods and services are often offered at various prices. How do providers determine these amounts and how do consumers decide whether those goods and services are worth the price attached? Both are complex processes, and both are dependent on the decision-making process.

Producers or providers of goods and services must cover the cost of providing those goods and services. The price of a hamburger at a fast-food restaurant must cover the cost of the burger, bread, condiments, wrappings, and labor to flip and prepare the burger. There must also be some money included to cover the overhead of the company (management, utilities, facilities, advertising, etc.). A business will only exist if there is profit to be made through its exchanges. So, after covering all of these costs, there must be a bit more money in the price to provide that profit.

As the price of something increases, the demand typically decreases. There are several reasons for this. Milk is a fundamental part of many American families' shopping list. When the price of milk remains stable, the amount purchased by families across the country stabilizes. If the price of milk increases slightly, there may be little or no impact on the amount purchased because consumers will tolerate small increases before they will change something that is considered both healthful and integral to their diets. However, when the price increases dramatically, more than 10%, families may reevaluate their need for milk.

Supply and demand work in predictable ways as long as the consumers do not find other ways to satisfy their needs. However, consumers react in diverse ways to changes in the price of goods they want. They may accommodate a price change by drinking less milk or they may substitute other liquids like water or juice where milk had been the drink of choice. They may change brands if other brands or generic brands are available at lower prices, or they may use canned or powdered milk products if they can be purchased for less and family members will accept these different products as substitutes. Another contemporary example of how consumers adjust to changes in supply and pricing is reflected in the rising gasoline prices of the last few years. Because the U.S. population has become accustomed to mobility, few consumers actually lowered the miles traveled or traded gas guzzling models for more efficient vehicles to accommodate the price increase. Some did turn to more public transportation as a substitute travel method to lower their costs. Many merely adjusted other expenditures to enable them to continue traveling as they had before.

When producers find that they have more products than consumers want, a surplus emerges. By lowering the price, producers may be able to stimulate consumer demand. The lure of a sale may convince a buyer that the purchase is necessary. Consumers may purchase larger quantities of something if they feel there will be a future need for that product and the current reduced price is lower than it will be at that future time.

When consumers want something, but producers have not anticipated that demand and there are not enough products to meet demand, there is a shortage situation and the price may increase. Buyers are willing to spend more money to get something that has a higher value regardless of whether that value is obvious. That value may be linked to its level of scarcity. For instance, pieces of artwork have been known to increase in value when the artist dies. Because there will be no more works by that person, past works may be considered to be collectibles or to be rare. Owning them creates an aura of prestige and privilege.

Prices do not always reflect the functional value of a product. Preferences, real or imaginary, may create a situation where the price of a product can be increased and consumers will still buy. Wine is a liquid that could be used to quench one's thirst. What is the difference between a $5 bottle and a $500 bottle? Quantity could be the same, but if the consumer believes that the more expensive bottle tastes better or that owning that bottle will increase his or her social value due to its rarity, the extra money may be rationalized, and the decision to purchase the more expensive bottle may be made.

Supply and Demand Interrupted—The Health Care System

As you are sitting in the doctor's office waiting for your appointment time, or when your physician can work you in regardless of your appointment time, do you notice a pricing board with fees and procedure charges posted for consumer viewing? Probably not. In the U.S. health care marketplace, prices are not determined by supply and demand, and competition is not the driving force. Actually, prices are usually set by the service providers, and the consumer would have a difficult time evaluating quality of services consumed. You can only have your appendix removed once. If you are not satisfied or you feel the charge was too much, what can you do? They won't put it back so you can try another doctor and hospital! Most providers and consumers of health care view these goods and services as priceless. Americans with health insurance are determined to optimize their personal health and that of family members. Health insurance makes services accessible by providing a safety net to subscribers.

For a monthly premium or fee, the insurance company agrees to pick up your medical bill once it reaches a point that you would not consider it an option if you were paying directly out of your pocket. Data gathered by Rosenbaum (1993) indicate that 90% of hospital charges and over

(Continued)

(Continued)

> 75% of doctor fees billed to American patients are actually paid by their insurance companies. With this kind of parachute, consumers do little comparison shopping for health care procedures they feel are necessary. In essence, the consumer depends on the provider for advice on what treatments are needed. Although it may seem like a conflict of interest, those providing the advice are also setting the price for those treatments. Even selection of the hospital or treatment facility is made from relatively few possible choices. Location and doctor affiliation most often determines the facility utilized. When supply is greater than demand, prices should fall. The medical field is different, however, because the providers are actually creating the demand for their own services. Studies show that the number of beds used by members of any community is closely linked to the number of beds available in that community (Rosenbaum, 1993).

INCOME FLUCTUATIONS

Individuals and families participating in the American economy have the opportunity to improve their financial position through additional education, job promotion, inheritance, and investment gains. They also face the possibility of losing their current position and falling to a lower socioeconomic level when crises occur—unemployment, loss of health, and loss of family providers. Adjusting to these changes in available resources is a complex process. Families will need to continue to meet the basic survival needs of family members regardless of financial position; however, their consumption patterns will change to accommodate rising or falling income situations.

Research reveals that expenditures by families can be analyzed using the following categories:

- Housing
- Utilities
- Food
- Transportation
- Medical care
- Insurance
- Clothing and personal care
- Education

Although not all-encompassing, these categories allow analysis of family expenditures that cross all socioeconomic levels and address basic survival and social needs of contemporary families. There are several groups that depend on information gathered about these categorical expenditures—marketers, producers, financial institutions, social scientists, and governmental agencies. The data gathered also provide insight on how changes in economic position affect family purchasing.

Food, while essential for survival, also has social implications. One person can only comfortably consume a limited amount of food. However, the type and cost of that food can vary greatly. A fast-food hamburger may be less than $1, but a steak or lobster tail may cost a great deal more. As families move up and down income levels, the percentage of income spent on food is relatively stable. It has also been reported that contemporary families spend between 15% and 19% of their annual income before taxes on food, either prepared at home or purchased away from home. The difference was within those two choices. Families with less than $10,000 annual income spent 13% of their income on food prepared at home and 6% of their income on prepared food purchased from a vendor. Families with more than $40,000 in annual income reported spending only 9% of their income on food prepared at home and 6% in restaurants. As income continues to rise, the percentage spent on food, both home cooked and fully prepared, continues to separate, but eventually levels off. Families with more than $1 million annual income may find it difficult to spend 19% on food: $190,000 is a lot of lobster dinners!

Housing costs across income levels indicate a steady 30% to 36% expenditure. Families in the lower income group must spend a slightly larger percentage on housing to meet minimum standards. Those on the other end of the income scale adjust size, materials, and location preferences to maintain their expenses at that level.

Photo 7.1   The purchase of food has many social implications.

Source: © Chuck Savage/Corbis.

Bo and Cher have been married for 5 years. They have been living in an apartment that is located close to both of their jobs. Currently their rent and utilities consume about 30% of their combined incomes. Both have just received promotions in their companies and find that their total income has jumped by more than 25%. Although their apartment is still functional for their needs, they feel social pressure to move to a location that reflects their new socioeconomic status. They will be entertaining more. Homeownership is expected of middle management in their social circle. They decide to purchase a home in the suburbs, increasing their housing costs to 35% of their new income and adding commuting expenses on top of that. Getting ahead can often translate into running even faster to maintain expectations!

Other studies have reported that certain expenditures have marked differences between family income levels. Gambling is one of those choices. Of families studied, those from low-income groups spent about 10% on recreation and gambling, whereas those in the higher income groups spent only 4%. However, that 4% was considerably higher in terms of actual dollars. Another expenditure showing differences by income level was tobacco. Households in the middle-income groups spent almost twice as much per week on tobacco as those in the lower income groups and more than one third more than those in the highest income groups.

So, do families functioning at extreme ends of the socioeconomic scale behave that much differently in the consumption of goods and services in the economic system? As a general rule, no. Families must meet the same basic needs of members. The amount of resources available determines which possible choices are attainable—the 50-cent can of generic soda or the $5,000 glass of wine. The selection is then drawn from the value base of the decision maker.

Thomas J. Stanley has written some interesting pieces on the spending habits of self-made millionaires. He conducted interviews and gathered survey data from people who had made their own millions, rather than inheriting or winning their fortunes. He found that these subjects live relatively simple lives. They often drive used cars, use coupons when purchasing goods, and reside in middle-class housing. Many even refuse to use debit and credit cards.

Stanley found a marked difference between these self-made men and women. He focused an entire book on these differences (2004). After surveying 1,165 affluent women, he reported that they were more generous, more frugal, and harder working than men in similar situations. They donated an average of 7% to charity, more than three times the amount average families report. These women often mended their own clothing and reported being value-driven purchasers.

CHANGES IN PREFERENCE

Economic theory can provide guidelines for both the producers and the consumers. However, consumers are human and have been known to be fickle. Other than price, there are three less visible factors that impact buying behavior—taste, fashion, and innovation. Individuals express unique preferences when presented with choices. The color of the refrigerator will not impact its performance, yet manufacturers offer several color and material options to customers. The concept of taste is an important part of the decision-making process in product selection. Taste is related to sensory response before, during, and after product consumption. Families, over time and when resources are available, develop preferences for brand names, recipes, furniture styles, and even types of toilet paper. The flavor, feel, smell, and aesthetic aspects of products draw different responses from different people. Over time, purchasing these favored products becomes ingrained in personal and family behavior. Price changes may have some impact on their favorite products, but if a preference is strong enough, they will accommodate price fluctuation.

Fashion is another deciding factor in product selection that reflects preference; however, fashion is an expression of preference on a much larger scale. Social groups develop preferences that become part of the membership criteria. Clothing is an obvious example of this concept. Skirt length, allowable skin exposure, and width of pant legs are all subject to acceptance or rejection of the social group. Although perfectly functional, pieces of clothing will be thrown away or donated to charity if they no longer reflect the tastes of the group. Seeking acceptance, individuals and families judge their current material possessions and future purchases on choices made by the majority of their social group.

New products that can function as a replacement of currently preferred products may enter the marketplace. These new choices may be innovative, such as the pop-top aluminum can that replaced the bottle cap, or they may be new flavors, new formulations, or merely packaged differently. Soda producers had to adjust to the emerging popularity of sports drinks to maintain market share. Most introduced their own fortified drinks and even entered the bottled water market to compete in the health-conscious market. Flat-screen TVs are replacing the square or rectangular sets that have been staples in American households.

Cellular phones have infiltrated the everyday lives of Americans across all socioeconomic levels. These handy portable telephones have been available to U.S. consumers since 1960, but were slow to sell during the end of the last century. Not so anymore. The four leading American cellular companies

(Continued)

(Continued)

have a total of 63.4 million users (Palpini, 2003). The small, wireless communicators have revolutionized communication around the globe. Almost anywhere and anytime cell phone users can "reach out and touch someone." The question has shifted from "do I need a cell phone?" to "which cell phone features can't I live without?" Borrowing from the futuristic Jetsons cartoon, one of the most popular versions of the cell phone unit is the camera phone. These photo-messaging machines were introduced in Japan slightly before hitting the U.S. market. More than 12 million digital cameras have been sold to Americans since their debut (Graham, 2004).

How could this market get any sweeter? Don't forget cell phone accessories! Entire stores are popping up all over the country to help consumers personalize their newest must-have communication tool. Designer cases, antennas, and programmable video games are just a few popular postpurchase options. Much like the TV set of decades ago, cellular phones are moving out of the luxury, want-to-have category into the staple communication device, everyone needs-to-have level. Just one more example of how inventions change both the marketplace and the decision-making processes of consumers.

Cell phones also provide interesting possibilities for social scientists who are interested in how this movement toward constant and convenient communication within families will impact relationships. One area of importance in this type of research is the dependence/independence aspect of adolescent decision making. Now that parents are always just a second away, will adolescents have less motivation to make independent decisions? Should I really call Mom when my Econ class has been cancelled or should I try to work it out by myself?

EMPLOYMENT

Human labor and skills, when traded for money, fuel the financial stream of an economy. Money available is then spent, saved, loaned, or lost depending on the behavior of the participant. Companies that determine their products will be in demand will hire employees and maintain production. When their products are no longer in demand, they will cut their workforce, resulting in unemployed family members.

Employment opportunities exist only because there is a demand for labor in the market. This demand for labor is determined by the demand for goods and services. So, families participate on both sides of this equation. Family members provide labor and create demand for goods and services by spending the income their jobs provide. Unemployment of family members results in a reversal of that process. When money is unavailable to exchange for goods and services, families must seek other resources and limit their spending at all levels.

The U.S. labor force consists of all people over the age of 16 who are seeking work or who are already employed, including both men and women and those past the typical retirement age. The labor force is defined and calculated to understand the impact of employment on the economy. On the production side, if people are not employed, they cannot be producing goods and services. On the consumption side, if paychecks are not available, goods and services cannot be purchased. The unemployment rate, or the percentage of people seeking employment, but without work at the current time, is another important measure to economists. Although the goal may be full employment of all those seeking jobs, it is not in the best interest of an economy to be at that point. A desired point supported by most economists and labor analysts is 4% unemployment. With that cushion of unemployed workers, the system can accommodate workers moving in and out of jobs while moderating employment costs.

Unemployment

Unemployment is often categorized into one of three types: frictional, cyclical, or structural. Frictional unemployment includes those workers who have decided to leave one job and look for another. Typically frictionally unemployed workers are out of the labor market for short periods of time. They may be seeking positions of higher status or may be returning to school to enhance their employable skills.

Cyclical unemployment is involuntary and is the result of production lags, recessions, or business restructuring. Some business sectors are more likely to contribute to cyclical unemployment because their success is closely tied to general economic conditions. Examples include automobile production, building construction, and manufacturing. When the economy slumps and money becomes tight, consumers do not buy large-ticket items like homes, cars, appliances, and furniture. Employee layoffs are the result of this drop in demand. Another group highly impacted by cyclical unemployment is young workers with little seniority and those preferring part-time schedules. They are most often the first to be fired and the last to be rehired.

Structural unemployment is also involuntary. It occurs when changes in the economy result in a loss of demand for certain types of jobs. Most common in contemporary America is the restructuring of jobs due to changing technological requirements. Current employees may no longer have adequate skills to operate new computerized systems or may be unwilling to retrain to accommodate the change. Occasionally a technological advancement results in the elimination of certain positions or even entire divisions. One computerized software program can accomplish in a matter of seconds what might have taken several payroll managers to enter and calculate manually. Automated telephone answering systems have eliminated the need for humans in many transactions.

Unemployment, regardless of the cause, creates individual and family hardships. Loss of income intensifies the scarcity of family resources, forcing adjustments in expenditures and eliminating many choices available in the decision-making process. Families may need to make severe changes to survive periods of unemployment, such as moving to more affordable housing, selling or giving up existing possessions, and relying on governmental services or the support of other family members. These decisions impact personal self-esteem and strain relationships. Psychologically and physically, unemployment has been shown to elevate incidences of depression, suicide, mental hospitalization, ulcers, and immune deficiencies (Welch & Welch, 2004).

Seth, 45 years old, had been working in middle management for a large distribution company for more than 20 years. As purchasing over the Internet became the preferred method of product access for most of the consumers in this market, Seth's company lost several large accounts. He was told his job had been eliminated early last year. Since that time, Seth has been actively seeking other jobs, but finds that both his age and lack of marketable skills are obstacles. He finds that he has lost much more than his job. He no longer has a routine schedule and finds it difficult to self-manage his activities. His motivation to seek another job is falling with each rejection. His role as provider to his family is gone, and he feels devalued and resentful as his wife and children depend on him more and more for household chores. His circle of friends has disappeared. Colleagues from his previous job have either moved on or have become frustrated with their own situations. Neighbors and family friends are busy working during the day and aren't available when Seth needs their company. Although his wife and children try to be supportive, the changes and restrictions brought on them by his loss of wages have negatively impacted their social status. Seth's depression and mood swings are driving his family further away. Even a new job won't heal all of these wounds.

Unemployment insurance (UI) is a nationwide program created by the Social Security Act of 1935 to provide partial wage replacement to unemployed workers while they conduct an active search for new work. UI is a federal–state program, based on federal law, but executed through state law. Employers finance the UI program by tax contributions. The UI program benefits the individual and the local community. Payments made directly to the individual ensure that at least some of life's necessities, such as food, shelter, and clothing, can be met while looking for work. For the most part, UI benefits are spent in the local community, which helps sustain the economic well-being of local businesses. It is not a 100% replacement program, however, so families must still adjust spending and reevaluate previous budgeting practices.

To receive unemployment insurance benefits, the individual must meet certain qualifying criteria, including previous earnings guidelines. Once qualified, he or she must show continued effort to secure a job through documentation of applications and rejections. Because states administer this program, benefits and qualifiers will vary from state to state. All states have maximum time limits that benefits will be dispersed. The program was designed to be a temporary safety net, not a permanent replacement for earnings.

Other programs, both public and private, are available to displaced workers. Many provide educational and skill-building opportunities while the worker is unemployed.

Women in the Labor Force

While the labor force includes only those actively working or seeking work, participation of women complicates the calculation. In the United States, there is an expectation of choice that is available to females, but not to males. Adult males are expected to provide for themselves and their families. Adult females are allowed to stay home and devote their energies to maintaining the household and participating in the social volunteer network, or to work for a wage in their homes or outside of their homes.

Historically, women have always participated in the work of the family and in the economic system. Their role before the 19th century was often viewed as one of support and team player. Agricultural families survived with cooperative participation of all family members. Women also participated in trade in both production and management capacities long before the women's movement of the mid-1900s. Preindustrialized Europe relied heavily on female craftswomen and entrepreneurs, depending on the social gender norms of the times. Industrialization and mass production reframed women's participation in the economy, however, and the roles of females have been publicly and privately debated over the last century.

In the United States, relatively few married women worked outside of the home for a wage between the Civil War and World War I. As the social climate changed after the turn of the 20th century, young women who did not choose to marry directly after completing high school in their mid-teens were encouraged to attend business schools, medical schools, and teachers' colleges to become secretaries, nurses, and K-12 teachers. An understood social expectation was for these young women to work in these positions for a few years and then leave the workforce, marry, and raise their families.

During the 1940s, when huge numbers of working men left their jobs to join the armed forces to fight in World War II, women, young and old, were the only pool available to fill empty production and management positions. As the 1950s unfolded, many women left these wage-paying jobs and returned to the home. However, the percentage of women in the labor force in 1947 dropped only 4% from the participation rate during the war. From 1950 to 2001, women have slowly continued to increase in both numbers and percentage points within the U.S. workforce. Currently, 46% of all American wage earners are female (U.S. Department of Labor, 2007). Seven out of 10 mothers are actively employed (U.S. Census Bureau, 2001).

Mary Harshfield finished public school in 1907 at age 16. She entered a local college, or "normal school," to complete training required at that time to teach at both the elementary and high school levels. In 1908, she took her exams, received her teaching certificate, and started teaching at her hometown's rural one-room K-12 school. Three years later, Mary stopped teaching, married a local farmer, and gave birth to 10 children over the next 18 years.

Of Mary's three daughters, one farmed with her husband and raised a family of two daughters. The other two women married, had children, but worked for a wage outside of the home for most of their adult lives. Mary's 16 granddaughters all worked before marriage, and 10 held full-time jobs outside of the home. Of her 25 great-granddaughters, only 2 did not work full time after their youngest child entered public school. All four generations of women have lived or are living in America's middle class, some in rural areas, others in large cities. This last century has brought about great changes in both the expectations and participation of women in the workplace and their place in the economic system.

Women cite the same two reasons for working outside of the home as their male counterparts: personal satisfaction and financial resources to support their families. Enrollments and diplomas from colleges and universities indicate that females are just as likely to seek professional training for career development as males. Gender differences within and between certain fields are also narrowing. Males are entering the fields of nursing and education in record numbers, and females are pursuing careers in engineering and technology.

Because it is a choice available to women, understanding why some wives and mothers work while others don't can be explored using an economic framework (Becker, 1991). The employment decision of a mother is based on a comparison of the value of her work (wage rate, child-care expenses, education capital) with the value of her time at home. The opportunity cost of not working is loss of advancement potential and job skills. The opportunity cost of working is the loss of investment in the home and children. The cost–benefit analysis in this decision depends on several factors: quality of child care available, participation of father in parenting and housekeeping, personal and social values, and type of position the mother holds. Professional women such as lawyers, physicians, and business executives may face severe setbacks in future advancement possibilities if they choose to leave their positions for any extended period of time. Those employed in other types of jobs may require additional education and training to reenter the job market to ensure their skill levels are appropriate to the changing technological environments in many fields.

Women are definitely a key part of the employment picture in the United States. Should the trend of female participation reverse itself, serious implications in production and consumption would result. Should they continue toward full participation, the issues of wage gaps and glass ceilings will magnify in scope. Workplace environments and policy could face dramatic changes to accommodate female preferences and needs.

When the labor force participation rate for women with infants dropped slightly between 1998 and 2000, the media rushed to publish articles, and headlines focused on women's innate desire to leave their careers and stay at home with their babies. In reality, the choice to participate in the labor market or not is a reality for all women in the United States. However, it is much more difficult for some than for others to be unemployed. The media's attention at that time was focused on White, married, middle-class, professional women leaving their jobs behind to focus on their families and children. Unless many working women are willing to rely on governmental subsidies, they do not have the choice to leave their paying jobs. Single women have little or no other financial support available to them. Those married to men working in middle- to lower income-producing jobs face drastic reductions in living standards should they quit working.

Dickson (2004) stated that the media's report on women's desire to leave the rat race of the business world was oversimplified. A survey of senior female executives in large U.S. companies revealed that these women want the top job just as much as their male counterparts. Both men and women in this survey reported problems with balancing their professional and personal lives. Contemporary men are more involved with their families and household management than those of decades ago. These findings diffuse the belief that women will be leaving the workforce in significant numbers in the near future.

Adolescents on the Job

Brock works evenings and weekends at a local supermarket to help his single mother pay the bills. Sharon works afternoons at a local bank through a vocational program at her high school. The money she makes is added to her personal college fund. Tyson works fast food whenever possible and fills in other free time with various jobs—lawn care, child care, errands, and deliveries. His money goes toward maintenance of and improvements on a sports car he purchased earlier this year. All three teens are juggling work and school demands for different reasons. They are part of the powerful adolescent job force and consumer movement in the economic system.

Another labor pool and consumer group is increasing in importance in the U.S. economy. Adolescents are holding down part- and even full-time jobs while completing high school requirements. Almost one half of American adolescents are employed—a much larger percentage than any other developed country (Berk, 1996; Greenhouse, 2001). U.S. teens spent $155 billion in 2000. Their participation in the marketplace has earned them the label *Skippies*, or school kids with purchasing power (Quart, 2003). Teens in middle- and upper-class families work for spending money to increase their material possessions and to build savings for the anticipated expenses of higher education. Those from families struggling financially often work to contribute to the family income. A relatively small percentage of teen workers are seeking enhancement of future career skills. Regardless of the motivation, adolescents are participating in the workforce in rapidly growing numbers.

The jobs that adolescents typically hold are usually limited to lower paying, lower skill positions in production, sales, and services. They are usually the first to be fired when demand drops and the last to be rehired. Teen participation in the workforce is therefore a complex concept. National teen unemployment rates are reported in much the same way general rates are gathered and analyzed. Although many teens work around the calendar, the greatest surge of teens in the workforce is seen during the summer months. Their paychecks continue to play an important part in the overall economic picture of the United States as they buy goods and services and participate in the tax and financial bases of the national economy.

Experts disagree with regard to perceived risks and benefits for working teens. Some believe that working modestly, or for just a few hours weekly, teaches responsibility and social skills and occupies idle time that might be spent in less productive activities. Managing their time and money earned is also cited as a positive benefit for the adolescent employee. Job experience during high school may also provide the teen with valuable work experience and insight into possible future vocations.

Others argue that working during high school undermines a teenager's educational and emotional development. Studies have found that teenagers working more than 20 hours per week were more likely to have lower grades, higher alcohol use, and inadequate relationships with parents and families (Greenhouse, 2001). Others report that students who work long hours often lack time and energy for homework and miss out on social and intellectual skill development through participation in school extracurricular activities.

MONEY

Reality Check

Home Sales and Interest Rates:
A Truly Inverted Relationship?

Economists have long held that when interest rates are low, people will be more willing to buy durable goods, especially high-ticket items like automobiles and houses. With the typical length of home mortgages falling between 15 and 30 years, the purchase of a home is one of the largest and longest commitments made by a family. Although owning a home is often viewed as the American dream and the answer to the basic need for shelter, it is generally accepted that there are numerous options other than ownership available to those seeking a place to call home.

Families basically have two housing options—rent or buy. When rental units are readily available, meet minimum living standards expected, and are within the price range possible for families, the decision to rent apartments, condominiums, and homes is a popular one. Renting eliminates monetary outflows for repairs, upkeep, outside maintenance, property taxes, and mortgage interest payments. The negative side to renting, however, is that home equity is never developed.

Families purchasing their own home have the benefit of selling it at a later time and hopefully recouping some of the money used in the purchase in that sales transaction. Lending institutions will also view home ownership positively in borrowing decisions families might initiate. Having a home with no mortgage on retirement provides an important asset for senior citizens, eliminating that monthly expense from their budgets. If we believe that homeownership is still one of the great American dreams of individuals and families, it is essential that we understand how homeownership can be facilitated.

Few families will have the funds available to pay for their first home with cash. Most new homeowners will borrow some, if not most, of the money to fund that purchase. Loans for homes are called *mortgages*. Mortgages are long-term liabilities for purchasers, usually 10-, 15-, or 30-year contracts. Interest is a predetermined percentage of the loan that the borrower agrees to pay the lender for use of this money. The lower the interest rate, the less the loan will cost the homeowners as they work toward repayment. For instance, Dean and Daphne Baker

(Continued)

(Continued)

purchase a home priced at $110,000. They take $10,000 from their savings to make the down payment and borrow $100,000 from a mortgage company. They agree on a 30-year mortgage to make their monthly payments as low as possible. How does the interest rate they receive on this loan impact their actual purchase?

At 6%, over 30 years, the Bakers' monthly payment will be approximately $599.55. If the interest rate is just slightly higher, 7%, their monthly payment would be approximately $665.30. That is almost a 10% difference each month. Over the 30-year time period, the payoff of a $100,000 loan at 6% would be almost $216,000. At 7%, the Bakers would actually pay almost $240,000 over the 30-year period. That 1% difference would equal $24,000 in total purchase price!

Over the last few years, the housing market in the United States has been strong. Interest rates have remained low, in terms of previous decades, and homeownership has looked favorable in a marketplace where rental prices have steadily risen. The monthly house payment in the example above would be smaller than most comparable rental houses would cost, and the Bakers would be accumulating assets—wealth. But what about the impact of interest over time? They would actually be paying more than twice the original price when the interest paid was figured into the equation. How could that be a good decision for them?

Home purchases are also based on the consumer's belief that the value of the house purchased will appreciate—increase over time. If the Bakers were to sell this home 5 years from now, and they could set the selling price higher than what they paid, there could be a profit in the transaction. If they had stayed in a rental, there would be no profit when they relocated. If they remained in this home for the entire 30 years, eventually they would have no more mortgage payments, and any price they could receive in the sale of this home would be money in their pockets.

Purchasing a home with a mortgage is a gamble. Low interest rates lessen the risk. Some economists warn that "bubbles" can result when decreasing interest rates, increasing rental costs, and rising home prices coexist. Homebuyers may be enticed to buy homes in the upper end of the price line they can afford when mortgage rates are low and the cost of renting is comparable to monthly house payments. The bubble bursts when they find that their debt load is uncomfortable and they are unable to sell their homes for the original purchase price or more. These homeowners, forced to sell because they cannot continue to pay their mortgages, will lose the savings they invested as down payments and the money they paid monthly while owning the home. This situation is especially devastating for those nearing retirement, who had hoped to use home equity for retirement income.

Money is anything that can be used for exchange. In the United States, buyers and sellers agree that currency—bills and coins—have inherent value and can be used in the exchange of goods and services. Some people believe that this currency must be supported by a cache of precious metals, such as gold and silver. The true value of paper and coin currency lies within its value of exchange. If you were suddenly transported to another planet carrying $1,000 in U.S. currency, you would find it impossible to use that money. Even traveling to other countries makes this concept apparent. Countries participating in the European Community have agreed on the Euro as their accepted currency. Few vendors will accept American or even British money for purchases. You must exchange foreign currency for domestic currency to participate in trade of any kind. Even if you use your debit or credit card for purchases in a country that does not use your country's currency, a conversion will be made through the card company to enable the transaction to be completed.

Considering the vast numbers of different currencies across the globe and the fact that even something like a pack of cigarettes can be used as exchange currency if the two people involved in the trade agree on it, how can we determine what the value of money actually is?

A $5 bill is worth whatever you can trade it for in any given circumstance. A currency's value is measured by the goods and services it will purchase in the marketplace. Economists define money in terms of its function. Money is used as a medium of exchange, a store of value, and a unit of account. Families are involved with all three monetary functions.

Throughout recorded history, there is evidence that once a society forms its general basis, a method to facilitate the exchange of goods and services emerged. Originally, it took the form of barter, where one good is directly exchanged for another. For instance, Neighbor A helps fix a fence for Neighbor B and is repaid when Neighbor B helps fix Neighbor A's broken axle. Or a chicken is traded for a sack of seed. The problem with this type of exchange system is that it only works when individuals have simultaneous, seemingly equal needs and resources. Monetary currency eliminates the need for the perfect time and situation. It serves as a medium of exchange that is accepted in all transaction, by all those involved regardless of time, place, or need.

To function as a medium of exchange, currency must hold value over time; that is, it must be a store of value. Other assets function in the same way, but are not as liquid or easily converted. For instance, a family may possess a home that is of value over time. That home could even increase in value, but until it is sold or borrowed against, there is nothing to exchange in transactions. Money is always liquid, although its value decreases with inflation and increases with appreciation, so there is some fluctuation to consider.

When money is supported by a tangible resource, like gold or silver, the economy is on a commodity standard. The United States used to back its money with gold, but now operates on a paper standard. U.S. money is backed by the people's willingness to accept it and by the strength of the nation's economy. Across the globe, the strength of the U.S. dollar is calculated against all other foreign currencies and markets. One U.S. dollar may be equal to 1.0 Euros on one day and fall to a .80 exchange the next week. If a dozen silk sweaters were priced at 4,600 Euros and a U.S. buyer placed the order in the second week instead of the first, his or her company would pay $1,128 (U.S. currency) more because of this change in the exchange rate. That would translate into a probable increase in the price of each sweater to the U.S. consumer of almost 25%.

Money, in the form of currency or electronic transfer, provides a common measure of the value of goods and services being exchanged. Countries express this measure of value using a base unit. In the United States, the base unit is the dollar. In Japan, the base unit is the yen. With a base unit, the value of everything can be expressed in terms of that unit (e.g., a car might be worth 40,000 times a dollar unit). Having this base unit makes it easy to create comparisons among the values of goods and services. Being aware of the value or price of something, in terms of money, gives both the seller and the buyer a basis for decision making. It provides a common denominator for both sides. This function of money, however, can be manipulated and misleading. Higher prices create the aura of higher quality and value when that is not always the case.

To participate in the national economy as consumers, families must understand the banking system even if they do not have checking and saving accounts. Money circulates through the banking system, thus providing storage and distribution functions. A bank receives deposits from individuals, families, and other groups. They store money and even pay interest to depositors on certain types of accounts. Banks then put those monetary deposits back into the economic system through loans to individuals and groups. The financial institution must keep some of the deposit available for depositors, should they want to make a withdrawal, but most of the deposited money is recirculated into the economy. Banks also provide a method for storing and growing wealth.

Jess has $25 directly deposited from his paycheck each week into a savings plan that earns 5% interest annually. At the end of 1 month, he has $100 in that account. At the end of a year, he will have approximately $1,200, plus the interest his deposits have earned over time. Jade buys a bracelet for $1,200 on credit at the beginning of the year.

She pays $100 a month, plus 8% interest. Who made the wiser decision in terms of utilizing that extra $25 a week? The answer isn't that obvious. Jess will have approximately $1,350. Jade will have a bracelet with no debt attached. If the value of that bracelet has increased to more than $1,350, her investment, should she agree to sell the jewelry, would have been more profitable. Participating in the investment realm requires an understanding of inflation and utility.

Inflation occurs when there is an increase in the general level of prices. Inflation of prices has become an expected phenomenon in our economy. An automobile that sold for $5,000 thirty years ago may cost $15,000 today. That looks like a tremendous leap, but when distributed over that many years, it lessens in intensity. An economy with an inflation rate of 2% to 3% per year doesn't have a serious inflation problem. However, when prices jump, across the board, by 7% to 10% or more, an economy can fall apart.

Inflation impacts some income groups more drastically than others. Individuals and families living on fixed incomes, such as Social Security payments, must cut their buying because their income will not rise as the prices do when inflation is active. Over time, this will result in dramatic declines in their standard of living. For this reason, cost of living adjustments (COLAs) are usually instituted each year for Social Security recipients. However, those adjustments have not kept pace with the inflation rates, and a general decline in purchasing power has resulted for this group of citizens. Another group with similar concerns is that of employees who contract for wages and salaries over long periods of time. They, too, will be negatively impacted in times of inflation. If a service union agrees to an annual wage increase of 3% over the next 5 years and inflation averages 4%, those workers will experience a decline in buying power each and every year under that contract.

Much like a typical faucet/drain arrangement, money flows into the economic system in the form of wages, salaries, winnings, and inheritance and flows out into the marketplace through purchases made. The economy may become unbalanced if both the faucet and the drain are not in equal use. The growing dependence on credit has impacted this balance already and threatens to cripple the economy if unchecked. The growing reluctance to invest and save money when interest rates are low also impacts the balance of money flow through the overall system.

The Martin family is thinking about buying a new plasma-screen TV set. They are thinking about either taking the money needed to purchase this item from their savings account or buying on a 1-year, interest-free loan promotion the store is offering. If the interest being paid on their current savings account is less than the inflation rate of the coming year, it would probably be a better decision to withdraw the price from savings and buy the TV. The TV will cost more next year than the money would have made in the bank, and there is no accurate way to judge whether the family's income can support the new loan, even interest-free.

When interest being paid on savings is lower than anticipated inflation, consumers are enticed into spending more and saving less. This trend would boost the economy in terms of production, employment, sales tax collected, and standard of living, but reduce the amount of money banks could loan to companies and individuals.

EXCHANGING NONMONETARY RESOURCES

Not all exchanges of human resources result in financial form. Some family members may exchange child care with other families in a cooperative arrangement. Other family members may exchange favors with neighbors or extended family that would otherwise require an exchange of money.

Grace belongs to a group of 20 adult females in her neighborhood. Each woman shops for and cooks one large meal for 20 families, packaging and freezing these meals in individual family portions. Once a month these meals are exchanged, and each family ultimately has dinner for every working day for an entire month. Instead of 20 individual families preparing meals every evening after a long day at work, each family is involved in only one large-scale preparation at a convenient time. This arrangement saves time and energy when both may be at their lowest availability. However, this effort requires great coordination and cooperation.

A more common cooperative arrangement among families is that of carpooling children to school and activities. By sharing the responsibility, time, and automotive costs, more time is available for other tasks. This, however, is reflective of a worldview (see Chapter 1) that sees time as "manageable." It would not make sense to someone who views time as uncontrollable.

These types of exchanges are impossible to calculate because there is no common unit involved for comparison of value. A family with rich connections to other family and community nonmonetary forms of exchange will have more resources available in their decision-making process and may accomplish more over time than a family that depends wholly on goods and services purchased through the marketplace. A young working couple with a relative or friend who is willing to care for their young children without pay may translate into thousands of dollars more in annual net income for that couple. However, this type of nonmonetary service will usually require the exchange of other resources, such as time, energy, and emotional support. The value and costs of these types of exchanges cannot be calculated in an economic system that is dependent on the dollar as a unit of exchange. These intangible resources may really be priceless.

We have explored the interconnections and interdependency of families and the economic system. They are inseparable in the context of family resource management and of major importance in family decision making. But to understand the connection between these two entities, it is important to understand how family decisions, collectively, impact something as complex and worldly as the global economy.

FAMILIES IN THE ECONOMY

Worldview

Tanshin Funin. Almost half a million married employees in Japan live separately from their families because they have been transferred by their employers in an expected system of worker development. Many Japanese firms follow a practice of developing employee skills by rotating workers from one job to another, from one department to another, and eventually from one office to another. This process provides economic benefits for the employee moving up in the company, but has substantial social ramifications. *Single posting,* or *tanshin funin*, is especially common among employees between the ages of 35 and 55. They establish small living quarters, often provided by the company, and live there during the work week. If possible, they travel to their family's home on weekends and company holidays.

Employees involved in this practice accept it because it involves promotion. They are unable to move their families with them for several reasons. The housing market in Japan is tight, and finding appropriate housing for spouses and children is difficult. It is also common for workers in this age group to be living with and partially supporting their aging parents. Relocation of these elderly family members would involve medical and social difficulties. Education, however, is an even bigger obstacle to family relocation. Admission to middle and high schools is based on test performance. Once admitted, leaving and finding comparable schooling opportunities would be virtually impossible. Living with both parents must be weighed against the opportunity costs of disrupting the children's educational opportunities and possibly limiting their future access to prestigious universities. Thus, mothers and children most often stay behind. This situation has been created by employment practices, housing shortages, and an inflexible educational system. Choices available in the family decision-making process have been greatly limited by their economic environment (Sugimoto, 1997).

Households constitute the largest spending group in the nation's economy, purchasing more goods and services than businesses, government, and foreign consumers combined (Welch & Welch, 2004). The United States had 104,705,000 households in 2000 (U.S. Bureau of the Census, 2001). The population at that time was 281 million people. The census categorizes a household as one or more people occupying a housing unit, such as a house or an apartment. These individuals do not need to be related to be grouped into the same household, so these data are not pure family data. At that time, the average household size was 2.6 people, slightly lower than previous decades.

Data are gathered concerning the income within these households to analyze the impact of household financial management on the national economy and public services provided. In 2001, 91% of these existing households were operating on earned and investment income. The remaining households were receiving Social Security or transfer payments from federal and state aid programs. There has been a growing reliance on transfer payments over the last few decades. These include old age, survivors, and disability insurance provided by the Social Security Act; unemployment and disability benefits to workers; public employee retirement benefits and veteran's benefits; and public assistance. The forecast is for even greater dependence on transfer payments as the Baby Boomers enter retirement.

Household incomes differ greatly from one unit to another. Those of married couples report much higher average incomes than do those headed by a single female—almost twice as high. Other factors that seem to impact household income are age of family members, education level of family adults, and geographical location of households.

Economists are, of course, interested in how these households spend their incomes. Often this is analyzed in terms of purchases of durable goods, nondurable goods, and services. Durable goods are expected to be used for more than 1 year. Automobiles, homes, furniture, and appliances are typical durable goods purchases. Things with shorter useful lifespans, nondurables, include gasoline, food, and hygiene products. Services, especially medical services, have increased in total expenditures dramatically over the last few years. In 2001, for example, 59% of household expenditures were for services, 29% for nondurables, and 12% for durable goods.

Household spending habits and trends help economists predict future economic developments and anticipate changes in production, distribution, and demand of goods and services. This analysis is based on the belief that individuals and families make economic decisions based on their desire to maximize their economic well-being. This balancing process is evident in the family decision-making process central to this textbook. This balance requires weighing advantages, benefits, disadvantages, costs, satisfaction, and impact of goals with each important decision regarding resource allocation within families.

Summary

Individuals and families interact with the national and global economies on a daily basis. This relationship is interdependent, as the economy relies on family members as both consumers and workers. Singly, one family's decisions will have little, if any, impact on even the local economy. Together, however, family households drive the U.S. economy. Buying, selling, working, and exchanging nonmonetary resources are all integral actions within the overall economic system. Family decision making, in terms of resource acquisition and expenditures, results in better choices and long-term planning when basic economic principles are understood and managed.

Questions for Review and Discussion

1. How does the concept of conspicuous consumption impact your choices of clothing? Career? Housing?

2. There is great debate across U.S. college campuses about students working more and devoting less time and energy to study. How would your experience differ if you were not allowed to make the choice to work or not to work while you attended college classes?

3. How would your life change if you were to suddenly inherit a large sum of money? Would this change your basic goals and aspirations?

4. Many people propose that contemporary consumers are becoming immune to the lure of sale prices in marketing. How do you and your friends and families view price reductions, and how does anticipation of sale prices impact your purchasing decisions?

5. How might wages in your community be impacted by the closure of a major employer and a surge of unemployed workers?

The Impact of Society on Family Decisions 8

Objectives

- Understand the impact of legislated consumer protection laws on the choices families have available in the decision-making process.

- Understand, contrast, and compare educational alternatives available in the United States.

- Be aware of individual and family tax liabilities.

- Be able to identify resources provided through governmental funding.

- Understand the importance of linking assistance available and existing family needs.

I am proud to be paying taxes in the United States. The only thing is I could be just as proud for half of the money.

—Arthur Godfrey

F amilies living in the United States work within specific legal parameters and social expectations that have evolved over the last two centuries. Understanding the obligations and benefits of living in such a society is a complex process. In this chapter, we explore four primary connections between families and the local, regional, and national social systems they contribute to and benefit from. These social constructions have tremendous impact on the choices available to decision makers as they struggle to meet needs with limited resources. These constructions include tax obligations, compulsory education, government-supported resource programs, and consumer protection legislation.

Individuals and the Tax System

Most employees remember the shock they experienced when they opened the envelope holding their very first paycheck. Although many realize that taxes will be taken out of their earnings, the realization of just how much those taxes will reduce the check is usually disheartening. Americans realize many benefits in exchange for the taxes they pay. Some argue the disparity of the tax system, feeling that people within other groups receive more than their fair share of these benefits. Regardless, the informed taxpayer has the ability to plan effectively for payment of his or her tax liability.

FEDERAL TAXES

Income tax, Social Security, and Medicare are the three primary types of federal taxes that wage earners pay. Employees working for wages and salaries rarely have to manage the regular payment of these taxes. Employers are required to deduct employee tax liabilities during the payroll process and to deposit those deductions directly into government accounts. The employee, however, provides the information necessary to ensure that the proper amount is deducted regularly by completing and submitting a W-4 Form (www.irs.gov/pub/irs-pdf/fw4.pdf). By answering questions concerning family situation and obligation, this form provides a number of dependents that should be used in the tax calculation each pay period. That number is used to determine how much income tax should be deposited.

Carlos is a single accountant with no dependents. He will have a higher tax liability than his friend Jonathan, who has a family of four. The American tax system considers the additional needs of children and dependents and utilizes that implicit value in calculating tax liability. Both men make the same amount of money, so they would seemingly have the same tax liability. However, Jonathan's cost of living is higher due to the needs of his family. When filing yearly income taxes, Carlos and Jonathan will enter their income and then calculate their deductions to determine their actual liability. Assuming that Carlos will have a higher liability, it is important that he deposit more each month to meet that liability. Otherwise he may need to come up with a large amount of money at that point to fulfill his obligation, and he may be penalized for not depositing more each month.

The government will refund any prepaid taxes that are overpaid; however, it will not pay interest on that amount. The Internal Revenue Service (IRS) will, however, charge the taxpayer interest and penalties for unpaid taxes. It is in the best interest of all taxpayers to be aware of their obligations and to be honest in each calculation. The IRS of the federal government receives quarterly and annual reports on employee earnings from employers. Those figures are used to substantiate employees' liability and deposits.

Self-employed people must also pay income taxes. Their rates are identical to those working for others, but they must handle the deposits and reporting themselves. Because employers match their employee federal tax deposits, the self-employed may seem unfairly taxed because they must pay the entire amount. There is an adjustment within the tax-figuring process to compensate for this, but income tax liability is often seen as an obstacle to self-employment.

Taxpayers receive goods and services in exchange for their tax dollars. Money collected by the federal government is used to fund a multitude of public benefits (Figure 8.1). During times of war and terrorist alerts, a larger portion of tax dollars is channeled to military spending. Federally funded programs that directly impact families include education, job training, employment, health, justice, environmental protection, transportation, and community development. Other programs with broader impact, but less specific to families, include veterans' benefits and services, international affairs, science, space, technology, and the general costs of running governmental offices and programs. Agricultural support, energy programs, and housing programs are also funded with tax dollars.

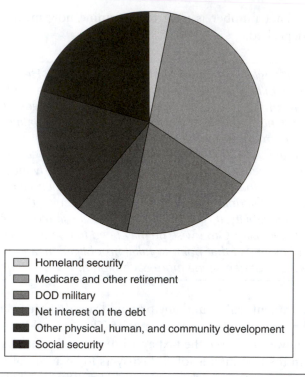

Figure 8.1   Federal Expenditures of Tax Dollars

Source: www.irs.gov/app/understandingtaxes.

STATE AND LOCAL TAXES

Individual states have the right to tax residents' income, although not all do so. States with no income tax liabilities include Alaska, Florida, Nevada, South Dakota, Texas, Washington, and Wyoming. New Hampshire and Tennessee assess state income tax only on dividends and interest received during the year. All other states have individual formulas for calculating a resident's income tax liability (Table 8.1). Funds collected through state income tax are used to support a variety of public programs and services. State and local taxes are used to support community programs, parks, and other public resources.

Individuals residing in and/or working in states that levy an income tax also must prepay their liability. Based on the information provided by the employee on Form W-4, state tax rates are used to calculate a probable tax liability. Money is deducted from each paycheck and is deposited in the state's account to ensure that the employee meets his or her year-end liability. If the taxpayer owes even more than he or she deposited over the year, that difference must be paid on or before the tax-filing deadline. There may be late payment penalties on underpayments.

Table 8.1   State Individual Income Taxes (Tax Rates for Tax Year 2006 as of January 1, 2006)

State	Tax Rates			Income Brackets		Personal Exemption			Federal Tax Deduction
	Low	High	No. of Brackets	Low	High	Single	Married	Child.	
ALABAMA	2.0	-5.0	3	500 (b)	-3,000 (b)	1,500	3,000	300	*
ALASKA	No State Income Tax								
ARIZONA	2.87	-5.04	5	10,000 (b)	-150,000 (b)	2,100	4,200	2,300	
ARKANSAS (a)	1.0	-7.0 (e)	6	3,399	-28,500	20 (c)	40 (c)	20 (c)	
CALIFORNIA (a)	1.0	-9.3 (x)	6	6,319 (b)	-41,477 (b)	87 (c)	174 (c)	272 (c)	
COLORADO	4.63		1	——Flat rate——		——None——			
CONNECTICUT	3.0	-5.0	2	10,000 (b)	-10,000 (b)	12,750 (f)	24,500 (f)	0	
DELAWARE	2.2	-5.95	6	5,000	-60,000	110 (c)	220(c)	110(c)	
FLORIDA	No State Income Tax								
GEORGIA	1.0	-6.0	6	750 (g)	-7,000 (g)	2,700	5,400	3,000	
HAWAII	1.4	-8.25	9	2,000 (b)	-40,000 (b)	1,040	2,080	1,040	
IDAHO (a)	1.6	-7.8	8	1,159 (h)	-23, (h)	3,300 (d)	6,600 (d)	3,300 (d)	
ILLINOIS	3.0		1	——Flat rate——		2,000	4,000	2,000	
INDIANA	3.4		1	——Flat rate——		1,000	2,000	1,000	
IOWA (a)	0.36	-8.98	9	1,269	-57,106	40 (c)	80 (c)	40 (c)	*

(Continued)

Table 8.1 (Continued)

State	Tax Rates			Income Brackets		Personal Exemption			Federal Tax Deduction
	Low	High	No. of Brackets	Low	High	Single	Married	Child.	
KANSAS	3.5	-6.45	3	15,000 (b)	-30,000 (b)	2,250	4,500	2,250	
KENTUCKY	2.0	-6.0	6	3,000	-75,000	20 (c)	40 (c)	20 (c)	
LOUISIANA	2.0	-6.0	3	12,500 (b)	-25,000 (b)	4,500 (i)	9,000 (i)	1,000 (i)	*
MAINE (a)	2.0	-8.5	4	4,550 (b)	-18,250 (b)	2,850	5,700	2,850	
MARYLAND	2.0	-4.75	4	1,000	-3,000	2,400	4,800	2,400	
MASSACHUSETTS (a)	5.3		1	——Flat rate——		3,575	7,150	1,000	
MICHIGAN (a)	3.9		1	——Flat rate——		3,100	6,200	3,100	
MINNESOTA (a)	5.35	-7.85	3	20,510 (j)	-67,360 (j)	3,300 (d)	6,600 (d)	3,300 (d)	
MISSISSIPPI	3.0	-5.0	3	5,000	-10,000	6,000	12,000	1,500	
MISSOURI	1.5	-6.0	10	1,000	9,000	2,100	4,200	1,200	* (s)
MONTANA (a)	1.0	-6.9	7	2,300	-13,900	1,900	3,800	1,900	* (s)
NEBRASKA (a)	2.56	-6.84	4	2,400 (k)	-26,500 (k)	103 (c)	206 (c)	103 (c)	
NEVADA	No State Income Tax								
NEW HAMPSHIRE	State Income Tax Is Limited to Dividends and Interest Income Only								
NEW JERSEY	1.4	-8.97	6	20,000 (l)	-500,000 (l)	1,000	2,000	1,500	

State	Tax Rates			Income Brackets		Personal Exemption			Federal Tax Deduction
	Low	High	No. of Brackets	Low	High	Single	Married	Child.	
NEW MEXICO	1.7	-5.3	4	5,500 (m)	-16,000 (m)	3,300 (d)	6,600 (d)	3,300 (d)	
NEW YORK	4.0	-6.85		8,000 (n)	-500,000 (n)	0	0	1,000	
NORTH CAROLINA (o)	6.0	-8.25	4	12,750 (o)	-120,000 (o)	3,300 (d)	6,600 (d)	3,300 (d)	
NORTH DAKOTA	2.1	-5.54 (p)	5	29,700 (p)	- 326,450 (p)	3,300 (d)	6,600 (d)	3,300 (d)	
OHIO (a)	0.712	-7.185	9	5,000	-200,000	1,300 (q)	2,600 (q)	1,300 (q)	
OKLAHOMA	0.5	-6.25 (r)	8	1,000 (b)	-10,000 (b)	1,000	2,000	1,000	* (r)
OREGON (a)	5.0	-9.0	3	2,650 (b)	-6,550 (b)	159 (c)	318 (c)	159 (c)	* (s)
PENNSYLVANIA	3.07		1	——— Flat rate ———		———None———			
RHODE ISLAND	25.0% Federal tax liability (t)			—	—	—	—	—	
SOUTH CAROLINA (a)	2.5	-7.0	6	2,570	-12,850	3,300 (d)	6,600 (d)	3,300 (d)	
SOUTH DAKOTA	No State Income Tax								
TENNESSEE	State Income Tax Is Limited to Dividends and Interest Income Only								
TEXAS	No State Income Tax								
UTAH	2.30	-7.0	6	863 (b)	-4,313 (b)	2,475 (d)	4,950 (d)	2,475 (d)	* (u)
VERMONT (a)	3.6	-9.5	5	29,900 (v)	326,450 (v)	3,300 (d)	6,600 (d)	3,300 (d)	

(Continued)

Table 8.1 (Continued)

State	Tax Rates			Income Brackets		Personal Exemption			Federal Tax Deduction
	Low	High	No. of Brackets	Low	High	Single	Married	Child.	
VIRGINIA	2.0	-5.75	4	3,000	-17,000	900	1,800	900	
WASHINGTON	No State Income Tax								
WEST VIRGINIA	3.0	-6.5	5	10,000	-60,000	2,000	4,000	2,000	
WISCONSIN	4.6	-6.75	4	8,840 (w)	-132,580 (w)	700	1,400	400	
WYOMING	No State Income Tax								
DIST. OF COLUMBIA	4.5	-9.0	3	10,000	-30,000	1,370	2,740	1,370	

Source: www.taxadmin.org/fta/rate/ind_inc.html.

(a) 17 states have statutory provision for automatic adjustment of tax brackets, personal exemption or standard deductions to the rate of inflation. Massachusetts, Michigan, Nebraska, and Ohio indexes the personal exemption amounts only.

(b) For joint returns, the taxes are twice the tax imposed on half the income.

(c) tax credits.

(d) These states allow personal exemption or standard deductions as provided in the IRC. Utah allows a personal exemption equal to three-fourths the federal exemptions.

(e) A special tax table is available for low income taxpayers reducing their tax payments.

(f) Combined personal exemptions and standard deduction. An additional tax credit is allowed ranging from 75% to 0% based on state adjusted gross income. Exemption amounts are phased out for higher income taxpayers until they are eliminated for households earning over $56,500.

(g) The tax brackets reported are for single individuals. For married households filing separately, the same rates apply to income brackets ranging from $500 to $5,000; and the income brackets range from $1,000 to $10,000 for joint filers.

(h) For joint returns, the tax is twice the tax imposed on half the income. A $10 filing tax is charge for each return and a $15 credit is allowed for each exemption.

(i) Combined personal exemption and standard deduction.

(j) The tax brackets reported are for single individual. For married couples filing jointly, the same rates apply for income under $31,150 to over $123,751. A 6.4% AMT rate is also applicable.

(k) The tax brackets reported are for single individual. For married couples filing jointly, the same rates apply for income under $4,000 to over $50,001.

(l) The tax brackets reported are for single individuals. For married couples filing jointly, the tax rates range from 1.4% to 8.97% (with 7 income brackets) applying to income brackets from $20,000 to over $500,000.

(m) The tax brackets reported are for single individuals. For married couples filing jointly, the same rates apply for income under $8,000 to over $24,000. Married households filing separately pay the tax imposed on half the income.

(n) The tax brackets reported are for single individuals. For married taxpayers, the same rates apply to income brackets ranging from $21,250 to $200,000. Lower exemption amounts allowed for high income taxpayers. Tax rate scheduled to decrease after tax year 2007.

(o) The tax brackets reported are for single individuals. For married taxpayers, the same rates apply to income brackets ranging from $51,200 to $336,551. An additional $300 personal exemption is allowed for joint returns or unmarried head of households.

(p) Plus an additional $20 per exemption tax credit.

(q) The rate range reported is for single persons not deducting federal income tax. For married persons filing jointly, the same rates apply to income brackets ranging from $2,000 to $15,000. Separate schedules, with rates ranging from 0.5% to 10%, apply to taxpayers deducting federal income taxes.

(r) Deduction is limited to $10,000 for joint returns and $5,000 for individuals in Missouri and to $5,000 in Oregon.

(s) Federal Tax Liability prior to the enactment of Economic Growth and Tax Relief Act of 2001.

(t) One half of the federal income taxes are deductible. Taxpayer has an option of using the standard brackets and rates with all deductions, or paying a flat 5.35% of income with limited deductions.

(u) The tax brackets reported are for single individuals. For married couples filing jointly, the same rates apply for income under $51,200 to over $336,551.

(v) The tax brackets reported are for single individuals. For married taxpayers, the same rates apply to income brackets ranging from $12,210 to $183,211. An additional $250 exemption is provided for each taxpayer or spouse age 65 or over.

(w) An additional 1% tax is imposed on taxable income over $1 million.

Communities may levy taxes on real estate, automobiles, and other personal property of citizens. This tax money is utilized for local and community purposes, such as street and road improvements, school funding, and protective services. These taxes are usually figured on an annual basis, with payment due at the beginning of the tax year, in installments during the year, or it may be collected in the year following the actual assessed year. Owners are responsible for payment of these taxes. However, many mortgage companies will pay the yearly real estate tax and collect that money with mortgage payments to ensure that the property is current on the tax rolls.

States and communities also have the right to impose sales tax on consumer purchases. These taxes impact all citizens equally and have a direct impact on family financial resources. The location of the actual purchase determines which tax rate applies. For instance, if the city closest to you has a 5% state sales tax rate and a 1% city rate, qualifying purchases made by you in that city will have an additional 6% added to their price. A $1.00 pen costs you $1.06. However, if you buy that same pen at a convenience store just outside the city limit, you would only pay the state rate, thus the final cost would be $1.05. That difference may not seem large, but when you are buying larger ticket items, such as furniture and automobiles, it can make a large difference. For instance, 1% of a $2,000 sofa is $20. On a $30,000 automobile purchase, you would pay $300 more if purchased in a city with that 1% sales tax.

When a consumer is traveling, local taxes can have a substantial impact on the travel budget. Many cities collect a tourism tax on hotel, travel, and recreational purchases of visitors. For instance, San Antonio has a hotel tax rate of 16.75%. A hotel room priced at $100 per night would actually cost a traveler $116.75 for each night's stay. Communities often use these types of taxes to fund construction and maintenance of facilities that both draw the travelers into their city and provide those visitors with access to things like sports, cultural events, and meeting facilities.

SOCIAL SECURITY

Federal tax liability is somewhat proportional. If you make more money, you will probably pay a higher percentage in taxes. Social Security is a uniform rate for all. Employees currently pay 6.2% of their gross income into the Social Security fund. Employers match that amount, for a total of 12.4% of earnings. The total Social Security tax liability is capped, however, because individuals only pay this amount on the first $97,500 (2007 level) of labor earnings.

Employee A makes $30,000 annually and $1,860 is deposited into the Social Security fund. Employee B makes $60,000 and $3,720 is her Social Security liability. Both have contributed 6.2% of their wages. If

Employee C makes $150,000, his or her liability stops at $97,500, so he or she pays $6,045 into Social Security. That translates into 4% of total wages. Those in the higher earnings bracket ultimately pay less in Social Security tax.

In exchange for the money paid into the Social Security fund, taxpayers receive many benefits, although usually deferred. The Social Security Administration pays retirement, disability, and family and survivors benefits. The most well-known benefit is the retirement income provided. Wage earners who have paid into the Social Security fund for at least the minimum length of time (determined by a point system) and reach the official age of retirement are eligible for monthly income payments as determined by benefit calculations. Currently employees earn "credits"— up to four each year. In 2006, one credit is earned for each $970 of wages or self-employment income. Most people need 40 credits, earned over their working lifetime, to receive retirement benefits. Once enough credits have been accumulated, benefit amounts are determined using the average earnings over the entire working lifetime. Theoretically, if you made more than your spouse, you will collect a higher monthly amount. The amount possible, however, is capped.

The age of retirement will also impact the amount you will receive in Social Security benefits. Currently, if you were born before 1938, your full retirement age will be 65. This age increases gradually to 67 for people born in 1960 or later. Some people retire before their full retirement age. If you retire at age 62, you will receive a reduced rate of payments. If you continue working after your full retirement age, you can receive higher benefits because of additional earnings and special credits for delayed retirement. Individuals must consider health, earning potential, and life expectancy when contemplating retirement before they reach the full retirement age.

Sal has just turned 62. If he retires now, he will receive a monthly check for $1,108. If he waits until his 65th birthday he will receive $1,573 each month, a difference of $465 monthly. Assume he does retire at age 62. When Sal reaches 75 years of age, he will have received approximately $173,000 (with no adjustment for increases). His twin brother, Ed, waits to retire until he is 65 years of age. When Ed turns 75, he will have collected approximately $188,000. So even though Ed has been receiving benefits for only 10 years and Sal has been retired for 13 years, Ed has already surpassed his brother in benefits received from Social Security.

This scenario impacts the decision-making process dramatically if all other variables are equal—personal health, health of spouse, and goals and objectives. If Sal's decision to retire early reflects his concern that his wife's health is failing, he may be willing to forgo the chance to collect more money for the opportunity to spend 3 more years with her while she is still able to enjoy their time together.

The concept of longevity has negatively impacted the Social Security program. When the program was originally introduced in 1935, the average life expectancy of working men (few women were considered in this plan) was not much over 65 years of age. The program was intended to provide a stable cushion of income to the elderly during the last few years of their life. Today's life expectancy for both men and women is approaching 80 years of age. On the average, then, retirees can be expected to draw from Social Security funds for at least 10 years, many for much longer. Today's retiree may well take out of the system more than he or she paid into it over his or her working life. That focuses partial weight for supporting this program onto payments made into the system by current wage earners. How will the pool grow large enough to support the current workforce when they reach retirement age if their funds are being used and not invested? It is forecasted by the Social Security Administration (2004) that, by 2042, the Social Security Trust Fund will be entirely depleted. By then, the number of Americans at retirement age will have doubled. There will not be enough younger people working to pay all of the benefits owed. Social Security, a compact between generations, is facing serious future problems.

Many current retirees are finding that Social Security benefits are not enough to cover their necessary expenses. Retirees can continue to work and draw their full benefits at the same time if they retired after age 65. If they opted for retirement earlier, there is a limit on how much can be earned without negatively impacting the monthly payment received.

Photo 8.1   The future of Social Security is questionable.

Source: © Brooks Kraft/Corbis.

Because the Social Security legislation was passed during a time when relatively few married females were in the workforce, a provision for wives who had not earned their own qualifying points was created. Although previously assumed that the nonworking spouse would be the woman, the terminology is "spouse," so the same provisions and regulations apply to all spouses, male or female. A spouse will receive 50% of the retired worker's full (age 65) benefit unless the spouse begins collecting benefits before reaching full retirement age. In that case, the amount of the spouse's benefit is permanently reduced by a percentage based on the number of months before he or she reaches age 65. If the spouse begins receiving benefits at age 62, the benefit amount would be 37.5%.

If the spouse has worked and accumulated enough points, she is eligible to receive the full amount calculated. If that amount is less than 50% of his or her spouse's benefit, the larger amount will be provided.

Marjorie did not work for a wage outside of her home. When her husband retired, he qualified for a monthly Social Security payment of $900. She is entitled to collect a payment of $450 based on 50% of his benefit. Joan did work for a long enough period of time to accumulate the necessary points to qualify for her own Social Security benefit. Her earnings history resulted in an initial monthly check of $750. Her husband collects $1,600 each month from Social Security. His record entitles Joan to a payment of $800 each month. She will forego the payment based on her own earnings to collect the larger check. She cannot receive both.

The term *spouse* also refers to ex-wife or ex-husband in many cases. If you are divorced (even if you have remarried), your ex-spouse may qualify for benefits on your record if you are 62 or older. To qualify on your record, your ex-spouse must

- have been married to you for at least 10 years,
- be at least 62 years old,
- be unmarried, and
- not be eligible for an equal or higher benefit on his or her own or someone else's Social Security record.

If your former spouse continues to work while receiving benefits, the same earning limits apply to him or her as apply to you. The amount of benefits your divorced spouse gets has no effect on the amount of benefits you or your current spouse may receive.

Social Security also has a disability benefit available to those with qualifying point accumulation (currently 6–20 credits in 3–10 years prior to disabling condition). Once disabled, a qualified worker must wait for

6 months to receive disability benefits. At that point, it must be determined and documented that the worker has a physical or mental impairment that is expected to keep him or her from doing "substantial" work for a year or more or is expected to die. The financial support provided through this benefit is not expected to fully replace one's prior earnings, but rather as a supplement, much like disability insurance plans.

Much like Social Security retirement, spouses and children may qualify for disability payments under the primary wage earner's account. Current or divorced spouses, minor children, or adult children disabled before age 22 may receive benefit payments. Each may qualify for up to 50% of the worker's benefit amount. The total amount disbursed depends on how many family members qualify.

Paulette, age 42, was diagnosed with a degenerative bone disease. Her monthly income averaged about $4,000. Although in pain, she continued to work full time until it became impossible for her to make the trip from her home to the workplace. She tried working from a home office, but that has become impossible, also. Six months ago, she applied for disability benefits. She has met all necessary criteria and will begin receiving a check for about $1,400 each month from the Social Security Administration. This payment will help her meet expenses, but other sources of support will be necessary to sustain her current standard of living.

Another benefit provided to qualifying workers through the Social Security Administration is survivor benefits. Once dead, certain members of the deceased's family may be eligible for monthly payments:

- spouses age 60 or older (50 or older if disabled),
- spouses of any age if caring for your children under the age of 16,
- unmarried children under 18 who are still in school (19 if still in school), and
- adult children who become disabled before the age of 22.

There is also a one-time death benefit paid to the surviving spouse of all qualified workers. Currently this benefit is $255.

Employees currently in the workforce can view the amount taken out of their paycheck to fund Social Security payments in two ways. First, it allows them to eventually qualify for retirement, disability, and survivor benefits—a type of insurance. Second, it provides the money necessary to fund these benefits for friends and family members who have already met qualifying criteria—social responsibility. The question looming over the system is, "will money be available to fund benefits when current workers fulfill their own qualifying criteria in decades to come?"

MEDICARE

Like Social Security deposits, employee wages are subject to Medicare taxes through a straight percentage calculation (1.45%). Employers match employee contributions, so the pool of funds to support this benefit is 2.9% of employee income. Unlike Social Security, there is no annual wage limit. Thus, Medicare liability is calculated evenly among the poor, middle class, and wealthy. The money collected is used to fund the Medicare health insurance program available to qualifying workers 65 years of age or older. There are certain disabilities that qualify individuals under the age of 65, including permanent kidney failure requiring dialysis or a kidney transplant.

The Original Medicare Plan is a "fee-for-service" plan, which means you are charged a fee for each health care service or supply you get. This original plan has two parts: Parts A and B. When a qualified worker reaches the age of 65, he or she automatically receives Medicare Part A (Hospital Insurance). This plan covers inpatient care in hospitals and skilled nursing facilities (not custodial or long-term care). It also helps cover hospice care and some home health care. If you or your spouse paid Medicare taxes while still employed, there is no monthly fee required. If you didn't pay Medicare taxes while you worked, you may be able to buy it with a monthly payment similar to other health insurance premiums. Part B is a supplemental health insurance plan to help cover doctors' services and outpatient hospital care. A monthly premium is required to receive these additional benefits ($93.50 in 2007). Participation in Medicare Part B is not required; however, those who cannot pay the premium may find assistance through state programs designed to support this federal program. Prescription drug plans are also available through Medicare, but vary by type, coverage, and cost.

What Individuals Pay When Participating in the Original Medicare Plan

Qualifying individuals select doctors, specialists, and medical facilities that accept Medicare patients. Generally a fee is charged each time a service is provided.

Covered Expenses:

Hospital Stays

Semiprivate room, meals, general nursing, services, and supplies.

Skilled Nursing Facility Care

Semiprivate room, meals, skilled nursing, and rehabilitative services (only after related 3-day inpatient hospital stays).

Home Health Care

Part-time or intermittent skilled nursing care and home health aide services, physical therapy, occupational therapy, speech-language therapy, medical social services, durable medical equipment, medical supplies, and other services.

Hospice Care

Drugs for symptom control and pain relief, medical and support services from a Medicare-approved hospice, and other services not otherwise covered by Medicare.

Blood

Pints of blood received during a hospital or skilled nursing facility stay.

Participant Co-Pay or Deductibles

Like private health insurance programs, participants are expected to pay a base amount each benefit period. A benefit period begins the day one enters the hospital or skilled nursing facility and ends when one hasn't received any hospital care for 60 days in a row. If someone enters a hospital after one benefit period has ended, a new benefit period begins, triggering a new deductible.

UNEMPLOYMENT INSURANCE

In general, states and the federal government work together to provide unemployment benefits to eligible workers who are unemployed through no fault of their own. States, under federal guidelines, set eligibility criteria and collect payroll taxes from employers to manage this program. In most states, employees do not pay into this fund. Although utilized as an important part of a family's coping strategy during times of unemployment, this fund is not intended to provide full compensation and is limited in scope.

To be eligible for unemployment benefits, the worker must have established at least a 1-year period of time, or a **base period**, to qualify for compensation. Most states use the first four out of the last five completed calendar quarters prior to filing of the claim. It must be established that the worker was not responsible for his or her situation. Newly unemployed workers must contact the state unemployment insurance agency as soon as possible to file a claim for benefits. There is a lag time of about 3 weeks between filing and the receipt of the first check.

Those receiving benefits must continue to file regular claims to support continued eligibility. These reports include progress information about the claimant's efforts to find another job. It is a general expectation that unemployment benefits will not continue after 26 weeks unless special chronic unemployment situations are determined by the state.

Families are connected to the tax system through both funding and usage. Members pay money into the various accounts, and they withdraw payments when they are deemed eligible. The concept of equity often fuels debates between and among the different socioeconomic groups. Are Americans getting what they pay for? Are some groups benefiting more than others? These questions provide dialogue for political campaigns and policy discussions. Another concept that triggers debate is the administration of the funding within these tax-based programs. Wasteful spending and unnecessary overhead costs are concerns of all taxpayers.

Government-Supported Assistance Programs

Individuals and families have both private and public programs available to supplement or replace resources lost through crises or acute circumstances. This assistance may take the form of money, vouchers, food, or actual services. **Public programs** are financed and/or supported by tax dollars. **Private programs** are financed through charitable contributions. Both public and private programs require some justification or qualifications for families to qualify for assistance. Public funds must have higher levels of accountability in terms of equity, fairness, and distribution. Private funds can be more or less discriminatory depending on the goals of the source of funding.

Worldview

Norway's Social Security and Health Service

By Målfrid Bolstad

Norway has extensive health services and a well-developed social safety net. All Norway residents have a right to economic assistance and other forms of community support during illness, old age, or unemployment. About 35% of the state's budget is spent on the Norwegian health and social welfare system. Two laws—the National Insurance Act and the Social Care Act—are the statutory mainstays of Norwegians' social rights.

(Continued)

(Continued)

The health and social welfare system in Norway is predominantly publicly financed through a combination of general and separate taxation. The national insurance, or social security, is a collective insurance scheme to which all in Norway belong. All wage earners contribute a fixed percentage of their earnings by paying the national insurance tax. In addition, employers contribute by means of a payroll tax. The latter is assessed as a percentage of wages paid by the employer. The self-employed contribute more to social security than wage earners do because they are exempted from the payroll tax. Nonworking spouses, the unemployed, students, and others without wages are exempted from social security tax, but they still qualify for social security benefits. They have the same rights to assistance and medical treatment as those with salaries. The size of unemployment compensation, sick pay, and pensions depends on the amount of income the individual has previously earned. Economic social assistance is allotted on the basis of an individual means test.

When You Have Children

When pregnant, women who have been employed for at least 6 of the last 10 months are entitled to a maternity leave with full pay, limited upward to six times the basic national insurance sum. The mother can choose between 42 weeks of leave with full pay or 52 weeks with 78% pay. Three weeks of this leave must be taken prior to the birth. Four weeks of the leave must be taken by the father (the paternity quota).

A time account scheme enables parents to refrain from using their entire benefit quota in one consecutive period. They can retain unused days in their accounts and use them freely within a 2-year period.

Women who haven't been employed and don't qualify for a paid maternity leave receive a NOK 32,138 grant upon giving birth.

A new reform—the cash benefits scheme—has been adopted for 1-year-olds from August 1998 and for 2-year-olds from January 1999. This scheme will benefit families that do not use child-care centers or have been offered less than 30 hours of day care per week. The amount of the cash benefit depends on the number of hours the child would be in day care. The full cash benefit totals NOK 3,000 per month.

Currently, 60% of all children between 1 and 5 years of age are in day care. There is still a shortage of child-care centers but the authorities' explicit goal is complete coverage by the year 2000. The Day Care Institutions Act of 5 May 1995 entered into force on 1 January 1996.

As of the autumn of 1997, children now begin first grade a year earlier—at age 6. Care for children at school before and after class hours is enshrined in a special regulation to the Primary and Lower Secondary Education Act and is being extended and developed for kids aged six to ten.

The author of the article, Målfrid Bolstad, is a freelance journalist.

Source: Produced by Nytt fra Norge for the Ministry of Foreign Affairs. June 2000. The author is responsible for the contents of the article. Reproduction permitted.

HEALTH AND HUMAN SERVICES

One of the most recognized U.S. agencies for assistance programs is the Department of Health and Human Services. This federal agency has a multitude of resources (see www.hhs.gov). Of nearly $700 million budgeted for 2007, more than one half will be paid out in Medicare benefits described earlier in this chapter. Medicaid, the state-level programs supported by these funds, will require the next largest amount. The remaining money in the budget is used to finance many other programs focusing on disease, safety, disasters, child and family services, and aging services (Figure 8.2).

For over 35 years, the Administration on Aging has provided home- and community-based services to millions of older persons through the programs funded under the Older Americans Act. These services include home-delivered meals (Meals on Wheels) and food and nutrition services in congregate settings. Other services made available by funding in this HHS-based agency include transportation, adult day care, legal assistance, and health-promotion programs. Ombudsmen are provided for nursing homes, providing an ongoing presence in long-term care facilities, monitoring care and conditions, and providing a voice for those who are unable to speak for themselves. The National Family Caregiver Support Program provides a variety of services to help people who are caring for family members who are chronically ill or who have disabilities.

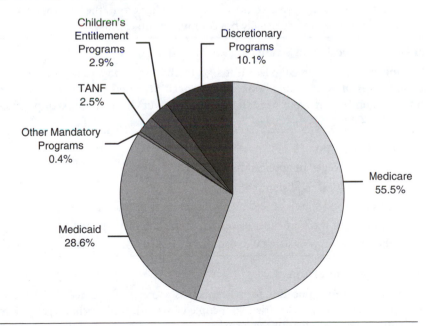

Figure 8.2   Federally Budgeted Program Expenditures

Source: www.hhs.gov/budget/07budget/overview.html.

THE DEPARTMENT OF AGRICULTURE

The U.S. Department of Agriculture (USDA) provides food assistance programs to citizens. The Food Stamp Program serves as the base of federal food assistance, providing crucial support to low-income households and individuals transitioning from welfare to work (Table 8.2). It provides families with Electronic Benefits Transfer (EBT) cards, which can be used to buy eligible food in authorized retail food stores. The Food Stamp Program helped put food on the table for some 10.3 million households and 23.9 million individuals each day in Fiscal Year 2004. Commodity food resources are also made available to qualifying families when the USDA purchases such foodstuffs from the agricultural producers in an effort to support the food producing segments of the country's population. Food safety, nutrition education, and research are also supported by this agency.

Table 8.2   How to Determine Eligibility for Food Stamp Program Participation

10 Steps to Help You Fill Your Grocery Bag Through The Food Stamp Program
Learn If You or Someone You Know Might Be Eligible for Food Stamps

❶	**Use the Internet Tool.**
	If you want to find out if you could be eligible, check out the Internet tool at www.hhs.gov. Your local library usually has computers you can use.
❷	**Call or Go to the Local Food Stamp Office.**
	If you think you might be eligible, call or go to the local food stamp office. Look in the blue pages of your phone book under "Social Services" or "Human Services" to find the number. If you need help finding your local food stamp office, call 1-800-221-5689.
❸	**Get an Application Form.**
	There are four ways to get an application form:
	• Pick it up at a local food stamp office,
	• Call the local food stamp office and ask the worker to mail it to you,
	• Ask the worker if there are other places where you can pick up the form, or
	• Print the form from your state's Web page (this is available in many states, but not all).
❹	**Fill Out the Application Form.**
	Fill out the food stamp application form as much as you can. If you need help, ask the food stamp worker. You can ask a friend or people who work at places like legal services or food banks to help you fill out the form.

❺ Return the Application Form to the Food Stamp Office.

Get the application form to the food stamp office as quickly as possible. If you are picking up your application form at a food stamp office, put your name, street address, and social security number on the form and sign it. Leave that part of the form (usually the first page) at the food stamp office. This starts the process and helps you to get healthy food sooner, if you are eligible. Take the rest of the form with you to fill out later.

❻ Make an Appointment for an Interview.

Make an appointment for an interview with a food stamp worker. If you are at a food stamp office, ask the worker to write down what you need to bring to the interview. If you are calling for an appointment, ask the worker what you should bring.

Here are examples of some papers that you might need to bring:

- Driver's license or birth certificate;
- Pay stubs;
- Letter showing money received from social security, SSI, VA, child support, etc.;
- Most recent rental agreement or letter from your landlord;
- Most recent mortgage statement;
- Utility bills, such as electricity, gas, and heating oil;
- Cancelled checks for day care for your child;
- Medical bills that you pay (if you are 60 or older, or disabled); and
- Court order or cancelled checks for child support payments.

❼ Get Papers or Other Information.

Get the papers or find the other information that the food stamp worker needs to finish your application. If you need help getting the papers, ask the food stamp worker, a relative, a friend, or a community representative to help you.

❽ Go to the Interview.

Go to the interview with the food stamp worker. Bring your papers with you. Ask the food stamp worker to make copies. Keep your original papers. If you need help filling out the application form or getting the information needed to finish your form, ask the food stamp worker. You may bring a friend or community representative to help you understand how to complete the process. If you can't go to the food stamp office for the interview, ask for a telephone interview. Or you can ask a friend or relative to go in your place.

❾ If You Are Approved, Go Grocery Shopping.

If you are approved for food stamps, happy shopping! Add lots of fruits, vegetables, whole-grain foods, and other good foods to your shopping cart. Ask your local food stamp office where you can learn more about smart, economical eating and physical activity for better health. Nutrition education may be available to you as a food stamp participant.

(Continued)

Table 8.2 (Continued)

	If You Are Not Approved, Ask Why. Call or visit the food stamp office to ask why you were not approved. You may ask to speak with the food stamp worker's boss. If you think there is a mistake, you may ask for a "fair hearing." This means that a state person will meet with you and the food stamp office to discuss your application. Fair hearings do not cost you any money.

Source: www.fns.usda.gov/fsp/.

The National School Lunch Program, initiated in 1946, is another USDA program. It provides free, reduced, and low-cost lunches to school children in public and nonprofit schools and in qualifying residential child-care institutions. A similar program, the School Breakfast Program, provides nutritious morning meals to children. Both of these programs have income eligibility guidelines that are adjusted periodically to reflect changes in the economy and wage base of participants. Other programs address the needs of elderly, pregnant, and breastfeeding women, as well as disaster relief.

THE FOOD AND DRUG ADMINISTRATION

In the News

DA Advises Consumers to Avoid Toothpaste From China Containing Harmful Chemical

FDA Detains One Contaminated Shipment, Issues Import Alert

The U.S. Food and Drug Administration (FDA) today warned consumers to avoid using tubes of toothpaste labeled as made in China, and issued an import alert to prevent toothpaste containing the poisonous chemical diethylene glycol (DEG) from entering the United States.

DEG is used in antifreeze and as a solvent.

Consumers should examine toothpaste products for labeling that says the product is made in China. Out of an abundance of caution, FDA suggests that consumers throw away toothpaste with that labeling. FDA is concerned that these products may contain "diethylene glycol," also known as "diglycol."

FDA is not aware of any U.S. reports of poisonings from toothpaste containing DEG. However, the agency is concerned about potential risks from chronic exposure to DEG and exposure to DEG in certain populations, such as children and individuals with kidney or liver disease. DEG in toothpaste has a low but meaningful risk of toxicity and injury to these populations. Toothpaste is not intended to be swallowed, but FDA is concerned about unintentional swallowing or ingestion of toothpaste containing DEG.

FDA has identified the following brands of toothpaste from China that contain DEG and are included in the import alert: Cooldent Fluoride; Cooldent Spearmint; Cooldent ICE; Dr. Cool, Everfresh Toothpaste; Superdent Toothpaste; Clean Rite Toothpaste; Oralmax Extreme; Oral Bright Fresh Spearmint Flavor; Bright Max Peppermint Flavor; ShiR Fresh Mint Fluoride Paste; DentaPro; DentaKleen; and DentaKleen Junior. Manufacturers of these products are: Goldcredit International Enterprises Limited; Goldcredit International Trading Company Limited; and Suzhou City Jinmao Daily Chemicals Company Limited. The products typically are sold at low-cost, "bargain" retail outlets.

Based on reports of contaminated toothpaste from China found in several countries, including Panama, FDA increased its scrutiny and began sampling toothpaste and other dental products manufactured in China that were imported into the United States.

FDA inspectors identified and detained one shipment of toothpaste at the U.S. border, containing about 3 percent DEG by weight. In addition, FDA inspectors found and tested toothpaste products from China located at a distribution center and a retail store. The highest level found was between 3–4 percent by weight. The product at the retail store was not labeled as containing DEG but was found to contain the substance.

DEG poisoning is an important public safety issue. The agency is aware of reports of patient deaths and injuries in other countries over the past several years from ingesting DEG-contaminated pharmaceutical preparations, such as cough syrups and acetaminophen syrup. FDA recently issued a guidance document to urge U.S. pharmaceutical manufacturers to be vigilant in assuring that glycerin, a sweetener commonly used worldwide in liquid over-the-counter and prescription drug products, is not contaminated with DEG.

Source: U.S. Food and Drug Administration. Retrieved from http://www.fda.gov/bbs/topics/NEWS/2007/NEW01646.html.

The FDA is dedicated to promoting and protecting the public health through monitoring the safety and effectiveness of certain types of products on the market. Products such as new drugs and medical devices must be proved safe and effective before the FDA will allow producing companies to sell them to private and public consumers. Other potentially harmful products, such as microwave ovens and over-the-counter drugs, are also under the FDA's jurisdiction.

To ultimately determine the safety of new products, the FDA requires science-based testing and research and diligent decision-making efforts concerning the risk versus benefit of such products on consumer health and safety. These requirements keep many new products off the market for long periods of time. Occasionally other countries will allow the marketing of such products before the United States.

> *Drug companies were working on an emergency contraceptive drug alternative for many years. One such product was approved for distribution in Europe long before it was legal to distribute the same medication from U.S. pharmacies. The FDA was not convinced of its safety and effectiveness. In the meantime, the drug's availability through the Internet market became controversial. After further testing and deliberations, this drug is now legally available in the United States and is even being considered for over-the-counter distribution. Deaths associated with this drug are forcing the FDA to reevaluate that decision.*

The FDA safeguards the nation's food supply by ensuring that all ingredients are safe and uncontaminated. It must also approve any new food additive before it can be used in food products available for sale in the United States. Infant formulas and dietary supplements are also under its jurisdiction, although standards for supplements are much less rigorous than for pharmaceuticals that may be sold for similar needs. Because a supplement is consumed by the purchaser, it must be safe and uncontaminated. The FDA does not, however, require these substances to verify the claims made by distributors (weight loss, improved sexual performance, etc.). Meat products, however, are regulated by the USDA.

Medical products under the FDA's regulations include medicines, biologics (vaccines, blood products, biotechnology products, and gene therapy), and medical devices. The devices regulated include tongue depressors, thermometers, heart pacemakers, and dialysis machines. Only the most complex new devices are reviewed, however, before marketing. The FDA even regulates drugs and devices for animals. Cosmetics are monitored for safety and accuracy in labeling, but are not reviewed or approved by this administration.

Labels on medications and food products must be accurate and informative. The FDA monitors existing labeling practices and institutes changes when determined to be necessary. The FDA's current role is still evolving, but it continues to blend law and science in an effort to protect consumers.

The ordinary trip to the grocery store is relatively free from worry about the safety of products available there because of the FDA—a tremendous service to American consumers, but not without a cost. The administration is funded through public tax dollars. The process for approving and withdrawing products for the marketplace is time consuming, however, and consumers get caught in the flow. Some medical patients will not have access to new drugs that may improve their condition because of the lag time between discovery and approval. Other consumers may suffer from the use of dangerous products during the time it takes to test, gather data about problems, and ultimately order these things off the market.

There are numerous other governmental programs providing services to the public. Families do have other sources of assistance from private organizations that provide goods and services to members or to the general public. The United States has a long tradition of neighbors helping neighbors and philanthropic activity.

Consumer Protection

Reality Check

A great deal of attention has been focused on why affordable housing is such a problem for many families in the United States. One impact on housing costs is the building regulations created and enforced by local governments. Examples of how these rules, codes, and standards impact housing costs include the following:

- Local regulations determine minimum lot sizes or how much ground must support a new structure. Even slight increases to these minimums reduce the number of houses possible in new developments. If the total cost that developers charge for their financial needs is set and the number of lots within that piece of ground drops from 12 to 10 because of lot size restrictions, each lot will be priced more than 16% higher, pushing the total cost of the house up that much.

- Many communities enforce impact fees and regulatory costs on each new home built in that municipality. Some studies show that such fees in some California communities add up to over $100,000 per home built.

- New energy codes enforced a nation-wide aim to increase energy efficiency in American homes. Although this goal is a long-range benefit to home buyers through reduced heating and cooling bills, initially these regulations can increase the cost of building, and thus the price of housing for consumers.

- Rising real estate taxes to support local governments and schools positively increase the cost of homeownership for families. Issues of equity surface when families without children feel they should not be burdened with the cost of providing schools to those who choose to have children. This issue is of increasing concern in communities with large retirement populations.

(Continued)

(Continued)

- The costs of securing and maintaining public utilities are passed from municipal governments to homeowners and general consumers. As regulations are enforced to alleviate the problems of garbage dumps and sanitation services, consumer prices for such services increase. Accessing municipal water sources are impacted with costs of increasing sanitation methods.

An illustration of governmental and other legal costs and their impact on the cost of housing:

Cost of building home: $170,000 including materials, labor, and lot

$12,000 real estate broker fee

$8,000 permits and fees

$10,000 profit to builder

Purchase price: $200,000

Down payment: $20,000 30-year mortgage at 7%

Amount financed: $180,000   Mortgage payment: $1,200.00

Annual real estate taxes: $2,400 $200.00 monthly

Home insurance required by lender: $100.00 monthly

Monthly payment: $1,500.00

If building codes required 5% less material, if labor costs and lot size restrictions weren't imposed that originally added 16% to the lot cost, and if local permits and fees were reduced by 50%, the purchase price could drop to $175,000. Even keeping real estate broker fees and builder profits at the same percentages, the cost of building and selling the home is reduced enough to lower the price more than 12%. The monthly mortgage payment could be reduced to $1,100. Real estate taxes would be lower because the purchase price impacts tax valuation, and insurance fees would be lower because of the replacement cost of the home. Essentially, the homeowner could choose to either buy a larger home or allocate the mortgage savings to other family resource needs. Higher energy costs due to the reduced building requirements would need to be at least $300 per month to justify the original monthly mortgage payment.

Although U.S. citizens have many protected rights that allow multiple choices during the decision-making process, some alternatives are regulated by laws designed to protect the consumer. Just focusing on the lowest level needs from Maslow's hierarchy, it is evident that regulation of food, housing, and water safety impacts choices. A family member may be able to hunt for game during restricted seasons and only with a legal permit. Food resulting from that activity can be consumed by the family; however, it cannot be sold to others without passing through a series of regulated processes. These processes will increase the final price of that meat. Family adults may be able to construct a dwelling that meets the basic needs, but often that structure must meet local, regional, and even national codes before an occupancy permit is issued. Meeting those standards will ultimately increase the cost of that dwelling. Parents of young children are restricted in terms of size and features when selecting an automobile. Child restraints are required by all states, and these devices require minimum seat space and seatbelt capabilities.

Consumer protection is a reflection of cultural beliefs that producers of goods and services cannot be fully entrusted to protect the safety of those who consume their goods and services. The Bureau of Consumer Protection's mandate is to protect consumers against possible unfair, deceptive, or fraudulent practices. The Bureau enforces a variety of consumer protection laws enacted by Congress, as well as trade regulation rules issued by the Federal Trade Commission (FTC). Its actions include individual company and industry-wide investigations, administrative and federal court litigation, rulemaking proceedings, and consumer and business education. In addition, the Bureau contributes to the FTC's ongoing efforts to inform Congress and other government entities of the impact that proposed actions could have on consumers. Specific areas of enforcement fall into seven categories—advertising, enforcement, financial practices, marketing practices, planning and information, international issues, and consumer and business education.

The Division of Advertising Practices protects consumers from deceptive and unsubstantiated advertising. Its law enforcement activities focus on

- Tobacco and alcohol advertising, including monitoring for unfair practices or deceptive claims, and reporting to Congress on cigarette and smokeless tobacco labeling, advertising, and promotion.

- Advertising claims for food and over-the-counter drugs, particularly those relating to nutritional or health benefits of foods and the safety and effectiveness of drugs or medical devices.

- Performance and energy-savings claims made for energy-related household and automotive products.

- Environmental performance claims made for consumer products, including claims that products are environmentally safe, ozone-friendly, or biodegradable.

- Infomercials, long-form (30-minute) broadcast advertising, to ensure that both the format and content of programs are nondeceptive.

- General advertising at the national and regional levels, particularly advertising making objective claims that are difficult for consumers to evaluate.

The Division of Enforcement conducts a wide variety of law enforcement activities to protect consumers, including (a) ensuring compliance with administrative and federal court orders entered in consumer protection cases; (b) conducting investigations and prosecuting civil actions to stop fraudulent, unfair, or deceptive marketing and advertising practices; and (c) enforcing consumer protection laws, rules, and guidelines.

The Division of Financial Practices enforces many of the nation's consumer credit statutes, including

- *The Consumer Leasing Act:* This law requires leasers to give consumers information on lease costs and terms. Products most often leased are cars, housing, business facilities, tools and equipment, and even such intangibles as airspace and trailer pads.

- *The Credit Practices Rule:* Americans are actively involved in the use of credit. Often consumers overextend themselves, and the Bureau of Consumer Protection must ensure that creditors cannot unduly harm the welfare of debtors. This law prohibits certain security interests and collection remedies in consumer credit contracts, confessions of judgment, wage assignments, waivers of exemption, and security interests in certain household goods. It is responsible for the protection of an individual's personal information gathered by creditors and for ensuring that all terms and conditions within credit contracts are presented fully and understandably to those seeking to borrow.

- *The Equal Credit Opportunity Act:* Protecting consumers from credit discrimination on the basis of sex, race, marital status, religion, national origin, age, or receipt of public assistance is the focus of this law.

- *The Fair Credit Billing Act and the Electronic Fund Transfer Act:* These Acts have been instituted to address the contemporary problems associated with the exchange of goods and payment using electronic methods. One important component of these laws is the establishment of procedures for resolving mistakes on credit card and electronic fund transfer accounts.

- *The Fair Credit Reporting Act:* Lenders require accurate information when determining whether a borrower is a good credit risk. Borrowers can be negatively impacted if inaccurate, negative information about their credit and payment practices is publicized.

This law ensures the accuracy and privacy of information kept by credit bureaus and consumer reporting agencies. It gives consumers the right to know what information credit bureaus and consumer reporting agencies are distributing about them to creditors, insurance companies, and employers.

- *The Fair Debt Collection Practices Act:* Creditors have tremendous power in the lending process; because they have a stronger interest in collecting what is due them than in considering the welfare of their debtors, this law was created to prohibit debt collectors from engaging in unfair, deceptive, or abusive practices, including overcharging, harassment, and disclosing consumers' debt to third parties.

- *Gramm–Leach–Bliley Act:* Information about a consumer's financial standing may increase that person's vulnerability to identity theft and unlawful manipulation. This Act provides the Commission's Privacy and Safeguards Rules, requiring financial institutions to maintain the privacy and security of consumer information.

- *The Holder-in-Due-Course Rule:* When a consumer purchases goods using credit, their debt is often passed to a third party. If the goods purchased are faulty or substandard, the issue of liability surfaces. Is it the original seller or creditor who is responsible for product performance? This law provides certain protections to consumers when the goods they buy on credit are not satisfactory.

- *The Truth in Lending Act:* This Act safeguards the consumer from creditor manipulation at the onset of a credit contract. Terms and phrases used in contracts may be difficult for average consumers to understand. Creditors are required to disclose in writing certain cost information, such as the annual percentage rate (APR), before consumers enter into credit transactions.

The Division of Marketing Practices responds quickly and decisively to the rapidly changing world of fraudulent marketing practices. It enforces federal consumer protection laws by filing actions in federal district court on behalf of the Commission to stop scams, prevent scam artists from repeating their fraudulent schemes in the future, freeze their assets, and obtain compensation for scam victims. The priorities of this division include

- Shutting down high-tech Internet and telephone scams that bilk consumers out of hundreds of millions of dollars annually,

- Halting deceptive **telemarketing** or **direct mail marketing schemes** that use false and misleading information to take consumers' money, and

- Stopping **pyramid schemes** and other fraudulent **investment scams**.

The Division of Planning and Information collects and analyzes data to target law enforcement and education efforts and measure the impact of activities related to the FTC's consumer protection mission. The division is responsible for various projects and functions, including

- *The Consumer Response Center:* Counselors respond to consumer complaints and inquiries received by telephone, mail, and e-mail.

- *The Identity Theft Program:* The division coordinates the FTC's Identity Theft Program. The agency has been directed by statute to serve as a central clearinghouse for identity theft complaints. Consumers can call or visit www.consumer.gov/idtheft.

- *The Consumer Sentinel:* This binational, multistate computerized consumer fraud database uses the Internet to provide secure access to over 200,000 consumer complaints for over 150 law enforcement organizations across the United States and Canada. The site offers law enforcement access to telemarketing, direct mail, and Internet complaints from the FTC's Consumer Information System database and from various law enforcement and private sector partners. The site also provides other information useful for investigations and prosecutions.

- *The International Coordination:* The division coordinates the FTC's international consumer protection work and helps facilitate international information sharing among consumer protection law enforcers.

- *Operations:* The division administers the core financial, administrative, and litigation support activities of the Bureau. It manages the agency's consumer protection redress activities and coordinates strategic planning and performance measurement.

The International Division of Consumer Protection seeks to promote consumer confidence in the international marketplace. Its activities focus on expanding international cooperation and information sharing through

- Negotiating and implementing bilateral consumer protection cooperation agreements. Agreements exist with consumer protection agencies in Canada, Australia, and the United Kingdom.

- Coordinating participation in the International Marketing Supervision Network (IMSN), an international network of consumer protection law enforcers in 30 countries.

- Coordinating and managing econsumer.gov, a Web site where consumers can file cross-border e-commerce complaints, which can be accessed by consumer protection law enforcers in 15 countries.

- Providing litigation support for enforcement actions with an international component—where wrongdoers, their assets, or their victims are abroad.

- Developing international consumer protection and e-commerce policies that promote consumer confidence while minimizing regulatory burden and promoting growth of the international B2C marketplace.

- Offering international technical assistance to developing countries in building consumer protection frameworks.

The Office of Consumer and Business Education (OCBE) plans and implements public education campaigns for consumers and industry on topics such as fraud, deception, and unfair practices. The OCBE also produces, promotes, and disseminates educational messages and materials to the widest possible audience through multifaceted communications and outreach programs. These efforts involve the use of print, broadcast, and electronic media, the World Wide Web (the OCBE maintains the Web pages of the Bureau of Consumer Protection and the Consumer.gov Web site), special events, and partnerships with government agencies, consumer groups, trade organizations, businesses, and other organizations.

Privately Funded Programs

Privately funded assistance programs are often faith-based, funded through donations channeled through religious organizations. Many private hospitals have foundations that seek funding from donor sources and then provide financial assistance to patients who could not afford them otherwise. St. Jude's Children's Hospital provides care to all patients regardless of ability to pay. It also funds research and health education programs. Habitat for Humanity has been addressing the need for family housing since its inception in 1976, building more than 175,000 homes for low-income families in more than 3,000 communities. Food pantries and clothing donation centers operate from local and regional centers. Many other needs are met through private assistance programs at local, state, regional, national, and international levels.

The challenge for professionals serving families is to identify needs and link people to these existing resources. The Internet has provided access to information and application procedures. Ironically, those most in need of these programs are the least likely to have access to computers or to have training necessary to search, understand, and complete application procedures.

Compulsory Education

This nationally held value has its roots in the belief that an educated citizenry is necessary to maintain a democratic government. Although not specified in the U.S. Constitution, public education was an expectation of the early leaders of this country. What that educational system will look like is left to the individual states, but federal policy and funding link these schools by providing guiding goals, objectives, and policies. Education provides opportunities to individuals and a knowledgeable workforce for employers. Families are impacted on many levels by the availability, quality, and choice of school systems for their children.

HISTORY

As early as the 1640s, inhabitants of what is now Massachusetts allocated some of their meager resources to publicly creating and supporting schools. Schooling at this time in American history resembled the private school patterns of today. Often they were part of local churches and included religious curriculum. In 1827, the Commonwealth of Massachusetts became the first state to make elementary instruction free to all citizens. By 1929, all 50 states, the District of Columbia, and Puerto Rico had enacted some form of compulsory school attendance laws. This form of public education is based on state-level efforts, so the exact requirements for attendance vary between and among states. Nonattendance is often presented as *truancy,* with legal punishment for a child within the age limits of expected attendance who does not meet minimum attendance requirements. Most often the legal ramifications are imposed on the parent or responsible adults as fines and/or imprisonment.

Many argue that the real basis of our contemporary compulsory school expectations stems from the Industrial Revolution. This movement created a high demand for an educated workforce, the reduction of family-centered production, and the emergence of childhood and adolescent protection from unhealthy employment participation. By the 1950s, a common, standardized educational experience became the rule, or the norm. Recent efforts to further standardize curriculum and assessment further illustrate this expectation.

THE FEDERAL LEVEL

Although only about 10% of funding for public education comes from federal money, this financial support is essential for local school systems to operate. At the federal level, there are three important departments interfacing with public schools—the Department of Education, the

Department of Health and Human Services, and the Department of Agriculture. Head Start and Early Head Start are comprehensive child development programs that serve children from birth to age 5, pregnant women, and their families. They are child-focused programs and have the overall goal of increasing the school readiness of young children in low-income families.

The Head Start program is administered by the Head Start Bureau, the Administration on Children, Youth and Families (ACYF), Administration for Children and Families (ACF), Department of Health and Human Services (DHHS). Grants are awarded by the ACF Regional Offices and the Head Start Bureau's American Indian–Alaska Native and Migrant and Seasonal Program Branches directly to local public agencies, private organizations, Indian Tribes, and school systems for the purpose of operating Head Start programs at the community level.

The Head Start program has a long tradition of delivering comprehensive and high-quality services designed to foster healthy development in low-income children. Head Start grantee and delegate agencies provide a range of individualized services in the areas of education and early childhood development: medical, dental, and mental health; nutrition; and parent involvement. In addition, the entire range of Head Start services is responsive and appropriate to each child and family's developmental, ethnic, cultural, and linguistic heritage and experience.

All Head Start programs must adhere to Program Performance Standards. The *Head Start Program Performance Standards* define the services that Head Start Programs are to provide to the children and families they serve. They constitute the expectations and requirements that Head Start grantees must meet. They are designed to ensure that the Head Start goals and objectives are implemented successfully, that the Head Start philosophy continues to thrive, and that all grantee and delegate agencies maintain the highest possible quality in the provision of Head Start services. The Head Start program has enrolled more than 23 million children since it began in 1965.

THE STATE LEVEL

Because public education is not addressed specifically in the Constitution, education of citizens falls within the realm of state governments. Control and coordination of public education within each state usually falls under the jurisdiction of state-level departments of education. These units centralize curriculum, teaching licensure and training, and special education expectations for public school sites across their states. Budgets of these departments are devoted to enhancement of school performance. The connection between federal programs and funds and state schools is also part of the mission of these departments. State taxes also support budgets for these schools, as determined by their legislators and voting constituents.

THE COMMUNITY LEVEL

Public education in the United States operates at the local level. Daily operations, budgeting and financial management, and policymaking begin at this level under the state guidelines. Free attendance for all children in each school district is a right. Administrators, teachers, staff, and parents deliver, monitor, and assess the education of children in their communities. Local school boards create policy and budgets for schools within their jurisdiction. Thus, public education is delivered locally, is coordinated at the state level, and has historically been marginally supported at the federal level.

FAMILY INVOLVEMENT

Parents in the United States do not have a choice about whether to educate their children. They do have options, however. These options are discussed later in this chapter. Parental involvement in education has been the subject of much debate. Some parents choose not to be involved in the educational system and have been accused of "dropping their children off for kindergarten and picking them up at high school graduation." Essentially, parents cannot avoid participation in the process. They are legally obligated to enforce compulsory attendance. Minimally, this would require efforts necessary to get their children to and from the school site as required. It also involves expenditures for necessary clothing, supplies, and fees required for school participation. Realistically, most parents are involved at a much higher level in the education of their children.

In early colonial education, parents were expected to be involved in curriculum selection and monitoring and teacher evaluation. During the early 1900s, schools became more bureaucratized, and school personnel became more professionally organized. This change led to a division of home life and school life, where parents were expected to support what was provided at school in their homes, while leaving the curriculum and teaching decisions to the staff and administrators (Barge & Loges, 2003). The role of parents in the education of their children has made a concentrated swing back toward fuller participation with state and federal laws and as a reflection of the national frustration with school and student performances. Parental involvement, while increasing, still differs between and among social groups. Several studies indicate that low-income minority parents are less involved than higher income nonminority parents. Others dispute those findings by reporting that minority parents have higher levels of participation in some areas and White parents are more involved in other areas due to the worldviews of these parents and what they believe their roles should be in the educational process (Desimone, 1999). When parents choose to be involved, resources necessary to facilitate that decision include time, knowledge, and energy. The perceived return of the investment of those resources must be positive.

Cordry and Wilson (2004) reported that approximately 77.4% of parents are actively involved in their children's education during grades K-5. This involvement decreases to an average of 67.4% of middle-school parents and 56.8% of high school families. These authors also report that active parental involvement has a positive effect on student morale, attitudes, and academic achievement. What, then, accounts for the "dropping out" of parents through the educational process?

Barge and Loges (2003) explored barriers to parental involvement. Low levels of education, socioeconomic status (SES), and their own negative experiences as students in the school systems are identified as factors. Teacher attitudes also negatively impact participation of parents (Epstein, 1992). More than 80% of Americans attend public schools. However, some parents are not convinced that public education is providing their children with appropriate teaching, curriculum, values, or morals. There are alternative routes to meeting their states' compulsory laws.

ALTERNATIVES TO PUBLIC EDUCATION

All children in the United States have the right to public education. Citizens paying taxes at both the federal and state levels are funding these services and facilities. When public education is perceived as less than desired, alternatives are explored. Three categories of alternative schooling are charter schools, home schooling, and private schools.

Charter Schools

The first charter schools were originally public school facilities. Parents and/or other organized groups proposed new, creative alternative curriculums and administration of existing schools that were struggling. Some states agreed to fund these alternative schools with per-student payments, whereas other states do not acknowledge or fund charter schools. Additional funding necessary was obtained through fundraising of the sponsoring parent or community group. States participating in this alternative process continued to monitor and support these schools. Essentially, the state is out-sourcing education of some students to the charter school sponsor groups. Some charter schools have been successful, whereas others have found the funding too difficult to manage.

Home Schooling

The practice of providing education in the home setting has roots in the U.S. pioneer experience. Until enough families settled in any one area and/or transportation methods improved, creating and maintaining common educational facilities did not make sense at any level. Parents assumed the responsibility of teaching basic literacy skills to their children within their homes. Arguably, parental control of their children's education is greatest in this form of instruction. Because the U.S. lawmakers acknowledge a certain level of privacy within parental rights, states do allow parents to provide state-required curriculum in the home setting. The U.S. Department of Education reported that approximately 1 million school-age children were being home-schooled in 2003. This number represented 2.2% of the student population.

The institution responsible for coordination of state schools oversees and grants permission for home schooling. Parents, or whoever is responsible for presenting curriculum, must be approved, and curriculum guidelines and materials are either supplied or approved by this body. This approach to education of children requires high levels of resource dedication, including time, energy, knowledge, space, and materials.

Private Schools

More than 10% of U.S. school-age children attend private schools. These schools do not receive public tax funding for general operations or faculty and staff payrolls. The financial base of these schools is a combination of pupil tuition and foundation funds. Some autonomy exists in private schooling in terms of curriculum and teacher expectations; however, to meet compulsory education requirements, these schools must follow state curriculum and teaching guidelines to some measure. Most private schools are religion-based. Other sponsoring institutions include military, boarding, and prep schools. Beyond the mandated curriculum, these schools are free to include instruction and expectations set forth by their funding sources.

MAKING EDUCATIONAL CHOICES

Families must ensure that children attend state-approved educational institutions or provide instruction in the home setting. The need has been presented by the compulsory education laws. Alternatives to meet that need include public education, private education, charter schools, or home-schooling. A few states also offer parents another choice through school vouchers. Some states allow families to choose alternatives to public education and will allow public funds to be diverted to these alternatives in the form of a voucher to be used for the educational program of their choice. As families evaluate these alternatives, their values, past experiences, and future goals will direct them to the type of education they provide for their children. That decision creates opportunity costs, but also results in educational experiences for the children involved. Parents and their school-age children should continually evaluate this decision and the results of their selection to ensure that the needs of family members are being satisfied. Once such a decision has been made, parents are free to change their minds and move their students to other acceptable educational settings.

Impact of Educational Choices on Family Resources

Knowledge and skills are essential resources that each member of a family contributes to the welfare of the entire group. The expectation of education is to provide and enhance the ability of family members to make good decisions. As children grow physically and cognitively, their ability to contribute to functions within family living increases. Individual families must decide how these new, expanding resources can contribute to overall functioning.

Time, and the management of family time, is greatly impacted by schooling decisions. All formal, out-of-home schooling works within a structured schedule. Many operate on a 9-month annual format, although several utilize a year-round calendar. Weekly and daily schedules resemble workplaces in many ways. Most schools operate on a Monday through Friday format and have a 6- to 7-hour class day.

Supply and Demand: An Application in Education

Compulsory education in the United States creates a large market for education. Public education is available to all children. Private education is accessible only to those who can pay for it or those who qualify for tuition waivers. Core curriculum, guided by the state, is generally similar in both. The quality of the education provided by any two school systems is rarely equal. Even within the public school network, there is disparity between and among publicly funded school sites. As recently as two decades ago, the public school available to children was determined by their place of residence. In many communities, that is still the deciding factor. If a neighborhood school was substandard in the parents' estimation, their choice was to accept the situation or pay tuition for their children to attend private schools.

The demand was guaranteed by law, and the supply of schools was determined by funding available through taxes collected. Quality was the unknown factor; because choices and resources are limited, ensuring equality across all public school sites was impossible. Many economists and others have proposed that parental choice would ultimately raise the level of quality across the board by adding an element of competition to the mix.

Summary

Families living in the United States have many freedoms. Societies, however, strive to protect members, and U.S. citizens must operate within several constraints intended to enhance their quality of life. Funding for large-scale programs and governmental expenses comes from collection of taxes. These tax obligations reduce the amount of resources available to families, but provide other resources important to social goals and family survival. Consumer protection efforts and educational programs directly impact resource acquisition and expenditure of both individuals and families. Family professionals seek to understand and match existing resources to existing needs, while also managing tax obligations and personal accountability.

Questions for Review and Discussion

1. The U.S. income tax system is criticized for being too complicated and for disproportional assessment—the wealthy seem to pay less. How do income, sales, Social Security, and Medicare taxes differ in that respect?

2. The FDA has a delicate balancing act to handle, meeting consumer needs for new, improved medications and foods and ensuring the safety of these new products. Identify three new products currently making news headlines and discuss how the FDA is managing that balance.

3. Who is ultimately responsible for consumer safety, the consumer or the government? Discuss.

4. How are public schools and the business model interdependent? Schedules? Curriculum?

5. What resources do the public schools provide families? What resource needs do they create for families?

Unit IV

Making Choices

The Decision-Making Process

- Recognize existing need(s)
- Identify alternatives to fulfill identified needs
- Evaluate identified alternatives
- Select and implement alternative

  Chapter   9. Managing the Future

  Chapter 10. Communication Within the Decision-Making Process

  Chapter 11. The Individual Within Family Decision Making

- Reflect and evaluate alternative selected

Managing the Future 9

Objectives

- Understand the planning process.
- Explore goal-setting and creation of implementation plans.
- Differentiate between long- and short-term goals and objectives.
- Understand the budgeting process.
- Explore the objectives of financial planning.
- Appreciate the need for family planning for emergencies/crises.

In preparing for battle I have always found that plans are useless, but planning is indispensable.

—Dwight D. Eisenhower

Decisions are worthless unless they are implemented. Once a decision is made, individuals or family units must complete a new series of operations and choices. They must develop a plan of action.

The Omega family has decided that their credit card debt is too large. They have reached an agreement that involves paying off current debt and reducing their dependence on the use of credit from now on. This type of decision requires long-term commitment and a strong plan designed to change their behavior.

Caren Bellows, a college senior, has decided that she needs to strengthen her resume before she begins looking for a job after graduation. Her advisor met with her, and together they decided that increasing Caren's campus activities would help prepare her for social expectations in her field of marketing. Caren plans to join two student organizations this semester and contribute 2 to 3 hours per week to a local soup kitchen. This plan is short term and focused.

Everyone is involved in the short-term planning process. This behavior is essential to human survival—meeting basic needs. Long-term planning is a universal trait across cultures and generations. However, cultural differences in how an individual believes he or she controls the future impact his or her willingness to engage in long-term planning and implementation of those types of strategies (see Chapter 1). Family resource management, as a process, is highly dependent on the planning process.

Goals, Objectives, and Standards

A **goal** is an end that one tries to attain. It is something that one wishes to reach or accomplish within a timeframe determined by the individual. **Objectives** are subsets of goals (Palomba & Banta, 1999). For instance, if the goal is to increase healthfulness to enhance quality of life, objectives within that goal may include weight management, exercise expectations, and nutritional changes. Objectives are more specific and measurable than the overall goal, acting as checkpoints to enable one to measure progress toward goal achievement.

Setting, pursuing, and achieving goals contribute to personal growth and satisfaction with life (Griffith & Graham, 2004). Goals help individuals guide and direct their behavior toward completion of tasks and objectives. Within the process of goal attainment are other tasks, such as self-regulation and problem-solving skills. Goals reflect basic values, attitudes, and beliefs. Goals are also bound by an individual's understanding and experience. Education is often cited as a goal of new immigrants. For parents from backgrounds of poverty and illiteracy, this may be structured elementary and high school opportunities for their children. For parents who are graduates of higher education institutions, a bachelor's degree may be part (an objective) of a larger goal—graduate degrees for their children. This does not mean that both sets of parents do not have high goals and expectations. It merely reflects the reality that each family has available based on knowledge of options and experience in the educational systems.

There are many ways to categorize goals. **Short-term goals** generally can be accomplished in less than 3 months. **Intermediate goals** will be accomplished in less than a year, and **long-range goals** usually require more than 1 year to complete.

Pamela agreed to work 3 extra hours per week between Thanksgiving and Christmas to make enough money to buy holiday presents for her family and friends. She is also spending more time studying to raise her final GPA before graduation in May. After graduation, she begins specialized study to become a radiologist. She has many goals of different duration operating at the same time.

Societal goals are reflected in rules and expectations within larger social groups. Reducing dependence of Americans on foreign oil is a goal expressed by the government and ecologists, alike. **Family goals** provide motivation for family members to work together to bring about positive changes for individuals within the group and for the family unit as a whole. **Personal goals** are specific to the individual. When goals are categorized by source, there will always be some overlap.

Sergio is a first-generation college graduate with several good job offers. He has reached an important personal goal. His entire family shares this success; however, his parents and siblings have sacrificed along the way to support this process. His promising career also meets the criteria of a societal goal, as he will move out of poverty and will be prepared to help his family do the same.

Recognizing that individuals juggle several goals simultaneously, it is important to understand how they manage to focus, prioritize, and endure. Goals must be reasonable, understood, measurable, and specific.

Kim wants to advance in her place of employment. Specifically, she wants to become an assistant manager and move up on the pay scale. A reasonable goal would be to focus on the next, logical position in the existing chain of command. She will want to involve her superiors in the process, so all that will be impacted by her goal are aware of her ambitions and how they may be able to assist her efforts, as well as how her personal goal might impact their positions. A couple of progressive steps should be agreed on—quarterly reviews and professional development opportunities. She will know she accomplished this goal when she is awarded the promotion and pay increase.

Family members responsible for or impacted by goals should be included in the creation of those goals. The level of acceptance and shared responsibility for achieving group goals increases when individuals involved feel their voices were heard in the decision-making process and their needs were considered by those ultimately setting them. Goals, and the objectives within them, provide direction, an element of control, and a shared understanding of where a family is currently operating, where it desires to be in the future, and how members of that family can contribute to the unit's success. Attainment of goals provides satisfaction and a sense of accomplishment, enhancing the life experience of family members and encouraging the successful completion of other goals.

Standards or perceived acceptable levels of adequacy within a family will also impact goals. For some students, a passing grade is sufficient. For others, only excellent grades are acceptable. Standards develop slowly over time, and family standards reflect a multigenerational developmental process. Young adults often face the task of realigning their standards of living, moving from an established home, fully furnished and functional, into their first independent apartments or shared housing. As the standard of living for middle-class Americans has continued to rise over the last three generations, young adults in those households have grown accustomed to high levels of comfort and even excess. Televisions, microwaves, and climate control are expectations, instead of options. They will experience discomfort when their own resources cannot support that level of living. Often this leads to overdependence on credit and the pledging of huge sums of future earnings for immediate gratification and enjoyment.

The Planning Process

Many decisions are complex in nature, requiring focused planning to fully implement. The decision to stop smoking requires both goal setting and a plan of action. Whether the method employed to accomplish that goal is to cease smoking immediately or approach it slowly and methodically, deliberate action is necessary. The planning process begins with a decision. This decision must be analyzed in terms of activities necessary to fulfill the inherent goal. The objectives, or key events, are plotted in terms of time and difficulty, and tasks are assigned and agreed on by those involved in the process. Some decisions are completely under the control of one individual, but in many family decisions, there is a need to delegate or assign specific tasks to certain members to complete the entire process. Those decisions and development of a time framework result in a plan—formal or informal. Implementation and eventual evaluation of the plan, regardless of whether it is completed, complete the planning process.

A plan is a course of action created to move a decision forward—toward goal accomplishment. Each plan is actually a set of multiple decisions and

> **The Planning Process**
>
> - Identification of a situation that requires action
> - Formulation of a plan
> - Implementation of that plan
> - Evaluation of plan's success or failure

actions arranged in sequence or steps. As plans formalize, **schedules** emerge. Examples of schedules include lists, timetables, calendars, electronic scheduling devices, and computer programs, all utilized to plot the way from beginning to end of tasks and appointments. Schedules depend on **sequencing**, or a mental process of laying out activities and resources needed to complete any particular task or goal. The complexity of these activities determines how much time, energy, and thought are required. Preparing a meal requires gathering of foodstuffs and equipment and a purposeful sequencing of tasks. Vegetables must be cleaned and often cut into edible pieces before they are cooked. Water must be drained from pasta before sauces are added. An electric coffee maker must be filled with water and ground coffee beans, and then the button to begin brewing can be activated. Doing any of these steps out of sequence may result in failure. Writing a research paper involves gathering of sources, organization of ideas, and then the actual writing or word processing of the actual paper. Sequencing is key to the planning process, whether deliberate and conscious, or habitual and subconscious.

Some actions require complete dedication and concentration. Completing a high-level algebraic equation or properly aligning a domino display are examples of such activities. Other activities may require less concentration, but limit the types of other activities you can be involved in simultaneously. Many activities require such low levels of attention that they can be done at the same time. **Independent activities** are unrelated to one another. In the morning, you can brush your teeth, comb your hair, and dress in any order you prefer. None of these activities is dependent on the other. **Interdependent activities** are more time and sequence specific. One activity within a series of activities must be completed before another in interdependent situations. You must obtain the title to an automobile before you can license and insure it. You must license and insure it to drive it legally. Ownership, licensing, and insuring are interdependent activities in that situation.

Many daily activities require little focus and allow us to **multitask**. You may do your homework with the TV and radio turned on and in the presence of friends and family. You might drive your car through traffic while conversing on your cell phone and eating fast food. The ability to multitask does increase our ability to accomplish more in less time. The quality of the end result and the safety of such behavior are questionable, however. Rubinstein, Meyer, and Evans (2001) found that, in all types of tasks, participants in their research lost time when they had to switch from one task to another. These time costs increased with the complexity of the tasks. They suggest that individuals go through two distinct stages when switching between tasks. *Goal shifting* involves the decision and action necessary to switch, and *rule activation* is the process needed to switch from the rules of the first task to the rules of the second.

Josh is watching his 2-year-old niece, talking to his girlfriend on the phone, and playing computer Solitaire. He is focused on explaining to his girlfriend why he will be late picking her up this evening when he hits a snag on the game. He deliberately shifts his focus to the game (goal shifting) and pulls up the rules and past strategies he has stored in his memory (rule activation). This half second of time lost to task switching can be critical if his niece has discovered an unprotected wall socket at the same time.

Decisions that have been repeated many times or those with little risk or investment involved are often implemented by one individual utilizing intuition and past experience. The household is running low on toilet paper. Any of the family members capable of purchasing supplies can implement the decision to purchase more. Toilet paper is a frequent purchase, so preferences do not need to be examined each and every time. It is a low-expense purchase, so pricing is not a high-level concern, especially in cases of emergency.

In group situations, such as families, brainstorming may be implemented to create a plan of action. Multiple members are asked to generate possible courses of action to address the decision. This approach to planning ensures diverse possibilities and creative options, but it is not an efficient approach. A large number of possible plans will need to be sorted, evaluated, ranked, and then decided on. When risk is high and time is available, families may find brainstorming to be both useful and effective.

Abbie has always wanted to travel internationally. As a senior in high school, she is eligible for the student exchange program in her district. She has an opportunity to spend the next semester in Spain. Because Abbie's mother is a single parent with two other children, Abbie's absence for that length of time will disrupt three other family members' lives. The family sits down to discuss how Abbie's dream can be realized with the least disruption to everyone else. One issue is how to transport her brother Jackson from middle school to home. Abbie has been able to pick him up in the family car each day and stay with him until their mother returns from work. Jackson suggests that he walk or ride his bike the 10 blocks each day. Mom's idea is to utilize the school's after-hours program, allowing Jackson to stay at school an extra 2 hours to work on assignments and participate in scheduled activities. Tenille, the oldest sister, offers to postpone her next semester of cosmetology coursework and work part-time instead to allow her to cover the late afternoon needs. While Mom's idea would probably rise to the top by itself, this process of brainstorming illuminates important information about both Jackson's and Tenille's needs. Jackson is seeking ways to become more independent and supportive within his family. Tenille is possibly not convinced that she is pursuing the right professional program of study. Abbie's absence will be handled, all family members were able to show support of her opportunity through offers of sacrifice, and important individual needs were expressed.

Obviously, brainstorming has advantages and disadvantages. It requires time, discussion, and teamwork. Not all ideas generated will be useful or practical. However, by allowing more members of the group to participate in the decision-making process, a higher level of agreement and commitment will exist when the final decision is made. This approach to decision-making also provides a higher level of creativity and originality.

TYPES OF PLANS

Many plans never reach a formalized, written state. They are merely stored in our mind or shared verbally with others. The probability of success, or completion of the goals and objectives within a plan, increases with the degree of formality of the plan. When a plan is made public, it is more likely to succeed than if it is held in secrecy. Once the specifics are announced to others, a level of accountability emerges. Informal or ad-hoc plans are created by individuals in all of their pursuits. Any purposeful action requires some level of planning. Structured and formal plans are most often used by multiple people who are working together to achieve a common goal. Examples include military strategies, career planning, and estate planning. It is common for less formal plans to be created as abstract ideas and remain in that form as they are maintained and put to use. More formal plans, although initially created with and as an abstract thought, are likely to be written down, drawn up, or otherwise stored in a form that is accessible to multiple people across time and space. This allows more reliable collaboration in the execution of the plan.

Jaime is going to the theater with friends. All four individuals are traveling from different parts of the city to meet at the theater prior to the curtain call. Jaime has never taken the subway system from his place of work to the theater district, so he accesses a printed map of the subway system, enters the particular stations and lines he will need to access into his PDA, informs his boss that he will be leaving a few minutes early, and sets off. While making a connection, he grabs a snack from a vending machine. His travel plans are more formal than his eating plan, but both are successfully achieved.

A **directional plan** moves an individual or group along a path toward completion of a goal. Career management is one example. To become an architect, you must first complete secondary school. Then you must complete an undergraduate degree that is compatible to a graduate degree in architecture. After receiving the graduate degree, you must complete supervised work experience for a certain period of time, take and pass licensing tests, and eventually present yourself to the public as a fully licensed professional.

Worldview

There are many reasons that people choose to immigrate to the United States. Push and pull factors include economic, social, and political motivations. Push factors are those that cause people in other countries to feel that they would be better off to leave the country because of low pay, lack of employment, underemployment, or the absence of family members who have chosen to leave before them. Exposure to endemic violence, persecution, and oppression are also push factors. Pull factors are those that give the immigrant the sense that the new country is pulling them away from their original country and may include the possibility of higher earnings, securing employment, joining family members, and a hope that they will have a better future than they envision in their current situation.

Scanning newspapers and analyzing political speeches illuminate three common myths about immigrants from Mexico and Central America: (a) These immigrants plan to stay in the United States permanently; (b) Latino immigrants drain public benefits and make little, if any, economic contributions; and (c) Spanish-speaking immigrants refuse to learn English and are determined not to assimilate into U.S. culture.

Schaefer (2007) found that Latino immigrants send a great deal of their earnings back to family members in their country of origin. He estimates that this equates to billions of dollars of earnings; however, he suggests that even those amounts are not necessarily a drain to the U.S. economy when the human capital represented in those wages is considered. The production of goods and services by these workers is fueling the exchange within the U.S. economy. This investment in family members still in their native country implies a continued commitment to their country of origin, suggesting a temporary mindset, rather than a permanent change of residence. Many surveys have indicated that at least one half of Mexican immigrants hope to return to Mexico at some future point (Lacy, 2007). Moving to another country to meet basic needs of their families does not necessarily equate to the abandonment of generations of history and personal investment in their native countries. Many Americans have moved to Europe and the Middle East to capitalize on high-paying, temporary kinds of employment without intending to permanently migrate to those locations.

Immigrants working in the United States are contributing to the economic base through labor and the tax system. Employers are required to collect and submit income tax to the Internal Revenue Service during the payroll process. If a worker is using a fraudulent identification number, the money is still deposited into the government's coffers. To draw public assistance, individuals must provide necessary documentation for qualification. Illegal workers and their families cannot readily access these types of programs (Lacy, 2007).

The use of English by newly immigrated workers is a much discussed and highly debated topic. Survival in the workplace and marketplace requires at least a rudimentary knowledge of the prevailing language. Lacy (2007) found that the majority of immigrants in her survey were actively working to improve their English speaking skills.

The findings dispelled four common myths about Latinos.

As presented in Chapter 1, within the discussion of worldview, groups of people differ in their beliefs about social relationships, management of their futures, and behaviors that are important to their groups. U.S. citizens are quick to attribute their cultural beliefs about job/career goals and materialistic acquisition to those who immigrate into their communities. Ties to and feelings for one's homeland are central to one's identity. Extended family relationships do not dissolve over geographical distances. Immigrating, whether legal or illegal in nature, is a decision that requires intense planning and complex family decision making. Priorities, goals, and objectives are driving forces. The demand to meet basic family needs, not necessarily to improve personal standards of living, is a strong motivational force.

Experienced planners know that plans must be **adaptive** to succeed. Rarely does an individual or family operate in a climate of complete control. Unexpected and uncontrollable events can make the original plan unworkable. These disruptions may be minor and require moderate changes, or they may be so dramatic that they require complete abandonment of the plan. **Contingency plans** are alternative plans created simultaneously with the original plan, anticipating the possibility of problems. The degree of risk and the importance of successful goal achievement determine whether contingency plans will be part of the planning process.

Melia is 16 and is looking for a summer job. She applies at a fast-food restaurant, a dog day-care site, and the local library. The fast-food job would allow her to work flexible hours, but if they don't offer her a job, her friend's mother owns the dog day care and her aunt works at the library. With two backup plans, Melia will probably have a summer job.

Proactive plans purposefully strive to avoid surprises and crises. They are designed with forethought and consideration of anticipated events. Proactive planners are controlling a situation by causing something to happen, rather than waiting to respond to it after it happens. Anticipating financial needs in retirement, a working adult may decide to contribute to an employer's retirement plan to supplement the Social Security payment expected. Although there is no way to know how much he or she will actually need to sustain the standard of living expected after retirement, having more money is obviously a better situation than not having enough.

Reactive planning is spontaneous, without forethought. These types of plans are almost always created quickly in response to an unwelcome event. A family living from one paycheck to another will be forced to react quickly to loss of employment or housing. They will have to lower their standards because they have no resources to draw on. They may decide to seek aid from other family members or friends or access public programs designed to help in such emergencies. A sudden total lack of income will force immediate action.

When a family engages in directional, purposeful planning processes in proactive ways, they are practicing **strategic planning** methods. Strategic planning often incorporates contingency planning and continual problem solving, too. Utilizing a strategy is necessary in high-risk situations, such a military combat, medical treatment for chronic and life-threatening diseases, and severe social crises. The generation of alternatives is especially important for decisions involving strategic issues (Tan & Platts, 2006). Because families are constrained by information available to them, experiential knowledge, and time and cost restrictions (Harrison, 1999), it is essential that they seek input from other sources when creating strategic plans.

Don has just had a mild heart attack. His physicians determine that there is severe blockage in two of his arteries. One form of treatment is less invasive than the other proposed, but possibly not as effective. Don's family has had little experience with such an illness and no family members are medical professionals. Because the family's medical insurance provides monetary support, the family seeks a second opinion from another medical specialist. She proposes that Don undergo the less invasive procedure at a leading medical facility. If, in her opinion and those of her colleagues, that procedure is not completely successful, Don will have the second procedure while still on the original operating table. In essence, she has proposed a contingency plan. Prior to the surgery, Don will be participating in drug therapy to enhance his chances of survival and recovery. After surgery he will begin a regime of medications, exercise, and behavior modification to further enhance the medical procedure. This plan includes elements of high risk, contingency planning, and proactive behaviors—all essential in this strategic planning process.

SCHEDULES

A plan may involve formal delineation of who, what, when, and where in a scheduled format. Families typically juggle multiple schedules of members as efficiently and effectively as possible. Utilizing lists, calendars with manual entry systems, and electronic scheduling devices, parents manage to get children to school, activities, and other social obligations. Adults work out ways to divide transportation and supervision duties while maintaining employment schedules and household management tasks.

This type of schedule is a written, detailed plan of activities, locations, and timeframes necessary to facilitate the completion of tasks. Schedules may also be in electronic or even mental format when an individual is capable of planning and remembering information effectively. The level of complexity and the number of people and activities requiring coordination will determine how formal a schedule will need to be to facilitate completion of all tasks desired.

Computer and Internet use has revolutionized the scheduling process. Hand-held devices, commonly referred to as personal digital assistants (PDAs), can be programmed to record appointments, remind the user of upcoming appointments, and maintain records of standing appointments across large time spans. Innovations in electronic devices, in terms of size and battery capacity, are already making PDAs obsolete. Many of these functions have become part of cell phone technology. Regularly scheduled credit payments, such as mortgage and utility bills, can be handled electronically by scheduling and authorizing them through a bank's computer network. Paychecks and payments from government programs can be scheduled to automatically be deposited from the payment source into your checking account.

Before leaving this discussion about the scheduling process, it is important to address a contemporary problem among American families— overscheduling. Parental work schedules, children's school schedules, extracurricular activities, and after-school lessons all must be coordinated for busy families. Dunn, Kinney, and Hofferth (2001) report that preadolescent children are spending more and more time in structured activities such as organized sports, private lessons, and paid leisure activities. Their parents encourage and support this participation in extracurricular activities because they believe it provides their children with opportunities to discover and enhance important lifelong skills.

Lareau (2007) found that working mothers were those largely responsible for scheduling and chauffeuring their children's activities. Hofferth (2003) found that the mother's education level is positively related to the number of activities her children juggle. If overscheduling of children is determined by researchers to be a problem, the college-educated women will have to be the first to set the limits (Lareau, 2007).

BUDGETING

A **budget** is another form of planning useful to families. It is a statement of monetary planning that defines income expected and expenses anticipated over a period of time. Most families with adult wage earners focus budgeting 1 month at a time. When used in conjunction with accurate record-keeping, budgets enable families to identify unnecessary spending and adjust expenses to better meet family goals and objectives. The initial creation of a budget requires gathering of information about past income and expenses. Records, receipts, cancelled checks, and other paper trails provide historical information important to budget creation.

Budgets are usually divided into two large categories—income and expenses. **Income** includes the salary or wages family members collect on a regular basis. Salaries are most often paid to professionals and managers. Wages are determined for workers who earn a certain amount for each hour or part of an hour they work.

Allison is a nurse. She earns $22 per hour at the local hospital. Her weekly gross pay is $880 or approximately $3,520 each month. She is limited to 40 hours each week unless her employer is willing to pay her overtime compensation—$33 per hour (time and a half). Stacia is the human resource manager at the same hospital. She is on a salary schedule earning $4,000 per month. There are no automatic overtime requirements for a salaried position. Allison may actually earn more per month if she works overtime occasionally.

When creating a family budget, it is necessary to gather income information from all working members who are expected to contribute to the budget plan. Weekly budgets can be created, but monthly budgets are more practical and less redundant. After adding all expected income, the **gross family income** is entered onto a budget form, paper or computer versions. Gross income is money earned before taxes and other scheduled deductions are subtracted. Refer back to Chapter 7 for more information on payroll taxes. Because these deductions will be made and the liability already exists, that money will not be available to spend. The amount of money available to spend after all deductions have been made is referred to as the **net income**. Other income that may be added to this section of the budget would include interest payments from savings accounts, payments received from federal programs such as Social Security survivor benefits, and qualifying payments from governmental sources for food stamps and other support programs. After all probable income amounts are determined and added together, the expendable income for a family has been determined.

Expenses must be determined to compare with the income calculated. There are two distinctive categories of expenses—variable and fixed. **Variable expenses** will not be exactly the same from one period to another. They include automobile expenses, clothing purchases, food, entertainment, gifts, medical, and utilities. **Fixed expenses** do not vary remarkably from one payment period to the next. They include mortgage payments or rent, automobile loans, child care, insurance, and some taxes. Together these expenses represent the outflow of money from the household for each budgeted period. Fixed expenses are easier to determine, but reviewing past expenditures in the variable category can provide a dependable way to estimate future payments for similar products and services.

When the total income is compared to the total anticipated expenses, a budget surplus or deficit will result. When there is a surplus, or more money available than required, the family will decide how to allocate the excess. It can be used to pay down large debts, support wish lists of family members, or be invested for future use. It is important to plan how surplus money will be allocated. Without a formalized plan known to key players in the family, this money may be used in ways that could eventually harm the family.

If a family has a surplus, it is important to consider the following:

- Have any expenses been underestimated?
- Has income been overestimated?
- Could this extra money be used to strengthen the family's economic position?

If a deficit emerges, consider these possibilities:

- Have any expenses been overestimated?
- Has income been underestimated?
- Are family goals and standards of living too high?
- Have all possible sources of income been identified?

Budgeting is a process, not a one-time event. Many families find budgeting tedious and constraining. Others practice quasibudgeting, recording income in their checkbooks, subtracting each and every payment in that same record, and then using reactive management as the money is depleted before expenses have all been paid or making unplanned purchases if a surplus appears toward the end of the payroll period.

A great deal of research has been conducted on family budgets and expenditures. Johnson, Rogers, and Tan (2001) reviewed 100 years of family budgeting in the United States (Table 9.1). The information collected revealed that the purpose of collecting these data has changed over time. In the first decade of the 20th century, family living conditions, including income and expenses, were explored to investigate the condition of women and child workers. Standards of living—minimum and fair—were determined at that time. After World War I, information was gathered to determine the impact of rapidly rising prices on working families. Terms like *sufficiency of food, respectable clothing, sanitary housing,* and *minimum essential sundries* were new standards set.

Table 9.1   Budget Categories and Average Expenditures by Families

Expenditure Category	Amount	Percent Share 1998
Total family budget	$41,487	
Food	6,657	16.0
Housing	14,648	35.3
Apparel	1,630	4.0
Transportation	6,697	16.1
Health care	1,979	4.8
Entertainment	2,480	6.0
Personal care	357	.9
Reading	190	.5
Education	470	1.1
Tobacco	383	.9
Miscellaneous	769	1.9
Personal insurance and pensions	4,483	10.8
Cash contributions	476	1.1

Source: From "A Century of Family Budgets in the United States," by D. S. Johnson, J. M. Rogers, and L. Tan, May 2001, *Monthly Labor Review*, p. 30. Copyright © 2001 by Monthly Labor Review. Reprinted with permission.

In response to the devastation to the American economy brought about by the depression period of the 1930s, two budget types were proposed. A maintenance budget met minimum need, but below standard conditions. The emergency budget was proposed as a way to cut the maintenance budget with the least amount of harm to family functioning. By the end of World War II, the economy was rebounding. Maintenance and subsistence levels were no longer the issue. Tax issues surfaced as money was raised to pay for the war. Congress was concerned that low-income families were being unfairly tapped for tax revenue. Efforts were made to determine a cost of living scale for analysis. From that time forward, the government has collected data periodically and has reported these findings as descriptive budgets of average households. The information gathered provides contemporary families with guidelines to compare their expenditures, providing important insights into their personal spending habits in relation to others.

Williams, Rosen, Hudman, and O'Malley (2004) focused attention on the challenges for low-income family budgets in recent years. Family interviews were conducted in three U.S. cities exploring work, spending patterns, financial challenges, priorities, and health care. They report that nationally, low-income families spend 7 out of 10 dollars on basic living expenses, including housing, transportation, and food. Income declined during 2003 due to a lagging economy. Family members reported working overtime and multiple jobs to make ends meet. One strategy identified was that of rotating bills, paying the most important first and paying portions of bills instead of complete balances if necessary. Many families, even those with insurance, reported large unpaid medical bills. These bills eventually result in bad credit ratings and insurance problems. Families struggling financially are more likely to lack health insurance, and thus seek health care only in emergency situations.

Family Financial Planning

Chances are that most of your future goals will, in some way, involve monetary resources. American social ideals revolve around many materialistic acquisitions—cars, homes, and possessions. As an increasingly mobile population with travel and leisure opportunities more of an expectation than a luxury for middle and upper income groups, it is important for adults to realize the importance of financial planning from an early age. In an environment of spending and credit usage, the value of saving money may be blurred for many. Important at any age, it is essential that good financial management begin early. If you begin saving just $33 a month right now, in 47 years, you could have over $1 million (assuming a 12% interest rate per year). Of course $1 million will not provide the same amount of goods and services in 47 years that it would today, but it could help replace your income once you retire!

Family needs change over the life course. Although a discussion of typical families across the life course is problematic due to the diversity of family compositions in contemporary society, there are periods of time where certain types of purchases and financial planning commonly occur (Table 9.2). During the first three decades of adulthood, two primary goals are explored and implemented: personal career or working life expectations and family formation.

Young adults are expected to be productive in American society, so career preparation and immediate employment are expectations. Education is an objective for many, intended to prepare them for initial employment and advancement opportunities in the future. The economy, health, family obligations, and other uncontrollable factors can have positive or negative effects on one's progress. From ages 20 to 50, adults typically accumulate a base of wealth to support their current needs and plan for future needs. At the same time, many individuals create their own family units and become independent of their original family group.

Table 9.2   Family Financial Life Cycle

Stage One: Early Adulthood to Middle Age
• Choose to remain single, marry, or form alternative family structure • Initiate long-term savings for future goals • Determine and fulfill insurance needs • Purchase a home • Plan career
Stage Two: Preretirement
• Adjust retirement planning if necessary • Create an estate plan • Adjust insurance to meet evolving needs • Establish retirement living plan
Stage Three: Retirement
• Reap retirement finances accumulated • Adjust to family changes (widowhood, family changes)

Photo 9.1   Moving a child into her next life stage is hard even when parents have planned for years.

Source: © Matt Rainey/Star Ledger/Corbis.

This experience in the United States often includes cohabitation, marriage, divorce, and remarriage. Occasionally widowhood is an unexpected experience. The number of dependents or children, partners, and parents one must provide for may vary greatly during these decades, or an individual may choose to remain single and independent.

Careers typically peak after the mid-50s are reached. In the past, this time was focused on approaching retirement, disengaging from the workplace, and developing plans for leisure activities. With the increasing life expectancy, it may be unrealistic to continue this pattern. A female retiring at age 65 can expect to live for at least 15 more years. The fastest growing segment of the population is 80 years of age and older. Can the economic system afford to move those over the age of 65 out of the employment sector? Do citizens want to leave businesses and careers they have worked to establish while they are still vital and healthy?

Acquisition of material goods (assets) follows patterns across a family life course as well. During family formation, housing, transportation, and the expenses of raising children place a large burden on income providers. Those choosing to parent may face the financial burden of college just as their careers peak and stabilize. Financial support may be required for aging parents, also. Downsizing housing at or near retirement age is a trend identified in recent decades, as is the purchase of secondary housing in retirement communities or resort areas. The concept of "active adults" is driving the housing market into new areas of development to meet the expected needs of those adults between retirement age and the new old age.

Financial planning in terms of investment savings has also followed patterns across the family life course. Many employers offer retirement savings plans to their workforce. This creates a large pool of young workers with early savings patterns. Those without employee-sponsored plans can purposefully invest in independent saving plans, but that group is much less likely to actually begin saving early in their careers. Tax and estate planning (see Chapter 12) has usually emerged between 40 and 60 years of age.

Reality Check

Eileen left her small hometown at the age of 19. It was during World War II, and she found employment as an office manager with a national brewery in the Pacific Northwest. She secured housing in a relatively safe neighborhood.

I found a one-bedroom flat on the third floor of a newer apartment building just eight bus stops away from my office. I didn't need a car, and my weekly paychecks more than covered my living expenses. It was a crazy time. Young men were rare, most in the service, but all of us working girls liked to party and we had a great time!

Eileen remained single for her entire life. She had a few steady men friends, but never felt the need to marry. At the age of 36, she met a man who had just lost his wife to cancer. They became a couple, but never married, and both maintained separate living quarters.

I lived in the same apartment for 55 years! The landlord wasn't very happy with me the last 20 years because rent caps were

(Continued)

(Continued)

instituted and he couldn't raise my rent as high as the market would allow. I worked for 25 years at the brewery and then for 35 years at the airplane factory—both nice office-type jobs. My bank account and retirement savings grew. Finally, at 79, I decided to retire and enjoy what was left of my life. Barton's health had gotten very poor, and his children wanted to move him 500 miles away into a care home. That would have broken my heart and his, so I moved into his house to take care of him. My nieces and nephews helped me move my things from that old apartment. I had so much junk to get rid of!

Eileen took care of Barton for 3 years. One day, when a niece hadn't heard from her in a while, a family friend was asked to check up on the two of them. He found Eileen in a diabetic coma and Barton in a state of shock. Important care decisions had to be made by both families. Because they were never married, Eileen could not make decisions for Barton's health care. His daughter moved him to southern California to be in a care home near her. Eileen's niece moved her back to that small town Eileen had fled so many years before.

I planned and saved for my retirement, but when it came down to it, I couldn't take care of myself after all. I miss my friends out there and I really miss Barton. I don't regret any of my life, though. It was a crazy time and I really lived it up good!

Retirement planning is an important activity for everyone. Although it is impossible to predict which relationships will continue in one's late adulthood, many adults plan for retirement and aging with certain family members and friends as expected sources of support. Choosing to remain single, or to marry and not to have children, eliminates spouses and/or children as possible sources of assistance in later life. Quality of life is not necessarily sacrificed with those decisions, however. Financial planning and solid legal documentation can ensure that one's personal needs will be fulfilled regardless.

Although the life course just discussed is a firmly held concept, it is not as common as believed. Poverty, chronic health conditions, and economic uncertainty play havoc on the lives of many Americans. Financial planning and budgeting are time and energy intensive, and many adults fail to set or follow original plans once they are created. When this happens, their financial future is dependent on life circumstances. To avoid this type of uncontrolled dependency, individuals and families need to be committed to financial planning and implementation.

Creating the Financial Plan

Individuals or couples need to start the planning process with a fresh perspective and an understanding of the flexibility required in long-term planning. One inherent goal of financial planning is management for worst-case scenarios. To expect the unexpected is a difficult concept for many to grasp. The odds that crises will occur in any family across a long period of time are high. Illness, unemployment, death, and economic crises are common experiences across generations. A plan creates alternatives and available financial resources to enable a family to work through these crises and move forward.

Expected expenses, such as college, travel, long-term care, and home buying, require the accumulation of wealth or savings over time. Meeting these anticipated needs requires strategic planning approaches and contingency arrangements. Retirement needs may seem too distant to motivate young families to plan, but everyone is encouraged to be proactive. Even if the Social Security funds are available several years from now, they are intended only as a supplement, not as full replacement of income. Actively managing the tax liability over a family's life course is also essential. Families need to keep as much of the assets they accumulate over time as possible to meet future needs while balancing their tax responsibilities.

A general understanding of financial investment and insurance management is necessary for all participating in long-term financial planning. It is important to recognize when savings and investments require professional guidance; however, it is important to remain actively involved in your family's savings plan. No one cares more about your money than you do! Be aware and alert.

As with all plans, it is best to begin identifying goals. These goals may be primarily long-term, short-term, or a mixture. Common financial goals for families include

- accumulation of an emergency fund
- eliminating current debt
- saving money for a down payment on a home
- creating a college fund
- funding home improvements
- financing a pregnancy and birth
- setting aside money for retirement

It is not uncommon for a single family to have multiple goals. It is important to keep the goals separate in nature, however, because certain types of investments are better for long-term than for short-term goals. It is also essential to realize and appreciate the fact that as goals are met, new ones will replace them. The life course is always presenting new challenges and redefining family needs.

Goals require plans of action. Each individual and family plan will be unique, reflecting the values and motivation associated with the particular goal. If creating the goal seems overwhelming, it may be helpful to employ a professional financial planner. The trade-off between the time spent studying and gathering data and the fees paid to such professionals must be carefully considered. Professionally developed or personally crafted, there are characteristics of good financial plans. These include *flexibility, liquidity, protection, and tax efficiency.*

The plan must be flexible enough to respond to changes in family needs and unforeseen crises. *Gresham's Law of Planning* states that short-term emergencies rise in priority, taking attention away from long-term goals.

Gerard and Petra have a special fund set aside for the eventual purchase of a condominium in a trendy part of the city. Every month they contribute $500 to that fund. This month Gerard accidentally broke the sliding glass door of their apartment. The couple decided to apply next month's contribution toward the door replacement.

Life is unpredictable, and families must remain flexible to deal with the curves they are thrown. Plans that are too rigid are not conducive to real-life experience and, thus, are doomed to fail.

Although it may seem responsible to secure savings, to avoid temptation, every family needs access to extra funds in times of emergency or temporary adjustments. **Liquidity** refers to the accessibility of funds when they are needed.

Troy was serious about buying a new car when he finished his initial job training in 2 years. He put $500 in 6-month certificates of deposit from every monthly paycheck. When his roommate left abruptly, Troy was stuck paying the entire monthly rent for 3 months while he searched for another roommate. He had already put $2,000 away for the car, but the first CD would not mature for another 2 months. If he withdrew that $500, he would lose up to $50 as a penalty for early withdrawal. He had to borrow $1,000 to meet his rental obligation.

Individuals and families need a certain level of emergency funding available, either in cash or easily liquidated savings plans. Once that fund is large enough to provide security, longer-term savings and riskier investments can be explored.

Although catastrophies are rarer than TV and movie scripts lead us to believe, they do happen. Risk management is fully discussed in Chapter 12, but it is important to include mention of insurance in this discussion of financial planning. Beyond the emergency funds available, individuals and families should have insurance protection in cases of large disastrous events, such as fire, major illness or disability, and death. Premium costs for these types of insurance must be budgeted carefully, and the rate of premiums must be considered in terms of affordability and risk minimization.

Rocky and Maddie are purchasing an engagement ring. The retailer offers insurance coverage in the event of loss. The annual premium for this insurance is $100. The young couple is on a tight budget. That amount of money would require cutting other expenses. Is it necessary? Would that $100 be better spent on renter's insurance or enhancement of a life insurance policy?

Tax liability is an essential part of citizenship. It is also an important consideration in financial planning. Many types of interest earned on investments are taxable. Some are not taxable. Investors need to ensure that their money is earning the maximum amount after taxes and inflation are accounted for. There may be certain times and circumstances where saving money is less profitable than spending it.

You have $10,000 from an inheritance. Your TV is not working anymore. If you invest that money in a savings account that yields 5% annually and you are in a high tax bracket, you may pay 30% of the interest in income taxes [$500 − 150 (tax) = 350 (real earnings)]. If, after a year, the cost of replacing that TV has risen from $1,000 to $1,500, you would have made a better decision to buy the TV, rather than investing the total inheritance.

Mortgage insurance is deductible in personal income tax formulas. When interest rates are low, it may be more financially sound to invest in real estate than in stocks, bonds, or certificates of deposit. Gains in those types of venues are taxable. Money paid on the real estate mortgage interest is deductible and the real estate may have appreciated in value.

Financial planning is crucial to the fulfillment of long-term goals. Because an important characteristic of families is sustaining the unit over time, financial preparation is essential for all families. General knowledge of personal finance premises is basic to the successful creation and implementation of these plans.

In the News

Gates's Charity Races to Spend Buffett Billions

By Stephanie Strom

Although it has long been the largest grant-making foundation in the nation, the *Bill and Melinda Gates Foundation* is facing an unparalleled challenge: how to give away more money—and do it much faster—than it ever has before.

Largely lost in the June announcement of *Warren E. Buffett*'s gift of $31 billion to the foundation were its terms. Mr. Buffet will make the contribution in annual increments. For tax reasons, starting in 2009, the foundation must give away every nickel that he contributed in the previous year.

At the current price of the Berkshire Hathaway stock Mr. Buffett will be donating, the foundation will have to distribute $3 billion annually, or a little more than twice what it distributed last year.

"It's like having a second child," said Dr. Helene D. Gayle, who left the foundation this year to become president of CARE USA, the international relief group. "It's not just twice the amount of work; rather, things change in vastly different ways."

In the next two years, the foundation plans to double its staff to about 600 people to handle the additional money, said Cheryl Scott, the foundation's new chief operating officer, and it is building a new headquarters complex in Seattle. "We're very thankful for the two years he gave us to ramp up," Ms. Scott said. "I think he understands that you don't just turn this kind of thing on and off."

"I've been a manager for close to 30 years, and this is a well-run organization," Ms. Scott added, "but if you put that kind of a load on the current process we have, it's not going to carry it through."

The foundation has said it intends to continue to focus its philanthropy on education and global health while adding a new area, global development, to help the poor in third world countries. Before Mr. Buffett's donation, the Gates Foundation had assets of almost $30 billion.

Dr. Gayle said the foundation's way of doing business had evolved from its early days, when it believed in giving out a few large grants, rather than many small grants, to avoid building a huge staff and becoming a big institution. Now, she said, it has a more formal, structured process. Increasingly, it creates horse races among potential recipients through requests for proposals, more like a business, Dr. Gayle said.

"That takes time and is very hard to do piece by piece, project by project when you're trying to get that much money out the door," Dr. Gayle said. "In addition to the traditional approach of requests for proposals for specific projects, they may need to look at ways of giving out money over longer terms and turning to institutions that have the capacity to spend large resources."

Externally, the immensity of the amount the foundation will have to give away each year is reviving debate about its size and influence.

"One out of every 10 foundation dollars spent is going to have the Gates name on it, and that gives it influence that is impossible to calculate," said Rick Cohen, executive director of the National Committee for Responsive Philanthropy, a research group.

"And as currently structured, just four people are deciding how to spend all that money," Mr. Cohen said, referring to Mr. and Mrs. Gates; William Gates Sr., Mr. Gates's father; and Patty Stonesifer, the foundation's co-chairwoman and president.

Mr. Cohen and others said the large amount of money also allowed governments and other donors an excuse not to spend their money.

In its 2007 budget proposal, for example, the Bush administration eliminated a $93.5 million program to underwrite the development of smaller schools, specifically citing the increase in support for those schools from "nonfederal funds" from the Gates Foundation and the Carnegie Corporation.

Then there is the issue of accountability. Foundations by and large police themselves because of the paucity of federal and state resources devoted to oversight of the nonprofit sector.

The Gates Foundation goes further than most in revealing its warts. Its Web site acknowledges various missteps and challenges, be they unexpected complications in starting its AIDS-related program in Botswana or problems with its efforts to develop small schools. Its new headquarters will have a visitors' center, a first for a major foundation.

"There is skepticism about whether a foundation can be a responsible and effective steward of this kind of money," Ms. Scott said. "For us, it's a question of teeing up the issue squarely, because it is a real one, and telling the story as fully and openly as we can. We do not want to be a black box."

Others say the critics' concerns are overblown because influence can be achieved with even small amounts of money.

"It doesn't take billions of dollars to influence public policy," said James Allen Smith, a philanthropic historian at *Georgetown University*. "It can be done with tens of millions or even a strategically placed few hundred thousand."

Dr. Smith said that although the Gates Foundation grants were typically many times the amount of an average foundation's, its donations paled in comparison with spending by government-financed organizations like the *National Institutes of Health*, which has an annual budget of $29 billion.

Foundation officials make the same point. "It's still, in absolute terms, a small amount of money, given the problems we're working on," said Raj Shah, who oversees the foundation's new financial services for the poor and efforts to improve agricultural productivity. Mr. Shah said the foundation's primary focus was on some 550 million households in the world that survive on less than $2 a day.

Mr. Shah's responsibilities include a new global development program. It is concerned with making financial and agricultural advances and water and sanitation

(Continued)

(Continued)

improvements for the poor. In Malawi, the foundation has underwritten the purchase of thumbprint readers used in establishing savings accounts for the rural poor.

The new endeavors, which grew out of a 16-month review aimed at determining how to expand the foundation's operations in ways that complement its work on global health issues, give it new opportunities to spend its money.

Dr. Gayle said the foundation's work had been evolving in the past year to include broader goals. In reproductive health, for example, it has been moving beyond grants supporting the delivery of services to broader goals like reducing maternal mortality, increasing access to contraception and providing education to girls.

The foundation had begun working toward an expansion more than a year before the Buffett gift was announced. The Gates' have long said they intend to give much of their fortune, pegged at $51 billion by Forbes magazine, to the foundation, and Mr. Gates is ceding day-to-day control of Microsoft to devote himself to foundation work.

Wealth, although the goal of so many, complicates one's life. It allows one the opportunity to indulge in material acquisition, but it can also result in feelings of guilt and shame from those indulgences. Both Buffett and Gates have enjoyed their social position and balanced that privilege with responsibility towards others. Their estate planning was conducted with a dedication to improve the world. That need to leave a positive legacy after ones demise is not always expressed among the famous and wealthy icons in society.

Emergency Action Plans

The global experiences of the last decade have highlighted the importance of preparation and planning for disasters. Despite the obvious importance of crisis planning, a recent Red Cross survey indicated that 67% of Americans believe such preparation is important, but only 16% are actually ready with plans in place (Pagan, 2006).

A good strategy for emergency planning is to identify all possible disasters the family might face. Conducting family discussion sessions about how everyone might respond in situations identified will illuminate strengths and weaknesses that currently exist in existing plans and family communication channels. The weaknesses can be discussed and better plans can be created to better prepare all family members for crisis action. Important questions to consider include the following:

Where would we (I) go if . . . ?

Who would I be responsible for if . . . ?

What possessions are important to take with me if . . . ?

One important lesson learned in recent disasters is that of supplies acquisition. In large-scale disasters, supplies of all kinds may be inaccessible. Pagan (2006) recommends that families have a safety stash of food and water, a first aid kit, and necessary medications. She also recommends that families have basic financial resources available in times of emergency—cash, checkbook, and credit cards. Important documentation such as birth certificates, Social Security cards, financial statements, and insurance identification cards should be stored in a waterproof container that is easily carried away from the disaster. Don't forget pets when creating this emergency plan. Their safety is often out of their own control.

How Plans Emerge

Chapter 10 delves into the importance of communication in family decision making. Communication patterns determine who and what will be involved in the planning process that emerges from decisions requiring action of family members. Chapter 11 discusses how leadership within families brings about implementation of plans and delegation of roles within those constructions. Communication and leadership are both important core concepts in the management of family resources.

Summary

Planning is a natural process for humans. The planning process enables individuals and families to focus current energies on future goals, leading to the long-term success of the family unit. Different approaches and strategies are necessary for different goals, and family members responsible for such decisions must be informed and prepared or aided by professionals in the field to be effective and efficient in maintaining the welfare of all members. Financial and emergency planning are two major types of plans instituted by families to prepare for the future.

Questions for Review and Discussion

1. What are important steps in financial planning?

2. Why do some plans fail?

3. How do goals and financial needs change over the life course of any family?

4. How does planning impact your daily life?

5. List five long-term goals you have for your future (20 years). What kinds of planning activities might you utilize to ensure that you will reach these goals?

Communication Within the Decision-Making Process

10

Objectives

- Describe the communication process.

- Apply the communication process to family decision-making.

- Explain family communication patterns.

- Explore power and conflict within family communication.

- Understand the impact of technology on family communication and decision making.

Half the world is composed of people who have something to say and can't, and the other half who have nothing to say and keep on saying it.

—Robert Frost

The decision-making process that guides families in identification of needs and selection of alternatives to meet those needs is heavily dependent on another process—the communication process. Galvin, Bylund, and Brommel (2004) view communication as a "symbolic, transactional process of creating and sharing meanings" (p. 23). Family communication illustrates this process of creating and sharing meanings as it unfolds to identify needs, alternatives, and ultimately the completion of the decision-making process.

The family systems theory refers to these shared understandings as family rules. Strong, DeVault, and Sayad (1998) explain family rules as patterned or characteristic responses, generally unwritten, that are formed over time and difficult to change. These rules fall within a hierarchy and are ranked in order of significance to the family unit. They are created consensually or through conscious and unconscious power struggles among family members. These rules may operate at overt levels (visible to family members) or at covert levels (hidden and unrecognized).

Communication Theory

The communication process operates within a framework (see Figure 10.1). Communication involves multiple senders, receivers, and messages, and is thus a complex process. Multiple points exist for noise to impact the message. Noise is anything that detracts from the pure, intentional message. It could be static on a telephone line (channel) or the bad mood of your friend (channel) who is taking a message to your teacher.

Message—Encoded by the sender

Channel—Sender selects and loads

Message sent through the channel to *Receiver*

Receiver gets message and decodes

Feedback is given by the *Receiver* to the *Sender*

Sender processes feedback

Figure 10.1   The Communication Process

Source: Adapted from Schermerhorn (1996).

In the News

Mommy, Tell My Professor He's Not Nice!

(Over)involved Baby Boomer Parents— and Cell Phones—Redefine Adulthood.

By Shannon Colavecchio-Van Sickler, Times Staff Writer

Parents of University of Florida students log on to their children's personal Gator-Link accounts to check grades, then call deans when they don't like what they see.

University of Central Florida parents call administrators to complain when their kids can't get into classes they want.

At Florida State University, parents of graduating seniors haggle with job recruiters. They want to make sure Junior gets a good salary and work schedule.

University administrators have a name for these baby boomer moms and dads who hover over their offspring's college lives.

"Helicopter parents," says Patrick Heaton, FSU's assistant dean of student affairs.

The worst of them—those who do unethical things, like write their kid's term papers—are branded "Black Hawks," a nod to the souped-up military helicopters.

"I also call them tether parents," says Heaton, who directs FSU's freshman orientation program. "It's like a leash. Students are afraid to make decisions about classes or anything without calling home."

Good luck finding a parent who admits being a helicopter, much less a Black Hawk. But across the nation, college administrators are struggling with what they say is a growing phenomenon, a product of the unique relationship between many boomer parents and their millennial-generation children.

Administrators say they know these parents mean well. But their frequent phone calls and unreasonable demands stunt student development and test the patience of college officials.

"Where parent behavior becomes a challenge for us is when they encourage dependence, and they become too involved because they are afraid their son or daughter will make a mistake," says Tom Miller, a University of South Florida dean of students.

"Our students are graduating," says Jeanna Mastrodicasa, associate dean of the UF honors college. "But they are not ready to go into the real world."

Administrators noticed the hovering problem a few years ago, when the first members of the so-called millennial generation entered college.

Millennials are the children of baby boomers, born between the early 1980s and 2000. Sociologists and higher education officials say this generation is unlike any

(Continued)

(Continued)

other, thanks to the child-rearing approach of their parents and the unprecedented influence of technology.

Many boomer parents carefully planned and fiercely protected their children, according to Millennials Rising: The Next Great Generation, by Neil Howe and William Strauss.

They saw their youngsters as "special," and they sheltered them. Parents outfitted their cars with Baby on Board stickers. They insisted their children wear bicycle helmets, knee pads and elbow guards. They scheduled children's every hour with organized extracurricular activities. They led the PTA and developed best-friend-like relationships with their children, says Mastrodicasa, co-author of a book on millennials.

Today, they keep in constant touch with their offspring via e-mail and cell phones. And when their children go off to college, parents stay just as involved.

Sometimes the attention is healthy and supportive. But in some cases, administrators say, their hovering is intrusive.

"The biggest change is technology," says Robin Leach, interim dean of students at FSU. "Where students in the past might just write home, now they're on the phone with their parents all day, every day. If something goes wrong or right, parents know about it very quickly."

An online survey in March by College Parents of America, an advocacy group formed 2½ years ago for the parents of college children, found that one out of three parents communicates with their child daily two to three times a day, typically via cell phone. More than half of the 839 parent respondents said their involvement with their children is "much more" than what they experienced with their own parents during their college years.

"When I went to college in the '70s, contact with my parents was standing at a pay phone on Sunday afternoon," says James Boyle, College Parents of America president. "And there was no expectation beyond that."

Freedom High School graduate Ashton Charles, 18, will attend UF in the fall. She says her mother is supportive but "not ridiculously overprotective."

They take yoga classes together. They watch Grey's Anatomy and Desperate Housewives. They use their cell phones to chat and send text messages.

Ashton figures their close relationship will continue even when she moves to Gainesville this fall.

"I'm sure I'll call her all the time when I'm here," Ashton says.

Pensacola resident Janet Summers was in Gainesville last month for her 18-year-old daughter Christine's freshman orientation. Summers' daughter Elizabeth already graduated from UF.

Summers says Elizabeth knew students whose parents called to wake them up for class or decided their class schedules. Some parents visited so often that others figured they had moved into town.

"It was so over the top, it helped me not to be that way," Summers says. "You just handicap them by being that way."

Last month, hundreds of parents filled a ballroom on UF's campus, where two-day freshman orientation sessions are being held all summer.

They laughed when Mastrodicasa told them not to expect report cards in the mail. But she wasn't kidding.

"This is very different from high school," she said. "It is so tempting for you to do it all for them. But let them do the work. This is how they'll learn to be grownups."

Paige Crandall, associate dean of students, told parents: "I know you want to fight their battles for them. But you need to give them their space. Starting today."

A generation ago, a lot of parents didn't even attend orientation, Mastrodicasa said. They let their children attend on their own.

Today universities expect a full house of moms and dads and other guardians, and many colleges are refashioning their programs with parent-only talks that politely convey the message: "Back off, your kid's not a kid anymore."

"We talk about the value of letting go," USF's Miller said.

UF officials separate students from parents for much of the two-day orientation. If not, "Mom will take notes and want to make decisions," Mastrodicasa says.

FSU students and parents also attend separate sessions, but that doesn't stop students from text messaging their parents for help before scheduling their first semester of classes, Heaton says.

At UCF, "we have parents who come and stay the whole first week of class, just to 'make sure they're okay,'" said spokeswoman Linda Gray, shaking her head. "They didn't use to do that."

In a recent online survey, "Helicopter Poll," by the career services provider Experience Inc., 38 percent of more than 400 college students admitted their parents participate in meetings with academic advisers.

One-quarter of the students polled think their parents are "overly involved" to the point of embarrassment or annoyance.

But Boyle, of College Parents of America, thinks concerns about helicopter parents are "overblown."

"It's better than the alternative, them not being involved at all," he says. "In every generation of parents, there are those that get too involved. I think it's a small percentage of parents who do things like try to personally intervene in a roommate dispute."

He says "smart schools" accept that parental involvement is higher with the millennial generation and respond by "catering to the parents."

"They are paying a large part of the tuition bill, and it's just good customer service," he says.

That is USF's approach, Miller said. USF, like an increasing number of universities, has a parents association. Other colleges are hiring parent "advocates."

This is the new reality, Miller said.

"When I was in college, had my parents actually called the dean, I would have been mortified. Now, it's very common."

Source: "But Professor, My Daughter Deserves an A!" by Shannon Colavecchio-Van Sickler. Copyright St. Petersburg Times, June 19, 2006. Reprinted with permission of the St. Petersburg Times.

FAMILY COMMUNICATION

The communication process is continuous and always changing. It is transactional, in that when people communicate they have a mutual impact on each other. This impact can be intrapersonal, interpersonal, within the group, or out to the external world. Communication can be oral or written, formal or informal, verbal or nonverbal.

Because communication plays a central role in the family, Koerner and Fitzpatrick (2002) suggest that any theory of family communication must include both intersubjectivity and interactivity. Intersubjectivity is the element of communication that involves shared meanings. When multiple members are interacting in the communication process, the understood meanings within messages are key to the successful outcome of the process. Individuals within the family system bring uniqueness to their encoding and decoding activities. However, family units have shared vocabularies and archived histories that serve as reference points for encoding and decoding messages. Interactivity is the way in which a family communicates. How family members interact with each other to get messages across is the focus of interactivity. Both are necessary to understand because they take place at the same time within a family.

Communication is at the center of family functioning because it is through communication that members are able to establish social reality (Baxter & Braithwaite, 2002). In addition, family members participate in the process because the focus is on relationship building and maintenance, rather than on the individual participants.

The encoding or decoding process is impacted by a variety of factors, and there are many variables that cause the message to be misunderstood. These misunderstandings are found in filters and distorters. Filters convince the sender and receiver that the message was not intended in its true form. *He really did not mean it like that.* Distorters convince the sender and/or the receiver that the message has a hidden meaning. What did he mean by that tone or that choice of words? Common filters are culture and wishful thinking. If a woman receives an e-mail with sexual overtones from her male boss, she and others may brush it off as something men say, but don't actually intend. If a parent receives a note from a child away at camp, "I hate it here," he or she may interpret it as, he hasn't adjusted yet, but it couldn't be that bad. An example of wishful thinking is common among young adolescents. He pushed me because that is his way of showing that he likes me.

Common distorters may result from the differences found between the two genders. Expectations and responses of men and women differ in regards to communication. Tannen (1990) argues that men typically use report talk, which is meant to convey information, and that women use rapport talk, which is meant to strengthen intimacy. Using Tannen's model, Edwards and Hamilton (2004) did not find that gender was the cause of difficulty in communication, but that differences between males and females are reconciled by the gender roles of dominance and nurturance.

In contrast to Tannen's earlier work, they believe that the characteristic of nurturance leads to cooperation, which actually reduces difficulty in communication between the sexes. Strong, DeVault, and Sayd (1998) report that in conversations where conflict is present, wives tend to send clearer messages to their husbands than their husbands send to them. Women are often more sensitive and responsive to messages received from their partners. Husbands tend to either give neutral messages or withdraw from the conversation. In arguments, wives set the emotional tone, escalating conflict with negative verbal and nonverbal messages and deescalating argument with an atmosphere of agreement. Wives tend to use emotional appeals and threats more than husbands, who tend to seek conciliation and try to postpone or end an argument.

Differing worldviews may also be a common distorter in communication. Cultures differ in terms of high and low context. The United States tends to operate in a low context, where words carry most of the meaning in a conversation. A high-context country allows body language and other behaviors to have equal, if not higher, meanings than the actual words used.

Jasmine wants to convert the basement storage room into a private room of her own. When she approaches her parents about this, her father utilizes a low-context response. "If you are willing to clean it out and fix it up, it's all yours." Jasmine's mother most often utilizes high context in her communication. "Jasmine, go for it." Her eyes roll upward as she says these four words, and her shoulders and hand gestures imply that she is sure Jasmine will never follow through on her promise, so the private room will never become a reality. Her words and mannerisms say two very different things. Jasmine knows from experience that her mother's implied messages are much more accurate. She can anticipate little, if any, support from her mother in her efforts to convert the storage room.

Worldview

Cultural Impact on Communication

How does the culture of individuals engaged in communication affect the communication process?

1. Different Communication Styles—Across cultures, some words and phrases are used in different ways. Nonverbal communication is also different across cultures. Facial expressions, gestures, personal distance, and sense of time can communicate different ideas across cultures. One family may see an increase in volume as a sign of exciting conversation, whereas another family might react with alarm.

(Continued)

(Continued)

2. Different Attitudes Toward Conflict—Some cultures view conflict as a positive, whereas others view it as something to be avoided. Some families may see conflict as necessary and are encouraged to deal directly with conflicts that arise. Other cultures would find open conflict embarrassing.

3. Different Decision-Making Styles—The roles that individuals play in decision making vary widely from culture to culture. Although some cultures value individual decision making, others prefer consensus.

4. Different Attitudes Toward Disclosure—In some cultures, it is not appropriate to be frank about emotions, the reasons behind a conflict or misunderstanding, or personal information. Other cultures would have no problem in sharing these kinds of details.

5. Different Approaches to Completing Tasks—People across cultures have different ways to complete tasks based on the resources available, beliefs about what is important, and their orientations to work. Even how cultures view relationships as they work together can impact how a task will be accomplished.

6. Different Approaches to Knowing—How people come to know things represents cultural differences. European cultures gather information based on measurement of facts. Other cultures may base their information on symbols or stories that have been passed down from generation to generation.

How would these differences affect an interracial marriage?
How would these differences affect an international couple living in the United States?

Source: www.wwcd.org/action/ampu/crosscult.html. Adapted from *Working on Common Cross-Cultural Communication Challenges,* DuPraw and Axner.

Families are the purveyors of culture. Members learn culture of the larger group through interaction with older family members. In reality, families have unique cultural frameworks within their own units. These shared understandings increase the complexity of the communication process when it functions within family decision-making situations.

Family Communication Patterns

Families usually follow two types of communication orientation: conformity and conversation (Koerner & Fitzpatrick, 1997). Although the family usually fits one or the other type of orientation, some families have a mix of orientations within the same family. A family that has a conformity orientation is one where common attitudes, beliefs, and values are expected. This family opposes conflict and stresses compliance to the decisions made by parents or older family members. Conversation orientation allows the family members of all ages the freedom to express their opinions openly and freely. From these two orientations, four family communication patterns emerge (see Table 10.1; Fitzpatrick & Ritchie, 1994). Consensual families are high in conversation and conformity. A consensual family is able to communicate with each other and desire to have agreement.

Table 10.1   Family Communication Patterns Versus Family Types

	Family Types	
Family Communication Patterns	High-Conversation Orientation	Low-Conversation Orientation
High-Conformity Orientation	Consensual	Protective
Low-Conformity Orientation	Pluralistic	Laissez-faire

Sources: Fitzpatrick and Ritchie (1994), Koerner and Fitzpatrick (1997), and Galvin, Bylund, and Brommel (2004).

Bob and Judy are in the process of deciding where to go for the family vacation. Although they have suggested some things to each other, they decided to ask their three teenage children for their suggestions. Judy tells them, "We want you to help make the decision because we want everyone to be happy and enjoy this vacation." Everyone made suggestions, and a vacation spot was determined.

The pluralistic family is one that is high in conversation, but low on conformity. These families are good at communication, but do not expect that everyone will agree.

Although the Phillips family had always attended church together, Paul, the oldest of the children, announced that he would not be going to church anymore. His parents were upset at first, but then sat down with him and had a conversation about his announcement. He explained that he wasn't sure that his beliefs matched those of the church and he didn't get anything out of the service. His parents listened and then talked about how faith was important to them. In the end, they said, "Paul, you know where we stand on this, but we will leave this decision up to you."

The protective family is low in conversation and high on conformity. This family expects everyone to follow the rules, and there is no need for communication about them.

Amanda just turned 16. The day she got her driver's license, she planned to go out with her friends. She was having so much fun that she completely forgot about the time. When she realized it was past her curfew, she immediately called her parents. When her dad answered the phone, he informed her that she would no longer have driving privileges for 2 weeks. He ended with, "You know the rules—now you will have to suffer the consequences. I don't care what excuse you have!"

The laissez-faire family is low in both conversation and conformity. This family does not communicate very much, and family members often carry on with their own lives outside the family.

Tim and Diane are high school friends. After they attended a friend's birthday party the night before, Diane noticed that Tim was wearing the same clothes the next day at school. When she asked about it, Tim told her that he had car trouble and spent the night at a friend's house. When Diane asked if his parents were worried, he said, "My parents don't even know. I don't have a curfew, and they are usually gone for work before I get up for school. I guess I don't know if they would be worried or not—we've never talked about it."

Family Communication Standards

Individuals often have a set of standards or beliefs about what the ideal relationship should include. Many of these standards involve communication. Someone may believe that a good relationship includes full disclosure and would be concerned if his or her partner ever held anything back. Others may believe that it is necessary to withhold information that could potentially hurt their partner. Communication varies greatly across families because all families are different. Differences between generations, between cultures, and even the degree of closeness within the family can alter the way a family communicates. Some grow up in families that talk very little, and others are raised in households where conversation takes place continuously. These differences can cause problems for couples as they form a new family. Caughlin (2003) identified 10 distinct communication standards of family communication (see Table 10.2).

Power is a subtle yet important element in family communication. The ability that one family member has to exercise power over another family member can be expressed in various ways.

Table 10.2   Caughlin Family Communication Standards (in order of frequency)

Communication Standard	Description
Intimate disclosure	Ability to discuss intimate topics such as one's feelings, drugs, and sex
Negativity/Conflict	A family's tendency to engage in certain conflict behaviors such as criticism, yelling, and swearing
Respect	Showing respect for other family members by not being rude, swearing, or talking back
Routine contact	Chatting, keeping up with other family members, importance of checking with others, importance of asking others what they mean rather than having the ability to mind-read
Creating/demonstrating cohesion	Importance of family being close or communicating to bond
Treating each other with equality	Everybody gets a say, parents talk to children as equals (vs. kids not supposed to talk), whether children get input in important decisions
Openness about problems	Expectations about whether family members should talk openly about potentially troublesome issues, problems, or disagreements
Politeness	The extent to which a family's communication is seen as proper and formal (rather than relaxed)
Discipline	Rule-setting, dealing with rule violations, curfews, groundings, etc. These include both rules that parents set for children and rules for the parents' behavior
Emotional/instrumental support	Manner or extent that family members provide each other with social support or acceptance when there is a difficulty

Source: From Caughlin, John P., "Family Communication Standards. What Counts as Excellent Family Communication and How Are Such Standards Associated With Family Satisfaction?" (2003). *Human Communication Research*. Blackwell Publishing, Ltd. Reprinted with permission of Blackwell Publishing, Ltd.

Power can be verbalized as the following:

- Withdrawal
  - ○ "I'm not speaking to you."
- Guilt induction
  - ○ "How could you ask me to do this?"

- Positive coercion
  - "Kiss me and help me move this sofa."
- Negotiation
  - "I'll do that if you do this."
- Deception
  - "I'll just charge it to the credit card and he'll never notice."
- Blackmail
  - "If you do that, I'll tell them about. . . ."
- Physical/verbal abuse
  - "Watch your back."

Where does power within a family unit originate? Szinovacz (1987) developed a view of family power and describes it as a dynamic, multidimensional process with power bases that are linked to individual family members. Adult members of families have the ability to reward, coerce, and ignore younger members when making decisions that impact all family members. Other than age and financial resources, expertise is another important power base. Children with higher technological skills may hold more power in situations involving computerization than parents. Newly immigrated parents often find themselves reliant on their children's ability to translate and communicate in the new language.

The balance of power within families is also reflective of the relationships between and among family members. Blood and Wolfe (1960) developed a resource theory of family power in their classic study. More power is given to the spouse of the family member with the most resources. In turn, the person gaining the most from the relationship at any given time will be most dependent on other family members. Such is the case of young children. Their survival depends on the actions of older family members. Adolescents sense lessening dependence as they mature, thus shifting the power balance in certain decision-making situations.

Family members may use resources to increase control within the family. McDonald (1980) identified five types of resources that are used as bases of family power:

1. Normative resources are those where culture or society identifies who should have the power in the family. For example, in a society where the traditional family is valued, the father will have more overall power, with the mother having power over the children.

2. Economic resources refer to monetary resources. Those that bring the money into the family will have more power and will probably make more of the financial decisions.

3. **Affective resources** are those that are more relational. An example would be a wife who withholds affection from her husband because she doesn't approve of his behavior.

4. **Personal resources** are inherent with the personality or appearance of the family member. The person who has an outgoing personality is much more likely to garner power within the family. Another example would be the youngest child who may charm the others into getting them to do anything for him or her.

5. **Cognitive resources** allow a family member to gain power because of his or her intelligence. This often includes the person who logically reasons strategies to gain power from the other family members. An example of this is the child who learns how to get what he or she wants by working his or her parents against each other.

Waller and Hill (1951) discuss the impact of the **principle of least interest**. In marriages and cohabitation situations, the partner with the least interest in continuing a relationship has the most power in it. The changing dynamics of male/female dependency over the last several decades has presented increased complexity in family decision making and communication. Some family theorists challenge the idea that women participating in the workforce have shifted the power balance within the family from one of subservient to one of equality.

> If power is defined as the ability to change the behavior of others intentionally, women, in fact, have a great deal of power. It is rooted in their role as nurturers and kin-keepers, and flows out of their capacity to support and direct the growth of others. (Kranichfeld, 1987, pp. 42–56)

Fitzpatrick (1988) views power dynamics and communication within the interactions of adult partners as either **symmetrical** or **complementary**. Symmetrical conversations occur when partners send similar messages that impact how the relationship is defined. Both individuals adopt the same tactics, but utilize different approaches within the communication process. **Competitive symmetry** occurs when both partners view the situation as a competition, where both aim to defeat the other. This creates a win/lose situation that results in escalating hostilities. Ammunition in this conversation is open to everything that has ever transpired between the two individuals. **Submissive symmetry** results when neither individual will accept responsibility for making a decision and taking action. The eventual goal is win/lose, to outlast the other in the process of passing the responsibility back and forth. **Neutralized symmetry** reflects the desire for a win/win outcome. Both individuals respect each other and seek to avoid assuming control over the other. Each gives a little and both gain. A **complementary interaction** results when both individuals adopt different tactics. One must accept the dominant position, and the other must accept the submissive position. This action is not to be confused with exertion of power, but rather with a give-and-take relationship where individuals work together for mutual enhancement of the unit.

The Everett family must decide what to do for Christmas this year. We assume that other members of the family are too young to participate fully in the decision:

Competitive Symmetry:

Mother: I don't want to go to your family's celebration; it's too far to travel.

Father: It's not much farther than your family. You just don't like my mother.

Mother: I don't like your mother, she's bossy and she can't cook.

Father: My mother's bossy. What about your mother?

Submissive Symmetry:

Mother: I don't care where we go; I just don't want to have it at our house.

Father: I don't care, either. My family won't be unhappy.

Mother: My family won't be unhappy, either. Maybe you should call your sister.

Father: Why don't you call your brother . . . ?

Neutralized Symmetry:

Father: Where did we go last year?

Mother: We went to my family for Christmas Eve and yours for Christmas Day.

Father: That worked for me. How about you?

Mother: I think it might be good to switch this year.

Father: That sounds fine.

Complementary Interaction:

Mother: My mother really wants us to come there this year.

Father: My parents will be disappointed, but they'll understand.

Mother: We'll find a way to make it up to them.

COMMUNICATION AND CONFLICT

Photo 10.1 All families have conflict.

Source: © Sean Locke/iStockphoto.

Not all communication in the family is positive. Some communication patterns incorporate negative tactics of manipulation through guilt or power. These communication habits are difficult to break and may cycle into tremendous problems and extraordinary circumstances for a family. Anticipation and prevention of conflict within the communication process are helpful, but conflicts will occur. Conflict is a state of disagreement or disharmony. It creates a stressful situation that is uncomfortable to one or to all parties involved. Conflict resolution is the negotiation of conflict toward a positive goal. This negotiation may involve a generation of consensus among participants or a majority rules process.

It is inevitable that there will be conflict in a family. Relationships are intimate, and an internal struggle of roles and expectations plays out over time. Each new family member creates more complexity in relationship building and maintenance. Each family member who leaves creates a chasm or a hole that needs bridging or filling. Our communication patterns evolve from our interaction with parents, caregivers, and siblings.

The most harmful conflicts within a family are interpersonal—those that exist between and among individual members. These conflicts shake the foundation of the family unit. Especially destructive communication in these situations includes direct verbal attacks on an individual. Things can be said and retrieved from past situations that damage the individual's perception of self and ultimately split families into opposing sides. This type of destructive communication has been associated with lower relationship satisfaction and higher divorce rates (Gottman & Notarius, 2000).

Money is a major source of marital conflict. Who makes it? Who decides how it will be allocated? Who sets priorities? Who enforces priorities? Another mitigating factor in money-based family conflict is the difficulty inherent in talking about money matters. People can be both secretive and defensive in such discussions. In addition, decisions about money affect everyone in the family, and power and control issues may come into play by those making the decisions (Jenkins, 2002). Olson and DeFrain (2003) suggest others reasons that finances cause problems for families. These include unrealistic expectations, inability to create and stick with a budget, heavy reliance on credit, differences in spending and saving habits, and family members' different meanings for money.

Some conflict within a family unit, or any group, is necessary and healthy. When communication focuses on the problem, not the individual, positive problem solving can occur. Kranichfeld (1987) suggests that resolution of family resource conflicts can result in three outcomes:

1. **Agreement**. Members agree without coercion or threats, giving freely without resentment. This agreement is based on perceived reciprocation at a later time.

2. **Bargaining**. Within relationships, equity is a goal. During the discussion, family goals and relationships are focus points.

3. **Coexistence**. When differences can't be resolved, they will be accepted. Discourse is absorbed within the family relationship without jeopardizing individual relationships.

Communication and Information Technology

Although radio, TV, the Internet, and cell phones are all means of communication common to American families, they also represent a large consumer market. What originally represented a way to connect to the outside world and as a form of entertainment for families has developed into a multimillion dollar industry that has had an effect on the family. The media now plays a role in the maintenance of family relationships and in their connection to society. Although the family has always been the center of socialization in preparing children to live in society, one aspect of the media is its socialization role. It is through radio, TV, and the Internet that we learn about the world and ourselves.

RADIO

Originally used as a way of communication for the military, the radio began to appear in American homes in the 1920s. As the first electronic media in the home, the radio was seen as an important window to the world. For the first time, Americans were able to have information in real time. At the same time, there were parents who were concerned about the effects of adult radio programming on their children. One parent organization in New

York complained that radio "was causing nightmares and other emotional problems among their young children" (Cooper, 1996, p. 21).

Although the radio is still a popular form of media, it has changed dramatically over the last decade. Public radio stations compete with private stations for audience share. Younger listeners are turning to portable electronic devices and downloaded copies of preferred music, avoiding the social, political, and economic implications of radio broadcasting. Purchase of these electronics, accessories, copy permission fees, and subscriptions to private radio broadcasting channels have added to the financial costs of audio entertainment.

TELEVISION

When the TV was first introduced in the 1950s, families placed this "appliance" in the living room or the most prominent place in the home. All members of the family had access and usually watched together. Wartella and Jennings (2001) report that, in the early days of TV, people believed it would benefit the family by keeping the family together, solving marital problems, and keeping problem children off of the streets.

TV viewing today is different from watching TV in the past. Passive TV viewers have become more active TV users (Atkin, 2001). As wealth increased, so did not only the size of homes, but the number of TVs in each home. Nielsen Media Research, Inc. (1998) reports that 99.4% of American households have at least one TV set. The cable and satellite industry provides the consumer with a multitude of options for specialized viewing. In addition, the opportunity to aggregate or stream video, as well as other technology such as scanning recorders (*Tivo*) serve to marry the TV with computer technology, which establishes individual viewing. The rise of Personal Video Recorders (PVRs) has also changed the way that families watch TV when one family member chooses programs to serve his or her individual preferences. As a result, TV viewing has become more of an individual activity. Today, multiset households have viewing units in bedrooms, kitchens, and even bathrooms.

In the late 1970s, the government began to investigate the effects of TV on the family. Pearl, Bouthilet, and Lazar (1982) conducted research that looked at children's aggressive and antisocial behavior, which was believed to be associated with TV viewing. Although most acknowledged that TV had some negative influence, it was generally considered the responsibility of the family to educate and instill morals. Not until the 1990s did parents organize to campaign for controls such as the V-chip or content labeling in addition to demanding antidrug commercials (Andreasen, 2001). In contrast to the view that all behavior exhibited on TV is negative, Bryant, Aust, and Venugopalan (2001) found that the majority of prime-time families were psychologically healthy and exhibited good communication skills.

Whatever position is taken on the value of TV within the family home, the messages received through this media format have had an impact on the social climate and social learning of the current generation. Signorielli and Morgan (2001) suggest that "television is one of the major players in the socialization process" (p. 333) and is more likely to portray family life as it already exists, rather than to affect changes in future family life. This position is likely to be argued and debated for some time.

TELEPHONES

The introduction of the telephone into the family represented a major change in communication. Although most were excited about the possibilities of being connected to the outside, some worried about the intrusion into the home and the loss of information out of the home that could weaken family relationships or compromise privacy. The technology of the mobile or cell phone was even more of a change in family communication and represents the fastest growing technology in history. In 2002, for example, 62% of U.S. adults owned cell phones (Schackner, 2002). Children and adolescents (10–19 years old) are also among those who own and use cell phones at 28% (Curry, 2001).

The original intention of the cell phone was for use in work-related situations and for safety or security. In time the advantages of cell phones expanded to include social interactions. Families use cell phones as a way to connect children, parents, and extended family members. Cell phones improve efficiency in time by providing immediate information, such as being able to ask someone a question and by coordinating events such as meeting at a restaurant. Ling and Yttri (1999) found that teenagers have created new forms of communication and interaction. Microcoordination is when social groups make plans over their cell phones to meet somewhere and activities are coordinated. Hypercoordination is when cell phones are used not only to coordinate activities, but they also include the development of group norms through emotional and social communication. Teenagers are also much more likely to integrate other media into their cell phone use, such as making Web connections, text messaging, digital camera capabilities, or gaming (Oksman & Turtiainen, 2004).

Along with the advantages, cell phones have also created some disadvantages. Most notable is the lack of boundaries between public and private space. Users are connected between home and work at all times, not allowing for a break between being at work and being at home. In addition, others are exposed to private conversations when users talk with others while in public places. Cell phone disruptions in business meetings, classes, and public gatherings have prompted the need for cell phone etiquette (see Reality Check—Cell Phone Etiquette). Another disadvantage may be social control. With a cell phone, others have the opportunity to know where you are and what you are doing at all times. This may give some a feeling of being monitored or under surveillance.

Reality Check

Cell Phone Etiquette

Don'ts

1. Never take a personal mobile call during a business meeting. This includes interviews and meetings with coworkers or subordinates.

2. Maintain at least a 10-foot zone from anyone while talking.

3. Never talk in elevators, libraries, museums, restaurants, theaters, dentist or doctor waiting rooms, places of worship, auditoriums, or other enclosed public spaces, such as hospitals emergency rooms or buses. Don't have any emotional conversations in public—ever.

4. Don't use loud and annoying ring tones that destroy concentration and eardrums. Grow up!

5. Never "multitask" by making calls while shopping, banking, waiting in line, or conducting other personal business.

Dos

1. Keep all cellular congress brief and to the point.

2. Use an earpiece in high-traffic or noisy locations. That lets you hear the amplification—how loud you sound at the other end—so you can modulate your voice.

3. Tell callers when you're on a cell phone and where you are—so they can anticipate distractions or disconnections.

4. Demand "quiet zones" and "phone-free areas" at work and in public venues.

5. Inform everyone on your stored-number list that you've just adopted the new rules for mobile manners. Ask them to do likewise. Please.

Source: Adapted from Joanna L. Krotz, Muse2Muse Productions, New York, NY.

Immediate access to others via cell phone technology has changed the communication patterns of families and other social groups. It, too, has resulted in a divide of haves and have nots. Those with the economic ability to purchase cutting-edge devices and to subscribe to expensive service plans are advantaged in a society where information is such an important resource. Some argue, however, that cell phone use creates an unnecessary dependence and a reduction of independent thinking. Legal issues of privacy and ownership of photographs and taped conversations are increasing heavy court loads. Regardless, the cell phone has quickly become an important part of social communication around the globe.

COMPUTERS

The computer was originally used in the home as a time-saving device. Word-processing and record-keeping capabilities were the reasons that Americans bought personal computers when they became available. Because families with children were more likely to own computers, marketing strategies for home computers focused on fear as a motivator for parents to provide their children with what they need to compete in the digital world (Wartella & Jennings, 2001). Although the computer was originally meant to be used for educational purposes, children use the computer more for entertainment and, according to Giacquinta, Bauer, and Levin (1993), game playing.

The Internet has also had an impact on the family. The Census Bureau reports that access to the Internet increased 139.1% from 1994 to 1997 (National Telecommunications and Information Administration, 1998). The Pew Internet and American Life Project (Fallows, 2004) reports that nearly two thirds of Americans are online, and daily living has changed dramatically (e.g., in the way we get news, communicate with others, and pay our bills). Grunwald Associates (2000) conducted a national survey of households and found that, according to parents, 80% of children use the Internet for school work at least once a month. However, the children surveyed seemed to have a different idea about the purpose of the Internet. The researchers noted that, although parents overestimated the amount of time their children used the Internet for school work, they also underestimated the amount of time children used it for entertainment. There was also a difference in the amount of time that parents thought their children were on the Internet compared to the amount reported by the children and how much time was spend alone as opposed to parental supervision.

Access to information, guidance, and material goods has grown exponentially with the continued growth of the computer industry and computer marketing services. This can be beneficial to families during the decision-making process if the increase in available information is not overwhelming. Time spent using the computer cannot be regained or redirected. It depletes certain kinds of family resources.

Tory was anxious to plan a vacation for herself and her two school-age children. She wanted to travel to the Florida area so that their paternal grandparents could join them for a day or two. When she "Googled" family Florida vacations, she received thousands of possible Web pages devoted to that topic. She continued to narrow her search by limiting the city, type of activity, and desired cost, but she still had hundreds of options. Her initial search had taken seconds to find the information, but hours to process it. Individuals must weigh the value of time with the increased value of options generated to meet their needs.

What makes the Internet different from the other forms of media is its interactivity. The ability to connect with others in real time makes this technology different than the one-sided media of radio and TV. Although more people became connected to the Internet and others through e-mail, interactive Web sites, and chat rooms, it also provided for more commercial activity. Advertising and selling products online represented a whole new industry. This form of technology has opened many new opportunities to the outside world, but at the same time can change the way that families interact with each other. Although the Internet has the capacity to strengthen family relationships through e-mail, it also has the capacity to isolate family members for long periods of time in individual activity. Parents and children may have more conflicts over access time. In addition, the constant availability of goods also creates tensions between what kids see and want and what parents are able and willing to buy.

By the end of the 20th century, people, especially parents, became more aware of the risks as well as advantages of being online. Hughes and Campbell (1998) identified six parental concerns for Internet use and children: (a) distribution of pornography, (b) sexual predators, (c) misinformation and hidden messages, (d) loss of privacy, (e) unscrupulous vendors, and (f) development of childhood behavior disorders including social isolation and Internet Addiction Disorder. In 1998, Congress responded to these concerns by passing the Children's Online Privacy Protection Act (COPPA), which regulated data collection for children under age 13.

Family structure, race, and income influence computer ownership, which contributes to what is known as the digital divide. Two-parent families are more likely to own computers and be connected to the Internet than single-parent households (National Telecommunications and Information Administration, 1998). The same study found that Euro-American households were three times more likely to have access to the Internet as African Americans or Hispanics, although Atwell (2001) suggests that the gap in access is more likely due to income and education differences than to race. Households with incomes over $75,000 are twice as likely to have Internet access than households with incomes of less than $40,000 (Grunwald Associates, 2000). Although the number of public schools with Internet access has increased, schools that serve the poorest populations have fewer computers and slower Web access (Williams, 2000).

Beginning with the radio, mass media has been a part of the home. As each new technology was introduced into the family setting, a debate about the impact of that media on the family began. Wartella and Jennings (2001) predict that, whatever media platforms are available in the future, our debate should be less about media use and more about how families educate, entertain, and communicate.

Application to Family Decision Making

For thousands of years, the family has been the primary organization for managing property, distributing resources, and setting the division of labor. An understanding of the basic communication process and mitigating problems prepares group members for stronger and more positive communication of needs and problem solving.

Communication plays a principal role in how families make decisions and solve problems. The verbal and nonverbal messages, the meaning of those messages, the use of power, and the process of conflict resolution all contribute to the family's ability to effectively manage the decisions of life.

Although the adults assume primary responsibility for family maintenance, children's voices and those of elderly members must be addressed. Empathy and patience are necessary. The ability to listen to other members is crucial. Miscommunication within the family can often be traced to

- inability to listen
- refusal to listen
- unwillingness to share feelings
- lack of understanding and multiple viewpoints
- refusal to acknowledge the legitimacy of another's point
- lack of time
- existence of and reliance on assumptions
- need for self above others (selfishness)
- weak self-esteem of members

Listening skills must be learned and practiced to facilitate a positive family communication process and good decision making.

Summary

Communication is essential for good decision making and interaction within the family. The process of communication involves senders, receivers, and messages having mutual impact on the members of the family. Family communication involves both intersubjectivity and interactivity. The way that messages are sent and received can lead to misunderstandings, as well as differences in gender and worldview. Families follow and develop unique communication patterns and standards. Within the process of family communication, power structures present challenges and opportunities. Communication can be both negative and positive. The negotiation of conflict resolution is necessary and healthy, moving the family toward a positive goal. Information technology can be an advantage and a disadvantage for families. Communication plays a major role in how families make decisions and solve problems.

Questions for Review and Discussion

1. Describe the theoretical framework that explains the communication process.

2. What is the difference between the elements of intersubjectivity and interactivity in family communication?

3. What role do filters and distorters play in misunderstandings?

4. What are the two types of communications orientations that families follow?

5. How do communications standards affect family communication?

6. How does power affect family communication?

7. Why is conflict necessary?

8. Explain how information technology can be both positive and negative for families.

The Individual Within Family Decision Making

11

Objectives

- Understand the concept of leadership and how it applies to management of family resources.

- Explore how leadership impacts the family decision-making process.

- Contemplate how group dynamics complicate family decision making.

Leadership is the art of getting someone else to do something you want done because he wants to do it.

—Dwight Eisenhower

Anytime more than one person is involved in the same decision-making process, the complexity of the process multiplies. Rarely will there be complete agreement and total participation of all family members in a group activity. Someone will emerge during the process as an obvious leader, depending on the situation, the intensity, and the ultimate impact that decision will have on him or her and the other individual members. The same person will not always assume leadership. Such a role requires personal investment; if a member of the family will not be positively or negatively impacted by the decision, he or she may choose not to invest personal resources necessary for leading the group at that time.

Leadership

Every group has leaders. Leadership is one of the most important functions of any organization. However, **leadership** is difficult to define. Nall (2005) provides a definition from the 1920s, suggesting that a leader imposes his or her will on those led. That is a different definition from that of Langone (2004), who defines a leader as one who sets the "future direction for an organization. Leadership involves looking at the environment and the organization's mission or purpose and making decisions about which visions, activities, and goals to pursue" (p. 82). It is the leader who makes sure that the goals of the organization are accomplished. It is the leader who affects the behaviors, attitudes, and actions of those who follow him or her.

Blank (2001) suggests that the skills of natural-born leaders can be divided into three categories: foundational skills, leadership direction skills, and leadership influence skills. Blank proposes that *foundational skills* are necessary for all other leadership skills and form the foundations for success. These skills are self-awareness, or the ability to understand their own behaviors; building a rapport, or the ability to work with others; and an ability to clarify the expectations of the group so that everyone understands. These skills may explain why some leaders successfully rise to the top from among the low-level workers. That person easily understands the followers and is able to speak their language.

Leadership direction skills are those that provide guidance. Often in the face of problems or change, it is hard for followers to take action. The effective leader provides that direction. Leadership direction also includes the ability to develop leaders from within the group. These skills are those that allow someone to think on his or her feet—to be an excellent problem solver even in the face of crises.

Leadership influence skills include those that build a base of commitment to the group and create motivation to move forward. Good leaders will influence by commitment rather than force. These skills involve a sense of trust that is built between leaders and their followers. The group is motivated by a common goal for the good of all.

One of the most important components in becoming a good leader is attitude. Attitude can sprawl over into actions and affect the outcomes of the organization. Maxwell (2003) explains that attitudes such as the inability to admit mistakes, not wanting to forgive, jealousy, arrogance, being critical, and a need to take all the credit keep a group from succeeding. Leaders must also keep the attitudes of their followers in check. When attitudes are positive, the group can use its potential toward success. A bad or negative attitude is contagious and can hamper motivation to move forward. A good leader is fully aware of human behavior and understands why people do what they do.

Within the organization of the family, leadership is important. Crittenden (2004) proposes that being a parent prepares people for leadership roles with four transferable skills: multitasking, interpersonal skills, growing human capabilities, and building strengths of character or virtue. Of course multitasking is evident for parents who must juggle home and work life. She suggests that "the ability to handle irrational and immature individuals of every age; understanding the importance of win-win negotiation; the ability to listen to others' concerns; to practice patience; express empathy; and respect individual differences" (p. 8) are all skills necessary for good leadership. Good leaders in the workplace as well as good parents are able to develop strengths in others by growing their capabilities. Good leaders are able to let people grow from their mistakes, but still provide the structure and feedback they need within a safe environment. Finally, a good leader and a good parent model integrity and accurate perspective, which help build character in others.

What is the difference between leadership in an organization and leadership in a family? Hyde and Thomas (2003) suggest that, in organizations, roles are more complex. Changes in leadership are much more likely because people are moving in and out of the environment more frequently. In families, the same players are present unless death or divorce occurs. The stability of the organization is not threatened by the loss of one individual, as it would be within a family, unless the leader was a dominant figure in the organization. However, the boundaries will need to be renegotiated, and an adjustment to relationships will probably have to take place.

It is easy to assume that parents, as adults, will be the natural leaders within family decision making. Multigenerational family structures, however, bring multiple sets of adults and parents together at times. Leadership is still necessary.

Grandma Ruby is 83 and a widow. She has five grown children and 22 grandchildren and great-grandchildren. Just recently her health has indicated that she should move from her home of 50 years to a facility that would provide some general supervision for her safety. Ruby has designated her youngest daughter, Elle, as her power of attorney for health care, but doesn't want to burden her with more legal obligations, so she asks the remaining four children to determine who will help her decide which housing option she should select and to help her with the formalities of selling her home and entering into a housing contract. The only son assumes he should have the job. The three remaining daughters argue and refuse to accept his leadership. Elle, noticing her mother's despair at the behavior of her siblings, steps in and takes charge. Although she is the youngest, and a female, Elle's social skills and her education have always set her apart from the others. Ruby, and her older children, will be more likely to accept decisions made by Elle.

Although research on leadership in the family is limited, it is logical that leadership principles would be similar rather than different. Effective parenting, strong families, efficient management, and other family functions suggest that family life requires intentional leadership.

THEORIES

Before exploring family leadership, we explore some leadership theories. Most theories of leadership can be divided between the two camps of behavioral theory and situational theory. Behavioral theories of leadership are based on the idea that a leader's personal qualities and techniques drive the kind of leader they become. As early as the 1950s, McGregor (1960) and others began to develop a model of leadership based on the question of whether leaders were born or made. The investigation on leadership resulted in the theory of X and Y as a method of effective leadership. According to this theory, the integration of both X (the organization's needs) and Y (the employee's needs) is necessary, and the effective leader is able to accomplish both. McGregor concludes by saying, "Management is severely hampered today in its attempts to innovate with respect to the human side of enterprise by the inadequacy of conventional organization theory" (p. 245). In addition, the work by Fleishman (1953) in The Ohio State University Leadership Studies was among the first to identify the role of culture and climate in organizations.

Other behavioral research in the 1950s led to a "newer theory of management" (Likert, 1961) that includes the principle of supportive relationships. Likert states, "The leadership and other processes of the organization must be such that . . . each member will . . . view the experience as supportive and one which builds and maintains his sense of personal worth and importance" (p. 103). Likert (1967) identified four main styles of leadership that focused on decision making. Although these styles—exploitive authoritative, benevolent authoritative, consultative, and participative—incorporate the degree of participation within the group, they generally still view the leader as making the final decision.

Using the information from the previous studies, Tannenbaum and Schmidt (1958) developed a leadership continuum model called the three-factor theory. According to this theory, manager factors, subordinate factors, and situation factors all combine to create the leadership situation. Manager factors, such as personal values, self-esteem, and leadership style, combine with subordinate factors such as the need for independence, willingness to assume responsibility, and problem-solving skills of the group. These factors, along with the situation factors of time limits, group effectiveness, and the nature of problem being solved, determine the effectiveness of the group.

Recently, Lefton and Buzzotta (2004) proposed a model of leadership behavior that incorporates four basic patterns. Based on the earlier research conducted in the 1940s and 1950s, the **dimensional model** has two dimensions (see Figure 11.1). One dimension is represented by dominance and submission, whereas the other dimension is represented by hostility and warmth. Dominance represents people who take control and lead. They want to have power over those around them. At the other end of the continuum is submission. These are people who want someone to tell them what to do. They do not want to control others or make decisions. Hostility includes self-absorption and insensitivity to other people's needs. Warmth, in contrast, is

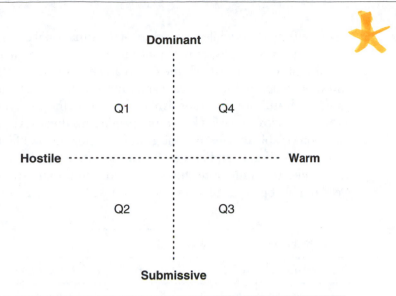

Figure 11.1   Dimensional Theory

Source: Lefton and Buzzotta (2004).

a consideration for others coupled with optimism. Hostile people tend not to trust others, whereas warm people are more open-minded about others. These dimensions then form four quadrants or four leadership styles.

Autocratic leaders (Q1) use power and intimidation to control others. This type of leadership style has one leader who makes all the decisions and is more concerned with outcomes than the process used to get there. Although much can be accomplished, the cost is high in terms of how people feel about the organization and how long they stay. Unassertive leaders (Q2) avoid true leadership by procrastinating, passing off decisions, and staying with traditional or old ways of doing things. They do not take risks and are often apathetic to what is going on around them. They tend to neither reward nor punish, which often causes those around them to be apathetic as well. Easygoing leaders (Q3) concentrate their leadership style on morale. They favor relationships rather than rules. Productivity is not as important as keeping people happy in the organization, which leads them to not value productive behavior and ambiguity. No one knows how well they are doing because praise is so easily given that they don't really know when their performance is unsatisfactory. Collaborative leaders (Q4) have the ideal leadership style. These leaders set goals and expect results while creating a positive environment where others feel valued and competent. The collaborative leader takes responsibility for the organization, but knows when to step in and when to back away.

Situational theories of leadership focus on the situational or outside factors that predict effective leadership. The contingency model, developed by Fiedler (1967), examines the relationship between the leadership style and leader effectiveness while being aware of the situational control of the leader. Situational favorability, or how much power and control a leader will have, is influenced by how much the group accepts and supports the leader, by how the leader is able to explain and carry out goals (structured tasks), and how much authority the leader is able to have over the group (see Figure 11.2). The leader's influence is a key component in this theory. The more influence someone is able to have over the group, the more favorable the situation for them as a leader. In addition to the leader's influence, the theory also brings in the idea that human relations are important for effective leadership. The leader must be aware of what is going on within the organization.

Unfriendly	1 2 3 4 5 6 7 8	Friendly
Uncooperative	1 2 3 4 5 6 7 8	Cooperative
Hostile	1 2 3 4 5 6 7 8	Supportive
Guarded	1 2 3 4 5 6 7 8	Open

Figure 11.2   Contingency Model

Source: Fiedler (1967).

The path-goal theory (House, 1971) is another situational theory. This theory is based on the idea that effective leaders are those who can motivate others by increasing rewards, clarifying goals, or meeting personal needs. Although there are some who do not support this theory, it does provide a link between good leadership and what motivated people to follow.

Finally, situational leadership theory (Hershey & Blanchard, 1992) is rooted in the idea that effective leadership can be measured by the relationship between the leader's actions and the followers' readiness. Using a matrix, task behavior and relationship behavior are used to form four leadership styles: the leader who participates and facilitates in decision-making, the leader who explains decisions and clarifies if necessary, the leader who makes the decisions and supervises tasks, and the leader who gives the task to the followers to make decisions on their own. Maturity is another aspect that is considered because the leader must decide whether the follower has the ability (willingness, confidence, responsibility, education, experience, etc.) to carry out the task.

LEADERSHIP STYLES

Today, the development of our understanding about leadership style tends not only to incorporate, but also to expand on these theories from the past. Three leadership styles seem to emerge as those relevant to predict

Photo 11.1 Transformational leadership involves teamwork.

Source: © Creasource/Corbis.

leadership effectiveness. They are transactional, transformational, and laissez-faire. Transactional leadership is often used to describe a combination of both leader behavior and situational details from both camps of theory. The transactional leader is one who uses interactions with followers to help make decisions, but is ultimately the one in control and usually commands the power in the organization. Leaders provide the incentives and regulation according to the performance of the followers, regardless of the outcomes of the organization. This leadership style is often found in top-down organizations where there is a definite hierarchy of structured leadership.

Although transactional leadership style has been effective in the past, the transformational leadership style has become more common and is desired in the workplace. It is not enough just to lead and to make decisions; the transformational leader casts the vision and provides the inspiration for the organization. Often the transformational leader is charismatic and able to empower followers to work beyond their potential. Bass and Avolio (1997) identified five characteristics of the transformational leader. These characteristics are (a) idealized attributes: influence on others, is credible, has integrity, is authentic, willing to make sacrifices, and encourages; (b) idealized behaviors: models behaviors that encourage others to look up to or want to emulate; (c) inspirational motivation: motivates others by increasing awareness and understanding of the goals, able to express the purpose and meaning of goals, and able to create vision; (d) intellectual stimulation: teaches followers to think beyond the ordinary and encourages them to develop independent thinking; and (e) individualized consideration: mentors others and provides opportunities that foster growth.

Another contemporary leadership style is the laissez-faire leadership style. In this style, the leader's involvement is decreased, especially in decision making, which allows followers to have more control over the outcomes of the organization. At first glance, this style appears to be a positive method of leadership for the followers, allowing them to have control over their work environment. However, certain factors must be present within the organization for the outcomes to be positive. People must be competent and motivated to make their own decisions and must be able to work well outside the watchful eye of the leader. This style also requires that the group does not need coordination of efforts, where each task is dependent on the other tasks in order for the job to be successful.

What style of leadership is best for the family? Let us take a look at the three contemporary leadership styles (transactional, transformational, and laissez-faire) and see how these leadership styles affect family functions. Transactional leadership is most often associated with the traditional family, where the father is the identified leader and the mother carries out the decisions of the father and enforces those decisions with the children.

The Osawa family consists of a father, mother, and two school-age children. Mr. Osawa works as an electrical engineer, and Mrs. Osawa is a full-time homemaker and mother. Mr. Osawa is the identified head of the house and makes the majority of the decisions. Although Mrs. Osawa is the one who purchases most of the food, clothing, and household items, Mr. Osawa controls the budget and pays the bills. If the children behave badly, Mr. Osawa is the one who decides what course of discipline is needed. If the children have consequences, it is up to Mrs. Osawa to make sure that they are carried out. Although Mr. Osawa asks for and listens to Mrs. Osawa's opinion, he makes the final decisions for the family. The Osawa family exhibits transactional leadership style.

Problems associated with the transactional leadership style within a family are similar to the problems of this style in a nonfamily organization. The divide between the leader and followers may be wide if the followers sense that the leader is not looking out for their best interest. When this happens, trust is broken between the two, and a lack of motivation to work toward a goal may result. In the case of the Osawa family, when the children became teenagers, the transactional model that worked before was not as effective.

Jerek Osawa just turned 17 and enjoys being with his friends and fellow soccer players. In fact, he would spend all of his free time with them if his father would allow. Although Jerek understands that there are times when he needs to be with his family and help out by doing chores around the house, it seems to him that he has more responsibility than his sister. He has started to resent the fact that he works harder and tries to find more excuses to be away from the house. Jerek avoids seeing his dad because he doesn't want to risk being given yet another job. He can't wait to turn 18 so that he can move out of the house and on his own. Mr. Osawa is annoyed that Jerek is never around to help out and that Jerek takes offense to everything he asks him to do. Mr. Osawa recalls that he would have never questioned his own father's authority, and even though he didn't always agree, he feared the consequences of disrespecting his father. What makes the transactional style of leadership less effective in both the workplace and the family today?

The family that exemplifies a transformational leadership style demonstrates a sense of shared purpose. Together, the family will discuss ways to solve problems collaboratively. Although the leader (or leaders, as in egalitarian relationships) will ultimately be the one to make the final decision, the family will work to meet each member's needs in a way to mutually benefit the whole family. In return, members trust and respect the leader because they know there are benefits.

The Garcia family consists of parents, Ric and Gloria, and their three children. The Garcias have always made decisions together, including how to raise their children. When a family situation arises, the Garcias sit down together and each person expresses his or her opinion and desires openly. Ric and Gloria then weigh the information and together as coleaders make a decision. Although not all problems are resolved just the way each one would like, they all have a sense that it was best for the family. Recently, 15-year-old Julia was invited to a friend's birthday party sleepover. When she asked her parents if she could go, they hesitated because they needed her to watch her younger brother and sister the morning after the sleepover. They knew she would be too tired and it would be difficult for her to be home by the time they needed to be at work the next morning. Julia was upset that she would miss her friend's party even though she knew that her role as caregiver for her siblings was important to the family. The family was able to collaborate together toward a solution: They decided that Julia would go to the party in the evening, but would not stay overnight. This solution was acceptable for all, and a sense of family unity was maintained.

Galbraith and Schvaneveldt (2005) suggested that there are many benefits for families that model the transformational leadership style, including "the involvement of children in a shared vision or cause; positive role modeling; family unity, trust, cooperation, and teamwork; a sense of responsibility among family members; the use of power in healthy ways; and a collective sense of ownership for overcoming problems and working toward positive individual and family outcomes" (p. 236). Families need good leadership just as much, if not more than, any organization. This type of leadership strengthens families and enables family members to successfully adapt and change to the environment around them.

Although the laissez-faire leadership style is not recommended for families, it is identified and practiced in many families. In fact, it may even be referred to as nonleadership because someone using this style resists taking the role of leader altogether. Within a family, the laissez-faire leader passes off dealing with important issues, postpones making decisions, and avoids getting involved in day-to-day family life (Galbraith & Schvaneveldt, 2005).

Gary and Janice Williams have been married for 28 years. Janice grew up in a traditional family. Her father was the "head of the house" and dictated the direction of the family. In her teen years, Janice resented her father's heavy hand and her mother's submissiveness. She vowed never to marry a man like that and she didn't. Throughout their marriage, Janice has had to make most of the decisions. It was difficult to get Gary to take a stand on anything. Janice felt uncomfortable in making decisions; although she didn't like the model of her own parents, she felt that her husband should take an interest at least some of the time. Early in their marriage, Janice would ask Gary's opinion. Gary didn't usually have an opinion and one day finally said, "Janice, I don't care what you do. Don't bother me with the details!" Although Gary doesn't want to make the decisions, he certainly lets Janice know when she makes a mistake. A few years ago, Janice gave their 16-year-old daughter permission to attend a party at a friend's house. It was there that their daughter began a long and painful journey into drugs. Ever since that night, Gary reminds Janice that it is her fault. "If you would have just paid a little more attention to what you let her do, she wouldn't be in this mess."

Although the laissez-faire leadership style may work in some corporate settings by allowing capable and motivated people to make their own decisions, this style is often detrimental to a growing family. Because a family includes both adults and children, the laissez-faire leadership style affects the entire family. All family members go unsatisfied. In the previous scenario, Gary is unhappy with the decisions of Janice and Janice is unhappy with Gary's uninvolvement. The children have missed the interaction of their father, have been affected by the conflict of their parents, and will not have a positive model of leadership to carry to their own families.

There are other factors that affect leadership within the family. Yu and Miller (2005) found that different generations prefer different leadership styles. Of course this would be important to know in an organizational or business setting, but also within the family setting where several generations are present. The **Baby Boom Generation** (those born between 1947 and 1964) has lived during a period of time that includes more than one phase of leadership style. In the early years, leadership probably focused on control and supervision. As a result, Baby Boomers tend to value loyalty to a leader and expect a chain of command within organizations.

Generation Xers (those born between 1965 and 1980) tend to value personal satisfaction and freedom, rather than loyalty. They are not afraid to change jobs several times because they are used to change and are more flexible. Generation Y is just now entering into the world of adulthood. They require even different criteria in leadership. Yu and Miller (2005) point out that they are as technologically savvy as those before them, but they have become so at a younger age. They are generally better educated, and they tend to be more articulate in expressing themselves and what they want. They are more interested in a more collaborative type of leadership and will follow someone if they have a need to learn from them. In a family, leadership where there is more than one generation can be a challenge.

Davenport and Prusak (1998) point to several studies that show no one style of leadership is better. They suggest that a successful leader should be able to develop a style that is best for his or her follower's needs and for each situation. Over time, the position-based leadership style, often referred to as "top–down" leadership, will probably be replaced with a more information-based or cooperative leadership style. Some may argue that this would be detrimental for families.

Misha and her husband have been married for almost 10 years and have two children who are now 5 and 8. When her children were born, Misha vowed never to repeat the kind of discipline style that her parents had while she was growing up. Misha's dad was authoritarian and a strict disciplinarian. When a rule was broken, there were consequences. Once when Misha was 16, she was a few minutes late. When she tried to explain that her car had a flat tire on the way home, her dad just put up his hand and said, "I don't want to hear it!" Even though Misha could see that her mother was sympathetic, she never questioned her husband's judgment. Misha's dad was the leader of the home. He made all the decisions and handed down all the discipline. Now that she has children of her own, Misha allows everyone in the family to make their own decisions. She and her husband have decided that a team approach is the best way for the family to live. Both children get to decide when, where, and what they would like to eat; when to sleep; and what they will do each day. Will this style of leadership work for the family? Why or why not?

In addition to generational leadership styles, there are also gender differences between the leadership styles of men and women. Although there is controversy as to whether men and women inherently have different leadership styles or they come as a result of what is expected of them because of their gender, there are some characteristics that cause men and women to lead differently. Eagly and Johannesen-Schmidt (2001) suggest that men exhibit more agentic characteristics, such as assertiveness, confidence, and competitiveness. Women exhibit more concern for others and are described as helpful and kind, which are more communal characteristics. Women tend to be more transformational and tend to be less likely to exhibit laissez-faire in their leadership style.

Worldview

Recognizing that gender leadership differences have been supported in research studies, what impact might female prominence within a society and the inheritance system described here have on other societal practices?

Nair Matrifocality

Anthropologist R. T. Smith (2001) refers to "'matrifocality'" as the kinship structure of a social system where the mother assumes structural prominence. Most anthropologists distinguish this from matriarchy.

The traditional Nair community in Kerala, South India, is matrifocal by their definition of "matrifocality." (Nowadays this system is rarely practiced. The members of the Nair community now live in nuclear families.) A traditional Nair matrifocal family is called as a Tarawad or Marumakkathayam family. A traditional Nair Tarawad consists of a mother and her children living together with their mother's surviving eldest brother or eldest surviving maternal uncle who is called as *Karanavan*. The Karanavan exercises full powers over the affairs of the family. The main significance of this system is that the heirs to the property were the women in the family and the men folk were only allowed to enjoy the benefits during their lifetime. The naming system of the Nair community had the prefix of their mother's family name and they adopted the maternal uncle's surname. The Marumakkathayam system of Kerala was a legal right that determined inheritance through the female line. Thus, if a family property was to be partitioned, all female members would receive one share, and all male members who were direct offspring of the family name would receive one share. Thus, a brother might receive only one share, whereas his sister and her children (and grandchildren by her daughters) would each receive a share. This right was removed by the Kerala Joint Hindu Family System (Abolition) Act, 1975.

Source: www.en.wikipedia.org/wiki/Matriarchy.

What is the difference between managing and leading? Blank (2001) found that managers perform tasks like leaders, but it doesn't make them a leader. Managers are given their role and expected to carry out the responsibilities. Leaders often take the role and guide followers to carry out the responsibilities. How does this work within the family? Is there a difference between a family manager and a family leader?

The Clements and the Lees are middle-class families that live in a large metropolitan area. Both families have similar household incomes, with all four parents working full time. Mrs. Clement is a manager. She is a master at scheduling, arranging, purchasing, and organizing. Although she performs much of the work herself, she does enforce the chores and responsibilities that she implemented over the years. In contrast, Mrs. Lee serves as a leader in her family. On Saturdays, Mrs. Lee gathers the whole family around the breakfast table to divide the weekly tasks, listen to the concerns of the family members, and together they make plans for upcoming events. What is the difference between the leadership style of Mrs. Clement and Mrs. Lee? If Mrs. Clement and Mrs. Lee are suddenly faced with life-threatening illnesses, what consequences will each family face in their effort to maintain family functions?

Group Dynamics

Photo 11.2   Individual choices affect families across generations.

Source: © Howard Pyle/zefa/Corbis.

Most family decisions are made by the group process. Husbands and wives, parents and children, and even extended family work toward a decision that affects the family. The process of making decisions involves various dynamics of the group that play an important role in the outcome. As stated at the beginning of the chapter, there are factors that differentiate leadership in the workplace from leadership in the family. These factors also point to the difference between how families make decisions and how other organizations make decisions. Sorrels and Myers (1983) found that family groups are less affected than other outside groups by focusing on one problem too long, a dominating member, inflexible status levels, or avoiding the emotional or personal dimension of the task. Similarities between outside groups and family groups included members who do not feel competent, lack of tolerance for other ideas, criticisms, pressures to conform, and the hidden agendas of the members.

Love, attachment, and other affective characteristics present the family as a group with different dynamics than other organizations. Just as attachment, love, and loyalty provide powerful affective components, so do rebellion, anger, jealousy, and resentment. Barsade (2002) found that emotional contagion is an important factor in group dynamics. As such, a group member's mood can have an effect on the group members' understanding, attitudes, and behaviors within the group. In addition, contagion for a positive mood was found to be just as powerful an influence as a negative mood.

Mary Ann had always been a positive and upbeat person. As a wife, she made it a point to encourage her husband in whatever he did. She also set a positive tone for the children by looking for the good in every situation and praised them for their accomplishments no matter how small. Her sister Ellen was just the opposite. She never failed to point out her husband's faults to him and corrected her children for their negative behaviors. She seemed to look only at the negative consequences for every circumstance, as if always knowing that something bad was about to happen. How does the mood of each sister affect their family? In any decision that these two sisters make, how will the outcome differ for each of their families?

Within the structure of the family, members also have a life-long investment in the success of the group. At the same time, the long-term nature of the relationships may have a negative effect on the group because of unresolved issues or past history preventing them from being able to effectively solve problems or make decisions.

Emran and Cyan have struggled with issues of managing money since the beginning of their relationship. Emran is a saver and Cyan is a spender. Now, decisions need to be made about how to finance the college education for their oldest daughter. Rather than rationally discussing whether to seek financial aid or take a second mortgage against their home, they cannot reach a decision without arguing and bringing up the past.

Merton and Kitt (1950) identified two types of groups to which people belong. People belong to a **membership group** by birth or life circumstance. This group membership is not voluntary. Membership is based on racial, ethnic, or sexual association. A reference group is a group to which members choose to belong. Families may belong to both types of groups. Within the family decision-making process, individuals bring a set of values, beliefs, and attitudes that, when combined with others in the family, produce unique dynamics.

In the News

The Amish Protest Against Evil

The Monitor's View

By Marilyn Gardner

The Amish of Lancaster County, often seen as living in an idyllic but archaic past, have given a powerful example for the future. Their actions since the school shootings that killed five Amish girls provide one of many ways to prevent such tragedies.

Previous school shootings, notably the 1999 murders at Columbine High School, have led to calls for any number of useful, preventive measures, such as tighter security, more federal gun control, anti-bullying training for young children, more parental vigilance in communities, and closer screening of wayward students. And perhaps, as a result, many shootings have been prevented.

Those Old Order Amish who live a secluded life near the school at Nickel Mines, Pa., have a different idea.

Their faith in the power of forgiveness led them to invite the widow of the non-Amish killer, Charles Carl Roberts IV, to the funeral for four of the slain girls. One Amish woman told a reporter, "It's our Christian love to show to her we have not any grudges against her."

This isn't surprising. It is common for the Amish to invite car drivers who have killed one of their community members to the funeral. Such a compassionate response reveals a belief that each individual is responsible to counter violence by expressing comfort—a sort of prayer in action.

After Monday's killings, the grandfather of one of the slain girls went to the home of Roberts's father, consoling and hugging him, pouring forth a love and innocence of the kind remembered of the girls in the school. "He extended the hope of forgiveness that we all need these days," said a Roberts' family spokesman, the Rev. Dwight Lefever of Living Faith Church of God. "God met us in that kitchen."

Such examples of forgiveness are often inspiring because, to many, they are so difficult and so rare. After previous school shootings, some families of victims have also sought to extend forgiveness to the killers of their children. The Amish, although known for a rigid shunning of members who adopt other ways, are emphatic about forgiveness, perhaps making it easier for them. It's one way they've held their communities together since the 18th century.

Like everyone, the Amish also seek justice for a crime, even as they struggle to forgive. Even so, as Abraham Lincoln said, "I have always found that mercy bears richer fruits than strict justice."

Such qualities are a corrective to the tendency to see evil as a real possibility and fear of it as necessary. "I don't understand it," said one Mennonite woman, speaking of the shooting, "but it's not from God. He wants us to love one another." Forgiveness helps resist the impression that humans can act like animals. It spreads a sensitivity to the needs of others, especially those whose inner torments might lead to shootings.

(Continued)

(Continued)

Some Amish saw Roberts as someone in need of help. Despite the guilt of his act, he was probably a man who needed to regain his child-like innocence, and heal his anger and the mental demons of the past.

While Roberts is now gone, the Amish example of forgiveness is a reminder that real safety lies less in acting out of fear to prevent violence and more on qualities such as forgiveness that better connect people. Such compassion reduces fears and reaches those prone to violence.

Source: "The Amish Protest Against Evil: The Monitor's View." By Marilyn Gardner. Reproduced with permission from the October 6, 2006, issue of *The Christian Science Monitor* (www.csmonitor.com). Copyright © 2007 The Christian Science Monitor. All rights reserved.

Leadership within families and communities greatly determines the success or failure of these social groups over time. How might forgiveness, rather than vengefulness, impact the healing process for an entire community?

Not all families make the same decisions, nor do the same decisions always produce the same outcomes. Factors such as social class, cultural or ethnic norms, communication styles, power structures, and previous family experience may also affect the dynamics of the family and the decisions they make. The socioeconomic status (SES) of the family may have an influence on the family. Vuchinich (1999) suggests that, although the question of whether social class or other outside social structures are linked to the decision-making process, it is likely that they will have an impact. For example, low-income families make decisions that may require them to select between two unfavorable choices, such as whether to buy medicine or food, or whether to take on a second job or apply for government assistance. An adolescent from a low-income family may not seek help from the family group to buy the sport shoes he needs because he knows it is not a possibility, whereas the adolescent from a family in a higher socioeconomic group may petition the family.

Cultural or ethnic norms also influence family group dynamics. The worldview of individual cultures can shape the way decisions are made in the family. For example, cultures that value a collective identity believe that decisions should be made based on what is best for everyone. For such a society, every decision is a family decision. In contrast, those in an individualist society would make decisions based on what is best only for them. Other cultural orientations enter into the decision-making processes of many family issues, including parenting, gender roles, and interactions between generations.

Tomoko is struggling to make a decision about the medical care for her mother, who is suffering in the last stages of cancer. Although she has lived in the United States most of her life, she still abides by the traditional

Japanese cultural orientation of filial piety, which gives a high degree of authority and respect to the elderly family member. Tomoko is torn by the desire to care for her mother in her home and yet understands how unequipped she is to handle the medications and procedures that will ease her mother's pain. She decides to leave the decision up to her mother.

Down the hall of the hospital where Tomoko's mother is a patient, another family has to make the same kind of decision. Stefano and his brothers and sisters have all gathered in the waiting room to talk to the doctors about their father's condition. Once they learn he has a terminal illness, they all agree that their father should not be told that he only has a few months to live. They are following a cultural norm designed to actively protect the patient as a function of love and respect. They decide to keep him as comfortable as possible and to continue to talk hopefully about his recovery.

One floor down, still another family has to make a decision about their elderly parent. This family makes their decision based on their personal needs. Jodi is married with a full-time job and a family. Vaughn is a busy accountant, a civic leader, and a father. Neither of them feels that they will be available to care for their father, and so they make the decision to admit him to a nursing home where he will get the attention he needs. How are the decisions that are made by all three families influenced by their culture?

The way the family communicates with each other impacts the dynamics of the group and their decisions. As in any group, there are members who are more vocal and those who express themselves very little. In addition, the family member who is able to articulate his or her message clearly and is able to quickly move the group to see his or her way of thinking has an advantage over the family member who cannot express him- or herself very well. Hsiung and Bagozzi (2003) found that influence and persuasion were important concepts within family decision making.

The dynamics in the family and the decisions that result are influenced by the power structures within the group. Family members who garner the most power within the family are likely to influence the decision-making process. In addition, when family members form coalitions, they may influence the decisions of the group by their majority representation.

Calvin and Melinda have three children. As the children have gotten older, family decisions have largely been made with input from the whole family. Calvin recently called a family meeting to discuss a promotion that he has been offered at work. The promotion involved moving several states away. The family members weighed the pros and cons of the decision, noting the increase in salary and perks of the new position. They also realized that they would be leaving well-established friendships and discussed several other negative outcomes for taking the new position. In the end, the children's protest of being uprooted in their last years of high school outweighed any of the positive outcomes that they identified for the new position. Calvin declined the promotion. How would the outcome of the decision have been different if Calvin held complete authoritarian power within the family?

The decisions that a family makes as a group may be influenced by past experience or behavior of the group members. Some of these behaviors are cyclical in nature and may continue generation after generation. A good example of this would be parenting behaviors. Seldom do parents discuss their parenting choices with their children. However, unless you make a conscious choice to change, you will probably parent your children similarly to the way you were parented (Simons, Conger, & Chao, 1992). The model that you saw becomes the behavior that you use, and it may continue for generations.

Another example can be found in family violence. Boulter (2004) reports that certain factors double the chances that a youth will commit a violent act. One of these factors is that children who are a witness to violence in the home are significantly and negatively affected by that experience. Children automatically observe and learn from their environment. Even parents who exhibit Type A personality traits (such as time consciousness, competitiveness, and control) tend to influence and pass those traits on to their children (Forgays, 1996). More controversy surrounds the influence of alcoholism or drug addiction on family members. Some believe that addictive behavior is genetic and, therefore, cannot be learned from others. Others suggest that the behavior is learned through the environment, by watching others. Most agree that some environmental influences play a role. The quality of the parental relationship (Miles, Silberg, & Pickens, 2005), the relationship to risk-taking within the family (Ellis, Zucker, & Fitzgerald, 1997), and parental mental health (Jacob & Johnson, 1997) are all environmental influences that have been found to affect the outcome of passing on alcoholic behavior from parent to child. The result of observing and learning from past experiences will have an impact on decision making both now and in the future.

Smith and Berg (1987) suggest that group dynamics include a series of paradoxical elements that are essential to group life. These paradoxes also apply to family group dynamics. Group members who experience these paradoxes may find that, while they may be painful, they produce growth for the group. One such paradox is that, although the group may want unity and consensus, often there is conflict. Conflict may not be pleasant, but it is necessary for change. For example, a married couple may not wish to have an argument over taking out the garbage, but it may be necessary for them to communicate about it so that a decision can be made and change can take place. Other paradoxes include the wishes of the individual versus the good of the group (a husband's desire to further his career vs. choosing what is best for his family), self-disclosure versus privacy (a daughter's need for help in a struggle with depression vs. her need to keep it private), and authority versus submissiveness (a son's need to parent an alcoholic father vs. his role as a child).

Groupthink

Groupthink explores how group dynamics can interfere with effective decision making. Groupthink was a word coined by Irving Janis in the early 1970s to describe what happens in groups when there is pressure to maintain unity and the group resists or ignores ideas that are contrary to the way the larger group is thinking. In his book, *Victims of Groupthink,* Janis (1972) argues that a group that is influenced by groupthink may fall victim to an overestimate of success and can fail even though the group may consist of otherwise intelligent and thinking people. He describes eight symptoms of groupthink that prevent good decision making.

The first symptom of groupthink involves the illusion of invulnerability, where group members believe they are invincible and that whatever decision they make will be the right one. Second, group members want to discredit or explain away any thoughts that are contrary to their thinking. In a sense, they ignore the warnings that their way of thinking may be flawed. Third, groupthink involves believing that they are making decisions based on morality, but they often do not consider the consequences of their actions. They often believe they are doing something for the "good of all" and are proud that they are thinking of others, but really haven't stopped to think about how it will affect everyone. Fourth, the group relies on mutual stereotypes to validate their thinking. No matter how inaccurate the stereotypes, all group members perpetuate those same attitudes about people or ideas. Fifth, groupthink involves pressure to conform to and agree with the thinking of the group. Dissenters are targeted and viewed as disloyal. Along with this pressure is the sixth symptom of self-censorship. When a group member does question or express opposition, he or she is censored or made to feel uncomfortable enough to keep their thoughts to themselves. The seventh symptom of groupthink is when the group members believe that everyone else agrees with the decision being made. Individuals may have a feeling that "if everyone else believes this is a good decision, then I don't need to question it." Silence within the group can add to this belief if no one speaks up. Finally, the eighth symptom is a group that includes what are known as "mindguards." These are self-appointed members who take on the role of protecting the group against anyone or anything that would cause disharmony. Janis (1982) further suggests that, to avoid groupthink, groups must employ vigilant decision-making practices, which includes encouraging group members to freely deliberate, allowing various points of view to emerge, gathering credible information to help make informed decisions, and having contingency plans in place once the decision is made. He warns that leaders of groups need to be impartial and open.

Although groupthink was developed within the arena of politics, family decision making can also find application.

Thomas and Marisol are part of a large extended family. Every Sunday night, they gather together for dinner. Over the course of the evening, various topics are discussed, including local events, national and international politics, and family issues. Although the discussions can sometimes become heated, everyone tends to agree. When Thomas first became a part of Marisol's family, he was thrilled to be a part of such a large and close group. His own family was not very close as a result of his parents' divorce early in his adolescence. However, now there are times when he feels that Marisol's family is so close and connected that they don't always see other points of view. For example, here is the conversation that transpired last Sunday night.

Marisol's brother: "Did anyone see the article in the paper about that new strip mall they are proposing? I can't believe that the city would let them build that thing so close to our neighborhood. What's next, a big Walmart next to the church?!"

Marisol's dad: "Yeah, I saw it. Those rich people think they can do whatever they want and the city just looks the other way."

Marisol's uncle: "Somebody should tell them that we don't want their BIG money around here! Nobody wants it."

Marisol's aunt: "I heard there's going to be a Starbucks. Who needs it—why would anyone pay four bucks for a cup of coffee?"

Thomas: "They might be trying to keep the younger generation around."

Marisol's brother: "We have gotten along just fine without them all these years and we will continue to do business as usual without them for years to come."

Marisol's mother: "Oh, come on now—we all want the same things, don't we! We are all alike in this neighborhood!"

No one said anything for a few seconds, and then Marisol said, "Who made that salad with the red peppers? I really like it—can I get that recipe?"

What are the symptoms of groupthink for this family? What role does Thomas play in the family? What role does Marisol's mother play? What are the dangers of groupthink for this family?

Janus (1982) also identifies antecedent conditions or existing characteristics that are likely to promote groupthink. These conditions include the insulation of the group from outside ideas, high cohesiveness within the group, impartial leadership, little knowledge of effective decision-making processes, homogeneous members, stress from external threats, and low self-esteem. These characteristics are found within families and make them vulnerable to groupthink. In the prior example, Marisol's family is cohesive and shares similar cultural and socioeconomic beliefs. They spoke about the past and the need to stay the same, which may indicate that they are unaware of or unwilling to investigate the reasons and need for change within the decision-making processes taking place in their community. It also appears that the leadership or strong personalities within the family do not want to consider outside opinions or other ways of looking at the situation. These are all reasons that it may be easy for this family to have fallen victim to groupthink.

Groups need to guard against falling into groupthink by developing strategies for preventing this type of faulty thinking. Such strategies include establishing an environment where alternatives and other ideas are welcomed and valued. In addition, the leader must not only take the lead in maintaining this open environment, but he or she must also work more as a facilitator than as a dictator, including accepting criticism (Janis & Mann, 1977). These strategies need to be considered within a family. Within an open environment, family members should be allowed to voice their divergent opinions toward a solution while maintaining respect for the leader. The transformational leadership style mentioned earlier in the chapter lends itself more to this strategy and works against the groupthink model.

Reality Check

Cults and Family Parallels

In 1997, thirty-nine members of the Heaven's Gate cult committed mass suicide in a mansion near San Diego. They claimed to be seeking redemption on a space ship that was following the Hale-Bopp comet. Like all organized religious cults, the group's leader, Applewhite, was successful in recruiting, training, and managing the cult members. What elements of leadership were present in this case? Was Applewhite a parental figure to his followers? Did their formation of a family-like unit perpetuate and/or facilitate their beliefs and actions?

Schwartz and Kaslow (2001) compared and contrasted the cult phenomenon of the 1970s and the turn-of-the-century time periods. Similarities included powerful, charismatic leadership and tight, heavily controlled member behaviors. Differences seem mostly embedded in purpose. Whether these now famous leaders actually believed what they preached is not the intriguing puzzle. How they were successful in convincing others of their bizarre purpose is the real mystery.

Charles Manson, leader of an infamous cult in the 1960s and 1970s, exhibited characteristics of charismatic leadership. He had an uncanny way of understanding his recruits—all young, idealistic, and psychologically damaged. Many professionals analyzing his group's development came to the conclusion that he preyed on their needs for a nurturing father figure and group affiliation. He and his members are still referred to as the Manson Family. Although never directly involved in murders and robberies himself, the courts determined that Manson was the

(Continued)

(Continued)

> mastermind and puppet-master of several heinous crimes. He remains in prison to this day, yet many of his original followers and some newer members still pledge their allegiance to this man and his beliefs.
>
> Schwartz and Kaslow (2001) believe the factors that make adolescents so vulnerable to cult recruiting include undeveloped decision-making skills, desire for peer acceptance and a sense of belonging, and high levels of idealism. They find that one of the fastest growing pools of recruits is senior citizens, and they postulate that this group of individuals shares many of those same factors.
>
> Walsh and Bor (1996) studied The Family, a religious movement or cult, to examine the psychological consequences of members' involvement. They determined that the longer individuals were in this group, the lower their need for mobility or freedom. The younger they were when they joined, the more they were concerned about disapproval and the more they worried about separation from the group. These behaviors parallel attachment patterns in kin family units.

In making decisions as a group, people often make different decisions than they would make if they were acting alone. This phenomenon is known as **group shift** and may appear as **risky shift** and **cautious shift** (Stoner, 1968). When risky shift occurs in decision making, group members may assume that the other group members hold more extreme views, causing them to adjust their views in favor of a more radical view than their own. Risky shift causes group members to take more risks as a group than they would if they were making an individual decision.

Darrin has been working in maintenance most of his adult life. In high school he began working at the local grocery store helping the maintenance director with various jobs after school and on weekends. After high school, he was hired as one of the maintenance personnel for the largest industry in the region. Twenty years later, he is still in the same job. Darrin has contemplated starting his own maintenance company, but has never really acted on it. Recently he expressed his dream to his brother at a family reunion. After talking about it for a few minutes, his brother gathered other relatives and soon the whole room was buzzing with ideas for Darrin. "You would be a great boss," his brother said. His cousin said, "You know everything there is to know about maintenance, after all, you have done it for 20 years—you could write the book on maintenance!" Leaving the reunion, Darrin was ready to initiate the plans to quit his job and start his own company. His family had given him the confidence to finally take the first step.

Darrin was making a risky shift in his decision to start a business. Although he would lose his stable income and start a business that had the potential to fail, he took the plunge because the group had given him confidence, and their collective attitude seemed to take away some of the burden of the decision. As with groupthink, Darrin may be making a mistake if he doesn't make his decision based on information that rationally and systematically guides him to the best decision.

Cautious shift reflects the opposite effect within the group. A group can be overly cautious in their decisions as well, especially following group discussion.

Antonio is getting married in 6 weeks. His fiancée is a beautiful girl who he has known since sixth grade. His coworkers tease him that he is the luckiest man alive, but lately he has been having some doubts about his decision to marry. One night while with his family, he expresses his concern. They all agree that he is mature, financially secure, and emotionally stable. His concerns lie in the uncertainty of marriage. Antonio agonizes, "Will I be a good husband? Will I be able to commit to this relationship long term? What if I find someone else?" Although his family feels that these fears may be a bit of "cold-feet," they listen and contemplate his dilemma. After much discussion, they agree that Antonio is not ready to marry. The following day, Antonio calls off the wedding.

Antonio's decision was made on the side of caution. Although later he may decide to marry, his family helped him to make a decision that was right for him at the time. His family gave him courage to make a decision that he did not feel comfortable making himself.

Myers and Lamm (1976) suggest that a result of group shift may have a polarized effect. They note that the decisions made after discussion tend to be more extreme to one side than the average of the opinions of individual group members before the discussion.

Summary

Leadership is an important function of any group, including families. A leader is one who can set the direction for the group and effectively lead the group in decision making. Leaders need foundational, direction, and leadership influence skills. A good leader is also aware of how attitude affects the outcome of the organization. Effective family leaders possess additional skills, including multitasking, interpersonal skills, growing human capabilities, and building character. Some leadership theories include the theory of X and Y, the three-factor theory, the dimensional theory,

(Continued)

(Continued)

the contingency model, the path-goal theory, and the situational leadership theory. Leadership effectiveness can be predicted by the transactional, transformational, and laissez-faire leadership styles.

Most family decisions are made by the group process. This process differs from nonfamily groups because of the presence of characteristics such as love, attachment, and a life-long investment in the group. Within the group process, families may make decisions based on social class, cultural or ethnic norms, communication styles, power structures, and past experience.

Families may be subject to groupthink when they fail to employ vigilant decision-making practices. To prevent faulty thinking, the group needs to establish an environment where alternatives are welcomed. Groups can make different decisions than they would if they were acting along. This process is known as group shift and can involve either risky shift or cautious shift.

Questions for Review and Discussion

1. How does an effective leader in the family differ from the leader in other organizations?

2. How does the leadership style of a parent influence his or her parenting style?

3. Discuss how the dynamics of a family can affect their decision making.

4. What are the consequences for a family caught in groupthink?

5. What type of family would opt for risky shift in making decisions? Cautious shift?

Unit V

Implementing and Evaluating Decisions

The Decision-Making Process

- Recognize existing need(s)
- Identify alternatives to fulfill identified needs
- Evaluate identified alternatives
- Select and implement alternative
  Chapter 12. Making It Happen
- Reflect and evaluate alternative selected
  Chapter 13. Defining Success
  Chapter 14. Current and Future Challenges

Making It Happen 12

Objectives

- Understand the need for flexibility in the implementation process.

- Explore the importance of motivation to plan success.

- Differentiate among different types of implementation strategies.

- Understand the need for accountability of those responsible for plan implementation.

- Become aware of the processes and importance of estate planning and risk management.

- Understand the value of postimplementation evaluation.

- Understand risk management and methods used in family management.

As long as the world is turning and spinning, we're gonna be dizzy and we're gonna make mistakes.

—Mel Brooks

Decisions rarely stand alone, disconnected from future processing. Usually, one decision leads to others, creating a continuous process that requires monitoring and adjustment. To reach goals, families must purposefully strive to fulfill objectives. In a dynamic environment, these objectives may require revision to reach ultimate success.

The Ito family has decided to reduce its utility bills and utilize the savings to strengthen their retirement funds. Their objectives included reducing the electric and gas bills by 25%. Methods utilized to reach that reduction included (a) weatherizing the doors and windows, (b) installing dimmers and timers on major household lighting, and (c) adjusting temperature thresholds for heating and air conditioning. The first year after implementing these measures, the Itos realized a savings of almost 30%. The next year, however, utilities increased rates by 15%, and it was an especially hard winter, requiring more heat than usual. The family's efforts are still important and are resulting in savings, but their objectives will need to be adjusted in light of the rate changes, which are uncontrollable factors. The plan is still working, but the expectations must be lowered or methods of reduction must be increased.

Family decisions and the resulting plans are not created or implemented in a vacuum. They are impacted by social, economic, and political changes. If members are unrealistic about the flexibility required to reach goals, they will become frustrated, and their participation may wane. Plans requiring group members' support are vulnerable to the attitudes and behaviors of individual members.

Implementation

One half of those who begin worksite exercise programs drop out within the first 6 months (Glasgow, Terborg, & Hollis, 1995). Less than one half of Americans over the age of 40 have been anticipating postretirement financial needs. Failure to implement plans is evident in many facets of contemporary family management. Why do families create plans and then fail to implement them? There are several possible explanations.

Most individuals and families have too many goals for their limited resources. When that happens, choices must be made about which goals are most important. In the process of prioritizing, some goals, and the plans to implement them, are abandoned altogether. Some are postponed to be revisited at a later, more conducive time.

Max had planned to finish college in eight semesters. Shortly after the second semester, he realized that, to pay for tuition, books, and living expenses, he would need more money than he originally budgeted. He decided to take a semester off and work full-time to boost his bank account. He is determined to resume studies next semester.

In this situation, Max is not abandoning his goal of obtaining a college education. He is postponing it—adjusting for reality factors. Should Max secure a full-time job that he likes and that has future potential, he may revisit his college goal and may decide not to go back to school.

Another reason that families don't fully implement plans is crisis management. Because a family operates in a dynamic, ever-changing environment, sudden, unexpected emergencies occur. Long-awaited vacation plans may be abruptly abandoned when a medical emergency or death occurs. Saving for new appliances may give way to repairing a family automobile. Job loss may derail many long-term plans. Resources must be diverted to handling these crises, and less important goals will be delayed or forgotten.

A third reason that family plans may not be fully implemented is attributed to Gresham's law of planning. This phenomenon (Chapter 9) occurs when short-term, more immediate needs shift priorities and extend deadlines away from established plans and into these short-term situations. Remodeling of a kitchen may be delayed when undetected water damage is discovered in the home's foundation.

Another reason for plan failure is loss of motivation. Chapter 11 discussed the complexity of group decision making. The same factors present during the decision and planning phases exist at implementation. It is important for all family members impacted by a plan to feel ownership of that plan. A leader will emerge with authority and responsibility necessary to monitor, adjust, and complete the plan. His or her leadership style must be appropriate for the plan and for all individuals involved. A common, shared vision must exist for members to maintain their motivation and level of effort toward goal completion. Four important concepts—strategy, delegation, accountability, and motivation—are keys to successful plan management.

STRATEGIES

Recent research in positive psychology (Seligman, 2002) and emotional intelligence (Bar-On & Parker, 2000) provide support for three groups of strategies: affect regulation, interpersonal, and problem solving/task management. Affect regulation deals with the emotional reactions experienced by family members during the implementation phase. Goals are often blocked or threatened, and people must learn to manage negative reactions such as anxiety, depression, and anger. Children may be expected to throw tantrums and express frustration vocally, but developmental theory suggests that there are different levels of behavior expected in times of disappointment. Adults usually have a repertoire of coping strategies that allow them to express affective thoughts and feelings. Relaxation, meditation, and stress-reduction skills are often part of successful strategies for managing affect during implementation. Optimism is an inherent desire to expect the best of things (Seligman, 2002). This affective tendency can be useful if it includes a rational evaluation of each situation. Pessimism is the tendency to believe that things will always turn out negatively. This affective reaction is not productive, and those expressing pessimistic attitudes almost always guarantee a drag on successful implementation.

Optimists report better adjustment to many types of stressors, including transition to college, pregnancy, chronically ill family members, and personal health threats (Jackson, Weiss, Lundquist, & Soderlind, 2002). Feather (1990) found that when people are confident that goals can be met, they are more likely to act and persist toward goal fulfillment. It is of interest to note that Jackson et al. (2002) also found that optimistic individuals are more likely to be married than are pessimists.

When informed that a new test had been implemented to determine proficiency in their foreign language course, Kale and Tristan react differently. Kale tells her friends that she is capable and willing to give the test her best shot. Tristan complains that everyone is out to get him, and he will never have time to adequately prepare for the test.

Kale's optimism will set her up for success if she is rationally assessing the circumstances—strong language skills and capability. It sets her up for disappointment, however, if she doesn't actually have what it takes. Tristan's pessimism will negatively impact his preparation and attitude toward the testing procedure, but it also provides him with an excuse if he does indeed fail. If family leaders can enhance the perceptions of mastery by communicating that the plan is sound, members have adequate resources, personal input and eventual rewards are valued, and progress is being made, the probability that members will remain engaged toward the completion of the goal is greatly enhanced.

Interpersonal strategies incorporate assertive communication without dominance of others involved. Using this strategy requires expression of one's willingness to cooperate and work with others toward a common goal. Active listening is part of this approach, as is offering or seeking support from others when needed. Problem-solving/task-management strategies involve self-monitoring and continual monitoring of the environment. Problems encountered during the implementation phase are viewed as nothing more than discrepancies between what is perceived and what is desired in terms of progress toward goal achievement.

Vernon is a problem solver. When his debate team seemed to be falling apart after months of success, he looked first at his own performance and effort and then at the differences in the competitions, past and recent. Julliette uses interpersonal strategies in her efforts to understand the problem with the same team. She calls a meeting to discuss team members' concerns and to explore the possibility of a group effort toward improvement. James, also a member of the team, is more likely to utilize affect regulation, exploring emotions expressed by himself and other team members to find reasons for the recent failures. All three have different approaches, but their strategies will be helpful if the goal is viewed to be the same—a stronger team effort.

Resilience is the ability to rebound from adversity, overcome obstacles, and achieve success even when one has experienced great losses in the past. Amatea, Smith-Adcock, and Villares (2006) present the family resilience perspective. This approach to understanding how family members and family units can succeed, even in adverse situations, considers each interaction between the home and outside environment as an opportunity to strengthen that family's ability to overcome adversity and fulfill family goals. Research focusing on obstacles faced by low-income families has supported this resilience perspective, citing a surprising resilience and creativity in these families when building strategies to help children in poverty overcome negative life situations.

Strategies for achieving goals are influenced by available resources, opportunities, and sources of support (Griffith & Graham, 2004). It is not enough just for a strategy to be in place. Day-to-day stress and competition for family resources can sap the energy out of any plan of action. It is important to make the strategy a priority by engaging all involved before and throughout implementation. This process requires clear communication of the plan's intent and structure and connecting each individual involved to the plan by defining his or her role and benefits expected on completion. Another important component of any strategy is continual assessment and feedback to all concerning the progress and necessary adjustments made along the way.

Brett, 5 years old, has just been diagnosed with juvenile diabetes. His condition reached a level of hospitalization, and a recovery and maintenance plan has been established for his situation. His mother insists on controlling the plan entirely, feeling that Brett's siblings are too young and that her husband has enough responsibility outside of the home. Shortly after Brett's return home, the stress level within the family peaks, and his maintenance plan is threatened. There have been no changes in the rest of the family's diet and exercise, and his siblings and friends don't understand the importance of his continual blood monitoring. They start to avoid him, and he becomes isolated and depressed. His father realizes that something must be done, but doesn't have the knowledge or skills to step in and work with his wife.

When any one individual in a family faces lifestyle changes, he or she needs the support of all other family members. They need to understand why and how these changes can impact everyone. They need to celebrate the successes and shoulder some responsibility for failures. Implementing any new type of behavioral change requires flexibility and a willingness of everyone in the family to adapt to change. Change brings about a measure of discomfort within the family, but is ever-present and necessary for family survival. Communication, engagement, and a shared vision help families implement important short- and long-term plans. Strategies that bring about success often become established patterns of actions and behaviors of individuals and family (Griffith & Graham, 2004).

DELEGATION

An important part of engagement of individuals during implementation is **delegation** of activities and responsibilities. Delegation is not "dumping" tasks on others, but rather an opportunity for leaders to help develop the skills of others involved in the implementation of a plan (Webb, 1991). By delegating parts of the implementation plan to others, the leader will be able to focus time and energy on other matters, and all members will grow and mature by fulfilling assigned responsibilities. They will also feel more connected to the entire plan when they are responsible for at least a part of it. Delegation is a complex activity, however, and there are some basic principles that will enhance the success of that process:

- Determine what requires your own attention and action and those things that may be accomplished by others without your direct supervision. Consider the mental and social maturity of those to whom you wish to delegate responsibilities.

- Realize that delegated actions may not always rise to meet your own personal standards. A younger child may not make perfect rows while mowing the grass. Ask yourself if these "imperfections" will critically harm the implementation process. If not, acknowledge progress, not the procedure.

- Don't underestimate the abilities of others. They may require some instruction and supervision, but each delegated task they accomplish prepares them for future, more complicated tasks.

- Focus on communication during the delegation process. Be clear and concise when expressing your expectations. Explain why you are delegating this task to him or her. Be open to questions the individual may have at the time he or she is given the responsibility and at intervals during the rest of the implementation process.

- Make delegated assignments easy enough to complete, but challenging and enjoyable at the same time.

- Because all decisions require future decisions, include assignments that require him or her to make some decisions and give him or her sufficient authority to do so.

- Always support and monitor family members involved in implementation. Remember to hold them accountable, but only for what is in their control. Avoid micromanaging them, but inform them of when and in what form you expect reports about their progress.

- When the implementation process has been completed, be fair and honest in the assessment of both the effort and end product of your delegated tasks. Complement when appropriate, and give constructive criticism when necessary. Be sure to include all participating members in the celebration of completion (Webb, 1991).

Maier (1968) found that communication is essential to successful delegation. There is a gap between the perceptions of the leader and those of other group members. The leader would like others to take more initiative and a more active role in decision making. Other group members perceive that the leader wants them to follow orders and to be conservative in doing so. These members, however, report that they would like more latitude in how they complete the tasks and more shared decision making. Untapped potential exists, but perceptions prevent implementation—a real possibility in family settings. Underestimating the actual capabilities of younger and older family members reduces total family productivity when delegation to these members is constrained.

ACCOUNTABILITY

All members involved in the implementation of a plan should have a balance between responsibility and authority. No one should be held accountable for something over which he or she has no control. Delegated tasks should reflect this balance. The distribution of responsibility across family members for the success of any plan should follow general guidelines of accountability:

- Ensure that each member fully understands his or her tasks within implementation and that each possesses the necessary resources to accomplish those tasks.

- Communicate expected feedback intervals and clarify who should be notified if something goes awry.

- Provide frequent feedback on the progress that results from the members' efforts, and balance positive and constructive criticism carefully.

An essential expectation of parenting and mentoring is that of guidance. Children and young adults learn responsibility by watching older family members and completing supervised tasks requiring developmental and age-appropriate levels of responsibility. A great deal of research and many educational programs address the concept of empowerment and the perceived benefits it provides to individuals within family and work settings.

Quinn and Spreitzer (1997) found two competing definitions of empowerment among business executives. One group believed that empowerment was about delegating decision making within a clear set of boundaries. The other group saw it more as risk-taking, growth, and change. Empowerment is not something a manager or leader does to subordinates, but rather a mind-set that individuals have about their role in the implementation process. Empowered family members see themselves as having choices, of being personally connected to the family unit, as confident about their abilities, and as capable of having an impact on the family's progress.

MOTIVATION

When an individual is part of a family group, his or her actions impact the outcomes of the other group members and the group as a whole (Dewitte & De Cremer, 2001), which creates a conflict between pursuing one's own self-interest and the group's interest. Dewitte and De Cremer refer to this as a mixed-motive situation. Self-control and delayed gratification become important in these situations. The ability to sacrifice for the group's long-term benefit will delay the possibility of reaching some short-term personal goals. When a family member can understand and conceptualize the future benefit to both him and her and the family unit, he or she is more likely to support the group's plan of action.

Long-term plans are especially vulnerable to delays and obstacles. Family members will be motivated toward goal achievement by all of the factors discussed earlier in this chapter. Specific strategies, however, are often necessary for certain groups. Adolescents, for example, have been found to be best motivated when they are given explanations for why a goal is valuable to them and how it will intrinsically benefit them and/or their families. Extrinsic motivators, such as financial success, power, and image, are less effective in goal accomplishment. Vansteenkiste et al. (2005) believe that extrinsic motivators during adolescence shift the focus to a more rigid, narrowly focused, and superficial involvement. They also found that adolescents are more motivated when they can identify with the personal importance of the activity with appropriate levels of autonomy within the tasks expected of them. Adults are more likely to respect the needs of other adults in terms of autonomy, but need to strive toward similar approaches when dealing with adolescent family members.

Marcus is 15 years old and working part time during the school year. His father insists that Marcus save 75% of his earnings. He wants his son to attend an Ivy League college and continually stresses how expensive that will be. Marcus' mother encourages him to save his money so he will have more options when he is ready to decide where he will go to college.

According to research on intrinsic and extrinsic goal motivation, Marcus will probably be more likely to save his money if he believes it will provide him with choices later. His mother's encouragement is based on intrinsic and autonomous factors. His father is more concerned with image (extrinsic) and uses a more controlling approach.

Children develop self-control, independence, and strategies to correct poor behavior through experiences with unpleasant circumstances and by making mistakes (Lynch, Hurford, & Cole, 2002). Parental enabling, or overprotectiveness and manipulation to insulate children from these uncomfortable learning experiences, has been found to negatively impact a child's ability to take responsibility for his or her behavior. Another similar concept, locus of control (Rotter, 1973), refers to one's belief that one has the ability to control the outcome of a task one has been assigned. Children and adults with an external locus of control believe that the environment and others in that environment have a substantial impact on their ability to achieve. Those with an internal locus of control believe they have control over what happens to them. An internal locus of control has been linked to resiliency in both children and adults.

Estate Planning

One of the most important and involved planning and implementation processes an individual or family undertakes is that of distribution of accumulated assets to the next generation. Estate planning is a process used to manage a family's future financial health and well-being. This concept is a reflection of the belief that future generations should profit from the work and savings plans of current family members. At times through recorded history, a family's holdings were passed to specific members of the next generation, often first-born males. Contemporary beliefs favor a more equitable distribution across genders. There are complex legal methods that will be applied to estate distribution if a family has not created a plan prior to the death of a family member.

An individual's estate consists of everything he or she has accumulated to date that has value, including property such as homes, vehicles, and furnishings. An estate also includes all financial holdings—certificates of deposit, stocks, bonds, and cash. To determine what someone's estate is worth, a list of assets is compiled and those current values are adjusted by the liabilities or credit owed against those assets. This final figure is often referred to as an estate's **net worth**. In essence, this is what an individual will pass on to his or her heirs on death. This inheritance can be managed prior to the owner's death to minimize the tax liability for future heirs and ensure that the estate is both protected and invested well.

Inheritance tax has fluctuated greatly at the federal level during the last decade. Laws have been passed to eliminate it over time, but it is scheduled to reappear in 2011 unless new terms are passed. Gift tax is another important factor to consider when planning estate giving. Each year an individual is permitted under law to give up to a certain amount of money to as many people as desired without those recipients being taxed on the gifted funds. Currently, $12,000 (2007) is the maximum allowed for gifting without tax liability.

> *Georgia has gifted each of her five grandchildren and two of her close friends $10,000 during 2006. She plans on doing the same in 2007 and 2008. Her grandchildren and friends do not have to pay taxes on these gifts, totaling $30,000 each over the 3-year period. If Georgia had given $30,000 to each in her will, on her death, that entire amount may have been taxable under current tax law.*

Estate taxes are complicated and vary from location to location. It is an important part of an estate plan to research these taxes, and professional guidance is available.

As mentioned before, individuals who die without legally qualified estate plans filed will be considered as intestate. Under these circumstances, there are complex legal steps that will be followed to settle the estate of the deceased. If an individual wishes to have more control over the disbursement of his or her estate, legal steps must be taken before death. A will is a legal document that explains how an individual wants to distribute his or her assets on death. Beneficiaries, similar to insurance terms, will be designated, and terms of distribution among those individuals will be stipulated. To handle the process of distribution, an executor is named in the will. That person is responsible for carrying out all wishes explained within the legal will. A will is an important estate planning technique; however, anything within a will must go through the probate process, the validation and legal processing of the will, and this process is often slow and costly.

There are two other important legal documents that should be considered in the estate planning process. A durable power of attorney is a document that protects your estate if you should become unable to make decisions on your own behalf due to physical or mental problems. This person, chosen by the individual, can act as his or her representative in a legal capacity. This role does not impact an existing will, only the actual time of incapacitation while an individual is still alive. Another more specific legal designation that provides for important decision making when someone is deemed unable to make medical decisions for him or herself is referred to as a living will. In this document, a health care proxy is designated to make life support decisions for an individual who has lost the capacity to make those types of decisions. Such a document is often requested on hospital admittance, although it is not required for treatment.

Understanding current laws regarding transfer of assets is a major factor for success within estate planning. A few are presented here, but it is important to seek legal counsel when contemplating sound estate plan decisions. Types of ownership and the use of trusts impact estate distribution in unique ways.

Joint ownership with right of survivorship is a method of transferring property without tax implications. When an asset, such as a home or vehicle, is owned jointly, that asset is automatically transferred to the surviving owner without probate. Community property is another form of joint ownership falling under marital laws of states. Community property in these states is anything acquired during a legal marriage. On death of either the husband or wife, the survivor will receive one half of community property, and the other one half will be disbursed through the plan within a will or state inheritance laws.

A trust is a legal entity created by the grantor to hold and manage inheritance property or money on the behalf of another person. If someone is concerned that one of his or her designated beneficiaries might be unable to manage inheritance, such a legal situation may be helpful.

Fred has accumulated a great deal of money during his adult life. He married late, and at age 70 he has two children still in elementary school. His wife died recently, and his health is failing. Fred is concerned about how his young children might survive if something happens to him, so he creates a trust fund for both of them. If he dies before they reach the age of 25, the money he has willed to them will be managed by his good friend and legal counsel, Rico. Through this legal arrangement, all living expenses will be provided through their inheritance on the approval of Rico until they reach the age stated in the trust documentation (25), on which each will gain full control of the money in his or her account.

Aspen is the single mother of Jacque, an adult with Down's syndrome. To ensure that Jacque will have adequate care if she should die first, Aspen has created a trust that will hold any life insurance paid out on her death in his name, available to help pay for the care and supervision he may need after her death.

Trusts ensure guidance and supervision of estate inheritance. They are especially useful in the following situations:

- To bypass the probate process

- To avoid legal challenges that wills often experience
- To reduce estate taxes
- To ensure professional management for those who are not deemed knowledgeable or responsible by the grantor
- To ensure confidentiality as a will becomes public record and trusts do not
- To provide for survivors with special needs
- To keep money responsibly until a child reaches the age of maturity
- To provide uncontestable inheritance to children from a marriage that is currently dissolved

There are several types of trusts that can be legally established during the estate planning process. Each type specifically answers tax or responsibility issues faced by the planner. Due to the complexity of establishing and implementing a trust, it is strongly advised that legal and financial expertise be utilized.

Most people recognize the importance of estate planning, but many do not develop or implement strategies that are in the best interest of them and their survivors. Any individual with responsibility toward others—partners, children, parents, siblings—should have a legal will drafted and on file. Beyond that component, the size of the estate and the complexity of relationships will determine the intricacy of one's estate plan.

Family Business Succession

Attitudes and behavior toward inheritance are changing, shifting the ways that families manage family-based businesses and how they engage in training of their successors ("Planning for Your Successor," 2005). Without adequate planning, family disputes and mismanaged estate tax issues may force family businesses to be broken into pieces or be sold in entirety to outside bidders when family founders are incapacitated or die. The transfer or distribution of a family business on the death of older members often strains family relations. There is a difficult balance to negotiate between business strategies to ensure current and future business success and the need to distribute assets fairly and equally to all survivors.

Planning for the transfer of a family business is essential for two important reasons. First, when families are mourning the loss of a parent or other family member, emotions are high. Second, dealing with complex business decisions and issues of future business leadership may be too much for family members to bear at this time, and decisions made under

Photo 12.1 Family businesses have been an important part of the nation's economic history.

Source: © Michael Prince/Corbis.

such stress may be challenged at a later time, pitting some family members against others. Succession planning should be an integral part of any family business. These plans should be shared and understood by all members who will be impacted.

Risk Management

Most decisions contain a degree of uncertainty, and successful implementation of any plan includes assessing possible risks and consequences (Heller, 1998). Williams et al. (2006) define *risk management* as a systematic process of identifying, assessing, managing, and monitoring risks and uncertainty in an effort to plan for and cope with possible negative outcomes. Risk can be managed by intuition or unconscious reasoning based on affect. Past experience provides a more understandable method of analyzing possible future risks; however, intuition is often credited for important decisions.

Williams et al. (2006) suggest three important steps in risk management:

1. Risk Recognition
2. Risk Prioritization
3. Risk Management

Risks within the context of the family include damaged relationships, financial insecurity, and family unit instability. These risks must be analyzed for possible consequences and likelihoods of actuality. Realizing that a family operates under continual risk possibilities, members must determine how much risk is acceptable to members. Unacceptable risks can be handled in one of four different ways. The situation or behaviors can be terminated. They can be treated or managed with control measures or contingency plans. The family may decide to accept the risk and live with whatever outcome occurs, or the family may transfer or move the risk impact to another entity, such as insurance.

Missy and Earl own and occupy a home on the California coastline. Neighboring homes have fallen into the ocean over the last few years. Their risks in this situation include danger to life, loss of the family's home, and/or possible damage to the existing structure. Realizing the risk factors, they can move from the home and try to sell it or parts of it (terminate). They can invest in structural reinforcement to try to prevent future damage (treat). They can try to convince themselves that whatever happens will happen and they will figure out how to deal with it at the time (tolerate). If possible, they may invest in an insurance policy that will pay damages if they do, indeed, occur (transfer). If the risk is too high, it is unlikely that an insurance company will offer coverage on the home.

There are always choices in situations of risk, and the level of acceptance will differ from family to family.

Worldview (Chapter 1) presents another way to understand the levels of difference in risk assessment among families and cultural groups. If you do not believe you have control over natural processes, such as erosion and hurricanes, you will not spend time and money trying to manage potential risk from those phenomena. Decisions made by families to not carry insurance are not always based on financial inability or lack of intelligent decision-making. Different perspectives lead to different choices in similar situations.

INSURANCE

Many risks exist for individuals and families over time. Fire, accidents, illness, and legal problems threaten the security of families on a daily basis.

As part of the risk management utilized by contemporary families, insurance plays an important role in resource management. From a worldview perspective, insuring people and things against loss stems from a belief that there is and should be a level of control over the unknown. The insured believes that future loss can be compensated, and that such monetary replacement will make things right again, at least to some degree.

Insurance is based on the concept of risk pooling, or the sharing of financial risks among many group members (Keown, 2003). Those purchasing insurance pay **premium**s to companies and receive the promise of future payment if they experience a catastrophic situation that is covered by that insurance policy. Chances are that they will never actually face that catastrophe. Insurance companies offer policies based on a calculated risk of their own. Mathematically, the probability that your family home will be destroyed is small. If you and 1 million of your neighbors purchase home insurance, you are pooling your premiums through the insurance agency. That agency has calculated the possibility of home loss among policy owners and has set the premium price to cover the expected claims each year.

Insurance Company A has sold home insurance policies to 2,000 families in New Port. Each family pays an average of $200 per year for this coverage ($400,000). Last year two homes insured by A are ruined by fire, with an insurance payout of $300,000. The $100,000 difference between payouts and premiums collected represents a profit for the company, which is then used to employ agents in the community and to finance the overall company's expenses.

Of course the 1,998 families that did not collect money from their insurance policies have paid $200 and have received only the security of knowing they were covered just in case such a disaster hits them personally. There are several types of insurance available to families seeking to protect themselves from possible devastating losses. Some commonalities across insurance providers are **deductibles, copays,** and **stop-loss limits**. As discussed in Chapter 8, a deductible is the amount the patient is responsible for before insurance coverage will activate. A copayment is the amount of money expected from the patient in addition to the insurance payment. A stop-loss limit is the total amount an insured person will be expected to pay in a designated time period.

Rogene has an automobile policy that has a $500 deductible. When a rock breaks her windshield, she discovers that the replacement cost of the glass is $450. She must pay the entire amount to repair the windshield, and she probably won't even contact her insurance company because she is responsible for the first $500 of each repair incident. Her health insurance policy has a $250 annual deductible. Each year she must pay the first $250 of medical expenses before her insurance *coverage initiates. After meeting her deductible, she has a copay of 20%. A $100 medical bill, after the deductible has been met, will cost her only $20. The other $80 will be paid by her insurance carrier. Her policy also has a $1,000 stop-loss feature. Once the $250 deductible has been met and she has paid 20% of charges up to $750 total, her insurance will begin to pay 100% of future bills during that same designated time period (usually an annual cycle).*

HEALTH INSURANCE

Most health insurance policies include a combination of hospital, surgical, and physician expense coverage. Hospital insurance will cover some of the costs resulting from a hospital stay, such as room charges, care and medication costs, and surgical facility usage. Most health insurance plans have limits set on acceptable fees charged their clients and on the length of hospital stay for each visit. Surgical coverage will pay a percentage of expenses for necessary operations that have been approved by the company. This coverage usually does not include experimental treatments. Policies may also cover doctor fees incurred outside of the hospital, such as office visits and lab fees.

Individuals and families without medical insurance face two possibilities in the event of a health emergency—do without treatment or access public assistance/private foundation funds to pay for treatment. General health care is lower among those who are uninsured than those with even minimum insurance support. An important part of most health care insurance plans is payment for regular health check-ups to identify possible problems early or to avoid the development of disease and sickness later.

Specific insurance coverage for dental and vision health coverage are available for additional premium payments. Those concerned about developing cancer during their lifetimes may purchase insurance plans to cover expenses associated with those kinds of illnesses and treatments. Once basic health insurance has become part of a family's overall life plan, money available for additional coverage (often referred to as *riders*) will impact the decision-making process. It is important that the need for these types of special plans be reevaluated over the life changes of a family.

When Barry, the youngest Kohn child, married, Mr. and Mrs. Kohn analyzed their new health insurance needs. Both parents use reading glasses, but do not need glasses for other types of functioning. Because the vision insurance plan they had covered one examination annually and one pair of glasses each year, it became obvious that this plan was no longer needed. At $20 per month ($240 per year), Mr. and Mrs. Kohn would be paying more to keep the policy than they would need to pay for two eye exams each year. The plan had been useful when their two youngest children were under their coverage because both required glasses or contacts at all times.

Managed health care is a concept that stems from the growing need of companies to provide health insurance coverage to employees. To reduce insurance costs and claims, medical providers are recruited who will agree to lower charges per visit or treatment with the advantage of volume numbers of guaranteed patients. Those using a managed health care plan are limited to those physicians on a preapproved list. Some are given the right to choose others with additional costs or higher copayments.

There are two distinct types of managed health care plans—health maintenance organizations (HMOs) and preferred provider organizations (PPOs). HMOs are prepaid insurance plans that allow members to use the services of participating doctors and medical facilities. Members pay a flat fee to belong, and copayments may be required. HMOs are efficient, saving up to 40% of medical costs (Keown, 2004). The perceived drawbacks to HMO plans include limited choices of providers, impersonal care, and complicated referral requirements.

PPOs fall somewhere between traditional health care plans and HMOs. Employers negotiate reduced rates with a group of physicians and facilities, creating a list from which their employees can choose. If the insured insist on utilizing care providers who have not contracted with the insurance group, they will have to pay a higher copay or penalty charge.

Health insurance is available through employers, associations, professional groups, and individual plans. Group plans cost about 25% less than similar individual policies because larger groups have more bargaining power to reduce service costs. Lower costs equate lower premium needs from participants. When insurance is not available through employers, individuals can seek other group affiliations (clubs, financial institutions, and professional organizations) to take advantage of these pooled, lower rate plans.

Reality Check

In the spring of 2006, Jessica and Brandon faced fear and braced for the battle of their lives. Brandon, fresh from a restaurant management training program, collapsed in the bathroom of their new home. Jessica, newly employed herself, received a memorable phone call later that day. Brandon had been diagnosed with leukemia. Within the week, Brandon was fully immersed in an aggressive treatment program in a hospital 200 miles from their home and employers. Jessica, torn among her husband's care regime, their 18-month-old daughter's needs, and the responsibilities of her new job, felt her world tilt on its axis.

Understanding our health insurance coverage was one of the first things on our minds. How much is this going to cost us, and how are we going to pay for it? I honestly can't say what we would have done without insurance. I suppose we would have had to sell our house and declare bankruptcy. We didn't have the money in savings to pay for the extremely high medical bills.

(Continued)

(Continued)

> *At first there was a $500 deductible that we had to meet. This was virtually met with just the doctor visits leading up to the diagnosis. Second, there was a $1,500 stop-loss, which meant that we would have a total of $1,500 out-of-pocket expenses (deductibles and copays) before the insurance company would begin paying 100% of the medical costs. What a relief that was to know that we only had to come up with $1,500. That is much better than the $248,000 spent over the first 6 weeks for Brandon's treatment and care.*

Medical costs were just part of the financial problems within this family's crisis. Brandon was 200 miles away from home. Jessica had personal expenses just trying to be with him, care for their daughter, and meet the needs of her job.

> *Luckily, I am an educated person, and I knew about other resources available. Insurance does not pay for the spouse's food or lodging. The hospital social worker made funds available for these expenses. Reducing those concerns allowed me to focus on my husband's needs and those of our daughter.*

In times of family crisis, money is not the only resource necessary for survival. Jessica found that her social networks of family, friends, and colleagues were helpful.

> *My workplace policies allowed me to put my husband's health as top priority. I left my office immediately after the diagnosis, knowing that my colleagues would cover for me as needed. I was allowed to do much of my normal workload via the computer and Internet. My employer provided me with the laptop computer, also. That allowed me to be near my husband and continue working when things slowed down. Working was routine, and I needed routine to balance the helplessness of the situation and the lack of control I felt.*

After a bone-marrow transplant, Brandon was able to return home. Jessica still bears the full responsibility of wage provider and insurance source. An expected full recovery will eventually see this family back on their original track—a dual-career, two-wage family. Until that time, they continue to draw from the resources that emerged during the crisis. Risk management paid off for them in many ways.

Health insurance is available to all in the United States with access to funds, policies, and qualifying states of health. Often young adults ages 18 to 30 view the chances of experiencing devastating illness and injury as improbable. They elect to use their money in more real-life ways, such as consuming goods and services. Although the possibility of illness and disability increase more quickly after age 30, it is unfortunate for those under 30 who have elected to forgo health insurance who do fall ill or suffer catastrophic injury. The lack of health insurance could have derailed Brandon and Jessica's future and forced them to accept less expensive, possibly less effective, treatment options.

LIFE INSURANCE

Life insurance provides protection against loss of income due to death. When family members are dependent on the income of an adult member, loss of that income would create economic strain. A single person with no dependents would not need more life insurance than would be necessary to cover his or her last expenses. A married person with small children may see life insurance as a way to partially replace income he or she might have contributed to the family if death had not occurred. On the death of the insured, a lump sum payment or installments are paid to the designated beneficiary. That person or persons can use that money to replace the lost income of the deceased.

If an individual determines that he or she should have life insurance, the next decision involves the amount of coverage desired. Experts suggest that an individual purchase enough life insurance to cover 5 to 15 years of lost income. A more complicated, but focused, approach is to forecast future needs of survivors.

Andrew Saw is 65 years old with no surviving spouse or debts. His end-of-life needs are simply burial expenses. If he does not have enough money saved for that, he may want to have a life insurance policy that will cover those costs. Anything above that amount would be distributed among his surviving family members. His son, Tan, is 40 with a wife and three children under the age of 10. Tan's wife does not work outside of the home, and their savings are still quite small. Tan may want to have enough life insurance to replace his income until his youngest child has completed his or her education. Other future costs he may wish to cover would include education, mortgage, and costs associated with replacement of his physical contributions to his family, such as lawn care and home maintenance.

There are three primary types of life insurance—term, whole, and universal. **Term insurance** is the simplest form of life insurance. You pay a set premium based on your life expectancy, as determined by statistical analysis of your risk factors. In return, your beneficiaries will receive a set amount of money on your death. These types of policies are only in effect for a limited amount of time or a certain term, such as 10 years. Once the term has expired, your insurance carrier may increase the amount of the premium without increasing the policy's value. The original policy may be cancelled at that time if you choose not to agree to pay the increased premium. If you did not die during that term of coverage, none of the money paid in premiums is available to you.

Whole life insurance provides both death benefits and an opportunity to accumulate savings through payment of premiums over time. The company invests a small portion of each premium into a savings account that grows with each premium and interest earned over time. This savings account is referred to as the cash value of the insurance policy. The policy owner can borrow against this cash value and retain the insurance or he or she may terminate the policy and collect the amount of money in the savings plan.

Universal life insurance combines term insurance and cash-value, tax-deferred savings. Premium payments are broken down into three parts: term insurance payment, savings, and administrative costs. The insured person can increase or decrease the premiums. A higher payment will result in larger amounts being deposited into the savings plan. A lower payment will result in less savings, and if the payment is too low to cover the administrative costs and term insurance portion, the short-fall can be pulled from accumulated savings, thus ensuring the life insurance remains in effect. This type of plan requires dedication and continual decision making on the part of the insured party. Temptation to pay less over extended periods of time could result in policy lapse if not monitored closely.

Should adults in the family decide to hedge the risk of death with life insurance, deciding how much to purchase and what type to buy are important decisions. Paying premiums can be done automatically through bank drafts, payroll deductions, or company-supplied coupons. Insurance payments are expenses for families and must be folded into regular family budget plans. Missed payments can result in insurance cancellation, and to reinstate policies, individuals may have to prove insurability at the present time.

Bruce and his wife were struggling to make monthly debt payments. They decided to let his life insurance policy lapse for a time and re-apply when their finances stabilized. Three months later, Bruce is diagnosed with leukemia. His health records will be reviewed by any life insurance company before he is issued a policy. Chances are low that any company will agree to provide him with coverage, even at high premium rates.

AUTOMOBILE INSURANCE

Photo 12.2   Insurance eases the trauma of a crisis.

Source: © Robert Kyllo/iStockphoto.

In the United States, there are 30 million accidents each year (Keown, 2004). That statistic implies that each driver has about a 20% chance per year to be involved in some type of automobile altercation. Automobile insurance is not an optional expense if an individual purchases a vehicle with the intention of driving that automobile on public streets and highways. All states require proof of insurance before vehicles can be licensed for operation. Coverage required differs from state to state, but there are two basic types of auto insurance available to consumers—liability and collision.

Liability coverage provides protection from lawsuits rising from an automobile accident. It will cover bodily injury to people physically hurt and resulting property damage. Medical expense coverage will pay medical bills and funeral expenses of passengers and the driver up to a predetermined limit. Uninsured motorist protection coverage is required in many states, protecting the victims should the responsible driver not have insurance.

Collision coverage provides monetary payment should your vehicle be stolen or damaged. Comprehensive physical damage coverage includes damage from fire, storms, and other major catastrophes. This type of coverage pays for losses regardless of who is determined to be at fault for the damage. It is recommended that the amount of coverage carried equal the cash value of the automobile, and most policies include a deductible.

The cost of automobile insurance is determined by many things, some under the control of the insured and some determined by statistical calculations of the insurance provider. The most important determinants of price include the following:

- Type of automobile. Insurance companies determine the risk of specific models of vehicles and factor that into the insurance premium. Style, power, and even color impact this determinant.

- Use of automobile. Probability of an accident increased with the type of driving and the frequency of use.

- Driver characteristics. Based on research data, insurance companies have determined the lifestyle or demographic risk factors that predict accidents. Young, unmarried males have a statistically greater chance of accident, thus they pay higher premiums for coverage. Age, sex, and marital status are factors folded into the premium prices.

- Driver's past record. Traffic violations and previous accidents and arrests will result in higher insurance rates.

- Geographic location. The more dense the population in an area, the greater the possibility of accident. Those living in urban areas will generally pay more for automobile insurance than those in less dense areas. Types of driving surfaces will also factor into the equation because rough, gravel-covered roads may result in more body damage during general use than will smoother, paved roads.

There are many discounts available to automobile drivers to reduce premium prices. Companies offer different types, but common discounts include those for good driving records, multiple automobiles under the same policy, completion of defensive driving courses, and good high school and college student records. Other methods of reducing premium costs include selecting higher deductibles, improving one's driving record, and selecting models that are less costly to insure.

HOME INSURANCE

Owning a home increases liability for families. Injuries sustained by nonfamily members while visiting are legal issues. Homeowners can be held responsible for injuries of all visitors occurring on their property regardless of permission or knowledge. Aside from liability, fires, flooding, and other catastrophes can damage or destroy homes, creating enormous physical and emotional stress for families. Home insurance is available to consumers to help manage such risks. Often referred to as homeowner's insurance, these policies cover more than just the dwelling. Sold in different combinations, insurance is available to cover loss due to natural disasters, man-made perils, and possible liability claims.

Property coverage under homeowner's insurance may include the cost associated with replacement of the dwelling, other structures on the property, personal property within the dwellings, and the loss of use of the dwelling during the time required to replace or repair the home. Not all policies include all of these issues, and it is important that homeowners fully understand the terms of the policy they purchase. There are also additional types of supplemental coverage available for specific situations. **Floaters** provide extended coverage for personal property such as jewelry, silver and gold articles, and valuable collectibles.

Because replacement cost is difficult to determine at the time of insuring and at the time of destruction, companies encourage owners to fully cover their dwellings. Many companies require that owners carry at least 80% of their home's full replacement cost (80% rule).

The St. Claire's home is valued at $200,000. Their insurance company requires that they carry at least a $160,000 policy. A recent storm resulted in $150,000 damage. The insurance payment will cover the entire loss. If less than 80% of the replacement cost is purchased, the homeowner must pay a coinsurance provision.

The liability insurance within a homeowner's policy protects the policyholder and his or her family from financial loss if someone injured on their property sues for damages and/or medical expenses. Although families rarely anticipate nasty legal battles over such things, this type of insurance hedges risk in a time when liability cases are at an all-time high. It is especially important if the family home has a swimming pool, hot tub, trampoline, or elevated exterior living areas.

The major determinants of policy cost are (a) the location of the home, (b) the home's structure, and (c) the level of coverage and type of policy desired. Geographic location determines the probability of loss due to certain kinds of weather conditions and levels of theft, vandalism, and general crime. Older structures and homes made from less durable materials are more costly to cover. Those constructed with above minimum standard or code-required materials and specifications may qualify for premium discounts. The more comprehensive the policy and the higher the replacement cost of the home, the larger the premium will be. There are a few ways to reduce costs, however. Selecting higher deductibles, installing security features, and using the same insurance provider for multiple policies (auto, homeowners, and health) will lower the premium costs.

Worldview

Tsunamis, Hurricanes, and Insurance

On December 26, 2004, a massive earthquake of 9.0 magnitude occurred under the Indian Ocean just off the coast of Indonesia, creating a series of tsunamis that resulted in enormous land and property destruction and loss of life throughout the Indian Ocean basin land area. Although difficult to be precise in casualty estimations in such a diverse and remote part of the world, it has been estimated that around 150,000 people in those 12 countries of Asia and Africa lost their lives during or immediately after the event ("Areas Hit by Tsunami," 2005). What impact did this catastrophe have on the international insurance industry? Imagine such a disaster in the United States. Insurance companies could be devastated if Americans had covered their lives and property for such damage.

As this area and its people worked to restore commerce, residential housing, and lives, relatively few insurance claims were filed. The worldview of the inhabitants of India, Indonesia, Sri Lanka, and Thailand exhibit much less need to control the present and the future, and even less to control natural forces such as the weather. The Euro-American worldview assumes that humans have a right to control the impact of weather as much as possible with man-made inventions. It also assumes that risk management, or things like insurance, are necessary to make sure that the future is protected. Without that belief in the need and the ability to control the future, people will not invest in products such as insurance. In general, human and property damage resulting from this natural disaster was, for the most part, not protected by insurance. Some estimates for actual insurance claims ranged from $88 to $136 million. A hurricane catastrophe experienced by the Caribbean and southeastern United States just months prior to this resulted in approximately 3,000 deaths, but $27 billion of insurance claims!

Completion and Reflection

Plans cease to exist due to three conditions: (a) they are abandoned, (b) they are modified or re-created into a new set of objectives and goals, or (c) they are completed. Not all plans should be pursued, especially when the monitoring process illuminates flaws in the plan or new circumstances that negate the plan. Abandoning a plan is the right thing to do if it no longer meets the needs of the individual or family or if it places the family in any type of jeopardy. A marathon runner preparing for an upcoming race may have to pull out of that race if he or she experiences physical injury. Abandonment is not always failure. When family members or individuals discard a plan, it may be due to the inappropriateness of the plan or the lack of commitment of those involved. Loss of commitment or motivation may illuminate flaws within the plan.

The planning process exists in a dynamic environment, and both needs and resources continue to change over time. Those changes may result in a misfit between the original plan and current circumstances. Many plans can be adjusted during implementation without completely abandoning them.

Shirley is a single female with a long employment history and a healthy retirement savings account. Her original will left her estate to her siblings, in equal amounts. Now, at the age of 60, she has lost two of those siblings to early death. Both in-laws remarried and had children with their second spouses. If Shirley left her will as it were, those previous in-laws could petition the courts for the part of her estate that would have gone to their spouses, Shirley's brothers. One of her living siblings has experienced a severe stroke and will require medical and care services for the rest of her life. Shirley creates a new will, redistributing her estate among her living siblings, but places the majority in a trust to care for her ill sister.

The original will was a good, solid plan. The circumstances, however, have changed, and the changes made in the new version prevent future problems and help address new needs identified.

Completion is a natural end to a plan well implemented. The decision-making process does not stop at that point, however. An important step is that of evaluation. A plan is not a success just because it has been successfully implemented. If the end result is not what was originally desired or if the individual's or family's needs have not been completely and positively met, acknowledging the flaws within the plan or within the implementation process is an important part of future planning. Repetition of past mistakes is detrimental to the health and well-being of a family. Learning from one's mistakes is important at all levels.

In the News

Government's Role

Planning, Response Are Faulted

By Josh White and Peter Whoriskey, Washington Post Staff Writers

Friday, September 2, 2005, Page A01

Tens of thousands of people remain stranded on the streets of New Orleans in desperate conditions because officials failed to plan for a serious levee breach and the federal response to Hurricane Katrina was slow, according to disaster experts and Louisiana government officials.

Though experts had long predicted that the city—which sits mostly below sea level and is surrounded by water—would face unprecedented devastation after an

(Continued)

(Continued)

immense hurricane, they said problems were worsened by a late evacuation order and insufficient emergency shelter for as many as 100,000 people.

Terry Ebbert, head of New Orleans's emergency operations, said the response from the Federal Emergency Management Agency was inadequate and that Louisiana officials have been overwhelmed.

"This is a national disgrace. FEMA has been here three days, yet there is no command and control," Ebbert told the Associated Press as he watched refugees evacuate the Superdome yesterday. "We can send massive amounts of aid to tsunami victims, but we can't bail out the city of New Orleans. We have got a mayor who has been pushing and asking, but we're not getting supplies."

In Mississippi, refugees and survivors also complained about the agonizingly slow pace of aid. Food and fuel were extremely limited in many of the hardest hit counties, and power and telephone communications were distant prospects for thousands of people. Isolated reports of shooting and lawlessness compounded the woes of weary survivors.

Officials said debris on highways slowed the arrival of relief supplies. But most of the bottlenecks had now been finally cleared, said Mississippi Development Authority spokesman Scott Hamilton, and supplies were on their way. The state was also planning to activate thousands of additional National Guard troops, to help maintain order.

Michael D. Brown, FEMA's director, offered an emphatic defense of the federal response, saying that his agency prepared for the storm but that the widespread, unexpected flooding kept rescuers out of the city. He urged the nation to "take a collective deep breath" and recognize that federal officials are doing all they can to save people.

Brown said personnel, equipment, supplies, trucks, and search and rescue teams were positioned in the region ahead of the hurricane

"There is never a contingency plan for something like this," said Johnny B. Bradberry, secretary of the Louisiana Department of Transportation and Development.

Experts said one of the major problems with the response effort was an ineffective evacuation that began just 24 hours before the storm hit. Though models for such a storm accurately portrayed the circumstances that arose—a levee breach, flooding, stagnant water, inaccessible portions of the city and large numbers of people unable to leave—more than 100,000 people remained when the storm hit.

Some people were simply too poor to pick up their lives, and others unwisely figured they could ride out the hurricane in their homes because they had done so in the past. But Rep William J. Jefferson (D-La.) said there was a failure to think about a "holistic approach to the evacuation effort."

Jack Harrald, director of the Institute for Crisis, Disaster and Risk Management at George Washington University, said researchers and academics have for years been studying New Orleans because of its particular vulnerabilities to disaster. In the Natural Hazards Observer in Nov. 2004, Shirley Laska, director of the Center for Hazards Assessment, Response and Technology at the University of New Orleans, predicted a direct hit could produce "conditions never before experienced in a North American disaster" and said evacuation problems would be severe.

"They didn't get people out. There was a late mandatory evacuation, and it's a very exposed position," Harrald said yesterday. "The realization of how serious the situation was not shared in all directions."

Whoriskey reported from Baton Rouge, Louisiana. Staff writers Bradley Graham, Dafna Linzer, and Shankar Vedantam in Washington, and Christopher Lee in Gulfport, Mississippi, contributed to this report.

Even years of studying, planning, and preparing in the abstract were ineffective when reality hit New Orleans. Implementation of plans was hampered by unexpected snags—loss of communication, slow governmental response, and the unexpected obstacles presented by poverty. Victims realized, often too late, that family crisis plans would have been helpful, especially when faced with separation of family members during the rescue operation.

Source: "Government's Role Planning, Response Are Faulted" by Josh White and Peter Whoriskey. Originally printed September 2, 2005. © 2005, The Washington Post. Reprinted with Permission.

Summary

Implementation of a decision is the setting of a plan into motion. Successful completion is dependent on many factors—the actual plan, the motivation of family members involved, and the changing context over the time necessary for completion. Risk management is necessary during creation of the plan and throughout implementation. Change is a complicated process for individuals and family units. Efforts to minimize stress and maximize benefits are important. Plans may fail or cease to be useful over time. Flexibility and continual monitoring are necessary at all times. Once completed, lessons learned during the implementation process should be used in future decision-making situations.

Questions for Review and Discussion

1. Strategy is an important concept in plan implementation. Give examples of two types of strategies presented in the chapter.

2. College can be a stressful time, full of planning and adjustment. What role would a person's resilience play in the event of a health crisis during his or her last semester?

3. At this point in your life, is a legal will important? Why or why not?

4. What types of insurance are essential for contemporary families? Which are discretionary? What differentiates the two?

5. Recall a plan you created that was eventually abandoned. What were the primary problems you experienced? Were they part of the planning process or did they evolve during the implementation process?

Defining Success 13

Objectives

- Be aware of the responsibility society has for the environment.

- Understand the concept of sustainability and why it is important for the future.

- Recognize the role that ethics plays in social responsibility.

- Identify the responsibility that family has in society.

- Be aware of different aspects of wellness and how it affects the family and society.

- Appreciate the responsibility of the individual to the family and society.

- Realize how happiness and personal satisfaction affect the individual and others.

Success is simply a matter of luck. Ask any failure.

—Earl Wilson

Any decision that is made must be evaluated to determine whether it has been successful. Families that have made good choices and feel good about the decisions they have made are more likely to feel a **social responsibility** to contribute to others around them. But social responsibility is highly subjective. How can we measure who does and does not contribute to society?

Harold and Jean are active in their community. They volunteer for several causes through their service organizations and collect money in their neighborhood for heart disease, diabetes, and muscular dystrophy. They are active in their church and political party affiliation and actively participate in the voluntary recycling program in their city. Harold and Jean would be considered socially responsible to their community and world.

What makes this couple more socially responsible than the couple who lives next door who have taken on the responsibility to care for their elderly parents on a daily basis for the past 10 years? Is a person who volunteers his or her time to work with nonprofit groups, but does not have time to give to his own family members, socially responsible? Questions such as these are the subject of the following chapter.

Societal Responsibility

Corporate social responsibility has been identified and studied within corporate America and around the world for some time. Konkolewsky (2004) suggested that, for business to be successful, it must be socially responsible and address the areas of people, planet, and profit. Maintaining the health and safety of workers, protecting the resources of our planet, ethical reporting, and production of a quality product are components of the expectations placed on a socially responsible business.

Reality Check

Artificial Obsolescence

Corporate America is always looking for ways to get customers to buy more of what they already use. "Artificial obsolescence" is the yearly introduction of changes in style, color, and small improvements in order to lure status-conscious consumers into replacing perfectly functional products. Did you know that this is not new? This practice actually dates back to the 1920s. Here is just one example.

In the early 1960s, Alka-Seltzer, the fizzy heartburn and acid indigestion pain-relief tablet, needed an update. Most people recognized Speedy, the "cartoon disk with a squeaky voice and pop eyes," who had been introduced in the early days of TV. However, by the 1960s, Alka-Seltzer had fallen out of favor with the younger drug-buying consumer. Alka-Seltzer's customers were mostly older people, and the product was not attracting many new buyers. It had become associated with people who drank too much and ate too much and was not appealing to that younger consumer.

Up to that point, pain-relief products had been advertised in commercials filled with negatives that would have given you pain if you didn't already have it. People ran around groaning, holding their heads and stomachs. In one commercial, a poor man went through a series of tortures, including hammers pounding his head and straitjackets tying him up. People did not watch unless they already had a headache or stomach problem and were looking for relief, so most of the time, from the advertiser's point of view, advertising was ineffective.

Finally, Tinker & Partners advertising think tank solved the problem by coming up with different reasons for people to take Alka-Seltzer and fashioning a series of entertaining commercials around those themes.

> [We] created the kickoff commercial that set the style for all the variety of commercials that followed. It was a truly wonderful, iconic commercial, an ovation to stomachs, a sweet-natured montage of big ones, little ones, slim ones, fat ones, all filmed at stomach level. There was a street digger's jackhammer stomach, a young chick's bare midriff, two men talking, facing each other, one with a flat stomach and one with a big round one, an array of stomachs presented with self-deprecating humor and sweet humanness to a happy, bouncy tune. "No matter what shape your stomach's in" was its opening phrase. Self-deprecating humor was new and popular in the sixties and unheard-of in drug commercials, when it appeared it was news. It was followed by 16 completely different commercials, each entertaining and stylish, each giving you a different reason to take Alka-Seltzer.

One of these commercials was based on an "Alka-Seltzer on the Rocks" theme that showed an appealing visual of nothing but two Alka-Seltzers dropping into a crystal glass of water. The important thing about this new commercial was that there were *two* Alka-Seltzers. Before that, both the Speedy commercials and the label on the package only promoted using one tablet at a time:

> We met an attractive doctor at Miles [Laboratories], Dorothy Carter, who demonstrated to us that in order for aspirin to break through the pain barrier it often required two aspirins, not one, to do the job. Because aspirin

(Continued)

(Continued)

is one of the ingredients that make Alka-Seltzer effective, we asked her whether two Alka-Seltzers would be better than one. Yes, two would work better than one.

But the directions on the package said to take only one. And all the old Speedy commercials demonstrated only one fizzing in water. [We] did a little dance with Dorothy Carter in the laboratory. What a stroke of good fortune that was! We changed the directions on the packages and began showing two Alka-Seltzers dropping into a glass of water in every commercial. Miles created portable foil packs that held two Alka-Seltzers each and sold them in new places, magazine stands, bars, fast-food restaurants, powder rooms—they became ubiquitous—and, naturally, Miles began selling twice as much Alka-Seltzer.

Alka-Seltzer's large sales increase was directly related to consumers' using two tables instead of one. In addition to an increase in the number of tablets used, Alka-Seltzer's new image was later fortified with the catchy and enduring "Plop, plop; fizz, fizz" jingle, which led consumer to believe that no one had ever used anything *less* than two Alka-Seltzers at a time.

Source: From *A Big Life in Advertising* by Mary Wells Lawrence, copyright © 2002 by Mary L. Book Corp. Used by permission of Alfred A. Knopf, a division of Random House, Inc.

Manning (2004) believes that business and the environment are linked because it makes sense to invest in the future, and it is also good for business when customers view them as socially and environmentally conscious. As more and more people become concerned about issues such as global warming, clean air and water, and energy consumption, the business community wants to avoid being seen as contributing to the problem. Branding (logos and other promotional material) that reflects products as being "green" or environmentally friendly has become an important business practice. "The New Greening of America" (Adler, 2006) gives insight into the current pulse of Americans about issues that surround the environment. In his *Newsweek* article, Adler writes about how business is looking at the "budget-conscience masses" and is "gathering cachet among an affluent new consumer category which marketers call 'LOHAS': Lifestyles of Health and Sustainability." "The people who used to drive the VW bus to the co-op are now driving the Volvo to Whole Foods,' exults David Brotherton, a Seattle consultant in corporate responsibility" (p. 48). Even Dow Jones and Company, which publishes the *Wall Street Journal* and other financial news, has a "Global Sustainability Index" to measure the performance of those businesses that are socially responsible to the environment.

Society as a whole has a responsibility to the planet ultimately for the benefit of those who inhabit the earth. How this is accomplished is a debate that rages on between environmentalists and those who want to use the land for economic gain. Politicians are often forced to take a stand when it comes to the environment and social responsibility involving resources. Presidents are rated on their environmental stance and at the same time are also being closely watched by those who make their living from the land.

One area where the two groups differ significantly is in food production. Product labeling can be confusing with words such as *environmentally safe*, *organic*, and *homegrown*. Most consumers don't know the difference, and without labeling standards in place there are vast differences in the products. Ecolabels imply that the food was produced in an environmentally preferable way. However, Lockeretz and Merrigan (2005) point out that, other than the governmentally mandated *organic* label, there is no federal oversight.

With the organic sector of the market growing at an annual rate of 20% a year, the demand from both consumers and producers for standardization will also increase. There are several benefits associated with food carrying ecolabels. Production that decreases water pollution and soil erosion, as well as being safe for wildlife, is an environmental benefit. It also involves nonenvironmental benefits such as animal rights and promoting local agriculture. Ecolabels promote social responsibility by requirements such as decent treatment of farm workers and fair trade practices that help small farmers remain competitive. These components do not help the food taste better or help to protect resources, but they are socially responsible.

Soil conservation is much less of an issue, especially to those who live in urban areas. However, those who understand the significance of the Dust Bowl have an appreciation for this form of preservation. April 14, 1935, known as "Black Sunday," is a day especially important to remember when it comes to soil conservation. It was on that day that a large part of the Great Plains was covered with dust so thick that it blocked out the sun. It was caused by plowed fields and a devastating drought that resulted in blowing and drifting soil similar to that of a blizzard. It was estimated that the fertile farmland of the Plains lost 850 million tons of soil during that time. As a result, the government established the Soil Conservation Service.

Improvements in soil practices have prevented soil loss; however, today there are new threats to the land. As the population grows, consumers demand more food production at lower prices while encroaching land development demands that this food be grown on small amounts of land. American farmers have successfully been able to produce the most inexpensive food in the world, but not without consequences. Although the government has established set-aside programs at a cost of $1.7 billion annually to withhold approximately 35 million acres of cropland from production (Baerenklau, 2005), soil depletion is a problem. John Hassell, executive director of the Conservation Technology Information Center, says, "Conservation-minded farmers and researchers need a revival, one that will restore their fervor for stewardship" ("Bring Back the Passion for Soil," 2005).

Water conservation is of more concern because everyone needs water. Water is essential to life. Humans need water not only to live, but also for the maintenance of many other ecosystems. Fresh water represents only a small amount of the world's water, and its availability is a limited and finite resource. Fresh water is found as surface water (lakes, rivers, reservoirs, etc.) or ground water (underground aquifers). Managing water resources is difficult. Competing users, especially in urban areas, stress the availability of water.

Legislation is sometimes necessary to arbitrate water rights and allocation of resources. Legal questions focus on the ownership of moving water. Does the state where the water originated own the water that flows through another state? Also, uncontrolled use of groundwater has caused water tables to fall, and it is estimated that we are removing twice as much water as is being replaced. For example, the Ogallala aquifer, which lies under parts of South Dakota, Nebraska, Colorado, Kansas, Oklahoma, New Mexico, and Texas, has decreased by 33% since 1950 and is being depleted three times faster than it is being replaced. Some aquifers in Arizona are being withdrawn 10 times faster than the replacement rate (Gleick, Wolff, & Chalecki, 2002). As the population grows and as irrigation and industrial uses for water increase, conservation of water could become a major crisis. The Organization for Economic Cooperation and Development believes that water is set to become a more important issue in all our lives around the world (Akasaka, 2006).

Most of us take it for granted that when we turn on the faucet water will be available, clean, safe, and tasteful. According to the U.S. Geological Survey (Hutson et al., 2004), the United States uses about 408 billion gallons of water per day. Most of this is not consumed, but used for other purposes such as industry and irrigation. Americans use over 100 gallons of water per day per person for drinking, cooking, washing, disposing waste, and other personal purposes, whereas the world average is about 26 gallons (Pimentel et al., 2004). Most people think nothing of letting water run while brushing their teeth or peeling vegetables.

Liz is in her senior year of college and has moved into a one-bedroom apartment. She lived in the dorms since beginning college and wanted to get away from the noise and roommates to concentrate on her studies. During the first night in her new apartment, she noticed a dripping sound while she was lying in bed, but she soon fell asleep. She didn't think about it again until the next night when she got up and discovered that her kitchen faucet had a slow, steady drip. She decided to call her landlord in the morning and shut her bedroom door to cut out the sound of the dripping. It was over a week before Liz got around to calling her landlord. He said he would take a look at it the following week because he would be out of town. Two weeks later, she called again, but got no answer. As the semester got busy, she didn't think too much about the drip, and she found that if she left the sponge under the faucet, she couldn't hear the dripping. By the end of the year, she had forgotten all about the annoying drip. As long as it didn't keep her awake at night, it wasn't a problem. What Liz didn't think about was the wasted water over that year's time. The average leaky faucet can waste from 1,000 to 2,000 gallons of water per year! Whose responsibility was the leaky faucet?

The debate about energy conservation is decades old. Once again it is often the consumer who drives the debate when prices cut into their budget. Whether it is home heating oil, natural gas, or gasoline, America has become dependent on energy. The debate involves our dependence on oil-producing countries, whether oil drilling should be allowed where the environment will be affected, the depletion of nonrenewable energy sources, the profits of oil refineries, and others.

Although efforts have raised awareness about conserving energy, some efforts do not produce results. For example, the *Annual Energy Outlook 2003 Report* (2003) projects that even with conservation efforts in place, the annual growth of household energy consumption will only be reduced by .3% by the year 2025 at the present rate. Americans paid $83 billion more for gasoline in 2005, compared to the prices they paid in February 2003, meaning the average family paid at least $2,000 more (Environmental Working Group, 2006). The Energy Star program is another government program that helps business and individuals protect the environment through energy efficiency. The Energy Policy Act of 2005 provides tax credits for home improvement, efficient cars, solar energy systems, and fuel cells. The U.S. Department of Energy (2007) reported that, in the first year, results show that the program saved enough energy to power 10 million homes and avoid greenhouse emissions from 12 million cars.

What is more important is that some of those costs are associated with wasted energy. Leaving lights on and the lack of insulation all contribute to higher costs. Americans have a frustration with what seems like a governmental lack of initiative in addressing the problems associated with energy consumption. Deutch (2005) suggests that the answer to U.S. energy problems is striving for independence with new and emerging energy technologies such as wind, solar, and fuel cells. As a result, some states are beginning to start their own programs to address the crisis (Tucker, 2006):

- Massachusetts is promoting hybrid cars by offering tax credits to corporations whose transportation fleets run on alternative fuels and income tax deductions to individuals who own hybrid cars.

- Pennsylvania is offering special funding for more energy-efficient factories.

- Utah and New York have updated building codes to meet energy conservation criteria.

- Minnesota has enacted the first mandate requiring diesel fuel to include at least 2% biofuel.

Making dramatic changes in our energy consumption will take time and money. Americans will have to be committed to making the changes necessary and waiting for the results.

The use of resources leads to the need for disposal. America is known as a throw-away society. We buy too much food and too many clothes, and our products become obsolete too quickly. Even the packaging that the products come in accounts for almost one third of the trash discarded. According to Hattam (2005), in 1 year, Americans discard millions of tons of garbage, including

- 26,888,000 tons of food
- 8,550,000 tons of furniture and furnishings
- 6,330,000 tons of clothing and footwear
- 5,190,000 tons of glass beer and soda bottles
- 4,200,000 tons of plastic wrap and bags
- 3,650,000 tons of junk mail
- 3,470,000 tons of diapers
- 3,160,000 tons of office paper
- 3,070,000 tons of tires

Photo 13.1   Recycling is reflected in family values.

Source: © DLILLC/Corbis.

Over the past three decades, the amount of garbage generated in the United States has increased by 87%, twice as fast as our population (Hattam, 2005). The average American produces 4.5 pounds of garbage each day, with more than 3 pounds of that going to landfills and other disposals. When we think of conservation and social responsibility with regard to trash, we may think of **recycling**. Some may think of the messy job of separating trash into bins or bags, hauling it to a recycling center, remembering the recycling pickup day, and other time-intensive ways that we dispose of household waste.

From 1990 to 2003, recycling rates in the United States almost doubled, from 16.2% to 30.6% (Greenspan, 2005). Although most believe that recycling is important, not everyone participates. Successful recycling programs have provided many large containers that were convenient for the customer (Ando & Gosselin, 2005). Many cities have added curbside pickup and have tried to make it more convenient for people to recycle. For example, Kansas City, Missouri, noticed that it had higher recycling participation rates only in the suburban areas. When it conducted a survey, it found that city residents would be more likely to recycle if they were given incentives ("Identifying Barriers to Curbside Recycling," 2005). Ando and Gosselin (2005) found that those living in multifamily dwellings are more likely to recycle if they have enough room to process recyclables and if the recycling bins are not too far away.

Container deposit legislation ("bottle laws") has been adopted by cities and states to require a deposit on carbonated, water, or alcoholic beverage containers. The benefits of the deposit include increased recycling and reduced litter along roadways and other public areas, prolonging the lifetime usability of landfills.

Although we think of recycling as a process of sorting trash and recyclables, it can include many other ways of reusing resources. The idea that "one man's trash is another man's treasure" seems to describe a good attitude about recycling. There are many ways to find a home for used and surplus goods. Selling items at garage or tag sales or donating them to nonprofit organizations and charities is better for our environment than sending them to the local landfill. The Internet has also emerged as a distribution system for recycling goods, with several sites devoted to selling used goods, including eBay.

The greening of America generally means some form of conservation. It can take many forms. When a company announces that it is "going green," it means that it is actively looking for ways to conserve natural resources, uses products that are environmentally friendly, or is searching for ways to reutilize resources. There are numerous ways that this can be accomplished. Examples are using heat- or motion-activated lights to save energy, installing low-flow faucets and toilets to save water, and using building materials and cleaning supplies that are nontoxic. "Green" roofs on city buildings are those that are partially or fully covered with plants.

Worldview

Recycling E-Waste

Most Americans believe that it is cheaper to buy a new computer rather than upgrade the old one. According to the Environmental Protection Agency (EPA), Americans discard more high-tech equipment than any other country in the world. What do we call this refuse? It is called **e-waste**. If you have never heard of it, you are not alone. Schneiderman (2005), contributing author for *Electronic Design*, says that 95% of the population doesn't know about e-waste either. But more than 4.6 million tons of it found its way to U.S. landfills in 2000, and this figure is expected to increase fourfold over the next few years. Consumer Reports research estimates that the typical household discards three to four products each year. Although the Electronic Waste Recycling Act of 2003 did identify and regulate the disposal of certain products, little is ever recycled. What is even more disturbing is that the majority of the e-waste slated for recycling is exported to areas such as China, India, or Pakistan. A 2002 documentary entitled, "Exporting Harm: The High-Tech Trashing of Asia," shows e-waste making its way to remote villages in China, where people are paid a dollar a day to break discarded computers and other electronic equipment into component materials to be recycled. The crisis for China is not the massive quantities of e-waste, but the toxic chemicals such as lead beryllium, cadmium, and mercury that workers are exposed to and that find their way to the water and soil of the region. The documentary states, "Rather than having to face the e-waste problem squarely, the United States has made use of a convenient, and until now, hidden escape valve—exporting the crisis to developing countries of Asia."

What is our responsibility to our own waste? What is our responsibility to a safe world? Does the Information Age have a dark side?

Benefits include insulation qualities that can reduce the heating and cooling costs and minimizing rain runoff (Kapos, 2005).

Other attempts at adding "green space" are becoming part of community development. Some cities have required set-aside space, including grass and trees for all new construction, or they have adopted conservation easement programs to preserve existing green space. These spaces not only add aesthetic value, but help soil and water conservation (Blaine & Lichtkoppler, 2004). Some communities around the country are discovering that land deemed unusable is finding new life when it is reclaimed as green space. One Montana town turned the land from a closed copper mine into a golf course that is now environmentally safe as well as an economic boost for the community. Similar uses are being found for landfill sites and sanitation pond systems (Ward, 2000).

Ultimately, society has a responsibility toward maintaining the earth, but at the same time we must live on it and use its resources to survive. The balance between the two is known as sustainability. Sustainability allows the resources of the earth, the people who inhabit the earth, and the economic activity that bring the resources to the people to all benefit without harm. According to Roberts (2004), the ideas that are central to sustainable development include the following:

- Establish effective and efficient use and management of natural resources
- Promote waste solutions
- Devise new methods and techniques in design, production, distribution, and disposal that minimize waste and environmental management
- Establish new economic activities for the production of environmental goods
- Promote high standards of environmental management
- Establish institutional structures that will assist in maintaining sustainable economic development

What is necessary to bring society to a point where sustainability is valued and economic development follows these ideas as best practices? In the past, legislative laws or governmental regulations have forced these changes. Creating an endangered species list is an example of this. Americans are slowly becoming aware of the environmental costs of economic development. Because of our insatiable consumption of resources, incentives will need to be set out for us to stop and take a look at the consequences to our world.

Carl and his family lived on the edge of a small town. Carl thought of himself as a good citizen. He paid his taxes and provided for his family. A few months ago, a new town ordinance was enacted to prohibit burning within the city limits. Carl had opposed the ordinance saying, "I have burned my trash out behind the garage for years. It isn't hurting anybody and I have a right to continue to do whatever I want on my own property." Other than just the convenience of disposing of their own trash, Carl and his family would now have to drive the trash to the waste disposal and recycling center a few miles away and pay a small fee. He noticed that his property taxes would also be going up to help pay for the new center. Against his wife's protests, Carl continued to burn his own trash. Although he was careful to burn when the wind was calm, one day the fire got away from him and began to burn in an adjacent field. Because there were plans to develop the field into property lots for new housing, the field that was once planted with crops was now covered with stubble and dry weeds and it burned quickly. The fire headed for the new houses nearby. The local fire department was finally able to contain the fire, but Carl was cited for his actions. Although Carl has the right to own and use his own property, he failed to recognize that the new ordinance was for the benefit of everyone, including himself. As the town expanded, there was a new risk for open fires getting out of control. The fumes from some of the products that were being burned were also a hazard to the people around him, including his family. Finally, the town was beginning to take responsibility for renewable and reusable resources by beginning a recycling program.

Most of what has been presented so far in this chapter has focused on the economic aspects of social responsibility. There is more of a motivation to make decisions and changes in our world if there is a cost involved or if it will ultimately benefit us economically. A good example of this is the understanding behind NIMBY (not in my backyard). Many people are in favor of something that seems to benefit the world or environment as long as it doesn't affect them personally. If it will cost them something or inconvenience them, then they are against it. However, economics are not the only consideration necessary for community development. Hochachka (2005) advances the idea of **interiority** as important to the sustainability of society. Interiority includes ethical or cultural needs that are less noticeable, but are necessary for social responsibility. Making decisions that are ethical and that take into account the cultural history of society is as important as whether it makes sense economically. Will the economic benefits of a new business outweigh the ethical concerns of their products? Will providing family services obtained by state and federal funding be worth it when the families they were meant to serve find them culturally offensive?

One ethical issue involves the social responsibility of protecting the weak, which is controversial and is debated at all levels of society. Issues such as protecting children from predators or prosecuting those who take advantage of the elderly seem clear. However, issues such as the stem-cell research, euthanasia, or abortion are not, and opinions change and sway over time. Schneider (2005) reports that between 1994 and 2004 the percentage of people who thought abortion should be "legal in all circumstances" dropped from 33% to 23%. Public opinion often reflects the influence of contemporary politics; however, many believe that society should have an attitude of concern and responsibility for the weakest among humans regardless of the political climate. Giving voice to those who are less likely to be heard, but are affected by decisions made by others, is a social responsibility. These include not only the vulnerable mentioned earlier, but others such as the mentally challenged, the homeless, and immigrants.

Social responsibility and family responsibility are similar in that they both require those involved to take a look at how actions affect others. Families are responsible for their members. A family member is irresponsible when he or she makes a decision that negatively impacts others in the family.

Mark and Shelly have been married for 14 years and have two children ages 8 and 10. Over the past year, Shelly started to examine her life because she was struggling with feelings of not being wanted or needed. After her examination, she made some changes in her life. First, she decided to spend more time with a man from work who had been encouraging her. Second, she decided to join a health club and a cycling club to get into shape and feel better about herself. Although Shelly began to have more confidence and was feeling better physically, she had made decisions that impacted her family negatively. Mark was jealous of the time she was spending with the man from work, and he had a hard time trusting her because he was sure that the relationship was more than a friendship. Her children noticed that she was never around to help them or attend their activities because she was always at the health club or at a cycling event. Although Shelly's decisions were important to her well-being, they were irresponsible as a family member. Shelly should have considered her own well-being, as well as that of the entire family.

To consider a family's well-being, we must examine wellness. Good health is more than physical well-being. It also includes life satisfaction. H. Dunn (1961) was the first to coin the term wellness and defined it as "an integrated method of functioning which is oriented toward maximizing the potential of which the individual is capable" (p. 4). Others followed with definitions that included the idea that wellness is a chosen lifestyle that can be defined as the active process of becoming aware of and making choices toward a more successful existence. Most definitions also incorporate the idea that wellness includes the total person, involving the body, mind, and spirit.

Myers, Sweeney, and Whitmer (2000) developed a theoretical holistic model of wellness over the lifespan called the Wheel of Wellness (WoW) that is based on the characteristics of a healthy person. The main components of the WoW are based on psychological theories of growth and behavior and include the major life tasks of work, friendship, love, and spirituality. Figure 13.1 illustrates the integration of these components. In other words, when a change takes place, it affects the other parts. It is necessary to understand this when we recognize how wellness changes over time and across the lifespan. The diagram identifies 12 tasks of

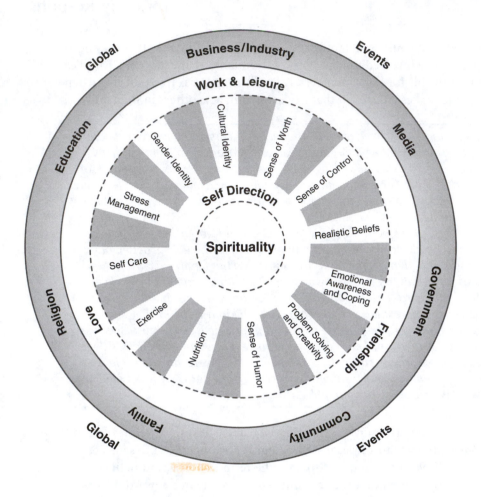

Figure 13.1   The Wheel of Wellness

Source: Copyright J. M. Witmer, T. J. Sweeney, & J. E. Myers, 1996. Reprinted with permission of the authors.

self-direction that are conceptualized as spokes on the wheel. These tasks include a sense of worth, sense of control, realistic beliefs, emotional awareness and management, problem solving and creativity, sense of humor, nutrition, exercise, self-care, stress management, gender identity, and cultural identity.

Wellness is a topic being considered in all aspects of society. Whether it is found in the workplace or within the medical community, it seems that wellness is being publicized as the answer to the problems of individuals, families, and society. Although wellness is an issue for all of society, we focus most of our discussion on the family's responsibility for wellness and use the tasks identified previously to focus on six areas of wellness: social, physical, occupational, spiritual, intellectual, and emotional.

SOCIAL WELLNESS

Social wellness involves many factors for a family. The conditions in which a family lives and works play a big part in the well-being of the family. Their connections to the community where they live provide a sense of belonging and provide them with security. A social network of friends and acquaintances can be called on for help when a family is experiencing difficulties. We have all witnessed countless fundraisers that are conducted by friends and neighbors who want to help a family that is going through a difficult time with medical bills or after a house fire.

The quality of the living environment is important for individuals. Research has shown that a green environment has a relationship with health and well-being. Living around green space not only has a positive effect on mental well-being, such as putting someone in a good mood or an increased ability to concentrate, but it also may lead to more physical activity like walking or bicycling (deVries, Groenewegen, & Spreewenberg, 2003). This doesn't mean that every family should live in rural areas outside the urban environment. Green space can be found in cities in the form of parks and recreation areas. If a family doesn't have its own green space or a park nearby, they may want to designate time to spend in green space.

Social wellness also includes social capital available for families. We assume that a family that is below the poverty level will experience low social wellness; however, it depends on the resources within the community where they live. If there are adequate resources such as low-income housing, food pantries, access to services, and other capital, the family will be more likely to survive or even move forward. The family that lives in an isolated setting where poverty is prevalent and services are not readily available will be less likely to succeed. Saegert and Evans (2003) found that certain environments with a concentration of poor households contribute to negative health results. However, they point out that social capital in the form of resources is not the only factor. Social support in the form of strong social ties to the community as well as cooperation and trust among neighbors also contributes to social wellness.

Much of social wellness depends on the family's sense of control over their situation. Racial discrimination, disrespect among groups within the community, income inequality, and residential segregation are situations that are often outside the control of the people involved. These conditions have been found to contribute to poor health and well-being of low-income, minority populations (James, Schulz, & Van Olphen, 2001).

In an interview with sociology professor Robert Bullard after the devastating Hurricane Katrina in New Orleans in 2006, he acknowledges the problems associated

(Continued)

(Continued)

> with flooding, homelessness, and crime. At the same time, he points out that the social problems that existed prior to the hurricane may have been even worse. Almost half of the children in the city lived below the poverty level and 67% are black. Minorities lived in the poorest conditions in the city, disproportionate to the population. In addition, with more than 125 refineries and chemical plants, the area had been called "Cancer Alley" because of the high cancer rates. Professor Bullard pointed to the fact that, for the first time, environmental injustice of what is going on in New Orleans is finally being exposed (Joseph, 2005).

Another aspect of social wellness for some families is cultural identification. Although the majority population in the United States does not necessarily identify with a particular cultural heritage, minorities are more likely to identify and find belonging with a certain ethnic group. Therefore, it is not surprising that studies show that, for minorities, ethnic identity (Rayle & Myers, 2004) is a significant predictor of wellness. Although cultural groups may experience discrimination and segregation, which can hinder wellness, some immigrant groups have formed strong and interdependent cultural networks that benefit families (Saegert & Evans, 2003).

OCCUPATIONAL WELLNESS

Wellness within the workplace is important for family life because it may be difficult to separate the two. For many family members, the work role consumes a good deal of their time and is increasing. The Families and Work Institute (1999) reports that U.S. workers' average weekly work hours increased from 43.1 in 1977 to 47.1 in 1997. The conflict that can be created between work and home has been associated with a variety of negative outcomes, including decreased family and occupational well-being, medical complaints, and psychological costs (Noor, 2002). Job burnout is a negative occupational outcome that is a result of stressors on the job, which can lead to mental and physical health concerns and job performance issues that affect the person's relationships at work as well as at home (Maslach, Schaufeil, & Leiter, 2001). The concept of spillover between work and family is well documented (Almedia, McDonald, & Grywacz, 2002). This concept is based on the idea that there is overlap between work and home.

Just before the end of the day, Celia's boss demanded that she finish a very detailed report by the time she left for the day. It meant that Celia had to drop the other project that she was working on and rush through the report to finish on time. Not only was it frustrating, but it put Celia in a bad mood and she was mad at her boss. When she got home, she barked orders to her children and yelled at her husband,

Brent, for not helping around the house. The rest of the evening was a disaster. Everyone was irritable until they all went to bed for the evening. The next day, Brent was still upset about what had happened the night before. He thought that Celia's accusations were unfounded and, as a result, he hadn't gotten much sleep. On his way to work, he made a plan to discuss his concerns with Celia that evening. At work, he found it hard to concentrate and snapped at his secretary for not being able to find a file that he needed. At lunch, he lost patience with his coworkers' comments about his mood and stormed out of the lunchroom. The last 24 hours for Celia and Brent can be characterized as spillover. Celia's problem at work spilled over into her home life, and Brent's problem at home spilled over into his work life.

Although most of the time the spillover effect is presented as harmful for families, Grosswald (2003) believes that it may not be necessarily always negative. She points out that talents and skills developed in both worlds can benefit each other. For example, skills such as negotiation learned in the workplace and the ability to organize and multitask learned at home can benefit both interchangeably.

Most people recognize that their occupation and their family life are connected, and that their satisfaction is essential to their life. A person's satisfaction with his or her work can be directly related to the meaning that he or she attaches to work. Based on the Meaning of Work International Research Team, there are six major dimensions of the meaning of work (Snir & Harpaz, 2002):

- Work Centrality—Work is a life role and is the most basic of activities for people within society. It is more important than leisure time.

- Economic Orientation—People work for and are motivated by the income that results from work. The reason that we work is to sustain life and meet our needs.

- Interpersonal Relations—Humans need interaction and a place to belong. We work for the satisfaction of being with others.

- Intrinsic Orientation—Individuals need challenges and strive to show competence in their work. They work because it creates interest and self-determination.

- Entitlement/Obligation—People work because they should work. It is expected within society, and they have a right to work.

By understanding their own orientation to work, individuals can create more realistic expectations of work that should lead to greater satisfaction. Marriage partners also need to understand the work orientations of each other to avoid misunderstandings. If both partners have a work centrality orientation, for example, it will not be a problem when one has to miss a family reunion because of work.

Although conflict between work and home can be a problem for both men and women, women seem to be affected more. The majority of the demands of both home and work life, especially if children are in the home, still fall on the woman. There are two models that explain the relationship between multiple roles and well-being that help to understand how women negotiate the demands of multiple roles.

The **scarcity hypothesis** says that human energy is limited and, when overloaded, presents conflict that results in guilt and anxiety. Therefore, according to this hypothesis, the more roles one has, the less one will experience well-being. In contrast, the **enhancement hypothesis** proposes that being able to handle multiple roles results in status, increased self-esteem, and privilege, which seem to compensate for the strain that multiple roles presents. Rao, Apte, and Subbakrishna (2003) suggested that most working women fall into the enhancement hypothesis because they seem to report higher well-being and lower psychological stress than women who stay home with their children. However, they also point out that the kind of job they have, the working conditions of that job, the amount of control they feel that they have, and the support they feel from both coworkers and family members, including their husband, make a difference in their well-being. Women who do not have favorable conditions and support may not have the same positive experience in the workplace.

Employers are beginning to recognize that wellness in the workplace is a great benefit to them. One way to attract and retain employees is to allow them to control the balance between their work and home life. Family-friendly policies that allow employees to choose alternative work arrangements that include flexible hours, working from home, a compressed workweek, or onsite child care are valued by workers with families. Employers realize that when there is a lack of work and family balance, employees are less satisfied with the job, and there may be an increase in negative job behaviors such as **absenteeism,** poor performance, or turnover. Another problem that is making waves in the business world involves "presenteeism," which represents the problems associated with workers who come to work but are not fully functioning because of a illness or medical condition that hinders their performance. If a worker has a severe medical problem, he or she usually stays home (absenteeism), but **presenteeism** has to do with chronic conditions that may not require missing work, such as allergies, back pain, headaches, and even depression. It is estimated that depression reduces performance at work by $35 billion a year (Hemp, 2004). Because presenteeism is likely to indirectly cost employers more than the direct medical costs that they pay, it is to an employer's advantage to emphasize wellness in the workplace.

In the News

Worksite Wellness

With increasing evidence supporting health promotion programs in the workplace, more companies than ever are implementing health and wellness strategies to reduce injuries, health care costs and long-term disability. According to the Wellness Councils of America (welcoa.org), more than 81% of businesses with 50 or more employees have some form of health promotion program—the most popular being exercise, stop-smoking classes, back care programs, and stress management. Most employers are offering wellness programs to offset the rising costs of health care. Yet many business leaders continue to ask themselves how to control massive increases in annual insurance premiums and health care costs.

For many companies, medical costs can consume half of corporate profits—or more. Some employers look to cost sharing, cost shifting, managed care plans, risk rating, and cash-based rebates or incentives. But these methods merely shift costs. Only worksite health promotion stands out as the long-term answer for keeping employees well in the first place. Worksite wellness is health care reform that works. Results from North America's finest companies, summarized here, are reason enough to think about an investment in your most important asset—your employees—and the impact this investment can have on your bottom line.

Reports show that healthier employees spend fewer days away from work due to illness, saving the company thousands and even millions of dollars on down time and temporary help. Wellness programs can also help alleviate depression and help employees manage their time and stress levels better, all of which are contributing factors to missed work days.

In one study, members of a **Travelers** fitness center were absent from work significantly fewer days than nonmembers and in another four year study, sick leave was reduced 19%.

WELCOA—1999

At **DuPont,** each dollar invested in workplace health promotion yielded $1.42 in lower absenteeism costs over a 2 year period.

American Journal of Public Health, September 1990

To prevent back injuries among its employees, a **county in California** offered classes and fitness training to all its workers. As a result, there was a significant decrease in sick days related to back injuries, producing a net cost-benefit ratio of 1 to 1.79.

WELCOA—1999

Northern Gas Company employees who participate in the company's corporate exercise program take 80% fewer sick days than non-exercising employees. Health Promotion and Education Programs, Riverside Occupation Health Services, 1991

(Continued)

(Continued)

> At **Mesa Petroleum**, wellness program participants were absent 1.6 fewer days per year than non-participants. Given the number of employees, this resulted in significant cost savings.
>
> The Benfield Group, St. Louis, Missouri, February 1996
>
> **Coors** has saved over $2.3 million in lost wages due to absenteeism and $1.9 million in rehabilitation costs and cost avoidance.
>
> Business and Health, November 1992
>
> ---
>
> *Source:* www.preventdisease.com/worksite_wellness/worksite_wellness.html.
>
> Individual wellness and family wellness are interconnected. When adults work for companies that care about wellness, regardless of the motivation, families will be better served.

SPIRITUAL WELLNESS

At the center of the Wheel of Wellness diagram is spirituality. It is more difficult to characterize spirituality because it has different meanings and is highly personal for each individual. The spiritual dimension can include aspects of purpose in life, moral or ethical beliefs, and the view of a person's place in the world. These ideas will permeate everything in life and become the foundation for decisions and behaviors.

Although most people equate spirituality and religion, there are distinctions. Religion is a part of spirituality. For many, religion is the way that they express their spirituality. It also means that practicing religion can expand a person's understanding of spirituality. That does not mean that those who choose not to participate in religion are not spiritual. Inward spirituality refers to comfort, peace, or an inner strength. Outward spirituality usually describes a connection to others or a feeling of being one with the world.

In the past, religion and medicine have had separate spheres. It was widely believed that religion would focus on the inner self, whereas medicine would focus on the physical self. Recently, spirituality has gained a place in wellness and health. Although the power of faith in healing has been an idea that has existed for a long time, more and more people are beginning to consider its benefits, although they don't understand it.

The Holistic Flow Model of Spiritual Wellness (Purdy & Dupey, 2005) describes the components of the spirit and how they affect life tasks. The model includes a belief in an organizing force in the universe, connectedness, faith, movement toward compassion, the ability to make meaning of life, and the ability to make meaning of death. It is thought that the person who is healthy in spirit will be more likely to integrate activities into his family life that develop and strengthen the components of spirituality.

What is the benefit of spiritual wellness for the family? Families that have tapped into spiritual wellness have created a foundation to form attitudes, behaviors, and purposes used in understanding themselves as individuals and in their interactions with others. A good example of this comes when a family faces adversity.

Ricardo and his family were going through a difficult time. Ricardo had recently become a U.S. citizen after moving his family from Mexico. At first it was difficult to find housing and a job, but they were eventually able to find a small house to rent not far from the distribution company where Ricardo worked. Recently, Ricardo heard rumors that his company would be laying off 20% of its employees, and because he was one of the most recent to be hired, he figured that he would be among those laid off. Every day he went to work he expected to get a notice from his boss. In addition to the stress of uncertainty with his job, last week his oldest daughter who had been experiencing some health problems was diagnosed with a rare and serious lung disease. Ricardo and his family recognize the role of spirituality in their lives. Although these things are never easy, they understand that life is always uncertain and that things happen for a reason. Ricardo is experiencing what is known as spiritual transcendence, which involves moving beyond the limits of human understanding. To help them get through this difficult time, he and his family need to draw their strength from their faith, their family, and their friends.

PHYSICAL WELLNESS

When someone says "wellness," the first things that come to mind are the physical aspects of nutrition and exercise. Health care costs are high and rising, and the consequences of poor health for the family are loss of income and increased risk of poverty. The early work of the World Health Organization (1947) defined *health* as "a state of . . . well-being," rather than a definition of someone who was just not sick or did not have disease. The idea that health should involve proactive prevention has not been the norm for most Americans, however. Understanding the differences in people's willingness to support the idea of wellness can be illustrated along a continuum, where at one end medicine is used to treat problems and the other end represents active prevention strategies.

Such a continuum is consistent with Haber's (2002) assessment of three types of prevention attitudes. Primary prevention represents the kind of interventions that target specific problems and implement exercise, good nutrition, stress management techniques, and immunizations in an effort to prevent disease or illness. Secondary prevention includes interventions such as screenings, which are designed to catch or detect early symptoms of disease or illness. Tertiary prevention is used to treat health issues after they have become a problem and focuses on treatment and stopping the further progression of the disease or illness. Promoting good health and wellness has many benefits for society as well as the family. However, it is often difficult to get people to choose prevention when they do not see an immediate need to change. Often by the time a change in diet or lifestyle is needed, it is already too late to make a difference.

In addition to the attitudes about health and wellness, there are other factors that families need to consider that affect the physical health of individual family members. Where the family is living and working, their skills and abilities to make good decisions, the genetic predisposition of the family, and the availability and competence of the health care system in their geographic location will all have an impact on the health of the family. Risk factors such as poverty, unemployment, illiteracy, inadequate housing, and social isolation have been identified as relevant to health and affect many American families (Millar & Hull, 1997).

One of the most pressing concerns for health in the United States today is obesity. Health risks such as hypertension, diabetes, and sleep apnea are common for those who are obese. Even weight cycling (repeatedly gaining and losing weight) and the use of some diet treatments are associated with increased cardiovascular risks such as heart disease, hypertension, and kidney disease (Ernsberger & Koletsky, 1999). Besides the health risks, obese individuals suffer mental health risks associated with the stigma associated with their size. The wellness approach puts the emphasis not on weight loss, but on prevention and reducing risk factors. Using this focus, a healthy lifestyle is the goal and leads to a more positive attitude.

Exercise is an important aspect of wellness because of the physical and psychological benefits. Obviously, physical activity aids in weight reduction and helps in overall health, but it also serves to lower risk factors associated with poor health. Research suggests that exercise offers mental health benefits, such as reduced depression, reduced anxiety, increased feelings of control, help in facing stress, and increased self-esteem (Okonski, 2003).

Participation in physical wellness programs also show mixed results in terms of success. Although more wellness programs are being implemented in the workplace, it appears that those who need them the most are not participating. In addition, the dropout rate is high, especially for women, due to time constraints, lack of support, or family responsibilities (Erickson & Gillespie, 2000).

INTELLECTUAL WELLNESS

In society, intellectual wellness is one aspect of the social capital within a community. Many rural communities are concerned about the "brain drain" of the educated young people who move to urban areas in search of better positions. This leaves a community with fewer resources or social capital. Within a family, intellectual wellness involves the preparation and improvement of life skills. It is natural to think first about the skills and knowledge that can be gained through education. However, other skills that are learned through relationships and life experience are also important to intellectual wellness.

We are living in the information age, and education can provide students with the information they need to succeed. Education is not only important for learning that will be needed throughout life (such as reading), but there are additional social skills that are learned as a result of the process of education. Dempsey (2004) believes that creativity, tolerance, appreciation of diversity, and social skills are necessary for the future.

There are disagreements about how education should prepare students for the future. Some believe that children need only basic knowledge, whereas others believe they need a variety of competencies, including technological skills. There are many parents who are concerned about whether the educational system is doing a good job. Some parents opt to teach their own children to ensure that they are taught the basics usually within a certain set of values that are important to them. Whether parents opt to send their children to public school or private school, or whether they choose to home school, it is important that they are involved with the education of their children.

Photo 13.2   Exercise improves family wellness in multiple ways.

Source: © Jernej Gartner/iStockphoto.

Parents who expect schools to meet all their children's educational needs will be disappointed in how well prepared they are for the future. It is parents' responsibility to teach or reinforce social skills, expose them to new ideas, and provide them with opportunities to work up to their potential. The key to this is a parent who is willing to spend time with his or her child.

It is especially important for parents to learn and practice good problem-solving and decision-making skills and then model them for their children. Families who go through difficult situations need good problem-solving strategies to succeed.

Jami and Delmar are wrestling with a situation concerning Delmar's mother, Margaret. Margaret is 83 years old and still lives in her home, although Jami and Delmar are worried that it is becoming more and more dangerous for her to live alone because she has fallen twice in the last month. Delmar wants to make sure that Margaret is safe, but is also concerned that she has a part in the decision making about her own future.

One evening, they all sat down to discuss the options. Over the course of the evening, they calmly looked at all the ways that Margaret could be safe, yet maintain her independence. They arrived at a solution that empowered them to make a rational decision that fit the needs of everyone concerned. Although the discussion was among the three of them, Jami and Delmar's two daughters witnessed the entire discussion. Although they did not have any input, the model that they saw will help them in the future to make good decisions themselves.

Economically, education contributes to wellness by adding resources to the family and, ultimately, to society. According to the Census Bureau, over a person's lifetime of work, high school graduates earn an average of $1.2 million, associate's degree holders earn about $1.6 million, and bachelor's degree holders earn about $2.1 million (Day & Newburger, 2002). There is a downside to viewing education only from an economic point of view. Hargreaves (2003) suggests that the "knowledge economy" is one where knowledge and education focus on the pursuit of growth and profit that leads down a path of corruption and greed. He proposes that the rise in corporate scandals and secrecy, as well as the widening gap between the rich and the poor, are all a result of placing the emphasis on economics.

Although there is no doubt that a good education is a resource that can be beneficial economically, there are nonmonetary benefits as well. Adam (2006) reports that increased life expectancy, better health, and higher voter participation are all benefits of higher education. According to a report published by the Carnegie Foundation, nonmonetary benefits of higher education include the tendency to be open-minded, more cultured, more rational, more consistent, and less authoritarian. In addition, these benefits seem to be passed along to succeeding generations (Rowley & Hurtado, 2002).

Unlike some of the other components of wellness discussed, intellectual wellness is difficult to measure. Social wellness can be measured in services that are offered and physical wellness can be measured in longer life expectancy, whereas intellectual wellness is dependent on numerous other variables. Some of these are the socioeconomic level of the family, the attitudes about formal education, the problem-solving abilities of the adults in the family, or the relationship between parents and children.

EMOTIONAL WELLNESS

A large part of emotional wellness is the ability to be comfortable with your own emotions, whether it is anger, fear, or love. This means being able to understand your feelings and appropriately express them to others. The best setting in which to practice emotional health is in the family. Children learn to manage their emotions in the safety of their own home. They usually learn, over the course of time, that throwing a tantrum to get what you want doesn't work or that getting angry in response to disappointment doesn't solve the problem and could lead to worse consequences.

Adults who have trouble identifying and expressing their emotions may choose to find other ways to manage their emotions, such as engaging in risky behaviors, which leads to emotional stress and possibly even health problems. Research shows that people who show negative emotions tend to have weak immune systems, more heart disease, more cancer, and may not live as long as those who exhibit more positive emotions (Laliberte, 1999).

Tony was driving home from work on a crowded toll way. Although it was the fastest route home, he dreaded the stop-and-go traffic and tollbooth delays. This day was particularly frustrating because there were a couple of car accidents that made travel even more difficult. "Why can't people just keep moving along? They don't need to know what happened!" he thought to himself as his lane slowly crept along past the wrecked cars and flashing lights. Finally, a break in the traffic allowed Tony to maneuver in and out of the lanes, picking up speed as he went. Things were looking up, and he could taste the cold brew he knew was waiting for him at home. Just as he reached the maximum speed, a car pulled in front of him and seemed to slow down, causing Tony to have to brake. He felt his temper flare. He had always had trouble with his temper. He had been kicked off the playground in elementary school, he had been kicked off the football team in high school, and his ex-wife had kicked him out of the house all because of his temper. The car in front of him was not going to get away with cutting him off! He accelerated and rammed the car in front, causing them both to careen off the road, rolling, and killing both drivers. Tony's road rage was the result of emotions that were out of control.

Emotional wellness also means that you have to accept yourself, including your limitations. Feeling that you have failed in your life is a sign of low self-esteem. Feelings of failure are painful and can interfere with enjoyment of life and well-being. It can cause problems with friendships and relationships. It can create anxiety, stress, loneliness, and depression. Good self-esteem requires individuals to live consciously aware of themselves and the world, accept themselves as they are, realize that they are responsible for their choices, stand up for their beliefs and values, identify and work toward goals, and honor their commitments (Branden, 1995). Self-esteem is basic to psychological health, achievement, personal happiness, and positive relationships in and outside the family.

Difficult situations disrupt emotional balance. There are times when anger, grief, jealousy, or other negative emotions come into our lives and can damage our personal and family relationships. Individuals and families who are able to adjust to change, cope with stress in a healthy way, and enjoy life regardless of its disappointments and frustrations are able to master emotional wellness.

The family that is resilient is able to make adjustments and changes that, although difficult, they know will benefit them in the long run. For example, although numerous studies have highlighted the negative effects of divorce on children, there are ways that families can turn this devastating period of life around. Some are calling for wellness strategies that will benefit children when their parents get divorced, including teaching skills that promote coping and resilience (Pedro-Carroll, 2001). Using practical steps may reduce some of the anxiety and stress of the situation and can help family members to cope with the situation.

Humor is an emotion that can be a part of wellness but is often overlooked. A sense of humor is more than being funny; it is a way of seeing the world. The American Association for Therapeutic Humor reported that happiness is directly related to humor; and those who can laugh at life's circumstances are 30% more likely to be happy than those who can't see the humor in life. There are many benefits of humor in our lives. Laughter can reduce stress, stimulate your immune system, reduce blood pressure, and lift your spirit. Sometimes we are so serious about our daily activities and work that we forget to have fun.

A healthy sense of humor can be a stress reliever and a valuable tool in relationships. The ability to laugh can help a person put problems in a more realistic perspective. Humor is important in marriage, both emotionally and physically. Humor in marriage brings couples closer together and keeps the relationship fresh. Family members who can laugh at themselves or at their situation usually feel stronger when problems arise. Everyone can relate a time in his or her life that, during a tense situation, it was humor that brought the levity needed to resolve the conflict and release the tension. To add humor to relationships, look for funny moments as you go through the day and share them with each other, recall humorous or embarrassing moments that have happened in the past, watch funny TV shows and movies together, and repeat funny words or phrases that only have meaning for the family.

Individual Responsibility

Responsibility from an individual viewpoint takes many forms. Giving back to the community, nation, or world can be accomplished by contributions of money, time, or other resources. Volunteer workers contribute billions of dollars into the economy each year (Boris, 1999). Yet there never seems to be enough volunteers to cover the need. Recently, some new information suggests that individuals do not contribute to social causes as much as in the past.

Putnam (2000) suggests that younger generations do not have the sense of civic duty that previous generations felt, especially those who came through the Depression and World War II. He proposes that earlier generations understood what it meant to pull together as a country and work toward a common goal. This idea seems to make sense when we see the change in the way Americans began to pull together after the 9/11 attacks. Other data seem to suggest that volunteerism is not in decline. Ladd (1999) found that volunteering actually rose from 26% in 1977 to 46% in 1991.

According to Rossi (2001), there are three primary sociodemographic variables that play a part in an individual's social responsibility: education, sex, and age. Those who have more education are more likely to be connected to social circles that are larger than those who are not educated beyond the high school level. They are more likely to contribute to society by volunteering, participating in service organizations, and giving to worthy causes financially. The higher the education of a person, the more he or she feels the need to be responsible to society without feeling the need to gain anything in return.

Sex is also a variable in individual social responsibility. Although both men and women contribute to social responsibility, it appears that there are some differences. Men are more likely to contribute money and financial resources, whereas women are more likely to contribute personal time. This finding would be consistent with the fact that women spend much of their lives as caregivers.

Age also plays a role in an individual's social responsibility. Throughout the life cycle, an individual's inclination to contribute to society increases. At midlife, when a person's work and family obligations may be decreasing, his or her desire and willingness to give back to society increases. This may be a result of maturation or generativity (i.e., mentoring, advising). The typical American volunteer is middle-age, educated, employed, a woman, and middle or upper class, and lives and is involved in a small town and is religiously involved (Eckstein, 2002).

As individuals, is it our responsibility to maintain our own personal satisfaction and happiness? Is it socially responsible to keep our personal well-being in check? It may be more beneficial to ask whether it is socially irresponsible to be unhappy. According to Erikson's (1963) psychosocial theory of development, humans move through a series of stages that are each marked by a crisis that leads to the need for resolution.

In adult life, the stages begin to focus on purpose and fulfillment in life. Those in early adulthood are either productive or they become bored and self-indulgent. At this stage of their lives, they either contribute to society, which leads to a sense of personal fulfillment, or they become a burden to society.

As they age, this stage gives way to two groups of people. There are those who face old age with integrity, knowing that they had a positive influence on others. The other group enters old age with regrets. They feel despair that there is not enough time left for another chance to make a difference. The first group comprises members who have taken responsibility for their own happiness and have gained wisdom in the process. The second group of people ends up blaming themselves and others.

Unhappiness contributes negatively to society. Unhappiness in the workplace leads to loss of productivity and high turnover. Unhappiness in family life results in divorce. Unhappiness in one's personal life causes individuals to shift resources toward things that we think will make us happy.

Nancy is concerned about her husband Doug. Over the past 2 years, she has noticed that Doug is less interested in doing what he used to do for fun, and he seems generally unhappy most of the time. The effects of his unhappiness are far-reaching. Personally, he has refused invitations from his friends to play golf, attend ball games, and go fishing. Most of the time, he sleeps or watches TV. As a result, he has gained a significant amount of weight.

Nancy wants to be supportive, but Doug gets mad every time she suggests a solution. Emotionally, she is worried and hurt, and recently she began to confide in a couple of friends about the problem. She has stopped trying to reason with Doug and feels that their marriage is in jeopardy.

Doug has become increasingly agitated with his teenage children. His reaction toward them has caused them to avoid any contact with him. They often sneak out of the house to prevent confrontation. At work, his boss has noticed his lack of productivity and pride in his work. His coworkers also avoid confrontation with him. Not wanting to fire him, his boss has recommended a transfer. Does Doug have a responsibility to himself, his family, and his employer to be happy? What are the costs for his unhappiness?

According to the U.S. Constitution, the pursuit of happiness is our right, although happiness may be highly subjective and hard to measure. What makes one person happy may not be the same for the next person. Many people think that money is the key to happiness. No doubt, those who are struggling to make ends meet would feel better if they could pay their bills. However, according to Frank (2000), there are rich people who are miserable and poor people who are happy. For some, winning the lottery has turned out to be a nightmare as they watch the money fly through their fingers as fast as it came.

Money is not the only measure of happiness. Measures of desire, intelligence, genetics, friendship, marriage, faith, charity, and age are also used to determine happiness (Davidhizar & Hart, 2006). Research shows that whether these measures cause happiness often depends on the individual and his or her circumstances. Physical health, stress, self-esteem, and personality can all affect someone's ability to be happy. One question that needs to be asked is whether these measures make someone happy or whether they are the choices of a happy person.

Emma and Jill were sisters. Both of them grew up in the same loving and encouraging family. Both were married to supportive husbands. Both of them received a good education and were successful in their careers. The only difference was that Jill was unhappy most of the time. It seemed that no matter what she did, she was never satisfied. When she got a raise, it was not enough. When she got a promotion, it was not enough. Jill was a perfectionist and, in many ways, it contributed to her unhappiness. Her happiness seems to be directly related to her personality style.

Money or income gained is usually as a result of work. Does moving up the pay scale make someone happier? The idea of the "hedonic treadmill" supposes that, as income rises, expectations also rise and we end up always wanting more by setting our benchmarks higher (Easterlin, 2001). Research also shows that job satisfaction may be more related to job status than the salary (Oswald, 2003).

Colby and Phelps (2001) suggested that an individual's work life should play more of a role in social responsibility. They reveal that many people today seem to be struggling with the meaning that work has in their lives and have lost the significance that the contributions of work have within society. Taking pride in paid work can be as important to society as the work that is volunteered. The work that is accomplished builds the economy and provides an important social good. Individuals who view work as a negative and only enjoy the weekends or time away from work are missing the sense of community and common purpose that work can inspire.

Finally, as a family member, it is the individual's responsibility to create and maintain a healthy family life. If the family is the basic unit of society, it becomes the foundation from which society builds. The breakdown of the family is the beginning of a breakdown in society, and the burden created by family problems falls on society. According to the structure-functional family theory discussed in Chapter 2, the family performs basic functions within society. When the family does not carry out these functions, society has to step in and use resources to meet the needs of that family. Although this safety net that is provided by society is necessary in some cases, if all families failed to take responsibility for its members, there would be chaos. Consider what would happen if all noncustodial divorced parents decided not to take responsibility to pay child support. The hardship created on society to meet the needs of these children would be overwhelming, and the government as well as the economy would be in serious trouble.

Taking responsibility for our families, our world, and ourselves is essential for survival. It is also the responsible family that feels successful.

Summary

Society has a responsibility to maintain the planet ultimately for the benefit of those who live on the earth. Individuals as well as business and industry must take responsibility for the sustainability of our future resources. Care must be taken to make sure that our food, soil, water, and energy are used wisely and that they are being conserved or replenished for the next generation. Interiority includes ethical or cultural needs that are less noticeable but are necessary for social responsibility. Families are responsible for their members. This responsibility includes different aspects of wellness: social, physical, occupational, spiritual, intellectual, and emotional. Individuals are also responsible for themselves. They must realize how happiness and personal satisfaction affects not only themselves but those around them and, ultimately, society.

Questions for Review and Discussion

1. Why is social responsibility important?

2. Why should the corporate world have responsibility to society?

3. What are the arguments between environmentalist and business? How can they reach a compromise?

4. Which environmental issue is more important for our world: food, soil, water, or energy?

5. What steps should America take to end the image of "the throw-away society?"

6. How does green space affect you? Is it necessary for society?

7. Is sustainability being accomplished in the United States? Around the world?

8. Why is interiority as important as economics to sustainability?

9. In what area of wellness does the American family need help the most? Why?

10. Does money make people happy?

Current and Future Challenges 14

Objectives

- Be aware of the impact that technology has on family resources and decisions.

- Recognize possible future changes to family structure.

- Identify current trends with possible future ramifications for family resource management.

- Understand the current and future challenges of managing natural resources effectively.

- Be aware of the forecasted changes in population demographics and possible associated changes.

In every conceivable manner, the family is link to our past, bridge to our future.

—Alex Haley

Chapters 1 to 13 explored both the context and progression within the decision-making process. This final chapter provides a view into the future

355

of family decision making and family resource management. Change is always a constant for families. Although challenging and uncomfortable, change provides the impetus for better decision making and the motivation to seek answers and enhance problem-solving skills.

What are the major changes forecasted that will impact family life in the near and distant future? Technology, family structure, availability of natural resources, and changing demographics will all force change in social policy, economic policy, and family functioning.

Technology

Before you even finish reading this paragraph, there will be new innovations announced in the field of technology. These newer, faster, more sophisticated tools will improve, complicate, and probably harm individuals and families in some way. There is no going back, however. Technology is imbedded in business, politics, and family life.

LIFESTYLE CHANGES

You are shutting down your laptop at work and ready to head out the door. Before you do, you hit a button on your computer that will automatically activate the thermostat in your apartment, switch your refrigerator drawer into an oven mode to heat your dinner, turn on entryway lighting, draw the curtains, and start filling your bath. Sound futuristic and contrived? It is all currently possible with the proper wiring and equipment. ZigBee, a network based on low-power, two-way radio microchips, can be installed on electrical devices and appliances, allowing you to control and monitor numerous devices remotely (Graham-Rowe, 2004). You could also access your sprinkler system, washing machine, and TV.

Online grocers have emerged as a new approach to an old business. In the St. Paul-Minneapolis, Minnesota, area, Simple Simon, Inc. provides grocery shopping directly from the PC with delivery directly to your door (Sheng, 2005). Another innovation proposed is the two-way refrigerator. This appliance would be placed against an outside wall with keyed access through the exterior wall. The grocery delivery person just drives up, opens the exterior door of the refrigerator, and places cold foods directly into the refrigerator. Even more timesaving is the proposed refrigerator that scans everything placed into it, scans and measures remaining quantities as items are removed and used, and automatically reorders items when the supply falls below an acceptable level.

Not only useful to busy adults, these innovations might possibly enable elderly and disabled individuals to function independently at much higher levels. Technology can be used to lessen the most dangerous obstacles, such as loneliness, isolation, and mobility. Constant supervision and social interaction can be provided through camera systems, e-mail programs, and audiovisual equipment. Groceries and medical supplies can be ordered and delivered easily. Motorized chairs, food preparation equipment, and cleaning appliances can lessen dependency on care providers. The biggest risk would be an overdependence on this technology, resulting in further isolation and loneliness (Monk et al., 2006).

Worldview

Cell Phones as Credit Cards

Are we heading for a time when money, credit cards, and debit cards are no longer necessary? Will the cell phone that keeps shrinking in size and growing in capabilities replace your wallet? The potential is there, but will the practicalities facilitate or impede the change?

As early as 1990, the credit card and vending machines became intertwined with sales of clothing—initially denim jeans. The fees required for use of credit cards were prohibitive for most vending machine purchases, and even fast-food companies held out for a while before they recognized the possible sales impact of accepting credit cards. But pulling that credit card out for purchases, juggling your cell phone simultaneously, and deciding which brand of soda you want from the vending machine may seem overly taxing to consumers. Why not just dial a number on your cell phone, point it at the vending machine, and hit the button? Instant gratification!

In 2006, MasterCard and Taiwan's Chinatrust Bank introduced a wristwatch with credit card capabilities. Visa looked to the Cingular wireless network for similar functions. A test marketing project at the Atlanta sports arena simplified purchases of tickets, concessions, songs, video clips, and even phone ringtones. Visa announced that these phone options would be widely available by late 2008.

Motorola looked inward and decided that this new technological capability could be used in self-promotion. The company introduced "robotic stores"—retail centers resembling vending machines that sold phones and accessories. Initially transactions are credit card-based. But imagine the possibility of purchasing a cell phone using your cell phone!

Technology is never without its glitches, however, and the ability to securely transfer funds through cell phones has been problematic. Japan and some European countries have initiated the cell phone purchasing option for customers (TECHWEB, 2007). Japan's NTT DoCoMo has experienced high customer demand for their mobile credit card system that transmits the payment process by holding the phone next to a cash register sensor (Mullins, 1997). The United States is moving much more slowly.

(Continued)

(Continued)

Some credit this snail's pace to the service carriers. With the potential for use so large, these companies fear the perils of too much, too soon ("American Giants Fight," 2007). They are seeking secure methods, stable business plans, and equitable profit sharing. Banking institutions and wireless network providers would become competitors (Bielski, 2007). If the service providers are enhancing the ability of consumers to utilize credit services, they feel entitled to part of the increased profit—through fees.

Although the major carriers are moving slowly, smaller market entities are trying their hand at this sales-enhancing technology. 7-Eleven has stepped into the waters in Dallas, promoting mobile payments through its own service. What does this mean to the U.S. consumer? Imagine purchasing your airline ticket for your next flight as you taxi into the airport (LaSusa, 2007). No lines, no waiting. Your credit card will become extinct. The evolutionary time period is just unclear.

HEALTH CARE

Individuals and families living in the United States already expect the highest level of health care available. Those with insurance coverage have many options for maintenance, treatment, and diagnosis available to them. Those without insurance may seek assistance from public and private programs, but will find their options much more limited. The latest developments in care, management, and medicines continue to feed consumers new hope. Struggles escalate between special interest groups lobbying for increased federal research spending on their particular disease. Resources are obviously not in step with demand or need. What does the future hold in terms of health care?

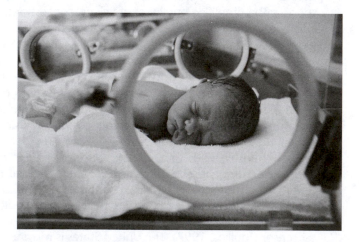

Photo 14.1   Medical technology presents opportunities and challenges.

Source: © Don Bayley/iStockphoto.

Newborn screening (NBS), the testing of newborn infants for up to 50 specific disorders, is the first program of population-wide genetic testing (Green, Dolan, & Murray, 2006). Two challenges emerge from such screening processes—establishment and maintenance of ethical standards and preparation of the public health system to accommodate and respond to these programs. Since the 1960s, a blood sample is drawn from almost all infants born in the United States. Most view the early detection of those problems as a positive step toward healthier lives. Some are concerned, however, that without stricter guidelines, these screening processes may become unmanageable. Once identified, how will these potential health problems be addressed? Will those with economic means be permitted to treat their own children while those in poverty are untreated? Will potential problems be treated as if they were existing problems, thus exposing infants to drug treatments and medical procedures that may be unnecessary?

Another infant health issue is the banking of umbilical cord blood. Blood found in a child's umbilical cord can be collected at birth and stored for future use. Storage can be in either a private or public bank. Once this blood is collected, it can be accessed when needed for medical treatment of the donor or other patients. If the blood is stored in a private bank, it can only be accessed for that individual unless permission is given for another to use it. Once in a public bank, that blood may be used by other patients. It is treated as a donation. These blood cells can treat a growing number of diseases and disorders. If a child has a family history of these medical problems, it may be a safety precaution for the family to bank the blood for possible use in the future. Banking is entirely up to the family. Because it does cost to contract for private storage, the practice is most common among those with monetary resources. Again, this raises the ethical question of privilege.

Stem-cell research is both hotly debated and scientifically intriguing. Medical research has the potential to extend the renewing capability of stem cells into treatments for several conditions—brain and spinal cord injuries, heart disease, neurological disease, and countless other types of diseases. Controversy about the source of these cells, especially when taken from human embryos, presents ethical questions that must be considered. As medical technology continues to provide new opportunities at ever-increasing speed, decisions about how, what, and why these new techniques should be utilized must be carefully analyzed.

On the other end of the lifespan, health care of the elderly is expected to be problematic in the next few decades. In 2046, 79 million baby boomers will be between the ages of 82 and 100 years (Della Cava, 2005). Although they will be the healthiest group of elders in history, aging bodies require increased health care. Advances in medicine, such as joint replacements and neurosurgical procedures, will increase both demand for and use of financial resources for medical expenses. Chronic diseases will increase with age, and the demand for pharmaceuticals to relieve symptoms, and even to cure those diseases, will tax the public program dollars.

Reality Check

The E-Patient

Akerkar and Bichile (2004) introduce the concept of the "e-patient." This new breed of medical patient is hitting the clinics and hospitals armed with information pulled from the Web. This quick-access reference leads to preconceived self-diagnosis and treatment options. E-patients are empowered by the information technology has provided them. Classical e-patients are younger and female. They are better educated and have higher incomes than other medical consumers.

Before the information age, medical knowledge belonged to the physician. Patients were expected to listen and comply. Now patients may be informing their physicians about new developments in medical treatments because that information is as readily available to them as it is to professionals. Informed patients are intelligent and actively engaged in the management of their personal conditions. This access to knowledge at the speed of light translates into an increased impatience. E-patients want quick, convenient, personalized services they have become accustomed to in other aspects of their lives.

How does this shift in expectations impact the trust between patient and care provider? While the 1900s were characterized as "Doctor knows best," empowered patients no longer depend on blind trust. Skepticism and weariness have emerged. In fact, the first point of contact in many health-based situations is the computer, rather than the physician. A survey of 500 online health seekers revealed that 55% gathered online information before visiting a doctor and 32% sought information about a particular doctor or hospital (Fox & Rainie, 2004).

EDUCATION

How will technology influence the future of education? Computerized instruction has already had a tremendous impact on university course and program offerings. Online courses provide opportunities for study to those in remote geographic locations and those with job and other time constraints. Distance education technology allows elementary and secondary schools to share instructors and curriculum efficiently and effectively. Computer use provides access to information at all times and from sources around the globe. Computer-designed instruction also enhances the ability to individualize study at all levels.

The increasing dependency on computers and technology for information access and exchange is not without its problems, however. Access (or lack of it) to computers in schools and private homes creates an economic divide that unfairly polarizes students at all educational levels in their ability to obtain necessary information. Increased sophistication of information presentation using graphics and other enhancement tools may lead to higher expectations and an increased valuation of presentation over content.

IMPACT

Although advances in technology provide many benefits, there are drawbacks. **Technostress** is a newly coined word used to describe the emotional state created by feelings of being overwhelmed by and underprepared for the rapid changes in information processing (Goldsborough, 2005). Advances in "time-saving machines" meant to save time may actually result in increased standards. The computer was touted as the way to a paperless society. That was believed to be environmentally beneficial. Many debate whether those computers reduced the use of paper or ultimately increased the consumption and ultimate disposal problems. Backup of computer data through hard-copy files is not uncommon.

Multiple computers, TVs, and video game systems have created a separatist environment in many homes. Individuals spend increasingly greater amounts of time separated, in different rooms attending to individual tasks alone. Younger generations are often more comfortable using technology, and the balance of power can be shifted when they have knowledge necessary to use new products while their parents and grandparents feel helpless and unprepared.

In the News

Self-Parking BMWs by 2009

By Errol Pierre-Louis

July 13, 2006

Following the trend of human control giving way to automation, BMW has developed an automated parking system that lets its vehicles park themselves. With a push of a button, your Beamer will slot itself into the garage while you watch from outside. The Mercedes S-Class and some Lexus models also have parking assistance systems, but the driver must remain in the vehicle in order to use them. According to **Wired News**, BMW plans to make remote control parking available within 3 years.

To set up the system, you'll install a reflective lens against the wall at the head of the parking space. A cam mounted on your BMW's front windshield will measure the distance and angle of the car relative to the lens. The car uses information from the sensors to calculate an entry trajectory and then navigates the vehicle into its parking spot.

This advanced parking assistance system builds on existing BMW technology such as *park distance control,* which uses ultrasonic sensors to help you judge the distance from your car to other cars and to unseen objects when you're parking. Parking assistance will use the same sensors to brake and steer around objects in the car's trajectory.

Family Structure

The increase and eventual leveling off of divorce rates over the last 50 years has already demonstrated a marked impact on family structure in the United States. The emerging trends of cohabitation and single parenting have challenged existing policies and opinions. It is reasonable, based on historical analysis, to expect evolving changes in family structure over time. These changes will ultimately impact family resource management.

MARRIAGE

The institution of marriage in the 21st century has changed. Cherlin (2004) notes that marriage may be in a process of deinstitutionalization as it becomes more individualized and the emphasis is placed more on personal choice and growth. Statistics show that the marriage rate has dropped. There are several reasons for this drop, including the tendency to delay marriage, an increase in unmarried cohabitation, and a decrease in remarriage for those who divorce (The National Marriage Project, 2006). For some, marriage is not a legal option. The United States, as a country, and individual states continue to struggle with legislation determining the legality of same-sex unions. *Marriage* and *civil union* are two terms imbedded in this battle for legitimate partner rights and responsibilities. Both reflect historical definitions of family and have far-reaching potential to impact current and future definitions of family structures.

There seems to be a difference between those who marry and those who choose not to marry. For those who are college-educated, the number of people who marry seems to have increased. The same group also shows a decline in divorce rates (Goldstein & Kenney, 2001). Studies show this group tends to be more egalitarian in their gender roles and have more satisfaction in their marriage when compared to other population groups (Schoen & Cheng, 2006). In contrast, trends show a decline in marriage for minority and lower income communities. This "marriage gap" is discussed in *The State of Our Unions* report. The report states, "America is becoming a nation divided not only by education and income levels but by unequal family structures" (The National Marriage Project, 2006, p. 16).

Although marriage rates have declined, marriage is still important to society. The authors of *Why Marriage Matters: Twenty-Six Conclusions From the Social Sciences* (Wilcox et al., 2005) identified three fundamental conclusions in their second edition about the value and purpose of marriage based on over 150 social science research studies:

1. Marriage is an important social good, associated with an impressively broad array of positive outcomes for children and adults alike.

2. Marriage is an important public good, associated with a range of economic, health, educational, and safety benefits that help local, state, and federal governments serve the common good.

3. The benefits of marriage extend to poor and minority communities, despite the fact that marriage is particularly fragile in these communities. (p. 9)

Trends for the future of marriage are difficult to predict. However, surveys of adolescents conducted annually at the University of Michigan, *Monitoring the Future,* may give some insight into the future of marriage and family life. The desire for marriage among this age group has increased, although they are more accepting of alternatives to marriage, especially unwed childbearing. Recent surveys reveal an unexpected drop in approval of unmarried cohabitation.

CHILDREN

Delaying marriage and the increasing number of women in the workforce have contributed to a drop in fertility rates over the last 30 years. In addition, the stigma of being childless is vanishing. In 2004, for instance, 1 out of 5 women in their 40s were childless, as opposed to only 1 out of 10 in 1976 (The National Marriage Project, 2006), and the number of households with children has dropped from one half to one third (Lawler Dye, 2005).

Perhaps more significant than fertility rates and family size to the future of the family are the changes in the social climate of parenting. This change in attitude can be found in many aspects of life within the United States. The advantages to being childfree are everywhere. From housing that emphasizes the amenities of single living to TV programs that portray parents as fools and glamorizes the single life, there seems to be an apparent shift from a child-raising society to a childfree adult society. Surveys of parents point out a growing number of people who view parenting as a disadvantage. More than just the idea that parenting can be physically difficult, Stearns (2003) writes that more and more parents are suffering anxiety about their ability to parent. He suggests that parents today are more worried than their own parents about competence and may feel guilty when they are not as satisfied with the experience as they expected. Research shows that parenting can also be associated with psychological problems and lower marital satisfaction (Twenge, Campbell, & Foster, 2003).

Although Longman (2004) suggests that the present generation is more likely to want at least one child as compared to the baby boom generation, the price is high in terms of economics. For women especially, motherhood means a "life-time wage penalty of five to nine percent per child" (p. 74). For some, the thought that parenting means more debt, smaller savings, and an inability to live within a certain lifestyle is enough to influence their childbearing decisions. It may be useful to apply this situation to the principle of revealed preferences. According to this principle, consumer behavior reveals true preferences. In this case, although many say they value the family and desire children of their own, their true values are revealed by the lower statistics on childbearing. One could argue that economics alone should not be used to predict the trends of childbearing because it is only based on the costs of parenting and not the emotional rewards.

Despite the recent trends and seemingly negative research on the benefits of parenting, people have not given up becoming parents. At some point, most will become parents. However, the trends toward postponing parenting and having fewer children will likely continue.

DIVORCE

Although divorce rates have risen sharply since 1960, they have leveled and declined slightly over the last two decades. Two factors seem to contribute the most in reducing the number of divorces. The age at marriage and higher educational levels contribute to the stability of marriage (Heaton, 2002). Other factors are higher income levels, waiting to have children, intact family of origin, and having a religious affiliation, especially for women (Bramlett & Mosher, 2002). If current trends remain, divorce will continue to decline in the future.

One issue that seems to be a source of controversy and likely will be a topic of discussion in the future in regard to divorce is the provision of the no-fault divorce law. During the 1970s and early 1980s, the divorce laws underwent what is commonly known as a "divorce revolution," where most states enacted no-fault laws as grounds for divorce. Until this time, spouses could only initiate divorce proceedings if they had proof that their spouse was guilty of marital misconduct. Reasons for the movement toward no-fault divorce included a desire to unburden the court system of divorce proceedings, promote more fairness in division of marital assets, and allow former partners the freedom to remarry. It was also the belief that no-fault laws would promote more reconciliation. Although there is evidence on both sides of the controversy, many states and other organizations are now considering the negative consequences of the no-fault divorce laws. The increase in divorce rates and the inability of many to get a fair economic settlement are some of those consequences (Mechoulan, 2005). One attempt to soften the effects of no-fault divorce has been the covenant marriage option, which only permits divorce in the cases of adultery, abuse, or abandonment. As a result of the recent push, policy changes and changes in divorce laws appear to be on the horizon.

Family scientists are more concerned about the consequences of divorce for children and their future relationships. Almost every study about the effects of divorce on children points to some negative effects; however, most have concluded that the effects do not have a universal impact on all children

(Amato, 2005). Risk factors such as economic hardship and exposure to stress certainly affect the well-being of children; however, the quality of parenting seems to be the best predictor of emotional and social well-being for children in all family structures. Amato (2005) suggests that future policies should focus not on lower divorce rates as much as improving economic well-being, strengthening parent/child relationships, and easing stress. Another recent change that may affect divorce in the future is the movement toward mediation or the "collaborative" divorce. In an effort to make the process of divorce less emotionally draining and less expensive, mediators are being chosen to litigate the divorce settlement outside of the court. If divorcing couples agree to the terms without going to court, the results are often more amicable, which is easier for both partners and less difficult for their children. Currently, the collaborative divorce model is being used in 35 states and promises to be used more in the future (Aronsohn, 2004).

Natural Resources

It has been the topic of great discussion for decades—alternative energy. Now seems to be the time for action. California's governor, Arnold Schwarzenegger, recently signed a bill mandating the use of solar panels on home roofs (Wagner, 2006). California developers of more than 50 new single-family homes must offer solar-energy systems as an option to all customers beginning in 2011. There are $2.9 billion in incentives to homeowners who install solar-electric systems. The goal is to have 1 million solar roofs in the state by 2018, reducing the output of greenhouse gasses by 3 million tons. Solar panels will limit home design choices. Families will need to adjust or redefine their definition of curb appeal in home design. They will need to be educated about the long-term benefits before they will be convinced to make larger expenditures during the design and building stages.

Automobiles are utilizing alternative forms of energy already. Ethanol, recycled cooking oil, and even electricity are possible fuels in a limited number of vehicles on the road. Manufacturers are developing new, more efficient automobiles that will be capable of using these alternative fuels. Urban areas are increasing efforts to expand public transportation, hoping to reduce the use of personal automobile congestion on roadways. It is not anticipated that individuals and families will ever purposefully reduce their desire to travel. Air travel will continue to increase as businesses and families expand geographically. Increasing numbers of older adults will pursue travel in their retirement.

A growing dependency on electricity must also be addressed. Harnessing wind and surf energy and converting those into useable forms of electricity are two important areas of research and design in the field of engineering. An emerging interest in portable energy sources parallels consumer demand for wireless technology and flexible products. Rechargeable fuel cells are gaining impetus in many areas of product design.

Feeding the billions of people currently on the planet is challenging. With expanding development of housing and industrial complexes, land available for food production is dwindling. New methods of food production that increase quantity without depleting soil sources must continue to emerge. Efficient methods of waste management will also be necessary. Chapter 13 explained social responsibility. The future will be positively or negatively impacted by the acceptance or rejection of this important concept.

Changing Demographics

Using demographic information is an important tool in not only under-standing the changes that are taking place, but to help policymakers and community leaders make informed decisions. Demographic forecasting is possible when emerging trends are identified from changing demographic information. Speaking at the 2005 National Conference of State Legislatures, William H. Frey, a demographer from the University of Michigan, stated that changing demographic information has led him to predict that the three emerging issues for the future are immigration, the aging of the baby boom generation, and the middle-class flight from urban areas to the interior west and southwest regions (State Legislatures, 2005).

DIVERSITY AND IMMIGRATION

Photo 14.2   Immigration presents economic and social controversy.

Source: © Matthias Wasserman/iStockphoto.

The United States was much more racially diverse in 2000 than in 1900, with the increase in diversity occurring mostly in the last part of the century. At the beginning of the century, 1 out of 8 persons was non-White, but at the end of the century, the ratio was 1 out of 4 (Hobbs & Stoops, 2002). In 2005, the nation's minority population totaled 98 million (33%) of the country's total of 296.4 million, or about 1 out of 3 according to national estimates released by the U.S. Census Bureau (2006b).

Both the White and African American populations represented a slightly smaller share of the U.S. total population in 1970 than they did in 1900, but in 2000 the population of other races than White or African American grew considerably and was comparable in size to the African American population (Hobbs & Stoops, 2002). The U.S. Census Bureau (2006b) reports that Hispanics continue to be the largest minority group at 42.7 million. With a 3.3% increase in population from July 1, 2004, to July 1, 2005, they are the fastest-growing minority group. By 2002, the Hispanic population surpassed the African American population as the largest minority. Estimates are that the nation's Hispanic and Asian populations will triple, and non-Hispanic Whites will represent about one half of the total population by 2050, according to interim population projections released by the U.S. Census Bureau (2004).

During the last few decades, immigration played a major role in changing the racial and ethnic composition in the United States. America is one of the most diverse countries in the world, and the open-door policies of immigration have made it possible for people from all over the world to come and make a life in the United States. Immigration was the major factor in the high percentage increases in the Asian and Pacific Islander (204%) and the Hispanic (142%) populations from 1980 to 2000 (Hobbs & Stoops, 2002). Despite the recent attacks on immigration following the terrorists' acts of September 11, 2001, immigration still continues. Controversy surrounding legal and illegal immigration continues to be the source of a great deal of debate among politicians and the public. There are no easy solutions, and the debate will likely continue into the future.

Recognizing and understanding the shift in the demographics of diversity is critical as we prepare for the future. The growth of diversity changes the dynamics of communities. Food migrates with people, but the authenticity of it changes when mixed with the likes and dislikes of others. Think of all the fast-food restaurants that serve an "Americanized" version of an ethnic food. The tortilla chip rivals the potato chip as America's snack food. Goods and services also change to meet the needs of the diverse groups. Business strategies and practices must change to fit the unique characteristics of the target market. Over time, the political process in America may also change; however, Ramakrishnan (2005) has found that even those immigrants who become citizens do not participate in politics. Once organized, he suggests that immigrants could play a significant role in changing the United States.

The Hispanic culture, now the largest minority group and the majority population in some places, has already changed American society. The Spanish language has been introduced in many ways from advertising and labeling to children's programming on TV. The worlds of music, entertainment, and sports include Latino talent with names like pop star Jennifer Lopez, actress Cameron Diaz, and Major League Baseball's Alex Rodriguez.

AGING POPULATION

The American Geriatrics Society (2006) reported that the number of elderly people is growing. At the turn of the 20th century, there were 3.1 million seniors. By 1994, the number increased to 33.2 million and is estimated to more than double by 2050 to 80 million seniors. By the year 2030, estimates are that one in every five people will be a senior citizen or 20% of the population. One reason for this dramatic increase is the aging of the baby boom generation, born between 1940 and 1960. The U.S. Census Bureau (2006a) reported that in 2006, almost 8,000 people are turning 60 each day.

The economic well-being of the elderly has improved because of the availability of Social Security, the introduction of Medicare, as well as increased education and earning ability. In the 1960s, 35% of those 65 or older had incomes below the poverty level, but by the 1990s this dropped to 10% (American Geriatrics Society, 2006). The Center for Health Communication (2004) predicts that the link between age and retirement will be coming to an end. The end of the 20th century brought a reversal in the trend toward early retirement. The age of retirement rose and is predicted to continue due to changes in Social Security that may force many to stay employed longer, technological advances that improve working conditions, and better health of older Americans.

It is evident that the changes in economic security, health, and longevity will give those who are aging considerable social power as they enter the next phase of their lives. Business and industry are already taking note of the likes and dislikes of the baby boom generation and are targeting them for a larger share of the consumer market. In the coming years, advertisers may need to switch from products that only target youth to those products that target older, more affluent, more technically savvy, and more health-conscious adults than previous generations at that age.

Although the future looks bright and positive for aging baby boomers, according to Nelson (2005), the chief operating officer at the American Association of Retired Persons (AARP), there are three issues that will plague older Americans in the future. They are

- Transforming the national health care system—rising medical costs, the number of Americans who aren't covered by health insurance, and better health care delivery are all issues that must be addressed.

- Strengthening the retirement system—the Social Security system needs to be made solvent and economically sound, people need to save more during their lifetime for additional funds in retirement, and they need to continue to work past retirement age while contributing to federal withholding funds.

- Creating more livable communities—barriers to "aging in place" need to be removed by providing adequate transportation, modifying housing to accommodate the elderly, and providing protection against fraud.

GEOGRAPHIC LOCATION AND HOUSING

Changing demographics of the typical household and other population shifts have led to changes in housing and urban development. The housing needs of families with children have fueled the housing trends in the past. The growth in minority populations, the aging of the baby boom generation, and the increase in single-parent families all require different housing choices (Grier, 2004). Although the new urbanism previously was said to be an emerging trend for those who wanted to move away from the suburban "sprawl," it appears that the "new suburbanism" is beginning to replace the desire for downtown revival and trendy loft spaces. Surveys find that more than 70% of Americans prefer a single-family home, with only 15% preference to space in an urban area. Reviving main streets in small towns, bringing business and industry outside the city, and building a community feeling are all ways to make suburban living more attractive. More than just an American phenomenon, suburban living is desired around the world, and immigrants dream of owning their own home when arriving in the United States (Kotkin, 2006).

The housing needs of the elderly will focus on maintaining their own homes with coordinated support services and physical modifications. However, Grier (2004) suggests that "empty nesters" don't want or need the large, suburban homes and choose to downsize to a smaller home that requires less maintenance and is more centrally located. Others may opt for urban neighborhoods or may even rent so they have the option to be more mobile. As baby boomers become empty nesters, they realize that the income from their large homes allows them to downsize in style and are choosing luxury over space in their new environments.

Wherever Americans live, there are also future implications in the way that they choose to engage in their community. According to the *General Social Survey* (2004), Americans are less connected to social networks. They report fewer close friends and have less ties to relatives than in the past. Many attribute this lack of connection to an increase in mobility. However, recent research shows that mobility rates have declined for individuals of all ages, especially among those in their 20s and those 65 and older. The study suggests that if we fail to make connections within our communities, it is not a result of increasing mobility (Wolf & Longino, 2005). The future of communities may be affected by the tendency of people to prefer isolation and make fewer connections to the outside world. As previously mentioned, the Internet has made it possible to shop, bank, and work in relative seclusion.

Summary

Families and how they manage the resources necessary to meet their needs and wants are dynamic in nature. Changes within the unit and changes in the external environment impact future needs and decision-making processes. Although it is impossible to predict the future, analysis of current trends allows projection of possible shifts. Technology is sure to continue bringing constant and confounding changes to individuals and families at many levels. Family structures have been and will probably continue to evolve to meet societal expectations and circumstances. Expected future crises in terms of natural resource demands and supply will present challenges. Alternative sources must be developed. Changes within the population will create new opportunities and problems for families to address. Change is both stressful and functional. Needs, and the resources available to meet these emerging needs, will continue to be a primary function of the family unit.

Questions for Review and Discussion

1. In what ways have recent advances in technology impacted your personal life? Your educational experience?

2. Have new inventions typically increased leisure time and activity?

3. How has technology shaped the educational process you are pursuing?

4. What major shifts in family structure will have the greatest impact on resource management?

5. What are some strategies that might increase participation in recycling efforts?

6. List five long-term effects on family resource management that may result from the aging of the general population.

Casebook

Casebook

THE ALPHA FAMILY

Members: Mother, 45 years old. Registered nurse with 15 years employment at the same hospital. She works four 10-hour days per week. Divorced from sons' father, remarried, but recently separated from second husband. She enjoys reading, movies, and spending time with her friends from work.

First Husband. Shared custody, although sons lived with mother across town. Child support ended; however, he does provide money to youngest son when justified. Remarried. No alimony settlement.

Second Husband. Currently in addiction rehabilitation program. Unemployed.

Oldest son, 25 years old. Serving in the military in Middle East. Father of a 3-year-old in the custody of child's mother. Unmarried.

Youngest son, 18 years old. Senior in high school. Severe asthma and allergic conditions. He enjoys spending time with his friends playing video games, attending school sporting events, and camping with his father on weekends.

The family has one housecat.

Strengths: Home was paid for through the divorce settlement. Home value is three times the mother's annual gross salary. Small sedan,

2 years old, has a loan against it for 50% of market value. Small sports car, 1 year old—gift from father to 18-year-old. Health insurance provided through mother's employer for reduced fee. Mother has a pension accumulation worth 1 year's gross salary. Liquid savings of $1,400.

Challenges: Although home is mortgage-free, taxes, insurance, utilities, and up-keep are the mother's responsibility. There is no loan against the son's car, but taxes, licensing, and insurance are liabilities. The family currently carries a credit card balance of two times the mother's monthly gross income. Although health insurance pays the majority of medical bills, this family has an average of $300 per month out-of-pocket medical expenses. The mother's pension is funded through a 3% monthly gross income investment directly from her paycheck.

THE BETA FAMILY

Members: Mr. Beta, 36 years old, is a city policeman of 8 years. He enjoys coaching his children's sports activities, attending sporting events, and participating in golf, adult basketball, and community projects.

Mrs. Beta, 36 years old, is a medical laboratory technologist. She has been working at the same facility for 12 years. She is active in the parent organization at the children's school, belongs to a women's health club, and transports her children to and from activities.

Oldest daughter is 10 years old. She participates in dance, swimming, and soccer.

Oldest son is 8 years old. He plays ice hockey and baseball and is a member of the local Boy Scouts.

Youngest son is 6 years old. He plays T-ball and is a Cub Scout.

The family has a small indoor dog and an aquarium with fish.

Strengths: Father works 3 days on, 3 days off, 6 am to 6 pm. Mother works 4 days on, 2 days off, 9 am to 7 pm. Family belongs to the local YMCA, which provides before- and after-school programs. Home is less than 5 years old and is valued at three times the combined gross annual incomes of both adults. It is mortgaged at 90% of its value. Family owns a 3-year-old pickup with no outstanding loan and a new sport utility vehicle with an outstanding loan of 75% purchase price. Health insurance is provided through either parent at a reduced rate, and the mother's company provides life insurance policies on both adults, worth five times the annual income of each. Both adults have pension balances equal to their annual income, and they continue to add to those funds by adding 5% of their gross incomes monthly.

Challenges: Taxes, mortgage, insurance, utilities, and up-keep of the new home are required monthly. Both vehicles must be licensed, taxed, insured, and maintained. The family has a credit card balance equal to 1 month's combined incomes. A recent furniture credit purchase has a balance equal to 80% of 1 month's combined incomes. The family is 1,000 miles away from the mother's family and 3,000 miles away from the father's family.

THE OMEGA FAMILY

Members: Husband is 68 years old and recently retired from his position as lead pharmacist in a local chain. He looks forward to golf, gardening, and being more active in local community projects and clubs.

The wife is 65 years old and is teaching full time in a local elementary school. She enjoys her work and doesn't plan to retire for a few years. She enjoys traveling and is a great supporter of the community cultural projects. Two adult children are married with children of their own—four total. They all live in a nearby city approximately 250 miles away.

The mother-in-law is 86 years old and has Alzheimer's disease. She cannot be left alone, but still enjoys socializing, watching TV, and needle point. Her other three adult children live out of state.

Strengths: The husband is currently drawing Social Security ($1,700 monthly) and Medicare benefits. He has a pension equal to five times his last annual gross income. This money can be tapped at any time, if needed, but will be taxable. The wife is also qualified for Medicare benefits and has a pension fund worth three times her annual salary if she should choose to retire. Together they have $200,000 liquid savings. Their home equity is $85,000, and the mortgage is equal to two times her salary. They have a 1-year-old sport utility vehicle and a 5-year-old small pick-up. Neither is encumbered by loans. Both have life insurance policies worth $180,000, with no additional premiums necessary. As a teacher, the wife still has medical insurance available through her employer for a reduced rate. The mother receives $700 per month from Social Security and qualifies for Medicare.

Challenges: Monthly this family must pay the mortgage and all necessary insurances on the home and automobiles. They have memberships to the local country club, community theater, university sports team events, and university alumni organization. They recently purchased a condominium unit in a Florida retirement community to use when they are both ready to move. The condo's value is four times her annual salary. They have leased this unit for 1 year for $2,000 per month. The mortgage on this unit is equal to one half of her monthly income, and there is a $450 monthly maintenance fee. The mother-in-law can no longer travel and requires constant monitoring for her safety.

The family has an elderly cat.

THE TAU FAMILY

Members: Grandmother, age 55, is the head of housekeeping at a local motel chain. She works Monday through Friday, 6 am to 2 pm. She is caring for her three grandchildren while her daughter serves a 5-year prison charge. She is active in her neighborhood and elementary school organizations. Although she is a widow, she has a large extended family in the community.

The oldest granddaughter is 13 years old, and she attends the middle school located approximately 1 mile from their home. She enjoys reading, watching TV, and spending time with her friends and cousins in the neighborhood.

The middle grandson is 9 years old, and he attends the neighborhood elementary school 3 blocks from their home. He enjoys playing with neighbor children, YMCA sports programs, and riding his bike.

The youngest grandson is 7 years old, and he attends a school for special needs children across town. He has behavioral and developmental disorders and requires medication and therapy treatments. He enjoys walks in the park, playing with toys, and listening to music.

Strengths: The children receive state assistance and Medicaid. Food stamps and other economic programs can be accessed to assist with their care. The grandmother has a close neighbor who stays with the children in the morning and makes sure they get to school. The grandmother, in turn, picks up this neighbor's children after school and watches them until early evening. When the grandfather died 3 years ago, an insurance policy on the mortgage paid for the house entirely. The home is a small three-bedroom, 50-year-old bungalow. It is valued at three times her annual gross income. There is also a 15-year-old sedan that was given to the grandmother by an uncle of her late husband. Health and life insurance are available through her employer for reduced rates. She also has accumulated a retirement savings equal to three times her annual gross income, and she continues to contribute 3% to that fund monthly.

Challenges: Believing that her daughter was innocent of charges, she took out a personal loan against her home for 30% of its value to pay for legal defense. This loan has an 8% interest rate and is payable over a 10-year period. The daughter is incarcerated 250 miles away, and the family tries to visit her at least twice a month.

THE ZETA FAMILY

Members: The adults in this family are cohabitating. The adult male is 38 years old and is divorced with a 12-year-old son who lives with his mother 200 miles away. He is a certified auto mechanic and has been employed by the same repair shop for 16 years. Workdays are Monday through Friday, 7:30 am to 5 pm and every other Saturday morning 8 am to noon. He enjoys spending time with coworkers, bowling, attending auto races, and riding his mountain bike in competitions.

The adult female is 37 years old, divorced, and the custodial parent of two daughters. She works 12 hours per week as a receptionist in a dental office. She enjoys scrap booking, cooking, and watching movies. Her family lives close by, and she spends a lot of time with her sisters and her mother.

Both daughters are in elementary school (first and third grades). They spend most of their free time playing with neighbor children or relatives and playing in the park down the block.

Strengths: Mother receives $200 per month for child support, and both children are covered by their father's medical insurance. The apartment this family is renting is within walking distance of both the school and the mother's place of employment. The mother has a 5-year-old van with no outstanding loan, and the father has a 10-year-old pickup that is debt-free. The male has $750 in liquid savings and a pension plan balance of two times his annual gross income. He also has insurance plans through his employer that cover his son and himself.

Challenges: The male pays $450 per month in child support and insists on visiting his son every other weekend. His son spends every other holiday with his father. The monthly rent is equal to one third of his monthly income and only water, sewer, and garbage are included. The adult female has no life or health insurance. Both vehicles require tax, licensing, and maintenance expenses. Auto and renter's insurance are also paid monthly. The girls' father does not visit or maintain contact, but his monthly payments have been dependable over the last year.

Case One

Read the description of your case family carefully.

- How similar is their current situation to your own situation in terms of family structure? How does it differ?

Obviously, certain choices have been made by the adults in your case family that have resulted in this current situation.

- Identify at least one choice that you would have made differently. Which of the worldview dimensions explains why your choice would have differed from the choice made by your case family?

Meet in your neighborhood groups. Present a summary of your case family's current situation to other participants.

- Do you identify more closely to one of the other families in the case neighborhood?
- If you could select your own case family to work with in these assignments, which would you choose? Why?

Case Two

To determine annual income of employed adults in your case family, visit the Web site provided. Gross income, or income before taxes are deducted, will be entered in Case One. Employee taxes will be part of a later assignment.

Using the spreadsheet provided, fill in as many of the accounts as possible with the information provided in your family's case file. Use the www.kelleybluebook.com Web site or another similar site to determine the value of the automobiles. Select any make and model you envision for this family.

Analyzing the income and outflow of monetary assets, identify current and future challenges your family might face. Discuss any possible advantages your family has based on both financial and human resources available to them. You will complete this entire budget sheet over the next few weeks, so save all entries from this point on.

Case Three

Using the weekly planner provided, plot out distinct periods of time for each family member that are obligated in advance. For instance, adults are obligated to work certain hours and certain days. Children are required to attend school for certain periods of time. Block out those time periods using a color code. Add in all obligated times for scheduled activities and sleep times. Realizing that there are certain auxiliary tasks required to manage a family (transportation time, laundry, cleaning, lawn care), block that time in the calendar, acknowledging that these tasks may occur at different times in actuality. Visually calculate the amount of time family members have available that is not obligated to something out of their control. Create a one- to two-page summary and discussion of this family's time management challenges and how they might meet them.

Case Four

This chapter has explored the identification of family needs, real and perceived. Society standards and expectations often help determine the kind of large-scale purchases families make. Homes and automobiles are two examples of this concept. Your case family has made decisions about housing and transportation. They may also have credit card debt or other long-term loan commitments.

Using the debt calculator provided, determine monthly payments your family must budget for based on their current debt load. Enter those payments on the budget spreadsheet. Determine their debt load by adding all monthly debt payments and dividing by the family's total gross income. Do you think your family has a healthy load? Create a one- to two-page summary of your findings and your professional analysis of their debt load.

Case Five

The budget category of "soft goods" includes many diverse types of expenditures. Food and clothing purchase behaviors of families have been researched over time. Although families are unique in their consumption patterns, an overall percentage of income can be used to approximate these expenses for your case family. American families typically spend between 13% and 16% of their gross income on food. This includes both in-home and out-of-home dining. School children may take their own lunch daily, purchase food on or off site, or participate in school lunch programs. Next, 6% to 8% of family income is spent on clothing, and another 1% is spent on personal care items such as cleansers, hair care, laundry items, and other hygiene supplies. Home décor purchases have not been researched as thoroughly.

To fill in the soft goods section of your case family budget sheet, first calculate the amounts using the percentages in the previous paragraph. Then cross-check the food amount by creating a 1-week menu/eating plan for your family and estimating the cost. Take that amount and multiply by 4 to compare to the monthly percentage originally determined. Make adjustments as you determine necessary. Décor purchases can be determined at a later time once a surplus or deficit has been determined.

In this case report (one to two pages), include your calculations, menu plan, and any adjustment justifications.

Case Six

Maintaining a home is a complex, continual process. Families will manage and exchange many types of resources to accomplish this. Much home maintenance can be done by family members if necessary. Contemporary families, however, have accepted the exchange of money for public or private services. For example, families could physically haul the garbage they generate in their homes to the public garbage facilities and pay a small fee to dispose of it there or they could subscribe to a garbage pick-up service, public or private, and have their garbage physically removed from their home on a regular basis. They can pool their physical attributes and clean the premises and laundry themselves or they can contract those chores out for a fee.

To complete the "Home Expenses" portion of the case family budget sheet, you will decide who is responsible for home maintenance and how often certain services are required. The mortgage, if required, was part of a previous case assignment. *Up-keep* is a general term used to describe physical maintenance requirements, such as exterior and interior painting, repair of the living premises, and any exterior renovations necessary. Renters have little responsibility for up-keep of their rental unit. Any damage caused by members of the family, however, is the responsibility of the renter. Newer homes require less up-keep than older homes. Put at least 5% of the monthly mortgage or rental payment aside for possible maintenance costs. Depending on the weather patterns of your location, lawn care, snow removal, and leaf removal will vary. Explore such service providers in your community and determine how much to allot for these things. Explain your decision-making process in this case report.

Renters do not have to pay real estate tax, but homeowners do. Condominium taxes are paid by the association and are part of the monthly fee. To determine the appropriate real estate tax for case families that own homes, call your local assessor's office and obtain the tax rate of your community. Take that and multiply it by your home's total value. That will determine annual tax liability. Divide that amount by 12 and enter that figure in the taxes column.

Utilities vary dramatically from home to home. Families make different decisions about types of energy to use, types of utilities to subscribe to, and what level of service they will require. Explore utility options and average costs online at local real estate Web pages. Homes for sale often list average utility bills. Estimate your family's needs in all remaining categories under "Home Expenses." Briefly describe and support your decisions in the report.

Case Seven

The case families all have vehicles that are used to transport family members to necessary work sites, appointments, and leisure activities. Families in large metropolitan areas can avoid this expense category when a dependable mass transportation system is available. Fees to use that system would need to be budgeted instead. Most Americans would find lack of vehicle availability limiting, however.

You have already determined the value and debt associated with your case family's vehicles. Other necessary budget items to maintain automobile ownership and use include fuel, taxes/licensing fees, and repairs/general maintenance. You can estimate fuel costs by calculating average miles driven on a weekly basis and multiplying that by 4. Online vehicle sites can provide you with estimated mileage per gallon of fuel. Use these figures to determine approximately how much your family would need to budget for automobile fuel monthly and enter that amount on the budget sheet.

New automobiles usually have a 3- to 5-year warranty for repairs and recalls. They would require only regular maintenance, such as oil and fluid changes and cleaning. Older vehicles will require additional funds for parts and replacement of tires. Using the information provided in the family description and accessing online automobile maintenance information or seeking assistance from family or professionals in auto mechanics, determine a reasonable amount your family should set aside monthly to cover these anticipated costs.

Annual taxes and licensing fees vary by location. Contact your local governmental offices to determine the process for figuring these expenses. Enter those amounts on the budget.

Case Eight

Chapter 8 explores the impact of society on family decisions. Case Eight requires that you apply this new knowledge by estimating monthly demands on the family resources to fulfill the need for entertainment. Employment taxes are also an important societal factor. Using the current Social Security tax and Medicare tax rates, calculate the monthly income after federal taxes for each adult family member. Explore state income tax rates in your area and determine the monthly liability for this. Adjust the after-tax incomes accordingly.

Dining out has already been calculated under the food expense category. At this point, map out a typical week of out-of-home food purchases, multiply by 4, and take that amount out of the original food budget and place in this "dining-out" category. Think about the remaining balance in the food budget. Would this still cover necessary foodstuffs to feed this family over the month? If not, make necessary adjustments.

Movies and theater expenditures would include admissions to any live or recorded performances a family might attend. Home video rentals should also be included. The descriptions of your families include cultural event preferences and memberships. This information provides clues as to your family's preferences and probable participation.

To calculate membership fees, visit organizational Web sites, telephone similar clubs in your area, and ask friends and family. Remember to convert annual fees into monthly allotments. Sports programs for children and adults also may require fees. Attending sporting events usually requires the purchase of tickets and may require parking or transportation fees.

Travel is a difficult category to estimate. Plan at least one annual family excursion fully and divide the total cost by 12 to determine the monthly budget amount needed. Consider holidays, birthdays, and other special events that might require travel expenses.

In the case report, explain the choices you have made for this family and discuss constraints and conflicts you encountered in the process. Being realistic and avoiding passing judgment on this family may be challenging. If this family has more or fewer resources than your family of origin, be objective when considering their expectations.

Attach a copy of your family budget sheet, completed to date.

Case Nine

The planning process is an important tool for family resource management. All resources can be used in this process, although the most easily identifiable application is financial planning. You have entered asset values and retirement pension plan balances. Case family members who are contributing to pension plans must also enter monthly contribution information as described in the case details. That amount should be placed under "savings" retirement. Liquid savings amounts are also presented in the case information and should appear on the budget sheet as assets. If you believe that your family should be setting aside a certain amount of money in savings that can be easily accessed in case of emergency, put that amount on the budget sheet under "savings" in the liquid slot. Some financial specialists suggest that a family should have 6 months income in savings as a safety net for large-scale emergencies. How might you accomplish this with a savings plan?

Are there possible large-cost purchases in your family's future? Car? Home? If you believe there may be, how would you suggest they save on a monthly basis to meet these goals?

If your family has children, should the adults be saving money on a regular basis to build a fund for educational expenses in the future? If so, indicate an amount for that purpose under other savings. If your family has money in savings that could be used to meet monthly expenses or to pay down credit liabilities, how would you allocate such withdrawals? If there are elderly members of your family, should funds be available for future care needs?

The case report for this assignment should be created in a financial analysis format. Begin by discussing the strengths present in the family's financial plan. Then present immediate and forecasted challenges. Provide practical advice to family members on how they might address these needs with a financial savings plan.

Case Ten

Communication skills are essential for the discovery of needs and resource identification in a family's decision-making process. To better understand the complexity of family communication, create a family relationship matrix illustrating all interpersonal relationships that will impact the flow of information during communication situations. For instance, a family composed of a newlywed couple has one primary relationship/communication link— spouse 1 to spouse 2 and spouse 2 to spouse 1.

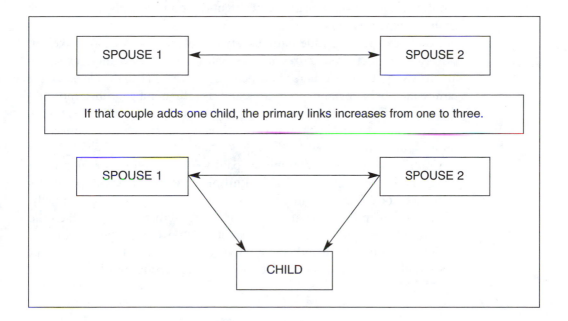

Each additional family member increases the number of primary links and, thus, the complexity of communication in that family. Create a visual of primary relationship/communication links only for your case family. Include parent, child, and significant adult relationships only.

Once you have created the visual relationship chart, analyze it and discuss the most problematic links at this point in time for the family. Which links are probably the weakest and most prone to experience noise and stress in times of crisis? Trace the following decisions through your family's chart:

1. The oldest female in the family requires a surgical procedure. A decision must be made as to where and when this will take place.

2. A major holiday is approaching. A decision must be made as to where family members will gather to celebrate.

Case Eleven

To complete the "Miscellaneous Expenses" portion of the budget sheet, be realistic and thorough. You have previously looked at the credit card debt and calculated a monthly payment. If you feel this needs adjustment, do so at this time. Explain in your report. Child support is part of the Tau family information, and alimony is not an issue for any of the case families. There are no outstanding education loans, but if you believe family members should be pursuing educational opportunities, add tuition expenses and explain. Family pets (when included in the family description) require different levels of care for health and grooming. Fully explain your monthly expense decision.

Beauty expenses include haircuts, styles, coloring, as well as make-up, skin care products, manicures, and pedicures. Some view these expenses are necessary, whereas others view them as luxuries. Try to decide based on family members' social expectations and age. Remember to use monthly figures only. Gifts are also discretionary expenses. Consider both the reasons for giving and the family's resources. Estimate yearly ranges and convert to monthly amounts.

Contributions include any money paid to organizations for support of programming, such as church, philanthropies, and public service programs (Humane Society, etc.). Some families set aside a flat percentage annually, whereas others preselect charities and amounts. Others just give when the opportunity presents itself. When financial support is not possible, many individuals donate time and energy. Giving back to others is an important value, and you should assume that these families practice this behavior.

Case Twelve

This case assignment will complete the insurance section of the family's budget sheet. Health/medical insurance is available as described. To determine the family's monthly payments to participate in these plans, visit the Web site provided by your instructor. Realizing your family's financial position and special needs due to life-cycle situations, select the insurance package that is best. If vision, dental, and other disease-specific policies are available on this site, balance the probability of family needs and the family's financial position in your decision. Enter monthly payment amounts on the budget sheet and explain your decision process completely in your case report. If your family members already have life insurance, determine whether it is sufficient. If not, make adjustments and include monthly payments necessary.

Use home insurance links provided to determine the appropriate amount of insurance and the monthly payments required. If you have a mortgage on your family's home, insurance is mandatory. Otherwise, home and renter's insurance are optional risk management tools.

Automobile insurance is required in most locations before licensing is allowed. View the links provided to determine what is required in your community. If there is an outstanding loan on automobiles, replacement insurance is usually required. Determine the monthly payments necessary to cover all automobiles, and enter that figure on your budget sheet.

If your family's condition indicates the need for additional types of insurance, such as disability, long-term care, and accidental death, and you believe it would be important for them to be covered for such things, add the cost of those policies. Explain these decisions thoroughly in the case report.

Case Thirteen

Through the last 12 cases, you have discovered the needs and resources within your assigned case family. This final case is reserved for you to adjust your budget sheet as necessary and to summarize what you have learned about the process of family resource management. You are now ready to move on and reassign this family to someone new. In a two- to three-page report, provide all the important information about your family, and explain the final budget sheet to your successor. Provide insight and suggestions for how they can continue to strengthen this family's resource management skills.

Glossary

Absenteeism (13)—prolonged absence of an owner from his or her property; chronic absence (as from work or school); also: the rate of such absence

Accessibility (1, 6)—ability to obtain when needed

Accommodate (7)—to make fit, suitable, or congruous; to bring into agreement or concord

Adaptive (9)—showing or having a capacity for or tendency toward adaptation

Affective resources (10)—resources that relate to feelings, preferences, and values

Affluenza (5)—an extreme form of materialism resulting from the excessive desire for material goods

Agentic traits (4)—personal success through self-enhancement or self-promotion

Agreement (10)—the act or fact of agreeing; harmony of opinion, action, or character

Artificial obsolescence (4)—a new need is created for consumers by industry that produces a demand by creating dissatisfaction with past models

Assimilate (5)—to take into the mind and thoroughly comprehend; to make similar; to absorb into the culture or mores of a population or group

Attitude (5)—a mental position with regard to a fact or state; a feeling or emotion toward a fact or state

Authority (4)—a conclusive statement or set of statements (as an official decision of a court) (2) a decision taken as a precedent (3): testimony; an individual cited or appealed to as an expert

Autonomy (12)—self-directing freedom and especially moral independence; a self-governing state

Availability (1)—ability to be used as needed

Baby boom generation (11)—people born between (and including) 1946 and 1964

Bargaining (10)—to negotiate over the terms of a purchase, agreement, or contract; to haggle; to come to terms

Barter (7)—to trade by exchanging one commodity for another; to trade or exchange

Base period (8)—a period of time that is used as a measurement yardstick for economic data; a base period may be a month, year, or average of years

Behaviors (5)—the manner of conducting oneself; anything that an organism does involving action and response to stimulation; the response of an individual, group, or species to its environment

Beneficiary (12)—the person designated to receive the income of a trust estate; the person named (as in an insurance policy) to receive proceeds or benefits

Benefit packages (6)—services an insurer, a government agency, a health plan, or an employer offers under the terms of a contract

Brainstorming (9)—a group problem-solving technique that involves the spontaneous contribution of ideas from all members of the group; the mulling over of ideas by one or more individuals in an attempt to devise or find a solution to a problem

Budget (9)—a plan for the coordination of resources and expenditures; the amount of money that is available for, required for, or assigned to a particular purpose

Budgeting (9)—to allocate funds; to plan or provide for the use of in detail

Bureaucratic (3)—of, relating to, or having the characteristics of a bureaucracy or bureaucrat

Business (1)—a commercial or mercantile activity engaged in as a means of livelihood

Cafeteria plans (6)—an employee benefit plan that allows employees to select among various group programs that best meet their specific needs

Capitalism (5)—an economic system characterized by private or corporate ownership of capital goods, by investments that are determined by private decision, and by prices, production, and the distribution of goods that are determined mainly by competition in a free market

Cautious shift (11)—the result of group social influence when individual group members become cautious

Certainty (6)—the quality or state of being certain especially on the basis of evidence

Circumstances (4)—a condition, fact, or event accompanying, conditioning, or determining another

Coexistence (10)—to exist together or at the same time; to live in peace with each other especially as a matter of policy

Cognitive resources (10)—mental skill abilities such as the ability to concentrate, memory, problem solving, and reasoning

Cohabitation (2)—to live together as or as if a married couple

Collective socialization (6)—a process by which children within a community social network are influenced by common behavioral expectations

Commodity (3)—an economic good

Communal traits (4)—a group's characteristics

Communication (10)—a process by which information is exchanged between individuals through a common system of symbols, signs, or behavior

Community property (12)—property held jointly by husband and wife

Companionate family (2)—a family where husbands and wives are partners who married because they loved each other, rather than out of a sense of moral duty

Competitive symmetry (10)—an interaction between two people where both want to define the interaction or dominate

Complementary interaction (10)—when each person in an interaction adopts a different tactic of conversation, with one being dominant and the other submissive

Compulsory education (8)—schooling required by law

Conceptual frameworks (2)—used in research to outline possible courses of action or to present a preferred approach to a system analysis project; built from a set of concepts linked to a planned or existing system of methods, behaviors, functions, relationships, and objects

Concreteness (6)—characterized by or belonging to immediate experience of actual things or events

Conflict (10)—the opposition of persons or forces that gives rise to the dramatic action in a drama or fiction

Conflict resolution (10)—the process of consensus arrived at after discussion of a disagreement between people

Conformity orientation (10)—parental assertion of power and control of communication in the family

Consensual families (10)—families that stress both the socio- and concept-orientation dimensions of communication, with the result that children are encouraged to explore the world about them, but to do so without disrupting the family's established social harmony

Conservation (13)—the preservation of a physical quantity during transformations or reactions

Conspicuous consumption (2)—spending large quantities of money, often extravagantly, to impress others

Consumer protection (8)—government regulation to protect the interests of consumers, for example by requiring businesses to disclose detailed information about products

Consumerism (7)—the promotion of the consumer's interests

Contingency plan (9)—a plan designed to deal with a particular problem, emergency, or state of affairs if it should occur

Conversation orientation (11)—family members of all ages have the freedom to express their opinions openly and freely

Copay (12)—the amount the insured pays in addition to the deductible of any judgment or settlement

Corporate social responsibility (13)—the awareness, acceptance, and management of the implications and effects of all corporate decision making

Cultural rituals (4)—practices that serve to unite a particular group by preserving cultural identity and heritage

Cultural transmission (4)—how culture is passed on through learning from one generation to another

Culture (1)—a set of learned beliefs, values, and behaviors of the way of life shared by the members of a society

Currency (7)—something (coins, treasury notes, and banknotes) that is in circulation as a medium of exchange

Cyclical unemployment (7)—the increase in unemployment that occurs as the economy goes into a slowdown or recession

Deductible (12)—the amount of the loss specified in such a clause

Deficit (9)—an excess of expenditure over revenue; a loss in business operations

Delayed gratification (12)—the ability to wait in order to obtain something that one wants

Delegation (12)—the assignment of authority and responsibility to another person to carry out specific activities

Demand (7)—the quantity of a commodity or service wanted at a specified price and time

Democratic family (2)—a family that emerged at the end of the 18th century as a separate and private group in society where they married for love and children were nurtured

Dependent (2)—one that is dependent; a person who relies on another for support

Digital divide (4, 10)—the gap between those people and communities who can access and make effective use of information technology and those who cannot

Dimensional model (11)—a model of leadership behavior that the dimensions of dominance, warmth, submissiveness, and hostility

Directional plan (9)—a strategic plan that guides the future of decision making

Disability benefit (8)—a benefit paid to active members when they are totally disabled and unable to work at any job for which they are qualified based on education, training, or experience

Discipline (1)—training that corrects, molds, or perfects mental faculties or moral character

Discounts (12)—a reduction made from the gross amount or value of something; a reduction made from a regular or list price

Distorter (10)—to twist out of a natural, normal, or original shape or condition

Distributive justice (6)—justice dispensed in the community to confer maximum value to those in need through the notions of fairness and consistency

Diversity (1)—the inclusion of diverse people (as people of different races or cultures) in a group or organization

Domestic partners (2)—the personal relationship between individuals who are living together and sharing a common domestic life together, but are not joined in any type of legal partnership, marriage or civil union

Durable goods (7)—goods that have a life span of 3 or more years

Durable power of attorney (12)—a written legal document by which an individual designates another person to act on his or her behalf

Ecolabels (13)—labels or logos that would indicate that a product has met a set of environmental standards

Economic resources (6, 10)—the basic inputs or component parts of an economy such as land, labor, and capital

Economics (7)—a social science concerned chiefly with description and analysis of the production, distribution, and consumption of goods and services

Effective (1)—producing a decided, decisive, or desired effect

Efficient (1)—being or involving the immediate agent in producing an effect

Empowerment (12)—to give official authority or legal power to

Enabling (12)—to provide with the means or opportunity

Enhancement hypothesis (13)—the idea that being able to handle multiple roles results in status, increased self-esteem, and privilege that compensates for the strain

Environmental resources (6)—anything an organism needs that can be taken from the environment

Estate (12)—the degree, quality, nature, and extent of one's interest in land or other property

Estate planning (12)—the process of planning for the efficient transfer of assets at one's death

Esteem needs (4)—a need to be respected, to have self-respect, and to respect others

Ethics (5)—the discipline dealing with what is good and bad and with moral duty and obligation

E-waste (13)—electronic waste including computers, entertainment electronics, mobile phones, and other items that have been discarded by their original users

Executor (12)—the person appointed by a testator to execute a will

Expenses (9)—something expended to secure a benefit or bring about a result

Extrinsic (12)—a characteristic which is not essential or inherent

Family (1)—the basic unit in society traditionally consisting of two parents rearing their children

Family goals (9)—broad statements of ideal future conditions that are desired by a family

Family stage (2)—an interval of time in which the roles and relationships within the family change in observable ways

Family values (5)—values especially of a traditional or conservative kind that are held to promote the sound functioning of the family and strengthen the fabric of society

Fashion (7)—a distinctive or peculiar and often habitual manner or way; mode of action or operation

Filter (10)—a way to convince the sender and receiver that the message wasn't intended in its true form

Financial plan (9)—a budgetary planning document reflecting the way an organization plans to use its financial and human resources in a given year

Five-step decision-making process (1)—a flexible decision-making framework that incorporates recognizing existing need, identifying alternatives to fulfill identified needs, evaluating identified alternatives, selecting and implementing alternatives, and reflecting and evaluating alternatives selected

Fixed expenses (9)—those expenses that remain the same regardless of circumstances

Flexibility (9)—characterized by a ready capability to adapt to new, different, or changing requirements

Floaters (12)—provide extended coverage for personal property

Frictional unemployment (7)—workers who have decided to leave one job and look for another, typically frictionally unemployed workers are out of the labor market for short periods of time

Functional value (7)—having a practical application or serving a useful purpose

Generations (5)—groups born in different time periods

Generation X (11)—the generation following the baby boom; born between 1965 and 1975

Gift tax (12)—a graduated federal tax paid by donors on gifts exceeding $10,000 per year per donor recipient

Goal (9)—something that somebody wants to achieve

Grantor (12)—somebody from whom something is transferred in a legal transaction

Greening (13)—creating a world with minimum negative impact on our environment

Gresham's law of planning (12)—a general tendency for programmed activities to overshadow nonprogrammed activities

Gross family income (9)—family income before taxes are removed

Group shift (11)—when making decisions as a group, people make decisions differently than they would if they were acting alone

Groupthink (11)—conformity in thought and behavior among the members of a group, especially an unthinking acceptance of majority opinions

Head of household (2)—the person whose name appears first in the census enumeration of a family or group of people living together

Health insurance (12)—insurance against loss by sickness or bodily injury

Hierarchy of needs (4)—Maslow's theory of motivation that states that we must achieve lower level needs, such as food, shelter, and safety, before we can achieve higher level needs, such as belonging, esteem, and self-actualization

Home insurance (12)—an insurance policy that combines insurance on the home, its contents, as well as liability insurance for accidents that may happen at the home

Homogamy (5)—purposeful selection of mates that have similar characteristics to your own

Households (7)—Group of individuals occupying a house, apartment, group of rooms, or a single room that is considered a housing unit

Human resources (6)—Human wisdom, experience, skill, labor, and enterprise

Human rights (5)—the rights one has because one is a human being; the right to life, freedom, and human dignity

Hybrid (13)—vehicles that run on alternative fuel

Hypercoordination (10)—when cell phones are used for coordination of activities and the development of group norms through emotional and social communication

Implementation power (6)—responsibility for day-to-day decisions

Impression management (2)—the process by which people try to control the impressions that other people form of them

Income (9)—the amount of money received over a period of time as payment for work, goods, or services, or as profit on capital

Independent activities (9)—activities that are unrelated to each other

Industrialization (7)—the adoption of industrial methods of production and manufacturing by a country or group, with all the associated changes in lifestyle, transport, and other aspects of society

Inflation (7)—an increase in the supply of currency or credit relative to the availability of goods and services, resulting in higher prices

Inheritance (2)—the succession of money, property, or a title that has been passed on from generation after generation

Inheritance tax (12)—a tax levied on property received by inheritance or legal succession, calculated according to the value of the property received

Insurance (12)—an arrangement by which a company gives customers financial protection against loss or harm, for example, theft or illness, in return for payment or premium

Intangible (7)—without material qualities, and so not able to be touched or seen

Interactivity (10)—the way in which a family communicates

Interchangeable (6)—resources that can be exchanged or substituted as a means to gain assets

Interdependent activities (9)—activities that are dependent on each other and are sequence-specific

Interfaith (2)—involving or occurring between people of different religious faiths

Interiority (13)—consideration of ethical and cultural needs before economic considerations

Intermediate goals (9)—goals that will be accomplished in less than 1 year

Intersubjectivity (10)—communicating shared meanings

Intestate (12)—a person who dies owning property without having made a valid will or other binding declaration

Intrinsic (12)—a characteristic or property of some thing or action that is essential and specific to that thing or action and that is wholly independent of any other object, action, or consequence

Intuition (9)—the understanding without apparent effort, quick and ready insight seemingly independent of previous experiences or empirical knowledge

Joint ownership with right of suvivorship (12)—property that is owned by two or more people which passes to the survivor upon the death of one

Labor force (7)—people ages 16 years or older who are employed or looking for work

Laissez-faire family (10)—a family that does not communicate with and does not connect to each other

Laissez-faire leadership (11)—a leadership style where the leader allows the followers to have more control over the outcomes of the organization

Leadership (11)—the ability of an individual to influence, motivate, and enable others to contribute toward the effectiveness and success of the groups of which they are members

Life insurance (12)—a contract between the policy owner and the insurer, where the insurer agrees to pay a sum of money upon the occurrence of the insured's death

Lifespan (4)—the period or length of time in which a person lived

Liquid (7)—see Liquidity

Liquidity (9)—an asset's ability to *quickly* be liquidated or converted through an action of buying or selling without causing a significant movement in the price and with minimum loss of value

Living wage (6)—the minimum hourly wage necessary for a person to achieve some specific standard of living

Living will (12)—a legal document that covers specific directives as to the course of treatment to be taken by caregivers

Locus of control (12)—theory in psychology that originally distinguished between two types of people—*internals,* who attribute events to their own control, and *externals,* who attribute events in their life to external circumstances

Long-range goals (9)—goals that usually require more than 1 year to complete

Manageability (6)—something that is capable of being managed or controlled

Managed health care (12)—service that is provided by a hospital or other group of clinics may be managed by an external company

Management (1)—the act of directing and controlling a large group of people for the purpose of coordinating and harmonizing the group toward accomplishing a goal beyond the scope of individual effort

Membership group (11)—a group where people belong as a result of birth or life circumstance

Microcoordination (10)—when cell phones are used only to coordinate activities

Mixed-motive situation (12)—a situation where someone's personal actions impact the outcomes of the other group members and the group as a whole

Modern family (2)—a family that consists of a breadwinning husband, a housewife, and their children

Money (7)—a good or token that functions as a medium of exchange that is socially and legally accepted in payment for goods and services and settlement of debts

Morals (5)—ethics, codes, values, principles, and customs of a person or society

Motives (5)—a thought pattern with feelings and values that leads to energized behavior

Multitask (9)—a human being's simultaneous handling of multiple tasks

Mutual definition (2)—shared by or common to two or more people or groups

Need (4)—the psychological feature that arouses an organism to action toward a goal and the reason for the action, giving purpose and direction to behavior

Needs assessment (4)—a systematic process to determine the needs of a defined population

Net income (9)—the income that a firm has after subtracting costs and expenses from the total revenue

Net worth (12)—the total assets minus total liabilities of an individual or a company

Neutralized symmetry (10)—a situation in which neither person in a conversation seeks to be dominant

Nondurable goods (7)—items that generally last for only a short time (3 years or less)

Nonrenewable resources (6)—resources such as coal, oil, and other fossil fuels that are finite in supply and replaced so slowly that they are soon depleted

Nontraditional family (1)—the family that doesn't fit the social norm of the traditional family

Normative resources (10)—family power that is given to those within the family that are identified by culture or society

Nuclear family (2)—the family group consisting of parents (usually a father and mother) and their children in one household

Objectives (9)—specific and measurable means for accomplishing goals

Occupational wellness (13)—wellness within the workplace

Old money (5)—families that have been wealthy for several generations

Opportunity cost (7)—an opportunity forgone; what is lost because a decision is made

Optimization (3)—the process of finding the solution that is the best fit to the available resources

Orchestration power (6)—responsibility for major decisions that often determine the lifestyle of the family

Orientations (1)—awareness of self in relation to time, place, and person; an integrated set of attitudes and beliefs

Overscheduling (9)—family activities where members are too busy; a contemporary problem for many families

Particularistic (6)—the exclusive devotion to the interests of one's own group

Personal goals (9)—goals that are specific to the individual

Personal resources (10)—resources that are inherent with the personality or appearance of the family member

Personality (4)—the consistent emotional, thought, and behavior patterns in a person

Philanthropy (5)—the act of donating money, goods, time, or effort to support a charitable cause, usually over an extended period of time and in regard to a defined objective

Physiological needs (4)—a person's most basic needs: food, shelter, and clothing

Plan (9)—a proposed or intended method of getting from one set of circumstances to another

Planned obsolescence (4)—the conscious decision on the part of a manufacturer to produce a consumer product that will become obsolete and/or nonfunctional in a defined time frame

Planning process (9)—a process that begins with a decision and includes identification of a situation that requires action, a formulation of a plan, and the implementation of that plan

Pluralistic family (10)—a family that communicates but does not expect everyone to agree

Polygyny (2)—the practice of a man having more than one wife at the same time

Postmodern family (2)—the contemporary family that is more diverse than in the past in terms of family structure and relationships

Power bases (10)—individual family members have power when making decisions that impact other family members

Predispositions (5)—an inclination beforehand to interpret statements in a particular way; a disposition in advance to react in a particular way

Preference (7)—a real or imagined "choice" between alternatives and the possibility of rank ordering of these alternatives, based on happiness, satisfaction, gratification, enjoyment, and utility they provide

Premiums (12)—payments to the insurance company to buy a policy and to keep it in force

Presenteeism (13)—the problems faced when employees come to work in spite of illness, which can have negative repercussions on business performance

Pricing (7)—the manual or automatic process of applying prices to purchase and sales orders

Principle of least interest (10)—the partner with the least interest in continuing the relationship has the most power in that relationship

Private programs (8)—privately funded assistance programs

Proactive plans (9)—plans that are designed with forethought and consideration of anticipated events

Probate (12)—the legal process of settling the estate of a deceased person

Production (4)—the making or creation of something, the process of manufacturing a product for sale

Protection (9)—the act of preventing somebody or something from being harmed or damaged

Protective family (10)—a family that does not communicate but expects everyone to follow the rules

Public programs (8)—publicly funded assistance programs

Qualitative research (2)—a research method that measures information based on opinions and values as opposed to statistical data; data can be collected through open-ended interviews, review of documents and artifacts, participant observations, or practice

Quality circles (3)—a group composed of workers who meet together to discuss workplace improvement and make presentations to management with their ideas

Quantitative research (2)—research that examines phenomenon through the numerical representation of observations and statistical analysis; data can be collected through structured interviews, experiments, or surveys and are reported numerically

Rapport talk (10)—conversation meant to strengthen intimacy; typically used by women

Rationing (4)—the controlled distribution of resources and scarce goods or services

Reactive plans (9)—plans that are spontaneous and without forethought

Recycling (13)—reprocessing of materials into new products

Report talk (10)—conversations meant to convey information; typically used by men

Reproduction (4)—a copy of something in an earlier style; the act of reproducing something

Resilience (12)—ability to adapt and to move forward

Resource (1, 6)—commodities and human resources used in the production of goods and services; anything identified to meet an existing or future need

Resource-allocation behavior (6)—the outward observable behavior in which people act on when they make decisions about how they use resources

Resourcefulness (6)—having inner resources; skillful or imaginative

Risk (6)—the probability of a known loss

Risky shift (11)—the group collectively agrees on a course of action that is likewise more extreme than they would have made if asked individually

Safety needs (4)—safety and security rank above all other desires and include physical security (safety from violence, delinquency, aggressions), moral and physiological security, family security, security of health, and security of personal property against crime

Scarcity hypothesis (13)—the idea that human energy is limited and, when overloaded, presents conflict that results in guilt and anxiety

Schedule (9)—a plan for carrying out a process or procedure, giving lists of intended events and times

School vouchers (8)—a certificate by which parents are given the ability to pay for the education of their children at a school of their choice, rather than the public school to which they were assigned

Selective interpretation (5)—purposeful dissemination of certain information in ways advantageous to the individual

Selective memory (5)—purposeful retrieval of certain information while ignoring other information stored in memory

Self-actualization (4)—a driving life force that will ultimately lead to maximizing one's abilities and determine the path of one's life

Sequencing (9)—doing things in a logical, predictable order

Services (7)—the nonmaterial equivalent of a good

Shortage (7)—when there is excess demand and limited supply

Short-term goals (9)—goals that will be achieved in the near future

Situation (5)—the general conditions that prevail in a place or society; the circumstances that somebody is in at a particular moment

Social needs (4)—those needs related to interaction with other people and include the need for friends, the need for belonging, and the need to give and receive love

Social resources (6)—resources that are felt and collectively owned

Social responsibility (13)—consumers must act with concern and sensitivity, aware of the impact of their actions on others, particularly the disadvantaged

Social wellness (13)—being aware of, participating in, and feeling connected to your community

Societal goals (9)—goals that are reflected in rules and expectations within larger social groups

Socioeconomic status (4)—the hierarchical distinctions between individuals or groups in societies or cultures based on social rank and monetary advantage

Standards (9)—a degree or level of requirement, excellence, or attainment

Stop-loss (12)—the maximum amount under traditional insurance that benefits are calculated on a proportional basis; after the stop-loss is met, coverage is paid at 100%

Strategic plan (9)—a tool used to outline a group's priorities and future goals

Structural unemployment (7)—unemployment caused by basic changes in the overall economy, as in demographics, technology, or industrial organization

Submissive symmetry (10)—an interaction where both accept the other's definition of interaction or submit

Substitute (7)—to replace something with another similar product or good

Supply (7)—a quantity of something on hand or available, as for use

Surplus (7, 9)—something that remains above what is used or needed

Survivor benefits (8)—Social Security taxes that are used to provide insurance for a worker's family should he or she die

Sustainability (13)—to endure without giving way or yielding

Sustainable development (4)—any construction that can be maintained over time without damaging the environment; development balancing near-term interests with the protection of the interests of future generations

Symbiotic (7)—any interdependent or mutually beneficial relationship between two persons, groups

Symbols (2)—something that represents something else by association, resemblance, or convention

Symmetrical conversations (10)—conversations that are balanced in regard to dominance

Taste (7)—a personal preference or liking

Tax efficiency (9)—financial planning that involves consideration of tax liability

Technostress (14)—the negative psychological link between people and introduction of new technologies

Term insurance (12)—low-cost insurance that is valid only for a stated period of time and has no cash surrender value or loan value

Theoretical perspective (2)—one's preference for a particular theory

Theory (2)—a theory is a broad generalization that explains a body of facts or phenomena

Traditional family (2)—a married couple and their biological child or children in one household

Transactional leadership (11)—guidance based in contingency, in that reward or punishment is contingent on performance

Transferability (6)—the quality of being exchangeable

Transformational leadership (11)—behavior that is founded on the belief that leaders and followers can raise each other to higher levels of motivation and morality

Trust (12)—something committed or entrusted to one to be used or cared for in the interest of another

Uncertainty (6)—a perception that ranges from falling short of certainty to an almost complete lack of conviction or knowledge especially about an outcome or a result

Unemployment rate (7)—the percentage of people seeking employment but without work at the current time

Universal life insurance (12)—a type of flexible permanent life insurance offering the low-cost protection of term life insurance as well as a savings element (like whole life insurance), which is invested to provide cash value buildup

Universal values (5)—beliefs existent or operative everywhere or under all conditions

Utility (6)—the quality or condition of being useful; usefulness

Value (5)—worth in usefulness or importance to the possessor; a principle, standard, or quality considered worthwhile or desirable

Value congruence (5)—the degree to which all members of the group agree on values about group processes and group work

Variable expenses (9)—costs that are not always consistent and that change due to circumstances within and external to the family

Vegetarian (5)—one who subsists on a diet composed primarily or wholly of vegetables, grains, fruits, nuts, and seeds, with or without eggs and dairy products

Vocational (3)—relating to, providing, or undergoing training in a special skill to be pursued in a trade or occupation

Volunteerism (6)—contributing one's time or talents for charitable, educational, social, political, or other worthwhile purposes, usually in one's community, freely and without regard for compensation

Want (4)—something desired, but not necessary

Wellness (13)—an interactive process of becoming aware of and practicing healthy choices to create a more successful and balanced lifestyle

Whole life insurance (12)—an insurance policy with cash value before it becomes payable upon death or maturity

Will (12)—a legally enforceable declaration directing the disposal of a decedent's property

Worldview (1)—the common concept of reality shared by a particular group of people, usually referred to as a culture or an ethnic group; an individual as well as a group phenomenon

Web Resources

www.afscme.org/wrkplace/fmla.htm

www.blackgoldmovie.com

www.census.gov

www.census.gov/population/socdemo/hh-fam/

www.consumer.gov/idtheft

www.csmonitor.com

www.dol.gov

www.fns.usda.gov/fsp/

www.hhs.gov

www.irs.gov

www.nbnnews.com

www.pbs.org/kcts/affluenza

www.sric-bi.com/VALS/types.shtml

www.taxadmin.org

www.umanitoba.ca/anthropology/tutor/marriage/polyandry.html

www.uswaternews.com

References

Adam, M. (2006). Does higher education count less? *Education Digest, 71*, 47–51.

Adler, J. (1997, December 15). A matter of faith. *Newsweek*, pp. 49–54.

Adler, J. (2006, July 17). Going green. *Newsweek*, pp. 43–52.

Affluenza. (2006). Retrieved July 6, 2006, from www.pbs.org/kcts/affluenza

Akasaka, K. (2006). Securing tomorrow's water. *OECD Observer, 254*, 11–14.

Akerkar, S. M., & Bichile, L. S. (2004). Doctor patient relationship: Changing dynamics in the information age. *Journal of Postgraduate Medicine, 50*, 120–124.

Aldrich, N. W. (1996). *Old money: The mythology of wealth in America.* New York: Allworth.

Allport, G. W. (1935). Attitudes. In C. Murchison (Ed.), *A handbook of social psychology.* Worchester, MA: Clark University Press.

Almedia, D. M., McDonald, D. A., & Grzywacz, J. G. (2002). Work-family spillover and daily reports of work and family stress in the adult labor force. *Family Relations, 51*, 28–37.

Amatea, E. S., Smith-Adcock, S., & Villares, E. (2006). From family deficit to family strength: Viewing families' contributions to children's learning from a family resilience perspective. *Professional School Counseling, 9*, 277–313.

Amato, P. R. (2005). The impact of family formation change on the cognitive, social, and emotional well-being of the next generation. *The Future of Children, 15*(2), 75–96.

American Association of Family and Consumer Sciences. (2003). Retrieved June 26, 2006, from www.aafcs.org

American Geriatrics Society Foundation for Health in Aging. (2006). Trends in the elderly population. Retrieved July 10, 2007, from www.healthinaging.org/agingintheknow/chapters_print_ch_trial.asp?ch=2

American giants fight over cell phone Internet services. (2007, April 23). *The Nikkei Weekly.* Retrieved April 24, 2007, from www.lexisnexis.com

Anderson, G. L. (1997). *The family in global transition.* New York: Paragon House Publishers.

Ando, A. W., & Gosselin, A. Y. (2005). Recycling in multifamily dwellings: Does convenience matter? *Economic Inquiry, 43*, 426–439.

Andreasen, M. (2001). Evolution in the family's use of television: An overview. In J. Bryant & J. A. Bryant (Eds.), *Television and the American family* (pp. 3–30). Mahwah, NJ: Lawrence Erlbaum.

Annual Energy Outlook 2003 Report. (2003). Washington, DC: Energy Information Administration.

Areas hit by tsunami had limited insurance. (2005, January 4). Retrieved July 10, 2007, from www.iht.com/articles/2005/01/03/business/insure/php

Aronsohn, M. (2004, June). *Collaborative divorce—developing model of the future.* American Association for Marital and Family Therapy–California Division Newsletter (cover page).

Arvey, R. D., Segal, N. L., Bouchard, T. J., & Abraham, L. M. (1989). Job satisfaction: Environmental and genetic components. *Journal of Applied Psychology, 74,* 187–192.

Atkin, D. (2001). Home ecology and children's television viewing in the new media environment. In J. Bryant & J. A. Bryant (Eds.), *Television and the American family* (pp. 49–74). Mahwah, NJ: Lawrence Erlbaum.

Atwell, P. (2001). The first and second digital divides. *Sociology of Education, 74,* 252–259.

Aulette Root, J. (2002). *Changing American families.* Boston: Allyn & Bacon.

Avellar, S., & Smock, P. J. (2003). Has the price of motherhood declined over time? A cross-cohort comparison of the motherhood wage penalty. *Journal of Marriage and the Family, 65,* 597–608.

Avery, R. J., & Stafford, K. (1991). Toward a scheduling congruity theory of family resource management. *Lifestyles: Family and Economic Issues, 12,* 325–344.

Baerenklau, K. A. (2005). Cost-effectiveness of the conservation reserve program: Discussion. *American Journal of Agricultural Economics, 87,* 1256–1258.

Bakan, D. (1966). Behaviorism and American urbanization. *Journal of the History of the Behavioral Sciences, 2,* 5–28.

Barge, J. K., & Loges, W. E. (2003). Parent, student, and teacher perceptions of parental involvement. *Journal of Applied Communication Research, 31,* 140–163.

Bar-On, R., & Parker, J. (2000). *The handbook of emotional intelligence theory, development, assessment, and application at home, school, and in the workplace.* San Francisco: Jossey-Bass.

Barsade, S. G. (2002). The ripple effect: Emotional contagion and its influence on group behavior. *Administrative Science Quarterly, 47,* 644–677.

Bass, B. M., & Avolio, B. J. (1997). *Full range leadership development: Manual for the Multifactor Leadership Questionnaire.* Redwood City, CA: Mind Garden.

Baxter, L. A., & Braithwaite, D. O. (2002). Performing marriage: Marriage renewal rituals a cultural performance. *Southern Communication Journal, 67,* 94–109.

Beblo, M. (2001). *Bargaining over time allocation economic modeling and econometric investigation of time use within families.* New York: Physica-Verlag.

Becker, G. S. (1991). *A treatise on the family.* Cambridge, MA: Harvard University Press.

Beder, S. (1998). Is planned obsolescence socially responsible? *Engineers Australia, 52.*

Beecher, C. E. (1869). *The American woman's home.* New York: J. B. Ford.

Bem, D. J. (1972). Self-perception theory. *Advanced Experimental Social Psychology, 6,* 1–62.

Berk, L. E. (1996). *Infants, children, and adolescents.* Boston: Allyn & Bacon.

Bertalanffy, L. V. (1969). *General system theory.* New York: G. Braziller.

Bielski, L. (2007, January). Pay by mobile phone wherever, whenever? The mobile wallet steps closer to ubiquity. *ABA Banking Journal,* pp. 31–35.

Bishop, K. (1989, May 31). San Francisco grants recognition to partnerships of single people. *New York Times,* pp. A11(N)–A17(L).

Blackwell, D. L., & Lichter, D. T. (2000). Mate selection among married and cohabitating couples. *Journal of Family Issues, 21*(3), 275–302.

Blaine, T. W., & Lichtkoppler, F. R. (2004). Willingness to pay for green space preservation: A comparison of soil and water conservation district clientele and the general public using the contingent valuation method. *Journal of Soil and Water Conservation, 59,* 203–209.

Blank, W. (2001). *The 108 skills of natural born leaders.* New York: AMACOM.

Blood, R. O., & Wolfe, D. M. (1960). *Husbands & wives.* Glencoe, IL: The Free Press.

Blum, R. W. (2002). *Mother's influence on teen sex: Connections that promote postponing sexual intercourse.* Minneapolis, MN: Center for Adolescent Health.

Bond, A. E., Mandleco, C. L., & Donnelly, M. (2003). Needs of family members of patients with severe traumatic brain injury: Implications for evidence-based practice. *Critical Care Nurse, 23,* 63–74.

Bonilla-Silva, E., & Forman, T. A. (2000). I am not a racist but . . . : Mapping White college students' racial ideology in the U.S.A. *Discourse and Society, 11,* 51–86.

Boris, E. T. (1999). The non-profit sector in the 1990s. In C. T. Clotfelter & T. Ehrlich (Eds.), *Philanthropy and the nonprofit sector in a changing America* (pp. 1–33). Bloomington, IN: Indiana University Press.

Bossard, J., & Boll, E. S. (1968). *Family situations.* New York: Greenwood.

Bossard, J. H., & Boll, E. S. (1943). *Ritual in family living.* Philadelphia: University of Pennsylvania Press.

Boulding, K. E. (1985). *Human betterment.* Beverly Hills, CA: Sage.

Boulter, L. (2004). Family–school connection and school violence prevention. *The Negro Educational Review, 55,* 27–40.

Bradbury, K. L. (2002, Winter). Education and wages in the 1980s and 1990s: Are all groups moving up together? *New England Economic Review,* pp. 19–46.

Bramlett, M. D., & Mosher, W. D. (2002). Cohabitation, marriage, divorce and remarriage in the United States. *National Center for Health Statistics, Vital and Health Statistics, 23*(22).

Branden, N. (1995). *The six pillars of self-esteem.* New York: Bantam.

Brazelton, B. T., & Greenspan, S. (2000, Fall). Our window to the future. *Newsweek* (Special Issue), pp. 34–36.

Bring back the passion for soil, water conservation: CTIC director. (2005, July 12). *Western Farm Press.*

Bristow, D. N., & Mowen, J. C. (1998). The consumer resource exchange model: Theoretical development and empirical evaluation. *Marketing Intelligence & Planning, 16,* 90–99.

Brown, P. L. (2000, March 10). Silicon Valley wealth brings new stresses on children. *New York Times,* p. 1A.

Brubaker, T. H., & Roberto, K. A. (1993). Family life education for the later years. *Family Relations, 42,* 212–221.

Bryant, C., DeWalt, K., Courtney, A., & Schwartz, J. (2003). *The cultural feast* (2nd ed.). Boston: Thomson Learning.

Bryant, J., Aust, C., & Venugopalan, G. (2001). How psychologically healthy are America's prime-time television families? In J. Bryant & J. A. Bryant (Eds.), *Television and the American family* (pp. 247–270). Mahwah, NJ: Lawrence Erlbaum.

Bryant, W. K. (1990). *The economic organization of the household.* New York: Cambridge University Press.

Bubolz, M. M., & Sontag, M. S. (1993). Human ecology theory. In P. G. Boss, W. J. Doherty, W. R. LaRossa, W. R. Schumm, & S. K. Steinmetz (Eds.), *Sourcebook of family theories and methods a contextual approach* (pp. 591–625). New York: Plenum.

Buckley, W. (1967). *Sociology and modern systems theory.* Englewood Cliffs, NJ: Prentice Hall.

Burgess, E., & Locke, H. (1945). *The family: From institution to companionship.* New York: American Book Company.

Caughlin, J. (2003). Family communication standards: What counts as excellent family communication and how are such standards associated with family satisfaction? *Human Communication Research, 29,* 5–40.

Center for Health Communication. (2004). *Reinventing aging: Baby boomers and civic engagement.* Boston, MA: Harvard School of Public Health.

Cherlin, A. J. (2004). The deinstitutionalization of American marriage. *Journal of Marriage and the Family, 66*(4), 848–862.

Chilman, C. S. (1983). *Adolescent sexuality in a changing American society social and psychological perspectives for the human services professions* (rev. ed.). New York: Wiley.

Clarke, R. (1973). *Ellen Swallows: The woman who founded ecology.* Chicago: Follett.

Cohen, R., & Roosevelt, E. (2002). *Dear Mrs. Roosevelt letters from children of the Great Depression.* Chapel Hill: University of North Carolina Press.

Colby, A., & Phelps, E. (2001). Social responsibility and paid work in contemporary American life. In A. S. Rossi (Ed.), *Caring and doing for others social responsibility in the domains of family, work, and community* (pp. 463–501). Chicago: University of Chicago Press.

Coleman, P. G. (2000). Aging and the satisfaction of psychological needs. *Psychological Inquiry, 11,* 291–294.

Collinge, R. A., & Ayers, R. M. (2000). *Economics by design principles and issues.* Upper Saddle River, NJ: Prentice Hall.

Coontz, S. (1992). *The way we never were: American families and the nostalgia trap.* New York: Basic Books.

Coontz, S. (2000). Historical perspectives on family studies. *Journal of Marriage and the Family, 62,* 283–297.

Cooper, C. A. (1996). *Violence on television congressional inquiry, public criticism, and industry response: A policy analysis.* Lanham, MD: University Press of America.

Cordry, S., & Wilson, J. D. (2004). Parents as first teacher. *Education, 125,* 56–57.

Crainer, S. (2000). *The management century: A critical review of 20th century thought and practice.* San Francisco: Jossey-Bass.

Crandall, R. W. (2001). The digital divide: Bridging the divide naturally. *Brookings Review, 19,* 38–41.

Crittenden, A. (2004). *If you've raised kids, you can manage anything leadership begins at home.* New York: Gotham Books.

Curry, S. (2001). Wireless trend taking hold. *Advertising Age, 72,* S2.

Cushman, E. M. (1945). *Management in homes.* New York: Macmillan.

Davenport, T. H., & Prusak, L. (1998). *Working knowledge: How organizations manage what they know.* Boston, MA: Harvard Business School Press.

Davidhizar, R., & Hart, A. (2006). Are you born a happy person or do you have to make it happen? *The Health Care Manager, 25,* 64–70.

Day, J. C., & Newburger, E. C. (2002). *The big payoff: Educational attainment and synthetic estimates of work-life earnings.* Washington, DC: Commerce Department of Economics and Statistics Administration, Census Bureau.

Deacon, F. M., & Firebaugh, R. E. (1975). *Family resource management: Principles and applications.* Boston: Allyn & Bacon.

DeFrain, J., & Stinnett, N. (2002). The family strengths perspective. In J. J. Ponzetti (Ed.), *International encyclopedia of marriage and family relationships* (pp. 637–672). New York: Macmillan.

DeGenova, M. K., & Rice, F. P. (2002). *Intimate relationships, marriages, and families* (5th ed.). New York: McGraw-Hill.

Della Cava, M. R. (2005, October 28). *2046: A boomer odyssey.* Retrieved July 11, 2007, from www.usatoday.com/news/health/2005-10-27-boomer-cover_x.htm

DeLorey, C. (2003). The health consequences of being female or male. *Healthcare Review, 16,* 12.

Dempsey, N. (2004). Building the knowledge society. *Observer, 242,* 7–8.

Desimone, L. (1999). Linking parent involvement with student achievement: Do race and income matter? *Journal of Educational Research, 93*(1), 11.

Deutch, P. J. (2005). Energy independence: High oil prices have everyone talking about energy independence again. *Foreign Policy, 151,* 20–25.

Devries, S., Groenewegen, P., & Spreevwenberg, P. (2003). Natural environments—healthy environments? An exploratory analysis of the relationships between green space and health. *Environment and Planning, 35,* 1717–1731.

Dewitte, S., & De Cremer, D. (2001). Self-control and cooperation: Different concepts, similar decisions? A question of the right perspective. *Journal of Psychology, 135*(2), 133–154.

Dickson, A. (2004, June 24). Survey: Most top women execs want CEO job. *Reuters.* Retrieved July 12, 2007, from www.ivc.ca/studies/us/index.htm

Doherty, W. J. (1997). *The intentional family how to build family ties in our modern world.* Reading, MA: Addison-Wesley.

Doyal, L., & Gough, I. (1991). *A theory of human need.* New York: Guilford.

Dunn, H. L. (1961). *High-level wellness.* Arlington, VA: R.W. Beatty.

Dunn, J. S., Kinney, D. A., & Hofferth, S. L.(2001). *Parental ideologies and children's after-school activities.* Unpublished manuscript, University of Michigan, Alfred P. Sloan Center for the Study of Working Families.

Dupont, H. (1994). *Emotional development, theory and applications a neo-Piagetian perspective.* Westport, CT: Praeger.

Eagly, A. H., & Johannesen-Schmidt, M. C. (2001). The leadership styles of men and women. *Journal of Social Issues, 57,* 781–798.

Easterlin, R. (2001). Income and happiness: Towards a unified theory. *Economic Journal, 111,* 465.

Eaves, L. J., Eysenck, H. J., & Martin, N. G. (1989). *Genes, culture, and personality an empirical approach.* San Diego: Academic Press.

Eckstein, S. (2002). Community as gift-giving: Collectivist roots of volunteerism. *American Sociological Review, 66,* 829–851.

Edleson, J. L., & Tan, N. T. (1993). Conflict and family violence: The tale of two families. In P. Boss (Ed.), *Sourcebook of family theories and methods a contextual approach* (pp. 382–384). New York: Plenum.

Edwards, R., & Hamilton, M. A. (2004). You need to understand my gender role: An empirical test of Tannen's model of gender and communication. *Sex Roles: A Journal of Research, 50*(7–8), 491–505.

Ellis, D. A., Zucker, R. A., & Fitzgerald, H. E. (1997). The role of family influences in development and risk. *Alcohol Health and Research World, 21,* 218–226.

Energy Information Administration. (2003). *Annual Energy Outlook 2003.* Washington, DC: Author.

Environmental Working Group. (2006). *Analysis.* Retrieved July 10, 2007, from www.ewg.org/reports/gaspricewatchdog/analysis.php

Epstein, J. L. (1992). *School and family partnerships* (Center on Families, Communities, and Schools, Rep. No. 6). Baltimore, MD: Johns Hopkins University Press.

Erickson, J. A., & Gillespie, C. W. (2000). Reasons women discontinue participation in an exercise and wellness program. *Physical Educator, 57,* 2–8.

Eriksen, T. H. (2001). *Tyranny of the moment fast and slow time in the information age.* Sterling, VA: Pluto.

Erikson, E. H. (1963). *Childhood and society.* New York: Norton.

Ernsberger, P., & Koletsky, R. J. (1999). Biomedical rationale for a wellness approach to obesity: An alternative to a focus on weight loss. *Journal of Social Issues, 55*(2), 221–260.

Eshleman, J. R. (1994). *The family: An introduction.* Boston: Allyn & Bacon.

Fallows, D. (2004). The Internet and daily life. The Pew Internet and American Life Project. Washington, DC: The Pew Charitable Trusts.

Families and Work Institute. (1999). *National study of the changing workforce. Guide to public use files.* New York: Author.

The Family and Medical Leave Act: AFSCME's comprehensive guide. (2007). Retrieved July 3, 2007, from www.afscme.org/publications/2281.cfm

Fayol, H. (1949). *General and industrial management.* London: Pitman.

Feather, N. T. (1990). Bridging the gap between values and actions: Recent applications of expectancy-value model. In R. M. Sorrentino & E. T. Higgins (Eds.), *Handbook of motivation and cognition foundations of social behavior* (pp. 151–192). New York: Guilford.

Featherman, D. (1980). Schooling and occupational careers: Constancy and change in worldly success. In O. G. Brim & J. Kagan (Eds.), *Constancy and change in human development* (pp. 675–738). Cambridge, MA: Harvard University Press.

Feldman, S. (2001). Building blocks. *American Teacher, 86,* 5.

Fiedler, F. E. (1967). *A theory of leadership effectiveness.* New York: McGraw-Hill.

Fishbein, M., & Ajzen, I. (1975). *Belief, attitude, intention, and behavior an introduction to theory and research.* Reading, MA: Addison-Wesley.

Fishbein, M., & Ajzen, I. (1980). *Understanding attitudes and predicting social behavior.* Englewood Cliffs, NJ: Prentice Hall.

Fitzpatrick, M. A. (1988). *Between husbands and wives communication in marriage.* Newbury Park, CA: Sage.

Fitzpatrick, M. A., & Ritchie, L. D. (1994). Communication schemata within the family: Multiple perspectives on family interaction. *Human Communication Research, 20,* 275–301.

Fleishman, F. E. (1953). Leadership climate, human relations training, and supervisory behavior. *Personnel Psychology, 6,* 205–222.

Foa, U. G. (1971). Interpersonal and economic resources. *Science, 171,* 345–351.

Foa, U. G. (1993). *Resource theory: Explorations and applications.* San Diego: Academic Press.

Folbre, N. (2001). *The invisible heart economics and family values.* New York: New Press.

Forgays, D. K. (1996). The relationship between type A parenting and adolescent perceptions of family environment. *Adolescence, 31,* 841–862.

Fox, J. J., & Bartholomae, S. (2000). Economic stress and families. In P. C. McKenry & S. J. Price (Eds.), *Families and change coping with stressful events and transitions* (pp. 250–278). Thousand Oaks, CA: Sage.

Fox, S., & Rainie, L. (2002). *Vital decisions.* Pew Internet and American Life Project, Part 6, Washington, DC.

Frank, R. H. (2000). *Luxury fever money and happiness in an era of excess.* Princeton, NJ: Princeton University Press.

Furnham, A. (1999). The saving and spending habits of young people. *Journal of Economic Psychology, 20,* 677–679.

Galbraith, K. A., & Schvaneveldt, J. D. (2005). Family leadership styles and family well-being. *Family and Consumer Sciences Research Journal, 33,* 220–239.

Galvin, K. M., Bylund, C. L., & Brommel, B. J. (2004). *Family communication cohesion and change* (6th ed.). Boston: Pearson.

General Social Survey (GSS). (2004). Storrs, CT: The Roper Center for Public Opinion Research/NORC.

Giacquinta, J. B., Bauer, J. A., & Levin, J. E. (1993). *Beyond technology's promise: An examination of children's educational computing at home.* New York: Cambridge University Press.

Gibbs, T., & Campbell, J. (1999). Practicing polygyny in Black America: Challenging definition. *The Western Journal of Black Studies, 23,* 144.

Gilbreth, F. B., Carey, E. G., & McKay, D. (2003). *Belles on their toes.* New York: Dell Yearling.

Glasglow, R. E., Terborg, J. R., & Hollis, J. F. (1995). Take heart: Results from the initial phase of a work-site wellness program. *American Journal of Public Health, 85,* 209–216.

Gleick, P. H., Wolff, E. L., & Chalecki, R. R. (2002). *The new economy of water: The risks and benefits of globalization and privatization of freshwater.* Oakland, CA: Pacific Institute for Studies in Development, Environment, and Security.

Goethals, G. R. (2003). A century of social psychology. In M. A. Hogg & J. Cooper (Eds.), *The Sage handbook of social psychology.* Thousand Oaks, CA: Sage.

Goldsborough, R. (2005). Regaining control over information technology. *Teacher Librarian, 33,* 51.

Goldstein, J. R., & Kenney, C. T. (2001). Marriage delayed or marriage foregone? New Cohort forecasts of first marriage for U.S. women. *American Sociological Review, 66*(4), 506–519.

Gordon, L. (1979). The struggle for reproductive freedom: Three stages of feminism. In Z. R. Eisenstein (Ed.), *Capitalist patriarchy and the case for socialist feminism* (pp. 107–136). New York: Monthly Review Press.

Gottman, J., & Notarius, C. (2000). Decade review: Observing marital interaction. *Journal of Marriage and Family, 62,* 927–947.

Gough, E. K. (1971). The origin of the family. *Journal of Marriage and Family, 33,* 760–771.

Graham, J. (2004). *Camera phones rival DVD players as fastest growing.* Retrieved January 29, 2004, from usatoday.com

Graham-Rowe, D. (2004). Radio chip heralds the smarter home. *New Scientist, 183,* 22–23.

Grant, J. (2002). Learning needs assessment: Assessing the need. *British Medical Journal, 324,* 156–159.

Green, N. S., Dolan, S. M., & Murray, T. H. (2006). Newborn screening: Complexities in universal genetic testing. *American Journal of Public Health, 96,* 1955–1959.

Greenhouse, S. (2001, January 29). Problems seen for teenagers who hold jobs. *New York Times,* pp. A1, A22.

Greenspan, J. (2005). Mixed (garbage) bag. *Audubon, 107,* 12–14.

Grier, J. (2004). Changing demographics drive diverse housing choices: Statistics from the 2000 census reveal a striking divergence from what has been considered the "typical" composition of the American household. *Partners in Community and Economic Development, 14*(3), 14–17.

Griffith, B. A., & Graham, C. C. (2004). Meeting needs and making meaning: The pursuit of goals. *Journal of Individual Psychology, 60,* 25–41.

Grosswald, B. (2003). Shift work and negative work-to-family spillover. *Journal of Sociology and Social Welfare, 30,* 31–56.

Grunwald Associates. (2000). *Safe and smart.* Retrieved June 30, 2006, from www.nsbf.org/safe-smart/br-overview.htm

Gupta, S. (1999). The effects of transitions in marital status on men's performance of housework. *Journal of Marriage and the Family, 61,* 700–711.

Gutis, P. S. (1989, May 28). Family redefines itself, and now the law follows. *New York Times,* p. 6.

Haber, D. (2002). Wellness general of the United States: A creative approach to promote family and community health. *Family and Community Health, 25,* 71–83.

Habitat for Humanity Web site. (n.d.). Retrieved July 11, 2007, from www.habitat.org

Hamilton, I. (Ed.). (1992). *Resources and industry.* New York: Oxford University Press.

Hargreaves, A. (2003). *Teaching in the knowledge society education in the age of insecurity.* New York: Teachers College Press.

Harrison, E. F. (1999). *The managerial decision-making process.* Boston: Houghton Mifflin.

Hattam, J. (2005). Reduce, reuse, rejoice. *Sierra, 90*(6), 42–43.

Hawley, A. H. (1986). *Human ecology: A theoretical essay.* Chicago: University of Chicago Press.

The health consequences of being female or male. (2003). *Healthcare Review.*

Heaton, T. B. (2002). Factors contributing to increased marital stability in the United States. *Journal of Family Issues, 23,* 392–409.

Heckert, T. M., Droste, H. E., Adams, P. J., Griffin, C. M., Roberts, L. L., Mueller, M. A., & Wallis, H. A. (2002, August). Gender differences in anticipated salary: Role of salary estimates for others, job characteristics, career path, and job inputs. *Sex Roles,* pp. 139–152.

Heller, R. (1998). *Making decisions.* New York: DK Publishing.

Hemp, P. (2004). Presenteeism: At work—but out of it. *Harvard Business Review, 82,* 49–58.

Henley, W., Lamond, E., Cunningham, W. & Grosseteste, R. (1890). *Walter of Henley's Husbandry.* London: Longmans, Green and Company.

Hersch, P. (1998). *A tribe apart a journey into the heart of American adolescence.* New York: Fawcett Columbine.

Hersey, P., Blanchard, K. H., & Johnson, D. E. (1992). *Management of organizational behavior: Leading human resources* (6th ed.). Upper Saddle River, NJ: Prentice Hall.

Hesiod. (1999). *Theogany and works and days.* Oxford, UK: Oxford University Press.

Hess, B. B. (1995). *Sociology.* New York: Allyn & Bacon.

Hewlett, S. A. (1991). *When the bough breaks: The cost of neglecting our children.* New York: Basic Books.

Hill, R. (1971). Modern systems theory and the family: A confrontation. *Social Science Information, 10,* 7–26.

Hobbs, F., & Stoops, N. (2002). *Demographic trends in the 20th century: Census 2000 Special Reports.* Washington, DC: U.S. Department of Commerce, Economics and Statistics Administration, U.S. Census Bureau.

Hockhachka, G. (2005). Integrating interiority in community development. *World Futures, 61,* 110–126.

Hofferth, S.L. (2003). Parental ideologies and children's after-school activities. *American Behavioral Scientist, 26,* 1359–1387.

Hooghe, M., & Stolle, D. (2003). *Introduction: Generating social capital civil society and institutions in comparative perspective.* New York: Macmillan.

House, R. J. (1971). A path-goal theory of leader effectiveness. *Administrative Science Quarterly, 16,* 321–338.

Howitt, R. (2001). *Rethinking resource management justice, sustainability and indigenous peoples.* New York: Routledge.

Hsiung, R. O., & Bagozzi, R. P. (2003). Validating the relationship qualities of influence and persuasion with the family. *Human Communication Research, 29,* 81–111.

Hughes, D., & Campbell, P. (1998). *Kids alone: Protecting your children in cyberspace.* Grand Rapids, MI: Revell.

Hughes, K. (2006). *The short life and long times of Mrs. Beeton.* Oxford: Oxford University Press.

Hutson, S. S., Barber, N. L., Kenny, J. F., Linsey, K. S., Lumia, D. S., & Maupin, M. A. (2005). *Estimated use of water in the United States in 2000* (U.S. Geological Survey Circular 1268). Retrieved July 10, 2007, from www.pubs.usgs.gov/circ/2004/circ1268

Hyde, P., & Thomas, A. B. (2003). When a leader dies. *Human Relations, 56,* 1005–1024.

Identifying barriers to curbside recycling among urban residents. (2005, November). *BioCycle, 46*(11), 15.

Illich, I. (1978). *Toward a history of needs.* New York: Pantheon.

Internal Revenue Service Web site. (n.d.). Retrieved July 11, 2007, from www.irs.gov

Irvin, B. L., & Acton, G. J. (1996). Stress mediation in caregivers of cognitively impaired adults: Theoretical model testing. *Nursing Research, 45,* 160–166.

Jackson, T., Weiss, K. E., Lundquist, J. J., & Soderlind, A. (2002). Perceptions of goal-directed activities of optimists and pessimists: A personal projects analysis. *Journal of Psychology, 136*(5), 521–533.

Jacob, T., & Johnson, S. (1997). Parenting influences on the development of alcohol abuse and dependence. *Alcohol Health and Research World, 21,* 204–213.

James, S. A., Schulz, A. J., & Van Olphen, J. (2001). Social capital, poverty, and community health: An exploration of linkages. In S. Saegert, J. P. Thompson, & M. R. Warren (Eds.), *Social capital and poor communities* (pp. 165–188). New York: Russell Sage.

Janis, I. L. (1972). *Victims of groupthink.* Boston: Houghton Mifflin.

Janis, I. L. (1982). *Groupthink psychological studies of policy decisions and fiascoes.* Boston: Houghton Mifflin.

Janis, I. L. (1989). *Crucial decisions: Leadership and policy making in crisis management.* New York: The Free Press.

Janis, I. L., & Mann, L. (1977). *Decision making: A psychological analysis of conflict, choice, and commitment.* New York: The Free Press.

Jenkins, C. L. (2001). Resource effects on access to long-term care for frail older people. *Journal of Aging and Social Policy, 13,* 35–52.

Jenkins, N. H. (2002). *You paid how much for that?! How to win at money without losing at love.* San Francisco: Jossey-Bass.

Johnson, B. R., & Jacobsen, C. K. (2005). Contact on context: An examination of social settings on Whites' attitudes toward interracial marriage. *Social Psychology Quarterly, 68*(4), 387–400.

Johnson, D. S., Rogers, J. M., & Tan, L. (2001, May). A century of family budgets in the United States. *Monthly Labor Review, 124*(5), 28.

Johnson, L. (1998). *Strengthening family and self.* Tinley Park, IL: Goodheart-Willcox.

Joseph, P. (2005). Race and poverty are out of the closet. *Sierra, 90,* 28–30.

Kalmijn, M. (1998). Intermarriage and homogamy: Causes, patterns, trends. *Annual Review of Sociology, 24,* 395–421.

Kanter, R. M. (1985). *The change masters.* New York: Simon & Schuster.

Kapos, S. (2005). Go green: "Greening" has new meaning for energy-aware developers. *Journal of Property Management, 70,* 34–40.

Kennedy, L. (1991). Farm succession in modern Ireland: Elements of a theory of inheritance. *Economic History Review, 44,* 477–499.

Keown, A. J. (2003). *Personal finance turning money into wealth.* Upper Saddle River, NJ: Prentice Hall.

Key, R. J., & Firebaugh, F. M. (1989). Family resource management: Preparing for the 21st century. *Journal of Home Economics, 81,* 13–17.

Kluckhohn, F. R., & Strodtbeck, F. L. (1961). *Variations in value orientations.* Evanston, IL: Row, Peterson.

Knight, K. (2004, May 15). Callies' 1.8 million pound heartache. *London Daily Mail,* pp. 34–35.

Knoll, M. M. (1963). Toward a conceptual framework in home management. *Journal of Home Economics, 55,* 335–339.

Koerner, A. K., & Fitzpatrick, M. A. (1997). Family type and conflict: The impact on conversation orientation and conformity orientation on conflict in the family. *Communication Studies, 48,* 59–74.

Koerner, A. K., & Fitzpatrick, M. A. (2002). Toward a theory of family communication. *Communication Theory, 12,* 70–91.

Kohlberg, L. (1984). *The psychology of moral development the nature and validity of moral stages.* New York: Harper & Row.

Konkolewsky, H. (2004). Protecting people, planet, and profit. *The Safety and Health Practitioner, 22,* 36–39.

Kotkin, J. (July 3, 2006). Building up the burbs: The suburbs are the world's future because most people love them, so why fight the sprawl? *Newsweek International* (cover story).

Kranichfeld, M. L. (1987). Rethinking family power. *Journal of Family Issues, 8,* 42–56.

Kroesche, M. (2002). *Home economics through the years: 1898–2002.* Lincoln, NE: University of Nebraska Press.

Kurtines, W. M., & Gewirtz, J. L. (Eds.). (1991). *Handbook of moral behavior and development.* Hillsdale, NJ: Lawrence Erlbaum.

Lacy, E. (2007). *University study dispels myths about state's Mexican immigrants.* Retrieved July 11, 2007, from www.uscnews.sc.edu/FORL330.html

Ladd, E. C. (1999). *The Ladd report.* New York: The Free Press.

Laliberte, R. (1999). How to manage your moods. *New Choices, 39,* 44–47.

Lam, N. M., & Graham, J. L. (2007). *China now: Doing business in the world's most dynamic market.* New York: McGraw-Hill.

Lamanna, M. A., & Riedmann, A. C. (2006). *Marriages and families making choices in a diverse society.* Belmont, CA: Wadsworth.

Langholtz, H., Marty, A., Ball, C., & Nolan, E. (2003). *Resource allocation behavior.* New York: Kluwer Academic Press.

Langone, C. A. (2004). The use of a citizen leader model for teaching strategic leadership. *Journal of Leadership Education, 3*(1), 82–88.

Lareau, A. (2007). *Unequal childhood: Class, race, and family life.* Berkeley, CA: University of California Press.

LaRossa, R., & Reitzes, D. C. (1993). Symbolic interactionism and family studies. In P. Boss, W. J. Doherty, L. LaRossa, W. R. Schumm, & S. K. Steinmetz (Eds.), *Sourcebook of family theories and methods a contextual approach* (pp. 135–162). New York: Plenum.

Laverie, D. A., Kleine, R. E., & Schultz, S. (2002). Re-examination and extension of Kleine, Kleine, and Kernan's social identity model of mundane consumption: The mediating role of the appraisal process. *Journal of Consumer Research, 28,* 1–25.

Lawler Dye, J. (2005). *Fertility of American women: June 2004* (Current Population Reports P20-555). Washington, DC: U.S. Census Bureau.

Lefton, R. E., & Buzzotta, V. R. (2004). *Leadership through people skills.* London: McGraw-Hill.

Lehrer, E. L. (1998). Religious intermarriage in the United States: Determinants and trends. *Social Science Research, 27,* 245–264.

Lenski, G. E., Nolan, P., & Lenski, J. (1995). *Human societies: An introduction to macrosociology.* New York: McGraw-Hill.

Leone, C., Wallace, H. M., & Modglin, K. (1999). The need for closure and the need for structure: Interrelationships, correlates, and outcomes. *The Journal of Psychology, 133,* 553–562.

Levinson, D. J. (1978). *The seasons of a man's life.* New York: Knopf.

Levinson, D. J. (1990). A theory of life structure development in adulthood. In C. N. Alexander & E. J. Langer (Eds.), *Higher states of human development* (pp. 35–54). New York: Oxford University Press.

Likert, R. (1961). *New patterns of management.* New York: McGraw-Hill.

Likert, R. (1967). *The human organization.* New York: McGraw-Hill.

Lindahl, K. M., & Malik, N. M. (1999). Observations of marital conflict and power. *Journal of Marriage and Family, 61,* 320–330.

Ling, R., & Yttri, B. (1999). *Nobody sits at home and waits for the telephone to ring: Micro and hyper-coordination through the use of the mobile telephone.* Retrieved January 17, 2005, from www.telenor.no/fou/program/nomadiske/articles/08.pdf

Lockeretz, W., & Merrigan, K. A. (2005). Selling to the eco-conscious food shopper. *Nutrition Today, 40,* 45–50.

Longman, P. (2004). *The empty cradle: How falling birthrates threaten world prosperity and what to do about it.* New York: Basic Books.

Lynch, S., Hurford, D. P., & Cole, A. (2002). Parental enabling attitudes and locus of control of at-risk and honors students. *Adolescence, 37,* 527–560.

Macdonald, M. (1995). Feminist economics: From theory to research. *The Canadian Journal of Economics, 28,* 159–176.

Maier, N. (1968). The subordinate's role in the delegation process. *Personnel Psychology, 21,* 179–191.

Mannes, G. (2006, February 1). Getting back to business: After time off to raise kids, returning to work can solve a host of problems. First step: Rebuild your network. *Money, 35*(2), 39.

Manning, D. J. (2004). Benefits of environmental stewardship. *Review of Business, 25,* 9–15.

Manning, G. L., & Reece, B. L. (2001). *Selling today creating customer value* (9th ed.). Upper Saddle River, NJ: Prentice Hall.

Marling, K. A. (1994). *As seen on TV the visual culture of everyday life in the 1950s.* Cambridge, MA: Harvard University Press.

Marshall, C., & Rossman, G. (1995). *Designing qualitative research.* Thousand Oaks, CA: Sage.

Marx, K., & Engels, F. (1967). *Capital.* New York: International Publishers.

Maslach, C., Schaufeil, W. B., & Leiter, M. P. (2001). Job burnout. *Annual Review of Psychology, 52,* 397–422.

Maslow, A. H. (1954). *Motivation and personality.* New York: Harper & Row.

Maslow, A. H., & Frager, R. (1987). *Motivation and personality* (rev. ed.). New York: Harper & Row.

Maslow, A. H., Stephens, D. C., Heil, G., & Maslow, A. H. (1998). *Maslow on management.* New York: Wiley.

Maxwell, J. C. (2003). *Attitude 101: What every leader needs to know.* Nashville, TN: Thomas Nelson Publishers.

McCracken, G. D. (1988). *Culture and consumption new approaches to the symbolic character of consumer goods and activities.* Bloomington: Indiana University Press.

McDermott, C. J. (2004). *Economics in real time: A theoretical reconstruction.* Ann Arbor, MI: University of Michigan Press.

McDonald, G. W. (1980). Family power: The assessment of a decade of theory and research, 1970–1979. *Journal of Marriage and Family, 42,* 841–854.

McGregor, D. (1960). *The human side of enterprise.* New York: McGraw-Hill.

Mead, G. H. (1964). *On social psychology.* Chicago: University of Chicago Press.

Mechoulan, S. (2005). Economic theory's stance on no-fault divorce. *Review of Economics of the Household, 3*(3), 337–360.

Merton, R. K., & Kitt, A. S. (1950). Contributions to the theory of reference group behavior. In R. K. Merton & P. F. Lazarsfeld (Eds.), *Studies in the scope and method of "The American soldier."* Glencoe, IL: The Free Press.

Meyers, S. A., Varkey, S., & Aguirre, A. M. (2002). Ecological correlates of family functioning. *The American Journal of Family Therapy, 30,* 257–273.

Miles, D. R., Silberg, J. L., & Pickens, R. W. (2005). Familial influences on alcohol use in adolescent female twins: Testing for genetic and environmental interactions. *Journal of Studies on Alcohol, 66,* 445–451.

Millar, J. S., & Hull, C. (1997). Measuring human wellness. *Social Indicators Research, 40,* 147–159.

Miller, B. C. (2002). Family influences on adolescent sexual and contraceptive behavior. *The Journal of Sex Research, 39,* 22–27.

Mintz, S., & Kellogg, S. (1988). *Domestic revolutions: A social history of American family life.* London: Collier Macmillan.

Mitchell, J. (1984). *Women, the longest revolution.* New York: Pantheon Books.

Monk, A., Hone, K., Lines, L., Dowdall, A., Baxter, G., Blythe, M., & Wright P. (2006). Towards a practical framework for managing the risks of selecting technology to support independent living. *Applied Ergonomics, 37,* 599–607.

Mullins, R. (1997, March 28). *Cell phones roam into new areas.* Retrieved April 24, 2007, from www.tampatrib.com

Murray, J. (1987). *The perceptions of sexuality, marriage, and family in early English pastoral manuals.* Unpublished doctoral dissertation, University of Toronto.

Murry, V. M. (2000). Challenges and life experiences of Black American families. In P. C. McKenry & S. J. Price (Eds.), *Families and change coping with stressful events and transitions.* Thousand Oaks, CA: Sage.

Myers, D. G., & Lamm, H. (1976). The group polarization phenomenon. *Psychological Bulletin, 83,* 602–627.

Myers, J. E., Sweeney, T. J., & Whitmer, J. M. (2000). The wheel of wellness counseling for wellness: A holistic model for treatment planning. *Journal of Counseling & Development, 78,* 251–266.

Nall, M. A. (2005). Strengthening families and securing communities. *Journal of Family and Consumer Sciences, 97,* 18–21.

The National Marriage Project. (2001). *The state of our unions 2001: The social health of marriage in America.* Piscataway, NJ: Rutgers University Press.

The National Marriage Project. (2006). *The state of our unions 2006.* Piscataway, NJ: Rutgers University Press.

National Study of the Changing Workforce. Guide to Public Use Files. (1999). New York: Families and Work Institute.

National Telecommunications and Information Administration. (1998). *Falling through the net: II. New data on the digital divide.* Washington, DC: U.S. Department of Commerce.

Nelson, T. (2005, September). *How America can afford to grow older: A vision for the future.* Speech presented at the West Virginia Governor's Summit on Aging conference, Chester, WV.

Nielsen Media Research, Inc. (1998). *U.S. TV household estimates.* Northbrook, IL: Author.

Noor, N. M. (2002). Work-family conflict, locus of control, and women's well-being: Tests of alternative pathways. *Journal of Social Psychology, 142,* 645–662.

Norton, A. J., & Moorman, J. E. (1987). Current trends in marriage and divorce among American women. *Journal of Marriage and the Family, 49,* 3–14.

Okerlund, V. W., & Parsons, R. J. (1995). Needs assessment update. *National Civic Review, 84,* 48–54.

Okonski, V. O. (2003). Exercise as a counseling intervention. *Journal of Mental Health Counseling, 25,* 45–57.

Oksman, V., & Turtiainen, J. (2004). Mobile communication as a social stage. *New Media and Society, 6,* 319–339.

Olson, D. H., & DeFrain, J. (2000). *Marriage and the family: Diversity and strengths* (3rd ed.). Mountain View, CA: Mayfield.

Olson, D. H., & DeFrain, J. (2003). *Marriages and families: Intimacy, diversity, and strengths* (4th ed.). Boston: McGraw-Hill.

Olson, D. H., & DeFrain, J. (2006). *Marriages and families: Intimacy, diversity, and strengths* (5th ed.). Boston: McGraw-Hill.

Olson, J. M., & Zanna, M. P. (1993). Attitudes and attitude change. *Annual Review of Psychology, 44,* 117–155.

Opt, S. K., & Loffrendo, D. A. (2000). Rethinking communication apprehension: A Myers–Briggs perspective. *The Journal of Psychology, 134,* 556–570.

Osmond, M. W., & Thorne, B. (1993). Feminist theories: The social construction of gender in families and society. In P. Boss (Ed.), *Sourcebook of family theories and methods a contextual approach* (pp. 591–625). New York: Plenum.

Oswald, A. (2003). Give all your staff a real bonus. *Times Higher Education Supplement, 1620,* 28–30.

Otto, H. A. (1962). What is a strong family? *Marriage and Family Living, 24,* 77–81.

Pagan, C. N. (2006, January). Do you have an emergency plan? *Prevention, 5,* 103–105.

Palomba, C. A., & Banta, T. W. (1999). *Assessment essentials planning, implementing, and improving assessment in higher education.* San Francisco: Jossey-Bass.

Palpini, K. (2003, February 24). *Cell phones riding high in area.* Retrieved July 19, 2004, from www.gazettenet.com/business

Pandya, S. M., & Coleman, B. (2000). *Caregiving and long-term care* (Rep. No. AARP FS82). Washington, DC: Public Policy Institute.

Paolucci, B., Hall, O. A., & Axinn, N. W. (1977). *Family decision making: An ecosystem approach.* New York: Wiley.

Parsons, T. (1968). *The structure of social action.* New York: The Free Press.

Payne, R. K. (1998). *A framework for understanding poverty.* Baytown, TX: RFT Publications.

Pearl, D., Bouthilet, L., & Lazar, J. B. (Eds.). (1982). *Television and behavior.* Rockville, MD: Government Printing Office.

Pedro-Carroll, J. (2001). The promotion of wellness in children and families: Challenges and opportunities. *American Psychologist, 56,* 993–1004.

Peters, M. F., & Massey, G. (1983). Chronic versus mundane stress in family stress theories: The case of Black families in White America. *Marriage and Family Review, 6,* 193–218.

Petley, J. (2001). *The media: The impact on our lives.* Austin, TX: Raintree Steck-Vaughn.

Pfeffer, J. (1987). Understanding the role of power in decision making. In J. M. Shafritz & J. S. Ott (Eds.), *Classics of organizational theory* (pp. 309–335). Chicago: Dorsey.

Pimentel, D., Berger, B., Filiberto, D., Newton, M., Wolfe, B., Karabinakis, E., Clark, S., Poon, E., Abbett, E., & Nandagopal, S. (2004). Water resources: Agricultural and environmental issues. *BioScience, 54,* 909–919.

Planning for your successor. (2005, December 23). Retrieved July 10, 2007, from www.fwi.co.uk

Pollin, R. (2002). What is a living wage? Considerations from Santa Monica, CA. *Review of Radical Political Economics, 34,* 257–273.

Pundt, H. (1980). *AHEA: A history of excellence.* Washington, DC: American Home Economics Association.

Purdy, M., & Dupey, P. (2005). Holistic flow model of spiritual wellness. *Counseling and Values, 49,* 95–107.

Putnam, R. D. (2000). *Bowling alone: The collapse and revival of American community.* New York: Simon & Schuster.

Quart, A. (2003). *Branded the buying and selling of teenagers.* Cambridge, MA: Perseus.

Quinn, R. E., & Spreitzer, G. M. (1997, Autumn). The road to empowerment: Seven questions every leader should consider. *Organizational Dynamics, 26,* 37–49.

Ramakrishnan, S. K. (2005). *Democracy in immigrant America: Changing demographic and political participation.* Palo Alto, CA: Stanford University Press.

Rao, K., Apte, M., & Subbakrishna, D. K. (2003). Coping and subjective well-being in women with multiple roles. *International Journal of Social Psychiatry, 49,* 175–184.

Rauber, P. (2003, January). When Uncle Sam wanted us. *Sierra, 88,* 32.

Rayle, A. D., & Myers, J. E. (2004). Counseling adolescents toward wellness: The roles of ethnic identity, acculturation, and mattering. *Professional School Counseling, 8,* 81–91.

Read, C. R. (1991). Achievement and career choices: Comparisons of males and females. *Roeper Review, 13,* 188–193.

Roberts, P. (2004). Wealth from waste: Local and regional economic development and the environment. *The Geographical Journal, 170,* 126–135.

Rodman, H. (1967). Marital power in France, Greece, Yugoslavia, and the United States: A cross-national discussion. *Journal of Marriage and the Family, 29,* 320–324.

Rosenbaum, D. (1993, October 26). America's economic outlaw: The U.S. health care system. *New York Times,* A1(N)–A1(L).

Rossi, A. S. (2001). *Caring and doing for others: Social responsibility in the domains of family, work, and community.* Chicago: University of Chicago Press.

Rothstein, B. (2001). Social capital in the social democratic welfare state. *Politics & Society, 29,* 207–210.

Rotter, J. (1973). A locus of control scale for children. *Journal of Consulting and Clinical Psychology, 40,* 148–154.

Rowley, L. L., & Hurtado, S. (2002). *The non-monetary benefits of an undergraduate education.* University of Michigan: Center for the Study of Higher and Postsecondary Education.

Rubinstein, J. S., Meyer, D. E., & Evans, J. E. (2001). Executive control of cognitive processes in task switching. *Journal of Experimental Psychology, 27,* 763–767.

Saegert, S., & Evans, G. W. (2003). Poverty, housing niches, and health in the United States. *Journal of Social Issues, 59,* 569–580.

Safilios-Rothschild, C. (1976). A macro and micro-examination of family power and love. *Journal of Marriage and the Family, 37,* 355–362.

Sage, A. P. (1999). Sustainable development: Issues in information, knowledge, and systems management. *Information Knowledge Systems Management, 1,* 185–224.

Scanzoni, J., & Marsiglio, W. (1993). New action theory and contemporary families. *Journal of Family Issues, 14,* 105–132.

Schackner, B. (2002, August 30). *More students opt for wireless phone: Colleges face loss of commissions. Knight Rider Tribune Business News.* Retrieved July, 11, 2007, from www.post-gazette.com/localnews/20020830cellphones0830p4 .asp#top

Schaefer, R. T. (2007). *Race and ethnicity in the United States* (4th ed.). Upper Saddle River, NJ: Pearson Education.

Schartz, L. L., & Kaslow, F. W. (2001). The cult phenomenon: A turn of the century update. *American Journal of Family Therapy, 29,* 13–22.

Schein, E. H. (2004). *Organizational culture and leadership* (3rd ed.). San Francisco: Jossey-Bass.

Schermerhorn, J. R., Naumes, W., Naumes, M. J., & Schermerhorn, J. R. (1996). *Management.* New York: Wiley.

Schneider, W. (2005). The strong and the weak. *National Journal, 37,* 1116.

Schneiderman, R. (2005). It's time to take out the trash. *Electronic Design,* pp. 77–80.

Schoen, R., & Cheng, Y. A. (2006). Partner choice and the differential retreat from marriage. *Journal of Marriage and Family, 68*(1), 1–10.

Sclafani, S. (2002). No child left behind. *Issues in Science and Technology, 19,* 43–47.

Seabald, H. (1986). Adolescents' shifting orientation toward parents and peers: A curvilinear trend over recent decades. *Journal of Marriage and the Family, 48,* 5–13.

Seligman, M. (2002). *Authentic happiness using the new positive psychology to realize your potential for lasting fulfillment.* New York: The Free Press.

Seufert-Barr, N. (1994, March). The smallest democracy: At the heart of society. *UN Chronicle,* pp. 43–45.

Sheng, M. L. (2005). The wired mother. *Technovation, 25,* 1071–1078.

Sherif, C. W., & Sherif, M. (1967). *Attitude, ego-involvement, and change.* New York: Wiley.

Siegel, C. (1998). The end of economic growth: The limits of human needs. *Earth Island Journal, 14,* 40–43.

Signorielli, N., & Morgan, M. (2001). Television and the family: The cultural perspective. In J. Bryant & J. A. Bryant (Eds.), *Television and the American family* (pp. 3–30). Mahwah, NJ: Lawrence Erlbaum.

Simons, R. L., Conger, R. D., & Chao, W. (1992). Gender differences in the intergenerational transmission of parenting beliefs. *Journal of Marriage and Family, 54,* 823–836.

Skipp, C., Ephron, D., & Hastings, M. (2006). Trouble at home. *Newsweek, 148,* 17.

Skolnick, A. (1993). Changes of heart: Family dynamics in historical perspective. In P. A. Cowan (Ed.), *Family, self, and society toward a new agenda for family research* (pp. 43–68). Hillsdale, NJ: Lawrence Erlbaum.

Skolnick, A., & Skolnick, J. (2005). *Family in transition.* Glenville, IL: Scott, Foresman.

Smith, K. K., & Berg, D. N. (1987). *Paradoxes of group life: Understanding conflict, paralysis, and movement in group dynamics.* San Francisco: Jossey-Bass.

Smith, R. T. (2001). Matrifocality. In N. J. Smelser & P. B. Baltes (Eds.), *International encyclopedia of the social and behavioral sciences* (Vol. 14, pp. 9416–9418). Kidhington, UK: Elsevier Science.

Snir, R., & Harpaz, I. (2002). Work-leisure relations: Leisure orientation and the meaning of work. *Journal of Leisure Research, 34,* 178–203.

Sokalski, H. J. (1994). The international year of the family. In K. Altergott (Ed.), *One world, many families* (pp. 3–7). Minneapolis: National Council on Family Relations.

Sorrels, J. P., & Myers, B. (1983). Comparison of group and family dynamics. *Human Relations, 36,* 477–492.

St. Jude Children's Research Hospital Web site. (n.d.). Retrieved July 11, 2007, from www.stjude.org

Stanley, T. J. (2004). *Millionaire women next door: The many journeys of successful American businesswomen.* Kansas City, MO: Andrews McMeel.

Starbuck, G. H. (2006). *Families in context.* Boulder, CO: Paradigm Publishers.

State Legislatures. (2005, October–November). Counting on the future. *Changing Demographics, 31*(9), 7.

Stearns, P. (2003). *Anxious parents: A history of modern childbearing in America.* New York: New York University Press.

Stein, H. W., & Brier, M. C. (2002). Raising responsible children of wealth. *Trusts & Estates, 140*(6), 42.

Stephens, D., & Heil, G. (1998). Introduction. In A. H. Maslow, D. C. Stephens, & G. Heil (Eds.), *Maslow on management* (pp. xv–xvii). New York: Wiley.

Sterner, T. (2003). *Policy instruments for environmental and natural resource management.* Stockholm, Sweden: Swedish International Development Cooperation Agency.

Stinnett, N. (1981). Strong families: A national study. *Family strengths: 3 roots of well-being* (pp. 33–42). Lincoln, NE: University of Nebraska Press.

Stinnett, N., DeFrain, N., & DeFrain, J. (1999). *Creating a strong family.* West Monroe, LA: Howard.

Stolle, D. (2003). The sources of social capital. In M. Hooghe & D. Stolle (Eds.), *Generating social capital: Civil society and institutions in comparative perspective* (pp. 19–42). New York: Palgrave Macmillan.

Stone, L. (1997). *Kinship and marriage.* Boulder, CO: Westview.

Stone, R. (1998). *Human resource management.* New York: Wiley.

Stoner, J. A. (1968). Risky and cautious shifts in group decisions: The influence of widely held values. *Journal of Experimental Social Psychology, 4,* 442–459.

Strong, B., Devault, C., & Sayad, B. W. (1998). *The marriage and family experience intimate relationships in a changing society.* Belmont, CA: Wadsworth.

Sugimoto, Y. (1997). *An introduction to Japanese society.* New York: Cambridge University Press.

Szinovacz, M. (1987). Family power. In M. B. Sussman & S. K. Steinmetz (Eds.), *Handbook of marriage and the family* (pp. 651–693). New York: Praeger.

Tadmor, N. (1996, May). The concept of household-family in eighteenth-century England. *Past and Present,* pp. 111–130.

Tan, K. H., & Platts, K. (2006). Effective strategic action planning: A process and tool. *Business Process Management Journal, 11,* 137–157.

Tan, L. (2000). Spending patterns of public-assisted families. *Monthly Labor Review, 123,* 29–35.

Tannen, D. (1990). *You just don't understand: Women and men in conversation.* New York: Morrow.

Tannenbaum, R., & Schmidt, W. (1958). How to choose a leadership pattern. *Harvard Business Review, 36,* 95–101.

Taylor, R. L. (2002). *Minority families in the United States: A multicultural perspective*. Upper Saddle River, NJ: Prentice Hall.

TECHWEB. (2007). Retrieved June 10, 2007, from www.informationweek.com/story/showArticle.jhtml?articleID=198700535

Tesser, A. (1992). On the importance of heritability in psychological research. *Psychological Review, 100*(10), 129–143.

Timmerman, G. M., & Acton, G. J. (2001). The relationship between basic need satisfaction and emotional eating. *Issues in Mental Health Nursing, 22,* 691–701.

Tomer, J. F. (2001). Economic man vs. heterodox men: The concepts of human nature in schools of economic thought. *The Journal of Socio-Economics, 30,* 281–293.

Torquati, J. C. (2002). Personal and social resources as predictors of parenting in homeless families. *Journal of Family Issues, 23,* 463–485.

Triplett, Norman. (1898). The dynamogenic factors in pacemaking and competition. *American Journal of Psychology, 9,* 507–533.

Tucker, P. (2006). Thinking globally, acting locally on energy use: U.S. states push bold fuel-conservation programs. *The Futurist, 40,* 8–10.

Turner, R. H. (1970). *Family interaction.* New York: Wiley.

Twenge, J. M., Campbell, W. K., & Foster, C. A. (2003). Parenthood and marital satisfaction: A meta-analytic review. *Journal of Marriage and the Family, 65,* 574–583.

University of Nebraska Benefits. (2006). Retrieved June 27, 2006, from www.unk.edu

U.S. Census Bureau. (1998, March). *Current population reports: Marital status and living arrangements* (Series P20-514). Washington, DC: U.S. Government Printing Office.

U.S. Census Bureau. (2001). *U.S. adults postponing marriage, census bureau reports. United States Department of Commerce News.* Washington, DC: U.S. Government Printing Office.

U.S. Census Bureau. (2002). *Statistical abstract of the United States: 2002* (122nd ed.). Washington, DC: U.S. Department of Commerce.

U.S. Census Bureau. (2004, March). *Census Bureau projects tripling of Hispanic and Asian populations in 50 years; non-Hispanic whites may drop to half of total population* (CB04-44). Washington, DC: Author.

U.S. Census Bureau. (2006). *Nation's population one-third minority* (CB06-72). Washington, DC: Author.

U.S. Census Bureau. (2006a, January). *Oldest baby boomers turn 60! Facts for features and special editions* (CB06-FFSE.01-2). Washington, DC: Author.

U.S. Census Bureau. (2006b, May). *Nation's population one-third minority* (CB06-72). Washington, DC: Author.

U.S. Department of Agriculture Web site. (n.d.). Retrieved July 11, 2007, from www.usda.gov

U.S. Department of Education Web site. (n.d.). Retrieved July 11, 2007, from www.ed.gov

U.S. Department of Energy. (2007). *Energy star.* Retrieved March 20, 2007, from www.energy.gov

U.S. Department of Labor. (2007). *Bureau of Labor Statistics Report* (No. 978). Washington, DC: Author.

U.S. Energy Information Administration. (2001, July 30). *2001 housing characteristics tables* (Press release).Washington, DC: Author.

U.S. Social Security Administration Web site. (n.d.). Retrieved July 11, 2007, from www.ssa.gov

Vansteenkiste, M., Simons, J., Lens, W., Soenens, B., & Matos, L. (2005). Examining the motivational impact of intrinsic versus extrinsic goal framing and autonomy-supportive versus internally controlling communication style on early adolescents' academic achievement. *Child Development, 76,* 483–501.

Vickers, C. (1984). *Themes in home management.* Washington, DC: American Home Economics Association.

Vuchinich, S. (1999). *Problem solving in families research and practice.* Thousand Oaks, CA: Sage.

Wagner, J. D. (2006). Solar power to be a required option in California. *Green Builder, 1,* 14.

Waller, W. W., & Hill, R. (1951). *The family, a dynamic interpretation.* New York: Warner Books.

Walsh, Y., & Bor, R. (1996). Psychological consequences of involvement in a new religious movement or cult. *Counseling Psychology Quarterly, 9,* 47–61.

Ward, J. (2000). From tee to greenspace. *American City and County, 115,* 26–39.

Ward, K. (2001). Perceived needs of parents of critically ill infants in a neonatal intensive care unit (NICU). *Pediatric Nursing, 27,* 281.

Wartella, E., & Jennings, N. (2001). New members of the family: The digital revolution in the home. *The Journal of Family Communication, 1,* 59–69.

Webb, D. M. (1991). Delegation. *Academic Search Premier, 69*(4), 40–42.

Weir, A. (2001). *Henry VIII: The king and his court.* New York: Ballantine.

Welch, P. J., & Welch, G. F. (2004). *Economics, theory and practice.* New York: Wiley.

Welcome to VALS. (n.d.). Retrieved June 28, 2006, from www.sricbi.com/VALS

Wensley, R. (1996). Isabella Beeton: Management as "everything in its place." *Business Strategy Review, 7,* 37–47.

Westermarck, E. (1971). *The history of human marriage.* New York: Johnson Reprint Corporation. (Original work published 1922)

White, J. M., & Klein, D. M. (2002). *Family theories.* Thousand Oaks, CA: Sage.

Whorton, J. C. (2000). Vegetarianism. In K. F. Kiple & K. C. Ornelas (Eds.), *The Cambridge world history of food* (pp. 1553–1564). New York: Cambridge University Press.

Wickrama, K. A., & Bryant, C. M. (2003). Community context of social resources and adolescent mental health. *Journal of Marriage and Family, 65,* 850–866.

Wilcox, W. B., Doherty, W. J., Fisher, H., Galston, W. A., Glenn, N. D., Gottman, J., Lerman, R., Mahoney, A., Markey, B., Markman, H. J., Nock, S., Popenoe, D., Rodriquez, G. G., Standly, S. M., Waite, L. J., & Wallerstein, J. (2005). *Why marriage matters: Twenty-six conclusions from the social sciences.* New York: Institute for American Values.

Wilkerson, I. (1991, December 2). Interracial marriage rises, acceptance lags. *New York Times,* pp. A1–A11.

Wilkinson, D. (1987). Ethnicity. In M. B. Sussman & S. K. Steinmetz (Eds.), *Handbook of marriage and the family* (pp. 183–210). New York: Plenum.

Williams, C. (2000). *Internet access in U.S. public schools and classrooms.* Washington, DC: U.S. Dept. of Education, Office of Educational Research and Improvement.

Williams, C., Rosen, J., Hudman, J., & O'Malley, M. (2004). *Challenges and trade-offs in low-income family budgets: Implications for health coverage.* Washington, DC: The Kaiser Commission on Medicaid and the Uninsured.

Williams, R., Dale, B., Bertsch, B., Van Der Wiele, T., Van Iwaarden, J., Smith, M., & Visser, R. (2006, November 1). Quality and risk management: What are the key issues? *The TQM Magazine, 18,* 67–86.

Wolf, D. A., & Longino, C. F., Jr. (2005). Our "increasingly mobile society"? The curious persistence of a false belief. *The Gerontologist, 45*(1), 5–12.

Woolley, F. (2003). Control over money in marriage. In S. A. Grossbard-Shechtman (Ed.), *Marriage and the economy theory and evidence from advanced industrial societies* (pp. 105–128). New York: Cambridge University Press.

World Health Organization. (1947). *Chronicle of the World Health Organization: Volume 1.* Geneva, Switzerland: Author.

Yorburg, B. (2002). *Family realities a global view.* Upper Saddle River, NJ: Prentice Hall.

Yu, H., & Miller, P. (2005). Leadership style: The X generation and baby boomers compared in different cultural contexts. *Leadership and Organizational Development Journal, 26,* 35–50.

Yu, L., Chan, C., & Ireland, C. (2006). *China's new culture of cool: Understanding the world's fastest-growing market.* Berkeley, CA: New Rider's Press.

Zimmerman, E. (1964). *Introduction to world resources.* New York: Harper & Row.

Zuckerman, M. (2000). Are you a risk taker? *Psychology Today, 33,* 52–57.

Zuluaga, B. H. (2000). Implementation of the Zuluaga-Raysmith (Z-R) model for assessment of perceived basic human needs in home health clients and caregivers. *Public Health Nursing, 17,* 317–324.

Author Index

Subject Index

About the Authors

Tami James Moore PhD, CFLE, is an Associate Professor at the University of Nebraska at Kearney. Dr. Moore has taught Family Resource Management for several years; she also focuses on Diversity Development.

Sylvia M. Asay, PhD, CFLE, is an Associate Professor at the University of Nebraska at Kearney. Dr. Asay has more than 15 years of classroom teaching experience, with a focus on Marriage and Family Relationships and International Family Strengths.

Both authors have advanced degrees and a special interest in curriculum development and pedagogy and have conducted research on the relationship between teaching and scholarship.